The French Civil Code in the Free City of Cracow (1815–1846)

Legal History Library

VOLUME 73

The titles published in this series are listed at *brill.com/lhl*

The French Civil Code in the Free City of Cracow (1815–1846)

By

Andrzej Dziadzio, Mateusz Mataniak, and Piotr Michalik

BRILL | NIJHOFF

LEIDEN | BOSTON

NATIONAL SCIENCE CENTRE
POLAND

This publication is a result of a research project by the Polish National Science Centre (project registration number: 2017/27/B/HS5/01308).

JAGIELLONIAN UNIVERSITY
IN KRAKÓW

This publication was funded by the Faculty of Law and Administration of the Jagiellonian University granted within the Priority Research Area Heritage under the programme "Excellence Initiative – Research University" at the Jagiellonian University in Cracow.

Language proofreaders: Michael Mulryan, Michał Szewczyk

Cover illustration: Composition of Figs. 8, 12, 18, 27, and 28 by Anna Michalik. Full source information for the individual images in this composition can be found in the List of Illustrations.

The Library of Congress Cataloging-in-Publication Data is available online at https://catalog.loc.gov
LC record available at https://lccn.loc.gov/2025002717

Typeface for the Latin, Greek, and Cyrillic scripts: "Brill". See and download: brill.com/brill-typeface.

ISSN 1874-1793
ISBN 978-90-04-68873-5 (hardback)
ISBN 978-90-04-68874-2 (e-book)
DOI 10.1163/9789004688742

This book is printed on acid-free paper and produced in a sustainable manner.

Contents

Figures and Tables

Figures

Tables

Abbreviations

AUJ	Archiwum Uniwersytetu Jagiellońskiego (Jagiellonian University Archives)
ANK	Archiwum Narodowe w Krakowie (National Archives in Cracow)
DGS	Dziennik Główny Senatu Rządzącego (Main Journal of the Ruling Senate)
DPKW	Dziennik Praw Księstwa Warszawskiego (Journal of Laws of the Duchy of Warsaw)
DZ.Pr.RK	Dziennik Praw Rzeczypospolitey Krakowskiey (Journal of Laws of the Republic of Cracow)
DPr.WMK	Dziennik Praw Wolnego Miasta Krakowa (Journal of the Laws of the Free City of Cracow)
DRRz.WMK	Dziennik Rozporządzeń Rządowych Wolnego, Niepodległego i Ściśle Neutralnego Miasta Krakowa i Jego Okręgu (Journal of Governmental Regulations)
DRz.WMK	Dziennik Rządowy Wolnego Miasta Krakowa i Jego Okręgu (Government Journal of the Free City of Cracow)
NC	Napoleonic Code
PSB	Polski Słownik Biograficzny

Introduction

Andrzej Dziadzio, Mateusz Mataniak and Piotr Michalik

The French Civil Code of 1804 (*Code civil des Français*)[1] is one of the most important landmarks of law in history, being a symbol of the European, and even global, century of codification.[2] Introduced in a number of European countries as the Napoleonic Code (*Code Napoléon*), it survived the fall of its creator in 1815 and became a permanent feature of the French, Belgian, West German (Rhineland, Baden), Swiss (Geneva), Polish, American (Louisiana) and Canadian (Quebec) legal systems in the 19th century. Moreover, its important influence on the formation of the 19th century civil codifications of the countries of the old continent (Netherlands, Italy, Romania, Portugal, Spain) and the other continents is unquestionable.[3] The widespread implementation of the French Code raises a number of research questions which cannot be easily answered.[4] Was the Imperial Code imposed on conquered countries or voluntarily adopted by local societies? Was the appeal of the law primarily due to the contents, or perhaps the form, of its norms? Was the driving force behind the code, the liberalisation of the construction of property rights or the secularisation of the institution of marriage? Was the attractiveness of the Code determined by the social resonance of the idea of equality before the law or the need for legal certainty, so important for the formation of modern states? Or, was the lasting adoption of the regulations of the Napoleonic Code determined by their rapid assimilation into local legal cultures? What determined this? Previous experience with the reception of foreign law, or the lack of native codification? A reliable answer to these and other questions can only be approached through a comprehensive analysis of the source material relating to the introduction and application of the French Code in a given country.[5]

The introduction of the French *Code civil* was one of the key events in legal history on Polish soil. It coincided with a watershed period due to the dynamics of political, social and economic processes. The Polish-Lithuanian Commonwealth, which had been a union of the Polish Kingdom and the Grand Duchy of Lithuania from 1569, lost its independence in 1795 as a result

1 *Code civil des Français* 1804.

2 See, *inter alia*: Halpérin 2018, 907–928.

3 See articles on the reception of the Civil Code in individual countries in: Halpérin ed. 2004a; *Le Code civil 1804–2004: Livre du Bicentenaire*, 2004; Hattenhauer and Schroeder eds. 2011.

4 Halpérin 2018, 926.

5 See below, pp. 4–5.

 | DOI:10.1163/9789004688742_002

of partitions by the neighbouring powers of Austria, Prussia and Russia. Berlin and Vienna, encompassing the Polish territories with Warsaw, Poznań (Prussia), Cracow and Lublin (Austria) in their partitions, proceeded to introduce their laws, including civil codifications, into the occupied territories: the Prussian *Landrecht* of 1794[6] and the West Galician Code of 1797.[7] However, this process was stalled by the defeat of Austria and Prussia and the failure of Russia in Napoleon's victorious wars against the anti-French coalition. Under the terms of the Peace of Tilsit in 1807, the French Emperor created the Duchy of Warsaw from the Polish lands of the Prussian partition, which constituted the 'eastern flank' of his Empire. On the legal and political level, this was reflected in the imposition on the new State of the Napoleonic constitution and civil code, which formally introduced the post-revolutionary principles of universality and equality before the law in hitherto feudal Poland.[8] In 1810, these changes also included a part of the Polish lands of the Austrian partition, with Cracow and Lublin annexed to the Duchy of Warsaw by the Peace of Schönbrunn in 1809, ending Napoleon's subsequent victorious war with Austria.

Effective in the Duchy of Warsaw as of 1 May 1808, the French Civil Code had officially been the Napoleonic Code from 1807 (*Code Napoléon*),[9] and under this name it remained in force in Poland for the following 138 years, until 1946. The decisions of the Congress of Vienna in 1815 were crucial to maintaining its force in the Polish lands after the fall of Napoleon. At that time, on the initiative of Tsar Alexander I, the Kingdom of Poland was reconstituted from most of the lands of the Duchy of Warsaw with its capital in Warsaw, with the Tsar as Polish King. The territory of the Kingdom did not, however, include the western departments with Poznań, which were incorporated back into Prussia, reinstating the *Landrecht* of 1794 there. The Kingdom of Poland also did not include Cracow, which, together with its district, was separated as the Free City of Cracow under the protectorate of the three victorious partitioning powers: Austria, Prussia and Russia. In both the Kingdom of Poland and the Free City of Cracow, however, the powers left the Napoleonic Code in force, with the assumption that it would soon be replaced by domestic codifications. Indeed, the Civil Code of the Kingdom of Poland, enacted in 1825, replaced

6 *Allgemeines Landrecht für die Königlich Preussischen Staaten* 1794.

7 *Ustawy cywilne dla Galicyi Zachodniey* 1797.

8 See Sójka-Zielińska 1993, 119–133.

9 *Code Napoléon* 1807. It is significant that, apart from minor amendments introduced in the Duchy of Warsaw and the Free City of Cracow, the authentic text of the Napoleonic Code was the French text of 1807. The Polish text recommended by the Government, and most often used in practice, was the translation by Father Franciszek Ksawery Szaniawski published in the Warsaw printing house of the Piarist Fathers in 1808: *Kodex Napoleona* 1808.

Book I and Titles V of Book III of the *Code civil*, significantly changing marriage law. In particular, civil marriage was abolished at that time and divorce was forbidden to Catholics; in 1836, jurisdiction in personal matrimonial matters was returned to church courts. For the remainder, i.e. the law of property, obligations and inheritance (Books II and III without Title XVIII on privileges and mortgages), the *Code Napoléon* in the course of the 19th century became a 'Polish' code, important also for emphasising the separateness of the increasingly Russified Polish Kingdom from the rest of the Russian Empire.[10]

However, the changes introduced by the Civil Code of the Kingdom of Poland did not take place in the Free City of Cracow, where, despite the advanced work on the codification of its own code, it eventually remained with the Napoleonic Code, amending it only in the field of guardianship law and mortgage law. As a result, in the Free City of Cracow, the provisions of the French Code remained in force until the end of its existence in 1846, when the city-state was incorporated into Austria. Finally, it was not until a patent of 1852 that Emperor Francis Joseph I repealed the validity of the *Code civil* in Cracow and its district, introducing the Austrian Civil Code of 1811 (ABGB, *Allgemeines Bürgerliches Gesetzbuch*),[11] with effect from 1855, and as regards matrimonial law from 1852. Thus, the city-state of Cracow was, in the era of the Holy Alliance, a unique enclave in Europe (along with Belgium, Baden[12] and Rhineland). Here, the validity and application of the secular model of marriage was enforced, with an obligatory civil wedding before a civil registrar[13] and a general admissibility of divorce,[14] forbidden to Catholics between 1816 and 1884, even in France.[15]

This monograph is intended by the co-authors to be a summary of their research on the validity and application of the French Civil Code of 1804 in the Free City of Cracow.[16] The Napoleonic Code was at that time applied in

10 See Kodrębski 1993, 135–142; Korobowicz 1993, 143–153; Lityński 1994, 253–269; Gaudemet 1999, 212–213.

11 *Powszechna księga ustaw cywilnych* 1811.

12 Laufs 2011, 1–17.

13 Who, in relation to Christians, were, as in Baden, clergymen who then performed a church wedding for the prospective spouses, and in relation to Jews, secular clerks: Michalik 2023. As to the introduction of civil weddings in England and Wales, see Probert 2021.

14 According to recent research on judgments made by Cracow's courts, also in relation to Catholics: Pomianowski 2022b.

15 Halpérin 2018, 917.

16 This research was carried out by the co-authors as a project team between 2018 and 2022 as part of the implementation of the Polish National Science Centre research grant OPUS 14, entitled *Prawo własności w orzecznictwie sądów Wolnego Miasta Krakowa. Z dziejów stosowania Kodeksu Napoleona* (*Code civil*) [UMO-2017/27/B/HS5/01308]. The team consisted of Project Manager Prof. Andrzej Dziadzio and researchers: Mateusz Mataniak, PhD and Piotr Michalik, PhD.

the following Cracow courts: the Court of First Instance, the Court of Appeal and Court of Third Instance (later merged into the Higher Court). Although the Free City of Cracow encompassed only a part of the Polish lands where the reception of the Napoleonic Code took place, it provides the most complete basis for conducting a source analysis of this phenomenon, and for the relatively long period of the first half of the 19th century. This is due to the fact that the Polish 19th-century State Archives suffered considerable damage in the course of the Second World War, however the Archives of the Free City of Cracow were unaffected, and are preserved almost in their entirety as part of the collection of the National Archives in Cracow.[17] The archives preserved complete books of court records in nearly 550 volumes, containing a wealth of litigation material: court judgments, trial records and writs of the parties. In addition, the Jagiellonian University Archives preserve the records of the sessions of the Faculty of Doctors and Professors of Law of the Jagiellonian University, which, in the years 1817–33, issued legal opinions on the possibility of an appeal in a case to the Court of Third Instance.[18] The Archives of the Free City of Cracow also include numerous books of State records documenting the activities of the various bodies of the Government, in particular the Ruling Senate which was the Government of the Free City of Cracow. Also deposited in the National Archives in Cracow are books of civil status records drawn up between 1810 and 1852, based on the regulations of the French Civil Code.

The research carried out on the basis of the above-mentioned archival material will significantly contribute to the development of legal-historical research on the presence of the Napoleonic Code in Poland, which had hitherto focused on legislative and institutional analysis.[19] An exception in this respect is the recently published monograph by Piotr Pomianowski,[20] the subject matter of which (divorce) is complementary to the research conducted by Piotr Michalik presented in this monograph (the introduction and regulation of civil weddings). Yet the co-authors' research presented here, taking into account the earlier literature, is based on their own findings, both at the legislative level (constitutional foundations, legislation), institutional level (organisation and functioning of the authorities, including courts and administration), as well as

17 For more, see Pańków 1954, 123–124. The collection of the Archives of the Free City of Cracow held at the National Archives in Cracow, consists of 4,818 units (*c*.240 linear metres of files).

18 These records have been compiled and published by Andrzej Dziadzio and Mateusz Mataniak in the collection Dziadzio and Mataniak eds. 2022.

19 See below pp. 5–6.

20 Pomianowski 2022b.

an examination of the judicial and clerical practice of applying the *Code civil*, providing a full picture of the analysed phenomenon.

The significance, as well as the spatial and temporal scope, of the validity and reception of the Napoleonic Code and its impact on local, regional and even global legal heritage, has been the subject of legal-historical analysis since the 19th century.[21] Its outcome has been a series of publications shaping the current state of research on the subject, which is now more than 200 years old, primarily written by French scholars. A sort of summary of their output was the collective works published on the occasion of the centenary and bicentenary of the Code: *Le Code civil 1804–1904: Livre du Centenaire; Le Code civil 1804–2004: Livre du Bicentenaire*;[22] and *1804–2004 Le Code civil. Un passé, un présent, un avenir*.[23] Understandably, French research focuses on domestic issues,[24] and, in comparative terms, mainly draws on the Western European context,[25] only exceptionally drawing attention to the applicability and reception of the *Code civil* on Polish soil.[26] For analogous reasons, the validity of the French Code in the Germanic geographical area has become the subject of more extensive analysis by German legal-historical scholarship. Nevertheless, its contemporary publications on the significance of the Napoleonic Code in the development of German private law, only address to a limited extent the issue of 19th century case law based on the provisions of the *Code civil*, which remained effective until the nationwide German Civil Code (BGB, *Bürgerliches Gesetzbuch*) came into force.[27]

The issue of the validity and reception of the Napoleonic Code has also been present in Polish legal history scholarship since the 19th century.[28] During the 20th century, it was generally examined in the context of an analysis of the history of the State and the law of the Duchy of Warsaw, the Kingdom of Poland and the Free City of Cracow, but there has been no analysis of the application

21 See Halpérin 2018, 916–918; Robinson, Fergus and Gordon 2000, 266–267; Gilissen 1979, 416–417; Lewaszkiewicz-Petrykowska ed. 1993; Cavanna 1994, 87–112; Basdevant-Gaudemet, Gaudemet 2000, 397–400; Grimaldi 2003, 80–96; Bouineau, Roux 2004, 66–97; Varga 2011, 137–139; Gergen 2014, 29–30; Ranieri 2005, 85–125; Schubert and Schmoeckel eds. 2005; Schubert ed. 1977; Schulze 1994, 9–36.

22 See above, footnote 3.

23 Lequette and Leveneur eds. 2004.

24 Carbonnier 2004, 17–37; Halpérin 2004b, 43–58.

25 Blanc-Jouvan 2004, 477–512.

26 Halpérin 2003, 132.

27 Mohnhaupt 2006, 50–51; Geyer 2009; Peters 2018; Haferkamp 2019, 15–16; Schubert 2011, 109–110; Laufs 2011, 13; Kannowski 2011, 217–218; Zwanzger 2018, 161–189; Gross 1993; Fehrenbach 1983; Löhnig 2012, 255–269; Schubert 1977, 129–184; Wadle 2002.

28 See Hube 1829, 297–339.

of the law.[29] The importance of the *Code civil* for Polish legal history was particularly apparent during watershed moments, i.e.: in connection with the restoration of Poland's independence in 1918[30] and the collapse of communist rule in 1989.[31] As in other countries, the occasion to summarise the research on the presence of the Napoleonic Code in Poland was its 200th anniversary.[32] Its commemoration resulted in a conference *200 lat kodyfikacji napoleońskich – 200 années des codifications napoléoniennes*, organised in Cracow on 15–16 October 2004 by the Polish Academy of Sciences and Jagiellonian University,[33] and the first Polish monograph on the *Code civil* by Katarzyna Sójka-Zielińska.[34] The second decade of the 21st century saw the increasing involvement of Polish scholars in the analysis of the application of French law on Polish soil as an important part of the European and world heritage of Napoleonic codification, as demonstrated by the works published in English and German by Anna Klimaszewska[35] and Piotr Pomianowski,[36] as well as those by the co-authors of this monograph: Andrzej Dziadzio,[37] Mateusz Mataniak[38] and Piotr Michalik.[39]

This monograph aims to answer at least some of the research questions about the heritage of the *Code civil*.[40] Undoubtedly, the crucial point in the discussion is the issue of the implementation of the great European codification of civil law in the realities of the Free City of Cracow, a peripheral city-state from the point of view of the European political centres, with a political, social and legal culture different from that of France. For this reason, it is the intention of the co-authors to make this monograph a compact whole, which presents in a comprehensive, yet concise, manner both the process of the implementation of the Napoleonic Code and the application of its norms

29 See, e.g. Sobociński 1964; Wachholz 1957.

30 See Grynwaser 1951, 15–174.

31 Lewaszkiewicz-Petrykowska ed. 1993.

32 *Nota bene*, this was also linked to the landmark event of the accession of the Republic of Poland to the European Union in 2004.

33 The papers and discussion contributions from the conference have been published in a volume dedicated to the anniversary of *Czasopismo Prawno-Historyczne*. See Olszewski ed. 2005, 9–184. Both in the papers (only one of which dealt directly with the application of the Napoleonic Code in Poland (Janicka 2005)) and in the discussion, the need for research on this issue was repeatedly pointed out.

34 Sójka-Zielińska 2008.

35 Klimaszewska 2020, 143–163.

36 Pomianowski 2022b.

37 Dziadzio 2020a; Dziadzio 2022b.

38 Mataniak 2020a; Mataniak 2022b.

39 Michalik 2020; Michalik 2023.

40 See above, p. 1.

in the Republic of Cracow. In the Chapter 1, *The multicentric legal system of the Free City of Cracow,* Andrzej Dziadzio introduces the reader to the legal and organisational conditions of the city-state, which was a particular creation of the Congress of Vienna, in which the interests of the protective powers (Austria, Russia and Prussia) were embodied. In the Chapter 2, *The judiciary of the Free City of Cracow*, Mateusz Mataniak delves into the essence of the functioning of the legal system of the Free City of Cracow, i.e. the organisation and practice of its judiciary, which had the responsibility of applying foreign law, including the *Code civil.*

While the first and second chapters show the structure in which the Napoleonic Code was adopted, the third and fourth chapters present the initial reaction of this structure to the 'foreign body' introduced into it, in the form of the French Civil Code. This makes apparent that the Code was alien to the social and economic conditions existing on Polish soil and the legal culture established there. In the Chapter 3, *Attempts to codify civil law and the enactment of legal principles*, Piotr Michalik shows how difficult the implementation of the norms of the Civil Code was in the conditions of the Free City of Cracow, and how complex the reasons for its success were. A sort of riposte to the latter is the Chapter 4, *The modifications of the Napoleonic Code in the Free City of Cracow*, in which Mateusz Mataniak presents those regulations of the French Code which were already modified or even rejected by the authorities of the Republic of Cracow at the stage of their attempted introduction. This chapter thus closes a description of the conditions in which the application of individual institutions of the Civil Code took place, which will be presented later in the monograph.

Chapters 5 to 8 are a presentation of the co-authors' most important findings on the reception of the Napoleonic Code in the Free City of Cracow. They show its essence expressed in the actual application of adopted French norms to the realities of everyday life in Polish society. It is the intention of the co-authors to show an analysis of this phenomenon in all the basic branches of law regulated by the Civil Code, while highlighting the institutions particularly characteristic of this code. In the Chapter 5, *Civil weddings and marriage certificates of the Jewish population*, Piotr Michalik presents the intricacies of the application of the secular model of personal and matrimonial law of the Napoleonic Code on the Jewish community, which constituted a significant part of the population of the Free City of Cracow. In the Chapter 6, *Servitudes, expropriations and possessory protection*, Mateusz Mataniak presents the problem of property law in the context of restrictions on the 'sacred' right to property, so important for the life of the inhabitants of the Republic of Cracow and the administrative activities of the authorities of this city-state. In the Chapter 7, *Form of contracts*,

Andrzej Dziadzio analyses the implementation of the 'flagship' principle of freedom of contract for the Civil Code's contract law against the background of court disputes concerning the validity of a concluded contract, which were an everyday occurrence in the Free City of Cracow. In the final chapter of the monograph, *Inheritance*, Piotr Michalik presents the position of the Cracovian courts in relation to the inheritance rules adopted in French inheritance law, with particular reference to the reserve system. Mateusz Mataniak then shows how these courts dealt with the rejection by the Napoleonic Code of the inheritance subjectivity of legal persons.

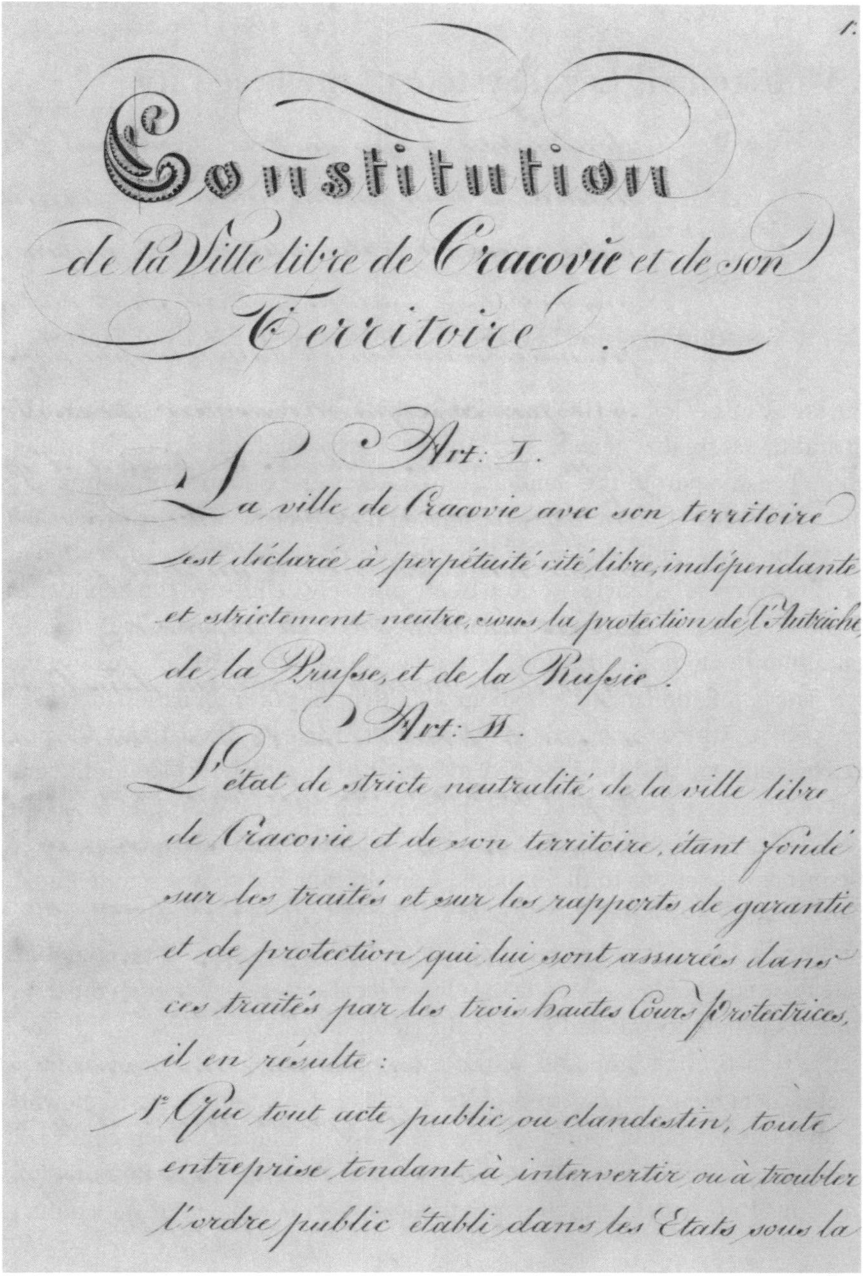

1.

Constitution

de la Ville libre de Cracovie et de son Territoire.

Art: I.

La ville de Cracovie avec son territoire est déclarée à perpétuité cité libre, indépendante et strictement neutre, sous la protection de l'Autriche, de la Prusse, et de la Russie.

Art: II.

L'état de stricte neutralité de la ville libre de Cracovie et de son territoire, étant fondé sur les traités et sur les rapports de garantie et de protection qui lui sont assurés dans ces traités par les trois hautes Cours Protectrices, il en résulte:

1° Que tout acte public ou clandestin, toute entreprise tendant à intervertir ou à troubler l'ordre public établi dans les Etats sous la

FIGURE 1 *Constitution of the Free City of Cracow from 1833*, (manuscript, paper, 1833)
SOURCE: NATIONAL ARCHIVES IN CRACOW, ANK, 29/200/19, 1; PHOTO IN PUBLIC DOMAIN (WIKIMEDIA COMMONS)

CHAPTER 1

A Multicentric Legal System of the Free City of Cracow

Andrzej Dziadzio

1 Constitutional and Legal Foundations of the Free City of Cracow

The Free City of Cracow (the so-called Republic of Cracow) was established by an additional treaty concluded by Austria, Prussia and Russia on 3 May 1815, which became part of the General (Final) Act of the Congress of Vienna of 9 June 1815. Article I of the treaty recognised that "Cracow and its district shall forever be a free, independent and strictly neutral city under the protection of the three powers".[1] Article II of the treaty precisely delineated the boundaries of the Free City of Cracow. It encompassed the area of Cracow with its surroundings (including Chrzanów, Trzebinia, Nowa Góra) with an area of 1,150 km^2. The population in 1815 was about 90,000 (in 1843 the population increased to 145,787, of which 10 per cent were Jews).[2] In Article VII of the treaty, the protective states granted the Free City a Constitution, which formed an integral part of the treaty concluded between them. The three powers announced the establishment of an Organising Commission, whose function was to develop the principles set out in the imposed Constitution and to oversee its implementation. The Commission was to be composed of three commissioners, the so-called residents, representing each of the three states. Three members were to be co-opted from among the elite of local society, drawn from the three estates: the nobility (landed gentry), the clergy and the burghers.

The Constitution, imposed by the three powers on 3 May 1815, was not a lengthy document; it consisted of 22 articles.[3] It contained the framework foundations for public order for the Free City of Cracow, which could still be supplemented in the course of the work of the Organising Commission. The Constitution defined Roman Catholicism as the religion of the country,

---

1 *Traité additionnel relatif à Cracovie entre l'Autriche, la Prusse et la Russie, signé à Vienne le 21 avril/3 mai 1815*. In: Tokarz ed. 1932, 4–8.

2 Bartel 1976, 8. In 1846, the Free City of Cracow ceased to exist and was incorporated into the Austrian Empire.

3 *Constitution de ıa Ville libre de Cracovie, 3 mai 1815*. In: Tokarz ed. 1932, 10–14.

 | DOI:10.1163/9789004688742_003

but at the same time declared equality of rights for all Christian religions. Tolerated religious cults were also to come under the protection of the law; the Constitution introduced the equality of all citizens before the law (Articles I–IV). The Government of the Free City of Cracow was the Senate, consisting of 12 members and the chairman. The representative body was the unicameral Assembly of Representatives with powers of the legislature. Nine members of the Senate, including its chairman, were elected by the Assembly of Representatives, while four were delegated by Jagiellonian University and the Cracow Chapter in equal numbers of two senators, one of whom was appointed for life, one temporarily for one year. Similarly, the Assembly of Representatives elected six senators for life and six temporarily. Three senators elected on a temporary basis stepped down each year. The Assembly of Representatives, the university and the Chapter filled the vacant seat (Articles V–VI). The Chairman of the Senate was elected for a three-year term with the possibility of re-election. The first composition of the Senate was appointed by the Organising Commission.

FIGURE 2 *Józef Brodowski, "The act of granting the constitution to the Free City of Cracow in 1818"*, (painting, oil on canvas, 1st half of the 19th century)
SOURCE: JAGIELLONIAN UNIVERSITY; PHOTO IN PUBLIC DOMAIN (WIKIMEDIA COMMONS)

The Assembly of Representatives was made up of deputies elected at municipal assemblies; the right to vote was based on the criteria of wealth and education. In addition to the elected deputies, the Assembly of Representatives also included three delegated senators, three prelates appointed by the Cathedral Chapter, three professors delegated by Jagiellonian University and six justices of the peace (Art. XI). The legislative powers of the Assembly of Representatives were severely limited; only a bill that had been debated and voted on by the Senate could be the subject of the Assembly's deliberations. The Chamber was not allowed to amend bills, including the budget bill, it could only accept or reject the bill. The Assembly of Representatives was not entitled to propose a constitutional amendment either. The Chamber did, however, exercise an important control function. Indeed, the representatives could, with a two-thirds majority, indict officials or also judges before the Sejm Court for the crime of theft of public money or abuse of power (Article X).[4]

Constitutional provisions were to be implemented, as mentioned, by the Organising Commission. To this end, the governments of the three powers issued an 'Instruction', which included an explanation of the main assumptions of the Constitution.[5] The Instruction identified priority issues for the Commission to address as soon as possible after its arrival in Cracow.[6] The Commission's task was first to appoint the initial composition of the Senate, which – according to the Constitution – headed the entire administration as the central governmental body. The subordination of the administration of the Free City of Cracow to the Senate was not, however, to mean that the Commission should withdraw from its activities. The Commission was to remain in constant contact with the Senate above all to discuss the provisions of the imposed Constitution with a view to elaborating on its content before publication in the Official Journal of the Free City of Cracow. The Protectors of the Free City of Cracow (Russia, Austria, Prussia) assumed that the Senate, with the consent of the Commission, would be able to amend the provisions of the Constitution, without, as the residents (i.e. plenipotentiaries of the

---

4 Ibidem, 11.

5 In full, the: *Instruction für die zur Organisation des Freistaats Krakau von den hohen drei Mächten Kommissarien, sowie man darüber in der gemeinschaftlich abgehaltenen Konferenz übereingekommen ist* (issued 4 July 1815), for which see Tokarz ed. 1932, 15. The publisher included the instruction in German, as the French version could not be found.

6 The Commission arrived in Cracow on 12 October 1815, but as early as 2 August 1815, the resolutions of the Congress of Vienna were announced in the Official Cracow Journal: *Gazeta Krakowska* No. 62 of 2 August 1815, 785–788. On 2 November 1815 the Organising Commission appointed the first composition of the Senate.

partitioning states) were instructed, violating the principles laid down in its original version.[7]

The limits of the permissible development of the content of the Constitution by the Senate were thus severely narrowed. The members of the Organising Commission were to ensure that the Senate did not reject the fundamental assumptions of the imposed Constitution. The Protective States expressed their view in the Instruction that the Constitution could also enter into force without a detailed elaboration of its provisions. It is therefore not surprising that the content of the 1818 Constitution overlapped almost entirely with its 1815 version.[8] However, the Senate succeeded in introducing two articles into the original text of the Constitution that gave it a more liberal dimension. One prohibited the confiscation of property, with the exception of the forfeiture to the treasury of criminal items (contraband). The other established a ban on pre-emptive censorship, allowing only judicial punitive censorship (Article XXIV).

An important part of the 1815 constitutional rules imposed by the Protectors of the Free City of Cracow, were the provisions concerning judicial law (civil, criminal and procedural) and the organisation of the general judiciary. Article XII of both Constitutions required the Assembly of Representatives to appoint a committee whose task was to prepare a code of civil, criminal and procedural law that would take into account local customs. In the Instruction given to the three residents, the governments of the Protective States explicitly stated that they had declined to designate a specific act in the constitution as the norm applicable in the Free City of Cracow.[9] However, it was their firm intention to replace the French law in force in Cracow, as a manifestation of Napoleonic usurpation, with new codes. Indeed, from 1810 onwards, both the *Code civil*[10] and the French *Code de procédure civile* were in force in Cracow. The Instruction therefore made a clear recommendation that the Organising Commission should work with the Representative Assembly to begin work immediately on the preparation of new acts. The Commission was to instruct the representatives of the Free City of Cracow of the great importance of introducing new

7 Tokarz ed., 1932, 17.

8 Dippel, ed. 2008, 139.

9 Tokarz ed. 1932, 17. § 9 of the Instruction said: "*Die Constitution schreibt kein bereits bestehendes Gesetzbuch als Norm für den Freistaat Krakau*".

10 The French Civil Code issued in 1804 originally had the name *Code civil*. In 1807 it was renamed *Code Napoléon* and retained this name in France until the fall of Napoleon I. Its Polish translation *Kodeks Napoleona* was introduced in 1807 in the Duchy of Warsaw and remained in force on Polish soil until the end of applicability of the code, i.e. until 1946. In the book, these names will be used interchangeably.

legislation. The Commission's task was to support the codification work, but also to ensure that the content of the drafts did not include regulations contrary to the Constitution. Until the new legislation was passed, the status quo was to be maintained.[11] In addition to maintaining the validity of French civil law, Austrian substantive and procedural criminal law, contained in the 1803 code, continued to apply in Cracow (the so-called *Franciscana*).

However, the history of the legal codification movement in the Free City of Cracow[12] took a different course than the members of the Organising Commission intended.[13] After its dissolution in August 1818, the Legislative Committee, with the consent of the Senate, completely abandoned work on the preparation of comprehensive codes, concentrating only on the drafting of acts that were dictated by a return to Polish legal tradition or by practical considerations.[14] In creating its own civil law, the Free City of Cracow followed the legislative path of the Kingdom of Poland, also established at the Congress of Vienna. It was a semi-sovereign state, remaining in a real union (common foreign policy) and personal union (common monarch) with Tsarist Russia. The Sejm of the Kingdom of Poland began its codification work precisely by amending those provisions of the *Code civil* which deviated from the old Polish legal order. Following the example of the Kingdom of Poland, mortgage law in the Free City of Cracow was amended first. This took place with the Act of 17 June 1822, in which more than half of the provisions were a literal repetition or reworking of the Mortgage Act of the Kingdom of Poland of 26 April 1818. In contrast to the Kingdom of Poland, however, the French provisions on personal law and matrimonial law were retained in the Free City of Cracow.[15]

---

11 Tokarz ed. 1932, 18. The Organising Commission fulfilled the task imposed on it in the legal act entitled "Provisional Solutions for the Judicial Authorities of the Free City of Cracow" of 5 December 1815, for which see: DRRz.WMK of 1816, 91–104.

12 This issue is addressed in Chapter 3.

13 It is possible to believe that even the Protectors themselves had, over time, come to terms with the prolonged presence of French law in the Free City of Krakow and left the amendment of legislation to the discretion of the bodies themselves, since Article XII of the 1818 constitution was amended, already stating, in a less ultimative form than in 1815, that "the Assembly of Representatives will undertake, if necessary, to *lay down and revise* (author emphasis) the civil, criminal and legal procedure codes".

14 This issue is addressed in Chapter 4.

15 Another code in force in the Free City of Cracow from 1810 onwards, besides the *Code civil*, was the French Commercial Code of 1807 (*Code de commerce*), supplemented by several specific acts, such as the Act of 5 January 1819 on the organisation of the stock exchange and on the establishment of the Commercial Council, or the Act on the rate of interest of 13 July 1844, insofar as it concerned interest in commercial activities.

2 The Opinions of Professors and Doctors of Law of Jagiellonian University on the Application of French Civil Law

Since the preparation of a comprehensive codification of civil law was abandoned, French civil procedure also remained valid in the Free City of Cracow. It was amended only in the part concerning enforcement proceedings by the Ordinance "Law on Judicial Enforcement", passed in 1823, and as regards the provisions on "proceedings before the Courts of the Peace" by the Act of 1825.[16] However, the course of judicial proceedings in civil cases differed from that of the Duchy of Warsaw. The constitution of 1815, in Article XV, introduced a new organisation of the judiciary, which provided for the existence of two judicial instances in the form of a Court of First Instance and a Court of Appeal, with the continuation of the Courts of the Peace of the earlier period. The Constitution omitted the organisation of the Court of Cassation, which had existed in the Duchy of Warsaw from 1810.

In its place, as it were, the constitution of the Free City of Cracow provided for an extraordinary appeal procedure in the form of a complaints process to the Professors and Doctors of Law of the Faculty of Law of Jagiellonian University. Under Article XV of the Constitution, the parties to civil proceedings were entitled to appeal the judgments of the Court of First Instance and the Court of Appeal, which were in conformity in content with the Faculty of Law of Jagiellonian University. The basis of an appeal against the issued judgments could be an alleged violation of the substantive law or the essential forms of court proceedings. The Faculty of Law, after reviewing the case, i.e. the judgments and the pleadings of the parties, would draw up a legal opinion in which it either found a violation of substantive or procedural law or, on the contrary, argued that no violation of law had occurred.

If the faculty opined that there was an infringement of the law in a case under consideration, this opened the way for a party to refer the appeal to the Court of Last (Third) Instance. A finding by the Faculty of Law that there were no grounds for appeal ended the case. The judgments became final, unless the Professors and Doctors of Law came to the conclusion that they differed in content. In such a case, there was always a right of appeal to the Court of Last (Third) Instance. In the years 1815–33, the Faculty of Law of Jagiellonian

16 The *Code civil* and the *Code de procédure civile* lost their binding force on 29 September 1855. Only in the area of matrimonial law did the *Code civil* remain in force until 20 April 1852. French law was therefore still in force nine years after the Free City of Cracow ceased to exist.

University thus performed an adjudicatory function *par excellence*.[17] This appeal measure adopted by the Constitution of the Free City of Cracow was an original and unique institution, unprecedented in other legal orders. Although, as already mentioned in the introduction, it combined elements of French cassation and the German procedure known as the *Aktenversendung*, neither of them found full expression in this hybrid Construction. A finding by the Faculty of Law on grounds for cassation before the Court of Last (Third) Instance did not mean that the contested judgments were repealed and the case sent back to the Court of Appeal, since the Court of Last Instance had the power to make a substantive ruling. The opinion of the Faculty of Law was not bound by it, since it could assume that there were no grounds for appeal and uphold the contested judgments.[18]

According to Article XV of the constitution of the Free City of Cracow, an appeal to the Faculty of Law of Jagiellonian University was not possible in cases where the Court of First Instance and the Court of Appeal had issued a unanimous judgment in a criminal case. Thus, a convicted person could not avail him or herself of the benefit of filing an appeal to the Court of Last (Third) Instance through the Faculty of Law in cases where the two lower courts had rendered concurring judgments. Only criminal cases ending in a sentence of death or infamy were to be submitted to the Court of Last Instance.

---

17 Patkaniowski 1964, 157. According to the constitution of 1815, Jagiellonian University was to play an important role not only as an academic centre, but was also given an extensive role in the political and judicial structures of the Free City of Cracow. Its representatives were members of both the Senate and the Assembly of Representatives (out of 22 articles of the constitution, the Cracow Academy was mentioned in eight, and an additional treaty of the three powers guaranteed its former privileges and property). Thus, the members of the Cracow Academy (since 1817 the Jagiellonian University) actively shaped the public life of the Free City of Cracow. Jagiellonian University, together with the so-called 'municipal party', presented a liberal and democratic attitude compared to the conservative policy of the majority of the Senate and its Chairman, Count Stanisław Wodzicki. Cracow's aristocratic and conservative spheres perceived the University's position in the Free City's political system as a "government within a government". They therefore aimed to weaken the influence of University professors on the administrative structures of the Republic of Cracow. The political conflict between the Chairman of the Senate and the Rector of the University, Professor Walenty Litwiński, ultimately led to a significant reduction in the autonomy of Jagiellonian University. The new constitution of the Free City of Cracow of 1833, while increasing the authority of the residents of the Great Powers over the authorities of the Free City of Cracow, at the same time abolished the function of the Faculty of Law of Jagiellonian University, provided for by Article XV of the 1815 and 1818 constitutions.

18 The procedure before the Faculty of Law of Jagiellonian University is discussed by Dziadzio 2020c, 189.

FIGURE 3 *Meeting place of the Faculty of Law of Jagiellonian University (Collegium Iuridicum) – current view*
PHOTO FROM 2018 IN PUBLIC DOMAIN (WIKIMEDIA COMMONS) – GNU FREE DOCUMENTATION LICENSE (CC BY 4.0)

Nevertheless, the Professors and Doctors of Law of Jagiellonian University – contrary to the literal wording of the Constitution – adopted the principle that in criminal cases as well it was possible to appeal to the Court of Last (Third) Instance on the basis of *opinio facultatis* in the event of grounds for cassation. This was because they assumed that the accused should not be in a worse legal position than a party to civil proceedings.[19] The legal faculty of Jagiellonian University, therefore, also issued opinions on violations of substantive or procedural law in criminal cases, but the percentage of these was small within the total number of rulings, which mainly concerned private law disputes.[20]

For 18 years, the Faculty of Law of Jagiellonian University of the Free City of Cracow exercised judicial supervision over the rulings of the Court of First Instance and the Court of Appeal by means of its opinions. The opinions of the Faculty of Law were of particular importance from the point of view of the multiplicity of legal systems in force in the Free City of Cracow. The courts had to apply Austrian law, regulating the legal relationship with the peasant population, still in the spirit of the feudal system. Yet, they were also bound by

---

19 Pauli 1970, 51.
20 See Dziadzio and Mataniak eds. 2022, 7–703.

provisions of constitutional rank, which presupposed the equal application of civil law to all persons, regardless of their estate affiliation. Peasant property was subject to administrative restrictions in the Free City of Cracow on the basis of Austrian regulations, which were still in force. Civil law relations with regard to peasant property were thus subject to a double regulation: the French Civil Code and Austrian administrative law. This legal state of affairs gave rise to doubts in judicial practice. For this reason, the legal opinions of the Faculty of Law were able to provide guidance to the courts in interpreting provisions derived from different legal orders.

In one of its opinions, the Faculty of Law presented its view on the relationship between the police (absolute) State legislation and the content of the liberal Constitution of the Free City of Cracow. It concerned inheritance rights to peasant property. The Faculty of Law instructed the courts on how they should proceed in such cases:

> Whereas according to the Imperial Austrian patent … all peasant land is to be considered as indivisible, and in the event of inheritance the co-successors should content themselves with paying off the valuation, and this according to the order of inheritance prescribed for the peasants; furthermore, that the fragmentation of peasant land, even if they possessed it by the right of ownership, is forbidden, and this by administrative law, or political solutions. Furthermore, taking into account that the introduction of the French Code and the Constitutions of the Duchy of Warsaw as well as the Constitution of the Free City of Cracow did not change this Act, because the Civil Code has no connection with the administrative sphere, and although the Constitutions declared that all are equal before the law, this equality extends only to personal rights, but not to political relations; indeed, the Constitution of the Free City of Cracow confirmed the legislation on the status of peasants issued by former governments, when it declared that the current rights of farmers were preserved[21]

21 Dziadzio and Mataniak eds. 2022, 244–245. Meeting of 22 July 1826, AUJ, WP I 57, 178–182. The competent authority for the division of peasant land was the Department of Internal Affairs and the Police. See the Regulation of the Ruling Senate of 4 May 1825 on the prohibition of the sale, exchange and division of peasant land without the knowledge of the municipal authorities and the consent of the Government authorities, DRz.WMK of 1825, Nos. 19 and 20, 77–78.

The above view of the Faculty of Law on the relationship between administrative acts and the Constitution was correct. For neither the principle of constitutional supremacy nor the hierarchy of sources of law was accepted at that time. The courts did not have the power to examine the compatibility of lower rank laws with acts. One can only raise an objection to that part of the opinion which refers to the text of the Constitution in order to justify the thesis that it did not repeal Austrian administrative laws. Indeed, in the phrase "the current rights of farmers were preserved", the Constitution meant to confirm their rights to the land they owned, rather than the restrictions stemming from the former acts.

FIGURE 4 *Design of the uniform of a professor of Jagiellonian University from 1828,* (drawing, paper, 1828)
SOURCE: JAGIELLONIAN UNIVERSITY ARCHIVES, AUJ, S I 544; PHOTO & PERMISSION BY JAGIELLONIAN UNIVERSITY ARCHIVES

3 The Austrian Criminal Law of the Free City of Cracow

Austrian law retained its binding force in the Free City of Cracow not only with regard to administrative-legal relations, but also criminal legislation. As mentioned above, the Austrian Criminal Code of Francis II (*Strafgesetz über Verbrechen und schwere Polizei-Übertretungen*) of 1803 remained in force. However, it did not apply in the Free City of Cracow as it had been introduced there during Austrian rule before 1809. Indeed, during the time of the Duchy of Warsaw, amendments were made to the Austrian Code by a decree of the Saxon King (the Duke of Warsaw) of 26 July 1810, which adapted the main assumptions of Napoleonic criminal law, i.e. the Criminal Procedure Code of 1808 and the Criminal Code of 1810. The amendment to the Austrian Code introduced, following French law, a division of offences into crimes, *délits* and contraventions. Applying this division of offences, the system of penalties was changed, which were divided into criminal, correctional and police penalties. The changes introduced were linked to the creation of a new system of common courts in the Duchy of Warsaw.

The inquisitorial procedure of the *Franciscana* was modified in the decree of 1810 with the incorporation of the fundamental principles of the modern French procedure into the Austrian code. Public, oral and open proceedings were introduced in place of the secret and written Austrian inquisitorial procedure. The concept of litigants was also introduced. A prosecutor became a new judicial body, whose task was to draw up and support the indictment before the court. The accused was granted the right to defence by being able to appoint a professional defence counsel. He was also granted the right to appeal against the judgment by way of appeal or cassation. Despite these progressive changes, however, the Royal Decree did not abolish the inquisitorial procedure. This is because the main phase of proceedings was still a secret and written investigation. Indeed, at the public trial, the principle of directness did not apply, as no fresh evidentiary proceedings were conducted, only the records of the investigation files were read out.[22] Nor was the principle of the judge's free assessment of evidence introduced, which was a hallmark of French legislation. The legal (formal) theory of evidence was still applied in criminal trials before Cracow's courts.

At this point, it should be noted that Cracow's lawyers, educated in Austrian law and still applying it, adhered to the legal theory of evidence. This

22 Pauli 1968, 23.

is demonstrated by the deliberations of the Legislative Assembly on the principles of future codes. The representatives of the Free City of Cracow were also in favour of transferring the legal theory of evidence to civil procedure, expressing their will that a future civil procedural law should determine the "number and quality of witnesses" needed for the court to accept complete evidence.[23] The Cracovian legislator thus espoused the principle of Austrian procedural law, rather than the free assessment of evidence promoted by French law.

In criminal cases, the judges of the Free City of Cracow generally ruled on the basis of Austrian criminal law. The progressive modifications made by the Royal Decree of 1810 were withdrawn at the request of the three protective courts by decree of the Ruling Senate on 2 July 1839. Seven years before the Free City of Cracow ceased to exist, the Austrian Code was applied in its original 1803 form. In the same year, the Protective States imposed on the Republic of Cracow the Military Penal Code of the Duchy of Modena (*Codice penale militare Estense*) as the Military Penal Code of the Militia of the Free City of Cracow. Promulgated in 1832 by Prince Francis IV, the code was translated into Polish and, on 22 May 1839, provisionally came into force by the Ruling Senate, pending its enactment by the Assembly of Representatives. Imposed in blatant violation of the Constitution, the code was reluctantly adopted in Cracow also because of its repressive nature (severe penalties, no appeal). The code was also never legalised by the Assembly of Representatives, as it was a telling manifestation of the extra-constitutional interference of the Protectors of the Free City of Cracow.[24] The practice based on the Military Code has been assessed critically in the legal-historical literature, as the case law of the separate militia court was in the spirit of maintaining the exaggerated severity of its provisions. In contrast, the application of the *Franciscana*'s provisions by Cracow's courts has been assessed positively in Polish scholarship. The analysis of the case law confirmed the correct interpretation of the norms of the code and the ruling line in the spirit of the lenient treatment of defendants. The tendency to liberalise the provisions of the Austrian Penal Code was clearly a dominant feature of the case law of Cracovian courts.[25]

---

23 *Gazeta Krakowska* No. 19 of 3 March 1818, 217.

24 Pauli 1982, 156–157.

25 Ibidem, 153–155.

4 The Case Law of Cracow's Courts at the Interface of French and Austrian Law

The liberalism of the Cracovian judiciary was also noticeable in the application of the provisions of the French *Code civil*, the strictness and formalism of which became clearly evident when confronted with Austrian civil law. Significant differences between Austrian law – i.e. the West Galician Code of 1797 (in force in Cracow until 1810) – and French law occurred above all with regard to divorce law and the form of contracts concluded (see Chapter 7: The Form of Contracts). The case law of divorce cases, in particular, is a perfect illustration of the use by Cracow's courts of legal norms derived from two separate, incompatible legal orders.

According to the *Code civil*, the right to divorce was enjoyed by any person regardless of religious denomination, while in Austria, Catholics did not benefit from divorce. Although in both legal systems the prerequisite for obtaining a divorce was adultery by one of the spouses, under Austrian law the right to request a divorce on this ground was enjoyed equally by both husband and wife.[26] Adultery as a ground for divorce was treated differently by the *Code civil*. A husband could always request a divorce on the grounds of his wife's adultery (Article 229 of the NC), but a wife only if the husband kept a concubine in the common residence (Article 230 of the NC). A separate independent ground for divorce was a provision in the NC according to which spouses could mutually request divorce on the grounds of rape, harshness or severe insults of one of them towards the other (Article 231 of the NC). Similarly, the West Galician Code considered coarse treatment of the spouses towards each other as a ground for divorce.[27]

French law put the wife at a disadvantage when it came to requesting a divorce on the grounds of her husband's adultery. This was because she could only obtain a divorce if she proved before the court that her husband had lived with his mistress in their common residence. A petition by a wife for divorce in the case of adultery committed by her husband in other circumstances was, in principle, inadmissible. On the other hand, any adultery of a wife proven in court proceedings led not only to a ruling a divorce, but also to a mandatory sentence of imprisonment by placement in a house of correction for between three months and two years (Article of 298 of the NC). Austrian law did not apply such strictness to a wife.

---

26 Dziadzio 2020a, 271–275.

27 For more, see e.g. Decourt-Hollender 2012, 329–378.

French law also diverged from Austrian law in terms of evidentiary proceedings. The *Code civil* defined the categories of evidence that could be admitted in a civil dispute. The evidence taken in divorce proceedings was subject to the judge's free assessment. Thus, a court in divorce proceedings was allowed to admit evidence from both eyewitness (*de visu*) and hearsay witness (*de auditu*) testimony. Accordingly, a court was allowed to accept the testimony of an earwitness as evidence of the act of adultery. In contrast, Austrian law had different rules of evidence in cases of the crime of adultery. Austrian criminal procedure – as mentioned above – was still based on the legal theory of evidence, according to which the testimony of two reliable eyewitnesses was necessary to prove the offence according to the principle: one witness is no witness (*testis unus, testis nullus*).

The duality of the legal order of the Free City of Cracow therefore played a major role in the course of divorce proceedings. This is because it opened up the field for interpretation of the law using the simultaneous validity of different rules and norms. It was particularly beneficial for the lawyers of the defendant wives, as they were able to successfully challenge the allegation of adultery committed if it was based on the testimony of a witness or witnesses, which constituted only indirect (circumstantial) evidence of marital infidelity. In their pleadings, they referred explicitly to the provisions of the *Franciscana*, which required evidence of the testimony of two eyewitnesses to prove the commission of an offence (§ 409).[28] The aim of the lawyers of wives sued for divorce was obvious; it was to protect their clients from mandatory imprisonment! As a rule, Cracow's courts usually accepted this argumentation if they did not have unequivocal and certain witness testimony in the case that the wife had committed adultery. On the other hand, it was less common that in evidentiary proceedings in a divorce case on the grounds of a wife's adultery, that the courts freely assessed indirect evidence presented in the husband's petition, and pronounced a divorce on this basis.[29] Evidentiary proceedings in divorce cases brought by a husband against his wife accused of adultery, were generally conducted by Cracow's judges according to the rules of the legal theory of evidence.[30] This kind of judicial practice was, on the one hand, a

---

28 Pomianowski 2018, 120–124.

29 Ibidem, 122. It was easier for the courts to invoke the principle of free assessment of evidence adopted in French law in a divorce case, when the circumstances showed that a well-known pharmacist from Cracow, and a professor at the Jagiellonian University, Józef Sawiczewski, had brought an action against his wife, who, according to witness testimony, "indulged in drunkenness and wandered about at night with men".

30 Ibidem, 124.

testimony to the judges' attachment to the principles of Austrian criminal procedure; on the other, it was also a manifestation of the deliberate circumvention of French law, which treated husband and wife unequally in the event of a request for divorce on the grounds of committed adultery.

However, the court's acceptance of the absence of legal proof of adultery – according to the rules of the Austrian Criminal Act – did not result in the dismissal of the petition, since there was still a likelihood of marital infidelity, which, under French law, could constitute grounds for divorce. The court, therefore, ultimately pronounced a divorce. However, the court based it not on a provision allowing divorce on the grounds of adultery, but on the premise of harshness and insults of the spouses towards each other, which were generally an inherent consequence of marital infidelity. By adopting a different legal basis for the judgment of divorce, the court avoided having to sentence the defendant's wife to a correctional institution.

Cracow's courts, in their rulings, also tried to limit the unequal treatment by French law of married women with regard to the right to request a divorce on the grounds of their husband's adultery. They ruled on the dissolution of marriage by divorce in the case of proven infidelity of the husband, even if he did not bring the mistress into the shared home. In such a case, the courts would change the legal basis of the ruling made, qualifying the husband's adultery as a special kind of grave insult to his wife. Undoubtedly, this way of applying the provisions of the NC did not correspond to either the intention of the legislator or the content of the legal norms, which clearly defined two independent and separate grounds for the court to pronounce a divorce. However, the interpretation of the law adopted by the courts was in line with the legal-natural idea of equality of the sexes in private law relations, which was implemented to a greater extent by Austrian than by French legislation. Cracow's courts considered it grounds for granting a divorce when the husband had committed marital infidelity in the shared home with any woman, e.g. a servant, and not only with one with whom he wanted to have a permanent relationship. In this respect, the case law in Cracow did not differ from the ruling practice of the Baden or French courts.[31]

The provision in the Civil Code on "qualified" adultery by the husband as grounds for the wife to file for divorce was also "creatively" – albeit *contra legem* – used by the Cracow courts to improve the inheritance rights of extramarital children. Napoleonic law prohibited children from incestuous and

31 See *Jahrbücher der Großherzogliche Badischen Oberhofgerichts*, Jahrgang 3 1825(1826), 14–19, https://dlc.mpdl.mpg.de/dlc/viewMulti/escidoc:14679 (accessed on 3 April 2023). For more, see Gross 1993.

adulterous relationships from inheriting their parents' property (Article 762 of the *Code civil*). Parents could only recognise natural non-marital children. If recognised, they could inherit from their parents, but not on an equal basis with marital children. The recognition by parents of children from incestuous and adulterous relationships was – according to the *Code civil* – legally impermissible, in contrast to Austrian law, in which there was no such prohibition. According to Austrian law, it was possible for a father to recognise a child from an extramarital adulterous relationship, who could inherit the entire estate from the deceased father, if he left neither other descendants nor a widow.

In French law, in the above situation, the estate was inherited only by the siblings or ascendants of the testator. Such a case was encountered by the judges of the Free City of Cracow, in which a sister claimed entitlement to the entire estate, despite the fact that her deceased brother had left an extra-marital son. During his lifetime he had formally acknowledged his illegitimate son, who was his only descendant. However, the court awarded the extramarital son – in accordance with French law – half of his father's estate, as it assumed that he was not the child born of an adulterous relationship. According to the court, a married man's relationship with an unmarried woman could not be considered adulterous if he had intimate relationships with her outside the home! The court of first instance therefore dismissed the claim for the entire inheritance on the grounds that the plaintiff had failed to prove that the brother had conceived an extramarital affair in a house where his wife also lived. This was the view of the Cracovian court derived from a provision of the *Code civil* which considered sexual relations with a concubine introduced into the shared house to be adultery of the husband as grounds for the wife to request a divorce. However, this original interpretation of the French Code did not last long. The Court of Appeal modified the judgment in favour of the plaintiff, in accordance with the content and spirit of the legislation of the *Code Napoléon*.[32]

5 Conclusion

The description of the legal order of the Free City of Cracow includes a mosaic of legal systems, the application of which made it necessary for Cracow's judges to familiarise themselves with provisions of varying content and origin. It was not uncommon for cases to have to refer to the old Polish law, the provisions of

---

32 For more on this subject, see Dziadzio 2020a, 269–277.

the West Galician Code, as well as the provisions of acts passed in the Free City of Cracow. These regulated private law relations anew, but took into account the principles of old Polish law, such as the one mentioned on privileges and mortgages of 17 June 1822. The act regulated the ownership of immovable property and the establishment of mortgages on it. The act adopted the principle, which differed from French law, that for an effective transfer of immovable property it was necessary to enter the contract of obligation (title of acquisition) in the mortgage books. The transfer of ownership of the property did not take place *solo consensu*, as in the case of the *Code Napoléon* provisions, but only after the registration of the title of acquisition in the mortgage books. This entry was constitutive and not, as under Napoleonic law, declaratory. A special mandatory form of a contract, transferring ownership of real estate, was also introduced. In order to be valid, the contract had to be concluded before a notary in the presence of two witnesses. The rules relating to mortgages were also changed. In contrast to the secret and general French mortgage, the mortgage law of the Free City of Cracow was based – with reference to the former Polish law – on the principles of openness and the high level of detail of mortgage entries, preserving the principle of priority of entry when satisfying creditors' claims.

Therefore, an important part of the judicial supervision carried out by the Law Faculty of Jagiellonian University became the assessment of the application of the provisions of the 1822 Act by the Mortgage Commission and the Court of Appeal, which was the appellate instance. Cases relating to decisions of the Mortgage Commission to enter or delete rights *in rem* in the mortgage lists, which were upheld by the Court of Appeal, frequently appeared in the rulings of the Faculty of Law.[33]

An analysis of the Law Faculty's opinions on the determination of rights *in rem* on real estate by the Mortgage Commission, shows that it generally accepted its decision, approved by the Court of Appeal's judgment, as correct. In one case, the faculty considered the lawfulness of the refusal to register mortgages in favour of, among others, hospitals, collegiate churches and Jagiellonian University, encumbering the real estate of the defendant party. According to the Faculty of Law, the appellant representative of the national Government had failed to prove compliance with the old law of the transfer of mortgage encumbrances on the defendant's hereditary estates by way of

33 Malec 2004, 75–96. The author correctly assumed that in the case of concurring rulings by the Mortgage Commission and the Court of Appeal, the dissatisfied party brought appeals to the Court of Third Instance through the Faculty of Law, but in a significant number of appeals (*c.*70 per cent), it found no grounds for cassation.

proof of the entry of the disputed sums in the court books. The Government's representative, relying on the provision of the NC that evidence by oath may be admitted in any case, demanded that it be submitted by the party to prove the possession of the document of the taking of the hereditary estates with the mortgage encumbrances. The Faculty of Law, rejecting the request of the Government's lawyer, declared the party's oath evidence inadmissible, since, as it argued, in its opinion:

> the right *in rem* should be proved not by a firm oath, but by a mortgage instrument under the above-mentioned constitutions [i.e. of 1523 and 1543]. Therefore, by revoking the right to enter these sums in the mortgage register, the courts did not commit any violation of the law, but rather complied with the explicit provisions of the above-mentioned constitutions, namely the 1588 constitution, vol.2 folio 1219 and of the 1511 constitution, vol.1 folio 377.[34]

In this opinion piece, the professors and doctors of the Faculty of Law of Jagiellonian University referred directly to the old Polish tradition of the legal trade in real estate, which was revived in the 1822 Act.

The undoubtedly positive aspect of the Law Faculty's supervision of the rulings of Cracovian courts with regard to the use of a decisive oath in court proceedings, was that it consistently instructed them that an oath was an extraordinary means of evidence with subsidiary application. In other words, the courts could not rely on a decisive oath as a means of proof if they had other evidence in the case, e.g. a letter presented by the defendant in which the plaintiff renounced a benefit claimed in the petition. The court in such a case was to rule on the basis of the document presented and not a decisive oath.[35]

The legal system of the Free City of Cracow was a rare example on Polish soil in the 19th century of the coexistence of different legal orders based on different axiological foundations. The legal mosaic of the Republic of Cracow was expressed primarily in the fact that civil law relations were regulated by the

---

34 Dziadzio and Mataniak eds. 2022, 327–329. Meeting of 22 March 1828, AUJ, WP I 58, 432–434.

35 Dziadzio and Mataniak eds. 2022, 236. Meeting of 3 June 1826, AUJ, WP I 57, 154–156. The Faculty in its opinion stated: "Considering further that proof by oath is extraordinary, and therefore only takes place where there are no ordinary ones, the courts of both instances, by giving place to the oath to be performed by Drobner, irrespective of the receipt given by him, insofar as the plaintiff has not claimed payment of the sum claimed for eight years, have infringed Article 1322 of the Civil Code".

provisions of the NC and French civil procedure. At the time, French civil law represented a breakthrough in the history of European jurisprudence, promoting the ideas of freedom of the person, property and contracts. In the field of procedural law, it popularised the principles of an open oral hearing and free assessment of evidence by the judge. Criminal cases, on the other hand, were heard by Cracow's courts on the basis of the Austrian Criminal Act of 1803, the so-called *Franciscana*, which contained both substantive and procedural criminal law provisions. In the area of procedural law, the Austrian law was based on the principles of secret and written inquisitorial proceedings and the legal theory of evidence. The inquisitorial criminal proceedings were only slightly modified by the modern rules of French procedure during the period when Cracow and its environs remained within the borders of the Duchy of Warsaw (1810–15).

FIGURE 5 *Map of the Free City of Cracow and its district from 1824*, (drawing, paper on canvas, 1824)
SOURCE: NATIONAL ARCHIVES IN CRACOW, ANK, 29/200/4218; PHOTO & PERMISSION BY NATIONAL ARCHIVES IN CRACOW

CHAPTER 2

The Judiciary of the Free City of Cracow

Mateusz Mataniak

1 The Structure of the Judiciary and Its Transformation

On 8 June 1816, the judiciary of the Free City of Cracow officially commenced its activities. The celebrations associated with this were of a dual character. First, it was religious in nature as a service was held in the Basilica of St Peter and Paul in Grodzka Street. Second, it was of a governmental nature; in the court building in the *Collegium Broscianum*, not far from the church, the chairman of the courts first welcomed the senators and residents of the Protective Powers, and then, together with the other judges, listened to commemorative speeches by Count Joseph de Sweerts-Spork, the representative of Austria, and Baron Ernest Wilhelm von Reibnitz, representing Prussia. A religious oath was also taken, which was read out by Father Wincenty Łańcucki, the archpriest of the Church of the Blessed Virgin Mary and Professor of Theology at the Academy of Cracow. Józef Nikorowicz, the Chairman of the Court of Appeal, also gave his speech.[1]

Starting the discussion with a basic issue, i.e. the structure of the judiciary, it should be noted that the decision-makers establishing the Republic of Cracow in no way drew from the solutions of the political model of the Polish-Lithuanian Commonwealth, i.e. Poland before 1795.[2] However, one can easily discern the influences characteristic of the two semi-sovereign State formations that emerged from parts of the pre-partition Polish lands, namely the Duchy of Warsaw (1807–14) and the Kingdom of Poland (1815–30). What is important here are both the structural issues – i.e. the division of the judiciary into Courts of the Peace, First Instance Tribunals and the Court of Appeal – as well as the basic principles of its functioning, namely the principle of the independence of the judiciary, the independence of judges and the openness of court proceedings. It was also quite common at the time to require judges to be

1 For a full account of the ceremony, see Dz. Rz. WMK: No.47 of 12 June 1816, 577–578 and No. 48 of 16 June 1816, 589–593.

2 The judiciary of the time was of an estate nature; one could distinguish between nobility courts (land courts, town courts and chamber courts), royal courts and, from the 16th century onwards, also General Tribunals (Crown and Lithuanian Tribunals), in addition to town, village and church courts. This is widely discussed by Uruszczak 2013, 255–271.

 | DOI:10.1163/9789004688742_004

adequately prepared professionally.[3] It should also be borne in mind that the relatively small size of the Free City of Cracow and the number of its inhabitants, influenced the fact that, under the conditions there, it was unnecessary to establish a Court of Cassation within the broad formula of a Council of State,[4] or separate commercial courts.[5] A very important modification in relation to the legal state before the Third Partition of Poland was certainly the abolition of the estate courts and the implementation of the principle of equality of all inhabitants before the law.[6]

The apparatus of the judiciary of the Free City of Cracow was shaped according to the principle of a three-tier system. It was made up of the Courts of the Peace ('Conciliation Offices'), the Tribunal (Court) of First Instance and the Court of Appeal. A Court of Third (Last) Instance was also established, which was in fact a Court of Appeal with an expanded composition (including the parties' persons of trust), whose role was to hear appeals against two judgements with different decisions, as well as against judgements identical in their content.[7] In the latter case, however, a favourable opinion from the Faculty of

3 With the possible exception of justices of the peace, who were to enjoy the confidence of the public in the first place, and who were usually recruited from among those who, in one way or another, had served the local population. See Chapter 4, Section 3. On the new position of judges in Europe at the turn of the 19th century, see Stolleis 2008, 207–208.

4 On the activities of the Council of State of the Duchy of Warsaw as a Court of Cassation, see Sobociński 1982, 141–182; Sobociński 1984, 5–43; Sobociński 1988, 97–133; Korobowicz 1998, 397–401.

5 The organisation and powers of the commercial tribunals were defined by Articles 631–661 of the Commercial Code. On the reasons for their non-implementation in the Republic of Cracow, see Fierich 1917, 148, 186–187.

6 On the judiciary in the Duchy of Warsaw and the Kingdom of Poland, see Ajnenkiel 2001, 72–73, 100–102, 109–111; Maciejewski 2016, 139–141, 150–151, 159; Cichoń 2021, 42–43.

7 The legal nature of an appeal to the Court of Third Instance may raise some doubts. Was it merely an appeal, only formally called a cassation? Fierich 1917, 137–138 correctly observed that the Court of Third Instance combined three elements: the French cassation judiciary, and through the introduction of the institution of university opinions – the German judiciary; and local ("peculiar") elements. However, he placed this court in the category of "ordinary courts for civil and criminal cases". At the same time, it was, according to Fierich, "a new type of supreme court". In 1827, in the course of work on the procedure before the Faculty of Law of Jagiellonian University, there were complaints that the procedure before the Court of Third Instance was not explicitly defined. However, the Court sometimes applied in practice the provisions of the Instructions for the Court of Cassation of the Duchy of Warsaw of 3 April 1810 (promulgated in DPKW, vol. 2, 151–185). On the other hand, due to the content of Article XV of the 1818 Constitution. ("the case will once again be sent back to the Court of Appeal but with a strengthened composition"), it can be assumed that the appellate procedure of the Code of Civil Procedure should have been applied. In any case, Fierich 1917, 230–231, argued that the Court of Third Instance occupied, in

Professors and Doctors of Law of Jagiellonian University was required, which had to conclude that there had been an infringement of (either substantive or formal) civil law in the courts' judgements.[8]

It comes as no surprise, then, that Cracow's judiciary had its constitutional basis in the form of the Basic Acts of 3 May 1815, 11 September 1818 and 29 July 1833.[9] The articles of the Constitution were creatively developed in the so-called 'organisational statutes' for the judiciary, which dated from 1816, 1833 and 1842.[10] It may be added that, although the organisation of the "judicial *magistratus*" in the 1816 statute was intended to be only provisional, it remained in force, with numerous modifications, until the end of the existence of the Republic of Cracow. The administration of justice at the lowest level of territorial division, i.e. municipal and rural communes, was carried out by justices of the peace. One level higher was the Court of First Instance, with three life judges and a number of temporary judges, i.e. appointed as necessary, for a two-year term. Generally, candidates for judges were put forward by the municipal assemblies; it was up to the deputies to the Assembly of Representatives, i.e. the parliament of the Free City of Cracow, to select them.[11] The qualifications of the candidates were examined by a special Sejm committee. Re-election of

relation to the Court of Appeal, the position of a court of third instance and not of a court of cassation. Indeed, an analysis of the case law allowed Fierich to conclude that, in its decisions, the Court of Third Instance approved the judgments of the courts of Second Instance, amended them within the limits of the conclusions formulated before it, or set aside the contested judgment and sent it back to the lower courts for re-examination. The concept of a cassation appeal does not appear explicitly until the 1833 Statute Organising the Judiciary, in section II "On Third-Instance Proceedings by Way of Cassation", where the content of a cassation appeal was defined in detail (Article 37). See also footnote 13 below, and Fierich 1917, 255–258.

8 On this topic, see above Chapter 1. See also Mataniak 2020b, 325–326.

9 On the constitutional foundations of the judiciary of the Free City of Cracow, see also Goclon 1990, 241, 258–261, 278–279, 284–285; Bartel 1981, 815–820. Older works, see Fierich 1917, 165–176, 182–199.

10 The *Urządzenie tymczasowego władz sądowniczych* of 1816 was not included in any of the categories of statutes, the division of which was established by the Organising Commission by resolution of 6 March 1818, promulgated by the Ruling Senate by means of a regulation of 24 March 1818, but was regarded as a transitive act which was to be amended after the new codes had been passed by the Assembly of Representatives. Thus, a distinction was made between: immutable statutes that could not be amended without the consent of the Protective Powers; statutes that could be amended by the Assembly of Representatives on the initiative of the Ruling Senate; statutes that could be amended only by decision of the Ruling Senate; statutes enacted by the Grand Council of Jagiellonian University: Meciszewski 1851, 116–122; Mieroszewski 1886, 351–352; Fierich 1917, 168–169.

11 On its activity, see Bartel 1984, 143–154.

a judge was allowed. In 1833, an additional requirement was introduced in that a person applying for the dignity of life judge had to previously have been a temporary judge; the term of office of the latter, moreover, was extended from two to six years. The courts issued judgments in civil and commercial cases, as well as criminal cases. Their jurisdiction, however, did not extend to disputes arising under administrative law, or to cases reserved to the jurisdiction of the Supreme Sejm Court. A clear reference to Article 4 of the NC was the duty of the judges to pass judgments in the cases entrusted to them. Moreover, because of the aforementioned principle of equality before the law, adjudication was to take place "without distinction as to the character and dignity of persons", regardless of the category of the dispute, except, of course, in cases reserved for the administrative route.

It was mandatory for three judges to take part in pronouncing judgements in the Court of First Instance, five judges in the Court of Appeal and seven judges in the Court of Third Instance (quasi-Cassation). There were four life judges in the Court of Appeal, including the court chairman and his deputy. The cassation appeals heard by the Court of the Third (Last) Instance involved not only appellate judges, in the usual number, but also three justices of the peace from Cracow, and two persons of trust of each party to the proceedings. In 1833, justices of the peace and persons of trust were replaced by the judges of the Tribunal. It was stipulated at the same time that no judges who had taken part in the judgment at a previous instance could be part of the adjudicating panel. Last but not least, the institution of the opinion of the Faculty of Professors and Doctors of Law of Jagiellonian University was then abolished, hence the admissibility of the appeal (cassation) was henceforth decided on its own by the Court of the Third (Last) Instance. Small civil cases (up to 600 Polish zloty) and cases of the so-called simple police were excluded from its jurisdiction.[12] The court was henceforth composed of the Chairman, four life judges and three temporary judges. It was divided into two divisions, with a view to correctly appoint judges for hearings in the Court of Third Instance, i.e. excluding the situation where a judge would be ruling on a case he had already been involved in. From 1833 onwards, the Court of Appeal had three life judges and two temporary judges in addition to the Chairman, with a full panel of five, including the Chairman. In the same year, the procedure for the examination of cassation appeals by the Court of the Third (Last) Instance was also laid

12 1833 also saw the establishment of sub-courts (in Polish: *sądy podsędkowskie*), which, however, adjudicated on criminal (minor) cases which are not of interest to us. See Fierich 1917, 255–256.

FIGURE 6 *Józef Peszka, portrait of Stanisław Wodzicki,* (painting, oil on canvas, 1819)
SOURCE: NATIONAL MUSEUM IN CRACOW, MNK II-A-457; PHOTO IN PUBLIC DOMAIN (CC0)

down in detail, with the principles of written, directness and material truth applying; the content of the cassation appeal was also specified in detail.[13]

Further significant changes in the Cracow judiciary occurred at the turn of the 1840s. In 1842, the activities of the Court of the Third (Last) Instance ceased, and thus the possibility to appeal against two unanimous verdicts in civil cases by way of cassation disappeared. The place of the former three instances was

13 *Statut Urządzający Sądownictwo* of 27 August 1833, DPr.WMK 1833, Chapter VI "On the Court of Third Instance", Section I "On Proceedings at Third Instance", Articles 31–35; Section II "On Proceedings at Third Instance by way of Cassation", Articles 36–60. These provisions were clearly linked to the Enforcement Act of 1823 and the Act on Courts of the Peace of 1825 (Title X "On an Appeal to the Court of Last Instance", Articles 68–72), which gave the possibility of filing a cassation appeal also against the judgments of these courts, which French legislation did not provide for: Fierich 1917, 190–191.

taken by the Tribunal and the Higher Court, which replaced the Court of Appeal. The former heard civil and commercial cases, in its various divisions, at first and second instance, while the Higher Court ruled as a third instance as long as there were different judgments at the first and second instances. An additional requirement was that the value of the subject-matter of the dispute exceeded 300 Polish zlotys (otherwise the judgment of the Tribunal in the second instance was final). In order to give the judiciary a "greater guarantee of equity", if the court examined a case as a court of first instance, it was to decide in a three-person composition, whereas if it proceeded as a court of second instance then the composition was to be five persons.[14] According to Wiktor Kopff, the author of a report of 1844 for the Sejm, the above-mentioned solutions significantly reduced the cost of trials, reduced barratry, and greatly accelerated the processing of complex civil cases.[15]

2 The Independence of the Judiciary and Supervision over Judges

A few words should also be devoted to an issue fundamental to the proper functioning of the judiciary – regardless of place and time – namely the already mentioned independence of the judiciary and judges. Based on the statements of representatives of governmental spheres, including the Residents of the Protective Powers, but also deputies of various political groups, it can be concluded that this issue was respected by all, remaining outside political disputes. The need to "ensure the independence of the judge in expressing his opinion" was repeatedly written about by the Residents to the Chairman of the Ruling Senate, while making it clear that it was, however, unacceptable for the judiciary to be "completely independent of any other power"; it was therefore always to be borne in mind that it was part of the "general administration".[16]

14 *Statut Organiczny dla Władz Sądowych* of 27 January 1842, DPr.WMK of 1842. Chapter VII. Division II "On the Organisation of the Superior Court in Respect of Civil and Commercial Cases" (Articles 79–80).

15 *Zdanie sprawy o stanie i położeniu Kraju W.M. Krakowa i Jego Okręgu w Zgromadzeniu Reprezentantów w r. 1844 przedłożone przez Senatora do tegoż Zgromadzenia delegowanego,* DPr.WMK of 1844, 77–81; ANK, 29/200/407 (WMK V-196), 811–816. These solutions were a result of a decree of the Ruling Senate, issued by order of the Conference of Residents. Fierich 1917, 258–259 pointed out that the Higher Court performed the functions of a court of review, and with considerable limitations.

16 Letter from the Residents to the Chairman of the Ruling Senate of 24 January 1824, ANK, 29/200/201 (WMK V-2), 395–396.

The fact that "the principles of justice should be closely linked to the duties of judges" was also pointed out by the deputy, Father Mateusz Dubiecki.[17]

Jan K. Kadłubowski spoke in the Sejm about the benefits to the State of electing officials, including judges, who are "fit, magnanimous, experienced, hard-working and unbending in their conduct". He also did not fail to raise the problem of the damage caused by lawyers "unfamiliar with the law, self-interested, perverse and malicious". He argued that in the Austrian period, "the scales of justice" were entrusted to "suitable men"; nowadays, candidates were not necessarily familiar with the laws, but were too often guided by "the lust for prestige" and exorbitant financial expectations. And yet it can hardly be denied that judges are entrusted with "the honour and property of the citizens", a judge who is "proficient and conscientious is therefore a great asset". But on the other hand, proper education was essential ("proficiency needs long experience"), Kadłubowski thus stipulated: "let us not be experienced on our property" and "let us beware of such [judges] who would be seduced by greed, anger, hatred, forgetful of the principles of law, duties of conscience and religion". In addition to experience, knowledge of the laws was essential, as well as "the ability to unfold innumerable formalities, detect perversity, stop delays, trace the intricate essence of things, discover crimes on criminals". In other words, the correct selection of judicial personnel guaranteed "the foundation of rest, the certainty of property, social peace, the security and happiness of the Nation"; it was, in fact, "the cornerstone of justice".[18]

Senator Józef Haller drew attention to yet another circumstance. This was the need to observe the constitutional requirements for those applying for a judicial post. The requirement to own real estate provided a guarantee of loyal behaviour and a genuine interest in the fate of the country, while the citizenship criterion was also found in other free city-states (Frankfurt, Hamburg, Bremen, Lübeck), in their "fundamental laws". It was therefore unacceptable to impose judges, including chairmen of the courts, against the will of the people (their will was expressed by the municipal assemblies and the Sejm). Such activities by the Reorganisation Commission and later by the Residents'

---

17 Speech of the deputy Father Mateusz Dubiecki, 1820, ANK, 29/200/41 (WMK II-21), 39–40. He also proclaimed that "any arbitrariness" was undesirable in judges, as opposed to "unbending of one's opinion".

18 Speech by Jan Kanty Kadłubowski, deputy of the Bobrek district municipality, 16 December 1826, ANK, 29/200/56 (WMK II-36), 369–370. The deputy was also the author of witty *bon mots*: "It is not the candidate for office but the Nation that should strive for a good official"; and "How can one expect [a judge] to be able to judge, when he cannot judge himself".

Conference, however, had already become a reality by the mid-1830s, only intensifying over time.[19]

At this point, then, the question of the disciplinary supervision over judges can be discussed. In the light of the 1816 Statute, it was defined rather vaguely. Supervision in disciplinary matters belonged to the Chairman of the Court of Appeal, in whose hands were the various measures necessary to maintain the "due order of the service" and to "expedite the course of justice". Yet, the exercise of "the rights over tribunals and officials used for justice" was entrusted to the Ruling Senate, including its Chairman. For the sake of the constitutional principle of the "independence of judicial judgments", the government was, of course, not allowed to interfere with the judges' "freedom to declare their opinion in judging".[20]

Governmental supervision over the "regularity of the course of cases" manifested itself in the following forms: (1) the Senate received reports ("periodic reports") from the Chairman of the Court of Appeal on cases heard by the courts; (2) the Senate could request to see the files of backlogged cases; (3) the Senate could take urgent measures against judges who were disregarding their duties.[21]

In 1829, modifications were made to the Statute Organising the Senate, whereby its chairman was given the right of supreme supervision over the execution of laws and regulations in all branches of the public service, both judicial and administrative. Accordingly, the heads of offices and chairmen of courts, and more specifically the Chairman of the Court of Appeal, through which the Senate supervised the lower judicial authorities (Article XVIII of the Constitution), sent to the Presidential Office of the Senate, every six months, lists describing the reputation of all subordinate officials. The Chairman of the Senate could also request the Senate to suspend an official from office, and

19 Speech by Senator Józef Haller of 5 September 1833, ANK, 29/200/202 (WMK V-3 B), 1457–1459. It was therefore inadmissible for the Reorganisation Commission to modify the list of candidates for judges already drawn up. Haller therefore proposed that the Assembly of Representatives request the Ruling Senate to ask the Reorganisation Commission to clarify the provisions of Articles VI, X and XV of the Constitution.

20 *Urządzenie tymczasowe dla Władz Sądowniczych Wolnego Miasta Krakowa*, promulgated by the letter of the Ruling Senate, Nos. 1904 and 1796 DGS, DRRz.WMK of 1816. The document was signed by the Commissioners of the Protective Powers: Ernest Reibnitz, Ignacy Miączyński and Joseph Sweerts-Spork.

21 *Konstytucja Wolnego Miasta Krakowa i Jego Okręgu* of 15 July/11 September 1818, Kallas and Krzymkowski eds. 2006, 188 (Article XVIII).

appoint a substitute, at the suspended official's expense, until the next Sejm, if the official was dependent on its appointment.[22]

In the 1842 Statute, the Senate retained formal influence over the appointment of chairmen and judges of the courts. *De facto*, its powers were significantly reduced, as the consent of the Conference of Residents, i.e. the diplomatic representatives of the Protective Powers, was henceforth required for the appointment of a chairman of a court, while the appointment of a judge of the Higher Court or a life judge of the Tribunal, was made conditional on the absence of objection from these Residents. Candidates for the Chairman of the Higher Court, as well as prosecutors and justices of the peace, were put forward by the Chairman of the Ruling Senate; in the case of the Chairman of the Tribunal and judges (as well as lower officials, apart from trainees), the notification was made by the Chairman of the Higher Court to the Senate. It was up to the latter to suspend the chairmen of courts (with the consent of the Residents), judges and prosecutors (after consulting the chairman of the relevant court) and lower officials from office and drawing their salaries ("*ab officio et salario*"); the opinion was given by the Chairman of the Higher Court. Removal from office could, in principle, only take place on the basis of a court judgment. Occasionally, an immoral lifestyle or gross disregard of duties could also be the reason; for the dismissal of a judge, the consent of the Residents was necessary (in the case of ordinary officials, the opinion of the Chairman of the Higher Court).[23]

It was also the Senate's responsibility to supervise the course of court cases ("supreme oversight of justice"), whereby it received up-to-date lists of civil, criminal and commercial cases, including backlogs, from the Chairman of the Higher Court. Through him, he also exercised authority over those employed by the judiciary (direct supervision was usually exercised by the Chairman of the Tribunal). Opinions on judges and other court officials were thus received by the Senate, in the form of so-called reputation lists.[24]

---

22 The Chairman of the Ruling Senate and the Chairman of the Court of Appeal thus exercised functions which, during the Duchy of Warsaw, belonged to the Minister of Justice. Fierich 1917, 176; Wachholz 1957, 265.

23 *Statut Organiczny dla Władz Sądowych* of 27 January 1842, DPr.WMK of 1842. Chapter XII "On the Appointment, Suspending in the Office or Dismissing from it the Judicial Officers" (Articles 108–112, 114–121). See the letter of the Ruling Senate to the Chairman of the Higher Court of 11 May 1842, "Ksiega normaliów Sądu Wyższego od 1842 r.", ANK, 29/200/4658 (WM 586), 1.

24 *Statut Organiczny dla Władz Sądowych* of 27 January 1842. Chapter XIII "On Supervision of the Judiciary"; Chapter XIV "On the Supervision of Persons Belonging to the Judiciary" (articles 126–129, 132–138).

FIGURE 7 *Portrait of Piotr Bartynowski* (*unknown author*), (painting, oil on canvas, mid-19th century)
SOURCE: JAGIELLONIAN UNIVERSITY MUSEUM, MUJ-41-M, PHOTO BY JANUSZ KOZINA; PERMISSION BY JAGIELLONIAN UNIVERSITY MUSEUM

Of a more serious nature was the criminal liability of officials, including those employed in the judiciary. From the beginning of the existence of the Free City of Cracow until 1839, the Supreme Sejm Court was appointed to enforce this, with the following members appointed on an *ad hoc* basis: deputies to the Sejm (five); senators (three); court chairmen, justices of the peace (four); and citizens of Cracow (three) appointed by the parties as persons of trust. Indictment before the Sejm Court was decided by parliament in a separate procedure. Liability related to offences of the "theft of the public penny, exorbitance or abuse" committed in connection with office.[25] The rules of its activities were further defined by the Statute of the Sejm of 1817.[26]

In addition to the high-profile case of Leon Chwalibogowski, prosecutor of the Court of First Instance and court cashier, accused of extorting bribes, and the cases of several justices of the peace,[27] records from the period show traces of proceedings implemented against judges, including Onufry Męciński, Jan Bąkowski and Józef Stróżecki, accused of abuse of office (the Sejm refused to prosecute any of them); and Wojciech Skarżyński, who resigned his office and died shortly afterwards, before the criminal proceedings were concluded.[28]

From 1840, the role of the Sejm Court was taken over by the Supreme Criminal Court. Its jurisdiction encompassed, in addition to ordinary criminal cases, acts almost identical to those heard by the Supreme Sejm Court (abuse of power, "embezzlement of official duties", exorbitance). In the event of suspicion that any of these offences had been committed, the Residents' Conference appointed a commission of inquiry, which was to include judges not only from Cracow but also those representing the Protective Powers. The commission was to initiate investigations, issue qualifying verdicts and then also carry out an "ordinary criminal inquisition". If the suspicion of prevarication proved to be well-founded, the perpetrator was to be handed over to the "ordinary punishment courts" to carry out "criminal proceedings".[29] The number of cases heard by the Supreme Criminal Court concerning clerical offences was small: between 1839–41 there were 20 cases, between 1844–45 there were only two cases.[30]

---

25 For more, see Pęksa 1999, 253–261; Fierich 1917, 236–245. The principles of judges' liability were also set out in Articles 505–516 of the Code of Civil Procedure.

26 *Statut tyczący się Urządzenia Zgromadzeń Politycznych* of 10 September 1817, promulgated by the letter of the Ruling Senate No. 2845 DGS, DRRz.WMK of 1817. Section VI "On the Manner of Proceedings in the Supreme Court" (Articles 136–147).

27 Pauli 1970, 126–127.

28 Letters from the Marshal of the Sejm (presiding in the Assembly of Representatives) to the Ruling Senate: of 15 January 1838, ANK, 29/200/62 (WMK II-42), 603–605; of 18 January 1838, ibidem, 615; Kopff 1906, 16–17.

29 *Statut Organiczny dla Władz Sądowych* of 27 January 1842. Chapter IX "On Criminal Cases in Which Exceptional Proceedings Take Place" (Articles 102–103). The application of the power of pardon by the Ruling Senate was made conditional on the approval of the "High Protective Courts", granted through the Residents.

30 *Wykaz rozgatunkowanych zbrodni przekazanych do instrukcji i osądzenia przez Trybunał za 1839 r.*, ANK, 29/200/1627 (WM 114); *Wykaz rozgatunkowanych zbrodni przekazanych do instrukcji i osądzenia przez Trybunał za 1840 r.*, ibidem.

3 The Qualifications of Judges

The issue of the level of education of Cracow's judges, and thus their suitability for their duties, is a debatable one, and is mainly influenced by discrepancies in the accounts of witnesses of the era. Stanisław Wodzicki, for many years the Chairman of the Ruling Senate, and therefore an influential and well-informed person, in his memoirs accused judges of a lack of competence and a susceptibility to bribery. It should be added, however, that Wodzicki was in acute political conflict with the intelligentsia-bourgeoisie community, so his account may be highly questionable. The information given by Ambroży Grabowski, a well-known Cracovian collector and amateur historian, is inconsistent. He wrote, *inter alia*:

> a judge in the Tribunal was Dydyński, a pretty stupid nobleman, supported in this dignity by Marcin Badeni, a minister of the Kingdom of Poland. He was simply a bankrupt landowner, who had never dreamt of the law, because he had never observed it and had no relevant education. Having been a judge for several years, he did not even go to courts, being ill or pretending to be, and collected his salary – until death finally took this *inutile pondus terrae* and freed the Treasury of the Republic from paying this dry beer.

In another place, Grabowski noted:

> A second similar judge was Józef Gołuchowski, a man otherwise of good character, but this is not the only condition for the judicial chair. He was, like the above-mentioned, a country farmer, but, successful, he grabbed Themis, never having learned the law. Yet he served for many years, drawing the salary of an appellate judge, and died as a retiree only in 1851.[31]

However, there is an account by Grabowski, in which he speaks in glowing terms about Cracow's justice system:

> The course of justice was swift and cases were dealt with one by one, as they came on the table. No one could accuse the judges of bribery, because these people were from the order of the most moral people called to judicial posts, and morality in this respect was strongly observed.[32]

---

31 Grabowski 1909, 133, 135; Mataniak 2020b, 329.

32 Grabowski 1909, 129.

Perhaps it should be assumed, then, that a lack of education did not stand in the way of honest adjudication, and that a sense of law and justice was more important than formal qualifications? But there may be another explanation: some judges did not have a legal education, but had considerable experience, which was a common phenomenon in the times of the noble Polish-Lithuanian Commonwealth. There was also certainly a group of judges who were very well educated and aware of the importance of the duties imposed on them; it is very likely that it was their views that had a serious, if not decisive, influence on the content of court rulings. In addition, it should be remembered that at least some judges had held various positions in the State apparatus of the Duchy of Warsaw, where an extensive training system, combined with demanding examinations, certainly improved the quality of the work of judges, advocates, etc.[33] A separate category were Cracow residents educated in Austrian law, usually graduates of the Franciscan University of Lviv.

It may be added in passing that concerns about judicial qualifications were not unusual in Europe at the time. Even at the end of the 18th century, the work of the judiciary, both in criminal and civil matters, was still the subject of widespread indignation and criticism; complaints were voiced in various social groups about the lengthiness of proceedings and the ruinous cost of seeking justice. Profit-hungry advocates and biased judges were also notorious.[34]

In the case of the Free City of Cracow, it is enough to become acquainted with the profiles of several judges to become convinced that the judiciary there did in fact comprise both experienced lawyers-practitioners and more ambitious individuals focused on improving their qualifications. For example, in 1833, the Sejm examined the qualifications of three candidates for judges: Wincenty Gołuchowski, Onufry Męciński and Ignacy Ostaszewski. As it turned out, none of them had any legal education (!), but all of them had a wealth of "experience in the judicial line", dating back to the Polish-Lithuanian Commonwealth.[35] Indeed, Ostaszewski had practised as an advocate at the land courts from 1790, and in 1808 became a notary at the Civil Tribunal of the Kalisz (subsequently Cracow) Department. During the period of the Free City of Cracow, he briefly became a judge of the Tribunal in 1816, then a deputy judge of the Court of Appeal, while in 1817, 1819–20 and 1822–23 he was a deputy to the Assembly of

33 Cichoń 2012, 45–58. See also Voutyras-Pierre 1992, 127–157.

34 Sójka-Zielińska 2000, 308–309.

35 "Diariusz Seymu Rzeczypospolitey Krakowskiey", 1833. Session 5. As the Chairman of the Selection Committee stated, "their school of life was the Bar, which provided training for future lawyers".

Representatives. His public activity culminated in a lucrative post as a notary in Cracow (1823–45).[36]

Józef Nikorowicz (1753–1833) also had a wealth of experience, but he graduated from a university (in his native Lviv) and went on to preside over the nobility courts in Tarnów and Cracow, and at one point even sat on the Vienna Legislative Commission. His successor as the Chairman of the Cracow Court of Appeal was another graduate of Lviv University, Franciszek Borgiasz Piekarski (1759–1834), who was Chairman of the Criminal Court for the Cracow and Radom Departments during the Duchy of Warsaw. In the Republic of Cracow, in addition to the judiciary, he was also active in numerous State institutions (the Peasant Commission, the Mortgage Commission), school institutions, and social organisations (the Charity Society, the Archbrotherhood of Mercy); he was also the author of numerous works on agronomy. Also a graduate from Lviv was Jakub Mąkolski (1782–1861), the son of a land notary from Cracow, who began his career as a prosecutor at the Criminal Court in Cracow, and went on to head the Court of First Instance and the Court of Appeal (1834).[37]

At Cracow Academy, but also at the universities of Breslau (present-day Wrocław) and Berlin, knowledge was acquired by Piotr Bartynowski (1795–1874). He was a long-time prosecutor and judge, a deputy to the Assembly of Representatives and a senator, in addition to being a lecturer in Roman law at Jagiellonian University (1829–33) and rector of that university (1860–61). Another academic was Mikołaj Hoszowski (1778–1828); he was a professor at Jagiellonian University's Department of Political Skills, in addition to being Marshal of the Sejms of the Free City of Cracow and a member of the Legislative Committee.[38]

Walenty Litwiński (1778–1823) was also a prosecutor and later a judge, who became famous above all though as an unrelenting defender of the autonomy of Jagiellonian University, of which he was a professor (in the Department

36 I. Ostaszewski's application to the Qualification Commission of 10 December 1818, ANK, 29/200/27 (WMK II-7), 165–166; *Gazeta Krakowska* No. 14 of 16 February 1817, 157–158; No. 99 of 12 December 1819, 1091; "Dyariusz czynności Seymu Rzeczypospolitey Krakowskiey roku 1822", ANK, 29/200/46 (WMK II-26), 10; "Diariusz Seymu Rzeczypospolitey Krakowskiey" of 1833. Session 5.

37 Hoszowski 1869, 15–20, 37–47; Wawel-Louis 1977, 170–176; Mataniak 2020b, 328–329.

38 Żukowski 2014, 16–17, 189–190. During his studies in Berlin, Bartynowski had the opportunity to listen to the lectures of Friedrich K. von Savigny, the founder of the historical school in jurisprudence.

FIGURE 8 *Józef Peszka, portrait of Walenty Litwiński,* (painting, oil on canvas, 1st half of the 19th century)
SOURCE: JAGIELLONIAN UNIVERSITY MUSEUM, MUJ-93-M, PHOTO BY JANUSZ KOZINA; PERMISSION BY JAGIELLONIAN UNIVERSITY MUSEUM

of Judicial Practice and Criminal Law) and then the rector for many years (1814–21).[39]

Józef Walenty Krzyżanowski (1799–1849) also graduated from Jagiellonian University. He was a prosecutor at the Tribunal, and later the Chairman of the Court of Third Instance. He represented a conspicuously patriotic stance: in

39 Litwiński also took care of the university's equipment, the proper staffing of the departments and the influx of students from outside Cracow. His conflict with the Chairman of the Ruling Senate, Stanisław Wodzicki, aroused great interest even among the statesmen of the Holy Alliance. For Litwiński was the *spiritus movens* of the bourgeois democratic opposition: Patkaniowski 1964, 162–163, 191–192; Żukowski 2014, 304–305; PSB, vol. XVII, 494–495.

1836 he was even expelled from the judiciary on the grounds that he had delivered a judgment acquitting participants in an independence conspiracy. In 1846, he served as Minister of Justice in the National Government of Jan Tyssowski, while in 1848 he was elected President of the Civic and National Committees; he was also briefly the President of the City Council (1848).[40] Tadeusz Krzyżanowski, who was not related to him, was also a graduate of Jagiellonian University. He was qualified to "hold court offices" in 1818, by passing an exam before the Voivodship Committee for the Cracow Voivodship, and his qualifications were confirmed – by way of a decision – by the Governor of the Kingdom of Poland (Józef Zajączek). He was an advocate in Lublin and then in Cracow (1819–21), after which he was elected a judge of the Court of First Instance, and finally a deputy judge of the Court of Appeal.[41]

Other graduates of the university in Cracow were Jacek Habowski; he was elected as a deputy judge from 1820, a judge of the Tribunal from 1826, and in the years 1817, 1817/18, 1825/26, a deputy to the Sejm and a member of the Extraordinary Legislative Assembly (1818).[42] Kazimierz Kozłowski was a secretary and adviser to the Municipal Office of the City of Cracow, a sub-judge (1810–16), and a judge of the Court of First Instance and Court of Appeal (1820–21), as well as a member of the Assembly of Representatives (1817, 1818/19).[43] Marcin Soczyński, between 1801 and 1816, was an advocate "in the public service", then a deputy judge of the Tribunal (1818) and a judge of the Court of Appeal (1820), as well as a deputy member of the Mortgage Commission and a deputy to the Sejm (1817, 1817/18, 1818/19, 1819/20, 1820/21, 1821/22).[44]

The most versatile lawyer of the Free City of Cracow, however, was certainly Wiktor Kopff (1805–89). In the 1830s, he travelled across Europe, during

40 Kasprzyk 2010, 779; Mataniak 2019a, 33–34.

41 Letter from T. Krzyżanowski to the Qualification Commission of 7 December 1823, ANK, 29/200/50 (WMK II-30), 531–534.

42 Application from J. Habowski to the Residents of 5 May 1828, ANK, 29/200/117 (WMK III-3), 261–262; *Gazeta Krakowska* No. 14 of 16 February 1817, 157; No. 5 of 18 January 1818, 49; No. 98 of 7 December 1817, 1191; No. 98 of 7 December 1825, 1215.

43 Application from Kazimierz Kozłowski to the Qualifying Commission, ANK, 29/200/27 (WMK II-7), 160–161; *Lista kandydatów mających prawem przepisaną kwalifikacyę na urząd Sędziego Czasowego Sądu Apelacyjnego* of 13 December 1818, ibidem, 159; *Gazeta Krakowska* No. 14 of 16 February 1817, 157; No. 99 of 13 December 1818, 1173; No. 102 of 20 December 1820, 1219; No. 101 of 19 December 1821, 1227.

44 Applications of Marcin Soczyński to the Qualification Commission: of 1818, ANK, 29/200/27 (WMK II-7), 189; of 5 December 1823, ANK, 29/200/50 (WMK II-30), 547–548; *Gazeta Krakowska* No. 14 of 16 February 1817, 158; No. 98 of 7 December 1817, 1191; No. 99 of 13 December 1818, 1173; No. 99 of 12 December 1819, 1091; No. 99 of 10 December 1820, 1181; No. 97 of 5 December 1821, 1177.

which he had the opportunity to familiarise himself with the latest trends in penitentiary science at the time (the result of his research trips was the 1834 Prison Statute of the Free City of Cracow). He also took part in the work around the construction of the railway line connecting Cracow with Silesia and the Warsaw–Vienna Railway. He is remembered by posterity as the author of numerous draft laws, for example an act on usury, church supervision, the Savings Bank, the House of Forced Labour and workshops for prisoners. He apparently also had artistic inclinations, as he became the chairman of the Theatre Directorate of the Free City of Cracow in 1842.[45]

It is difficult to state unequivocally whether, in the first half of the 19th century, a judges' proper training in the subject matter should also be understood as their ability to adapt the NC (and the other codifications) to the needs of everyday life. The editors of the NC, on the false assumption of its completeness and clarity, directed judges to decide cases in a definitive manner. Its Article 4 left no doubt about this: "The judge who shall refuse to determine under pretext of the silence, obscurity, or insufficiency of the law, shall be liable to be proceeded against as guilty of a refusal of justice".[46] Or perhaps it was sufficient to be able to read the provisions literally, ignoring the historical and theoretical threads? The fact is that between 1800 and 1830, the so-called "exegesis school" also known as the dogmatic or classical school, reigned undivided in French civilist thought. Its founders and disciples believed that the NC constituted a closed whole in which, by means of traditional methods of interpretation, the solution to almost all conceivable cases could be found. The role of lawyers was only to apply it in practice, without the possibility of a freer interpretative analysis of the text.[47] However, the issue of the proper interpretation of laws

45 PSB, vol. XIV, Wrocław–Warszawa–Kraków 1968–69, 18–19 (I. Homola); Mataniak 2017c, 216–217.

46 The foremost Polish expert on the NC pointed to the abandonment, in the course of the French codification work, of the Enlightenment idea of the judge as a passive executor of laws, following Montesquieu's advice, in favour of a judge-interpreter, adapting the codifications to the needs of life: Sójka-Zielińska 1999, 219–220; Sójka-Zielińska 2000, 312–313; Sójka-Zielińska 2005, 34–35, 37–41.

47 Sójka-Zielińska 2008, 161–166. Also at the core of the curriculum of the professional law schools of France at the time was a literal reading of the NC. The main representatives of the current of exegesis were Claude-Étienne Delvincourt, Jean-Baptiste-Victor Proudhon and Charles Bonaventure Toullier. In the early days of the school, its representatives were guided by the thought of the editors of the NC that it should nevertheless show some connection with social life; hence the interpretation with reference to various sources, e.g. philosophical-legal works. For more, see Gilissen 1979, 473–475; Rémy 1985, 91–105; Atias 1985, 107–123; Gaudemet 1999, 363–366; Basdevant-Gaudemet, Gaudemet 2000, 383–384; Rémy 2003/2004, 22–23; Gordley 2014, 147–148, 153.

was pointed out by the senator-lawyer Józef Haller. In the Sejm, he expressed the opinion that, in case of doubt, it was not the "literal meaning" but the "general spirit and principles of the Act" that should be decisive.[48]

Notwithstanding the above, it is a fact that, until the early 1830s, the selection of judges was carried out by the Assembly of Representatives, following the opinion of the Sejm selection committee. Applicants for the dignity of a judge had to meet conditions set by criteria of age, education and wealth. These were: being at least 30 years of age, having completed university studies in one of the cities of the former Polish-Lithuanian Commonwealth (later this could also be a university in one of the neighbouring countries) combined with obtaining a doctorate in law, as well as sufficiently long practice with a court scribe and an advocate, and owning real estate with a value of at least 8,000 Polish zlotys, acquired at least one year before taking up the post.[49] In addition, due to the complicated nature of the legislation in force in the Free City of Cracow, the judges had to be familiar in practice not only with French law, but also with its numerous modifications made by decrees of the Saxon king, as well as with Austrian law and pre-partition Polish law.[50]

We also have no reason to doubt that it was only concern for the proper level of judicial personnel that drove the authors of the regulations to introduce Government examinations for those applying for positions in the judiciary. In order to take them, one had not only to have completed a law degree, but also to have completed a three-year judicial apprenticeship, confirmed by an appropriate certificate.[51] The statute of 27 January 1842, classified judges as clerks of the third class, alongside advocates, notaries, court scribes as well as prosecutors and sub-prosecutors. All those listed were to prepare for examinations in the following subjects: (1) the Constitutional Act of 1833, together with the organic statutes developing the constitution; (2) decrees, laws and regulations concerning court law and the organisation of courts that were in force in the Free City of Cracow, including those dating from the Austrian era (up

48 Speech by Senator Józef Haller of 5 September 1833, ANK, 29/200/202 (WMK V-3B), 1457–1459.

49 Articles XV, XVIII–XIX of the 1818 Constitution. In the case of chairmen of courts and judges of second instance, there was also a requirement of at least two years' judicial practice and the exercise of the mandate of a deputy to the Sejm for one term.

50 Dziadzio and Mataniak eds. 2022, 11–12; Fierich 1917, 247–248. As acts were drafted in different languages, a good judge had to know French, German and Latin in addition to Polish. On the judicial profession in countries of the Roman-Germanic tradition, see David and Brierley 1985, 139–141.

51 Candidates also submitted a curriculum vitae ("description of life course") and a certificate of graduation.

to 1809) and the Duchy of Warsaw; (3) legal regulations issued by the Russian, Austrian and Prussian governments, if knowledge of them was necessary due to international relations ("mutual relations between the border countries and the country of the Free City of Cracow"); (4) Roman law; (5) Canon law, (6) old Polish law with procedure; (7) the NC (*Code civil*), together with the law of the Free City of Cracow modifying it (with "reference to the new national laws") and Austrian law; (8) the French Code of Civil Procedure (*Code de procedure civile*) of 1806; (9) the French Code of Commerce (*Code de commerce*) of 1807; and (10) the Austrian Criminal Code of 1803 (*Franciscana*), together with court procedure. The examination consisted of two parts: the first stage was oral, after successful completion of which the candidate proceeded to the written stage. It consisted of solving case-studies ("preparing an essay") on civil and criminal law; they could also concern an "administrative or jurisdictional dispute".[52] It is worth mentioning that the organisational structure of the Faculty of Law of Jagiellonian University – the university that educated lawyers in Cracow – as well as its curriculum, were, in principle, correlated with the above examination requirements.[53]

The sets of examination questions are also certainly worth a closer look. The minutes of the judicial examination taken by Maksymilian Grabowski, *nota bene* the son of the above-mentioned Ambroży, have survived to the present day. The oral questions, on private law only, were as follows: (1) what is renewal, how can it take place under French law, what effect does it have with respect to mortgages, privileges and warranties?; (2) whether and how does it differ under Austrian law?; (3) how could renewal take place under Roman law?; (4) what is the difference between renewal when a new creditor replaces an old one and an assignment of claims?; (5) what is the effect of a transfer under Article 1247 of the NC?; (6) what rights serve the assignee under French and Austrian law?; (7) what is the assignee is obliged to do?; (8) what might be the subject matter of the assignee?; (9) when might a judge be held liable, and in which cases does the law recognise liability under penalty of compensation for damages and lost profits?; (10) when should payment of the bill of exchange

52 The detailed requirements were laid down in a regulation of the Ruling Senate of 27 April 1842, No. 2124 DGS, *O applikacji i examinach sądowych*, DPr.WMK of 1842. The examining commission was to be composed of the Chairman of the Court of First Instance and four Government commissioners. After taking the examination, the candidate received a "certificate of suitability", taking into account the following grading scale: excellently disposed, sufficiently disposed, unfit. See Mataniak 2020b, 326–327.

53 For more, see Patkaniowski 1964, 159–162, 165–167, 171–172, 174–177, 213–214; Mataniak 2022b, 293–296.

take place?; (11) should partial payment of the bill of exchange take place?; (12) can, under the current law, the debtor defend on the basis of non-collection of the currency?; (13) in which cases is there an *ad hoc* court and to whom does it depend to establish such a court?; (14) what were the courts in Poland, and what cases belonged to the Sejm, assessor's, court and referendary courts?; (15) are priests according to the ecclesiastical laws are obliged to pay taxes?; (16) what are ecclesiastical benefices?; (17) what types of evidence belong to our code, and what does each of them consist of?; (18) can a pledge be given with the reservation that the creditor may keep it for himself if the debtor fails to fulfil his obligation?; (19) can a contract by which a person has created a lifetime income for himself be invalidated by his creditors according to Austrian law?; (20) when does paternal authority cease according to Austrian law?; (21) what is meant by a "merger of creditors" in commercial law?; (22) how must one proceed if one wishes to obtain the rectification of a civil status certificate?; (23) is it possible, under Polish law, for a minor to legally administer his own property?; (24) is an extorted contract valid under Roman law?; (25) what are disorderly successions and when do they take place?; and (26) can a final judgment be overturned and by what means?[54]

4 Budgets of the Judiciary, Salaries, Leaves of Absence, Retirement Pensions[55]

The judiciary was made up not only of judges, but also of so-called *oficjaliści*, i.e. clerical staff paid from the Public Treasury. These included secretaries, clerks and the keepers of the court register (administration journalists), as well as court archivists. A separate group consisted of court scribes, the conservator of mortgages (also known as the Regent of Mortgage Records) and audience ushers, who watched over order in the courtroom. Nor should we forget the delivery ushers, who supported themselves by the fees charged to the parties, as well as prosecutors and bailiffs. Attorneys and notaries, who were closely connected with the judiciary but did not directly belong to it, require a

54 *Protokół egzaminu przed Komisją Sądowo-Egzaminacyjną na urzędy II i III klasy* of 13 May 1851, ANK, 29/200/1814 (WM 150), no pagination. The examination took place in the audience hall of the Tribunal, in the presence of the Chairman of the Higher Court, Józef Majer, the judge of the Higher Court, Felicjan Dudrewicz, the judges of the Tribunal, Józef Pareński and Jan Czernicki, and the prosecutor, Ignacy Ciszewski.

55 The discussion presented in this section is an abridged and modified version of the article: M. Mataniak 2019b.

FIGURE 9 *Seal of the Judicial Examination Commision of the Free City of Cracow*, (seal matrix, brass, 1st half of the 19th century)
SOURCE: NATIONAL ARCHIVES IN CRACOW, ANK, 29/661/212; PHOTO & PERMISSION BY NATIONAL ARCHIVES IN CRACOW

separate description. Generally speaking, the number of people practising the profession of a clerk was very high in Cracow, which was certainly influenced by the attractiveness of this way of earning a living. As Hilary Meciszewski wrote about the local phenomenon of "office mania": "Being a court or administrative official, not to mention the ultimate dream, i.e. the post of senator, was a desire of many. The underlying cause was primarily the economic situation, caused by restrictions on the development of industry and commerce". He added: "The endeavour, therefore, to hold the offices of senators and judges was replaced by another industrial enterprise in Cracow; public office became a speculation to which time was devoted and for which no small expense was undertaken".[56]

Consequently, expenditure from the Public Treasury on the judiciary was substantial, although it did not differ significantly from the funds allocated to other branches of Government administration. In the first budget for 1816/

56 Meciszewski 1840, 140.

17, granted to Cracow by the Organising Commission, it amounted to 132,600 Polish zlotys, of which a total of 71,700 Polish zlotys was allocated to the Tribunal and Courts of the Peace, and 60,900 Polish zlotys to the Court of Appeal (the expenditure budget totalled 756,040 Polish zlotys 10 grosz).[57]

Judges' salaries were financed from the State budget ("Judiciary"). They were at a good level and were similar to the salaries of senior officials (Chairman of the Ruling Senate, Director of Construction) and mid-level officials (adjunct in the Department of Internal Affairs, Director of the Main Archives). For example, according to the budget for 1820/21, the Chairman of the Court of Appeal earned 10,000 Polish zlotys a year, his deputy 6,000 zlotys, the other judges 5,000 zlotys each. The Chairman of the Tribunal received 8,000 zlotys, life and temporary judges received 4,000–5,000 zlotys each. The salaries of judges of the Court of Third Instance were similar to those of the Court of Appeal.[58]

As for the salaries of other officials: a Government prosecutor at the Court of Appeal could count on 4,800 zlotys a year, a court clerk received 3,000 zlotys, a secretary 2,400 zlotys, an archivist 2,200 zlotys, a journalist 2,000 zlotys, two clerks 1,500 zlotys each, an usher 700 zlotys, and his assistant-servant 600 zlotys. Also included were the costs of running the court office, for which a lump sum ("*salvo calculo*") of 2,500 złotys was set. The subsidy for the Tribunal Office was considerably higher (6,000 zlotys). The Office of the Conservator of Mortgages received only 600 zlotys. Compared with the previous financial year, in 1820/21 expenditure on the judiciary increased slightly, from 134,500 zlotys to 138,200 zlotys.[59] According to the figures for 1833–37, the Chairman of the Court of Third Instance earned 10,000 zlotys, the two life judges 5,000 zlotys each. The following also worked at the court: a prosecutor (4,000 zlotys),

---

57 Resolution of the Organising Commission of 14 June 1816, *Zatwierdzenie Budgetu Rozchodów z epoki od 1 VI 1816 do 1 VII 1817*, ANK, 29/200/66 (WM 15), 202–203. For comparison: 137,160 zlotys were allocated for the Senate, 133,337 zlotys 22 grosz for the Department of Internal Affairs, for the Public Revenue Department 63,633 zlotys, for the Police Department 87,865 zlotys, for the Militia 138,323 zlotys, for retirement salaries 1,200 zlotys, for extraordinary expenses 61,921 zlotys 12 gr.

58 *Budget Rozchodów na Rok 1820/21*, "Budgeta oryginalne Przychodów jako Rozchodów Wolnego Miasta Krakowa i Jego Okręgu z lat 1817/18–1826/27 przez Zgromadzenie Reprezentantów uchwalone", ANK, 29/200/67 (WM 16), 299–300, 310, (Title III: "Judiciary"). Expenditure on the judiciary amounted to 138,200 zlotys, which accounted for *c*.12 per cent of State expenditure (the expenditure budget totalled 1,329,351 zlotys 29 grosz).

59 Ibidem. Expenditure on the judiciary of the peace remained unchanged (five scribes earned 2,000 Polish zlotys each, the cost of maintaining five offices was set at 600 zlotys). Budgetary expenditure was reduced from 1,331,692 zlotys 17 grosz to 1,329,351 zlotys 29 grosz.

a scribe (3,000 zlotys), an archivist (1,500 zlotys), a journalist (1,300 zlotys), an usher (400 zlotys) and a servant (300 zlotys).[60]

In 1833, the salary of the Chairman of the Court of Appeal was reduced to 8,000 zloty, retaining the 1,000 zloty supplement for Chairman J. Mąkolski; the three life judges, as well as the two temporary judges, each received 5,000 zloty. The salary of the prosecutor was reduced to 3,500 zlotys, that of the scribe to 2,800 zlotys, that of the secretary to 2,200 zlotys and that of the journalist to 1,800 zlotys.[61] As far as the Court of First Instance is concerned, the salary of the Chairman was reduced to 7,000 zlotys, that of the first life judge (presiding judge in the division) to 4,000 zlotys. Three life judges, like the three temporary ones, received 4,000 zlotys each; the public prosecutor received 3,000 zlotys; a newly appointed sub-prosecutor could expect 2,000 zlotys; two scribes received 2,800 zlotys each; a secretary 2,400 zlotys; an archivist 2,000 zlotys; a journalist 1,500 zlotys; five court clerks 1,200 zlotys each; two ushers 600 zlotys each; two servants 450 zlotys each; the court cashier 2,600 zlotys; and the cashier's controller 1,500 zlotys (an increase of 300 zlotys); the "*salvo calculo*" office costs were set at 5,000 zlotys. Also on the judiciary's staff was the Regent of Mortgage Acts with a salary of 3,600 zlotys (including office costs), who paid a deposit before taking up his post, as well as five justices of the peace and sub-courts.[62] The budget of the judiciary passed in 1833 amounted to 192,500 zlotys (the State expenditure reached 1,775,766 zlotys and 15 grosz).[63] An analysis of the 1838–41 budget shows that salaries did not change significantly.[64] Effective

60 "Budgeta oryginalne Przychodów jako Rozchodów Wolnego Miasta Krakowa i Jego Okręgu z lat 1833/37–1838/41 przez Zgromadzenie Reprezentantów uchwalone", ANK, 29/200/71 (WM 20), 130–131. The Reorganisation Commission blocked the creation of the post of a court secretary, which had to be accepted by the Sejm Treasury Committee.

61 Ibidem, 130–131, 168–169. There was no change in the salaries of the archivist (2,200 Polish zlotys), two clerks (1,200 zlotys each), the usher (700 zlotys), the servant (400 zlotys) and the costs of the court office (2,500 zlotys).

62 Ibidem, 130–133, 168–169. Five scribes of the courts of peace received 2,000 zlotys each, court premises cost 600 zlotys each, an allowance for the court office in Chrzanów amounted to 200 zlotys, five ushers received 500 zlotys each, the building maintenance cost 500 zlotys. Sub-courts: five sub-judges received 2,000 zlotys each, five sub-scribes received 1,200 zlotys each, five ushers with servants received a total of 2,000 zlotys, the cost of operating one office was estimated at 500 zlotys. The costs of operation of three sub-jails (2,500 zlotys) were transferred to Title X ("National Buildings", ibidem, 160–161). The salaries of two life assessors of the Tribunal (in 1827/28 they received 3,000 zlotys each) were cancelled.

63 Ibidem, 70–171. In 1827/28 this was 1,569,724 Polish zlotys 11 grosz. In comparison, in 1833 the expenditure on the Ruling Senate with departments amounted to 266,121 zlotys.

64 *Budget Rozchodu nr Rok 1838/41, czyli na czas od dnia 1 czerwca 1838 do 31 grudnia 1841 roku*, ANK, 29/200/71 (WM 20), 522–523, 526–531. Title I "National Administration", § 1: "Salaries

from 1 January 1845, the last budget of the Free City of Cracow took into account the reorganisation of the judiciary carried out between 1839 and 1842.

The 1833 Statute provided that all court officials were entitled to a six-week leave of absence ("rest time") each year, on condition that this did not cause any disruption to the functioning of the courts (that "the Courts should be in action without interruption").[65] In 1836, the Ruling Senate, under the authority of the "Protective Courts", repealed Article 85 of the same Statute, putting court officials on an equal footing with other officials in this respect.[66] Further changes were introduced by statute in 1842. The leave of court chairmen, judges and prosecutors was reduced to a maximum of 28 days, with the possibility of it being spread over shorter periods if the functioning of the judiciary was not threatened. The leave was granted by the Ruling Senate. The length of leave for other officials was reduced to only five days, with the possibility to extend it, at the request of the Chairman of the Higher Court and with the approval of the Ruling Senate.[67]

From 1833 onwards, judges enjoyed the benefits of an old-age pension scheme. Previously, provision for old age depended on the decision of the Sejm and the Government, "in recognition of merit". The new arrangement was that, when salaries were paid, the newly created Pension Commission deducted 4 per cent from them as a contribution to the Pension Society, membership of which was compulsory. In the event of shortfalls in the Society's coffers, pensions were subsidised from the State budget. The system was based on a progressive method: the amount of the pension, but also of the widow's and orphan's allowance, depended on the length of service: working 15 years resulted in a pension entitlement of 25 per cent of the highest salary, 35 years of service up to 100 per cent. In the intermediate period, the pension increased annually by 3/20 of the amount calculated in relation to one-quarter of the basic salary; the right to a pension was granted to the judge's wife, as well as to minor children. In order to start collecting the pension, the relevant documentation had to

of Administrative and Judicial Officers Attached to Persons"; Title II "Judiciary". The expenditure budget amounted to 1,812 224 zlotys 3 grosz (ibidem, 562–563).

65 *Statut Urządzający Sądownictwo* of 27 August 1833. Chapter VIII "General Solutions" (Article 85). The requirement of continuity of office also applied to the Courts of the Peace and sub-courts.

66 Regulation of the Ruling Senate of 8 November 1836, No. 6538 DGS, *Urządzenie o urlopach Urzędników Sądowych*, DPr.WMK of 1836 (Articles 1–2). They were to receive leave under the terms of Article 13 of the Senate Statute of 1833.

67 *Statut Organiczny dla Władz Sądowych* of 27 January 1842. Chapter XVII "On Holidays for Judicial Officers and Granting them Permission to be Away from their Duties" (Articles 149, 152).

be presented. The Pension Act also precisely defined the circumstances that would result in the loss of the right to a pension. These were: a) leaving the service before reaching the minimum "years of service"; b) conviction of a crime with a public punishment, combined with a deprivation of office or civil rights; c) expulsion from the service due to bad conduct; d) "entry into the service of a foreign government".[68] The aforementioned Pension Commission operated under the supervision of the Ruling Senate. In addition to delegates from the Government, Jagiellonian University, secondary schools and the National Militia, it also included a representative from the judiciary.[69]

Among the privileges of judges, as was the case with professors at Jagiellonian University, was the right to wear an official uniform. Its pattern, based on designs from the Duchy of Warsaw, was approved by the Organising Commission in 1816. It was dominated by a navy blue and crimson colour scheme. The uniform consisted of a "top dress of German cut", a white waistcoat, black or white trousers, a "plain hat with a silver safety pin made from a ribbon or cord, and a white bow", and buttons with the coat of arms of the Free City of Cracow.[70]

5 The Day-to-Day Activities of the Courts

As mentioned at the beginning of the chapter, the seat of Cracow's courts was located in the so-called 'post-Jesuit buildings' (*Collegium Broscianum*) in Grodzka Street. As early as 1796, they housed the offices of the Imperial Royal Court of Appeal for Western Galicia and the Cracovian Court of the Nobility. By the resolution of 20 September 1818, the entire second floor was transferred for the use of the Tribunal and Court of Appeal.[71]

68 For more, see Mataniak 2017a, 289–318; Mataniak 2017b, 493–519.

69 In the years 1841–47 they were successively judges of the Higher Court, Konstanty Hoszowski and Felicjan Dudrewicz. Proclamation of the Presiding Officer of the Pension Commission of 16 June 1844 no. 1538, DRz.WMK No. 81–82 of 3 July 1844, 330–331; *Kalendarzyk polityczny krakowski na rok 1844* 1844, 56–57; *Kalendarzyk polityczny krakowski na rok 1846* 1846, 48–49.

70 Regulation of the Ruling Senate of 14 September 1816 No. 3298 DGS, ANK, 29/200/206 (WMK V-7), 39–46; Resolution of the Organising Commission of 2 September 1816 No. 530, ibidem, 39. The pattern of the uniforms was slightly modified in: Regulation of the Ruling Senate of 9 February 1818 No. 372 DGS, ibidem, 111–112, 119. For a depiction of the uniforms and more information, see Mataniak 2022b, 313–317.

71 Szymborski 2014, 98–100, 104–105. The ground floor and the first floor were left at the disposal of the Government authorities. The monumental wardrobes in which court records were once kept are still preserved in the building.

FIGURE 10 *Seat of courts of the Free City of Cracow* (*Collegium Broscianum*), (drawing, paper, 1871)
SOURCE: NATIONAL ARCHIVES IN CRACOW, ANK, 29/671/182; PHOTO & PERMISSION BY NATIONAL ARCHIVES IN CRACOW

According to the 1843 inventory, the court's premises comprised: three session rooms of Divisions I–III, a deliberation (presidential) room, a prosecutor's room, the offices of the secretariat (which comprised the offices for the lodgement of documents, recording clerks and secretary, as well as the bureau), three chambers of the Tribunal' Archives, a six-chamber Criminal Inquisitor's Office, two court cashier's rooms, a criminal deposit office, a watchman's room, three offices of the Court Scribes of Divisions I–III, and the office of the Regent of Mortgages Acts.[72]

When necessary, renovations were carried out in the courtrooms, or necessary items of equipment (stationery, stamps, tables and chairs, etc.) were purchased.[73] For example, in 1850, in response to a request from the Chairman of the Tribunal, the Government authorised the city treasury to purchase four

72 *Inwentarz wszelkich Effektów i Utensyliów do obecnego składu Trybunału i Biór jego przeznaczonych sporządzony, z 1843 roku*, of 3 March 1843, ANK, 29/200/1818 (WM 154), no pagination.

73 See the announcement of the Department of Internal Affairs of April 30, 1833, DRz.WMK No. 11 of 4 May 1833, 39.

chairs with handrails and 28 small chairs, necessary for the tribunal rooms, "in place of those there, which had become worn out".[74] In 1849, the Chairman of the Tribunal reported an annual requirement of 130 reams of paper (one ream was equivalent to about 480 pieces), 7,000 goose quills, ten pencils, eight ink-wells and 30 *garniecs* (about 82 litres) of black ink.[75]

The daily order of the work of the courts was specified in 1816. The court started its work at 9 a.m. In both its divisions, so-called economic subjects were heard on Monday, civil cases on Tuesday and Thursday, commercial cases on Wednesday and Friday, and criminal and correctional cases on Saturday. A deviation from the above order was only possible in urgent situations ("inadmissible delays").[76] The table below gives an idea of the adjudicatory effort of the courts of the Free City of Cracow.

The above data should be supplemented with the information that conciliation judiciary ("economic cases"; voluntary jurisdiction, "*iurisdictionis voluntaria*") also played a very important role in the judicial practice of the Free City of Cracow. According to the data for the period 1 June 1819–31 May 1820 alone, 3,897 cases were heard in the Court of First Instance, and 1,949 in the Court of Appeal. In the reporting year 1824/25, the court dealt with as many as 4,520 economic applications, while the Court of Appeal dealt with 2,396.[77]

6 Court Officials, Notaries, Advocates

In my discussion, some attention should also be paid to the other court officials. First of all, court scribes deserve mention. Both the Code of Civil Procedure

74 Letter from the Chairman of the Administrative Council to the Chairman of the Court of 6 May 1850, No. 5162, ANK, 29/200/1818 (WM 154), no pagination; letter from the Chairman of the Tribunal to the Council of 2 May 1850, No. 644, ibidem. The chairs were to be "made of walnut wood, on springs, upholstered in green leather, green, the backs of all were to be padded".

75 *Wykaz materialiów potrzebnych dla* CK. *Trybunału na rok 1849*, ANK, 29/200/1818, (WM 154), no pagination. And also 300 pounds (about 150 kg) of tallow candles, 3 pounds (about 1.5 kg) of amber "for incense", 36 brooms, 6 brass candlesticks and 13 decanters with glasses.

76 Announcement by the Chairman of the Court of First Instance, Bernard Dwernicki of 15 June 1816, supplement to DRz.WMK No. 49 of 19 June 1816, 608. Every Monday, Wednesday and Friday, starting at 3 p.m., a separate department was to additionally deal with pre-inquisition matters in criminal and correctional cases, as well as with instructions in these cases.

77 In the reporting year 1825/26 there were 4,806 and 2,566 cases respectively, in the reporting year 1826/27 there were 4,873 and 2,865 cases.

TABLE 1 Number of civil cases adjudicated (as regard Courts of the Peace also settled and conciliated cases) by the courts of the Free City of Cracow (1816–44)

Year/type of court	Courts of the Peace	Tribunal of First Instance	Court of Appeal	Court of Third (Last) Instance	Total
1816/17[a]	941	939	135	12	2,027
1817/18[b]	715	726	159	21	1,621
1818/19[c]	520	480	114	21	1,107
1819/20	1,012	506	223	35	1,776
1821/22	1,046	544	194	41	1,825
1822/23	1,028	554	212	41	1,835
1823/24	1,123	556	221	47	1,947
1824/25	1,156	505	255	50	1,966
1825/26	2,380	544	285	49	3,258
1826/27	4,123	686	302	57	5,168
1827/28	no data	no data	no data	no data	5,291
1828/29	no data	no data	no data	no data	6,053
1829/30	no data	no data	no data	no data	5,794
1830/31	no data	no data	no data	no data	6,607
1831/32	no data	no data	bd.	no data	5,014
1832/33	4,533	667 (incl. commercial cases)	413	72	5,685
1833/37	22,604; on average 5,652 annually	2,830; on average 707 annually	1,602; on average 400 annually	428; on average 107 annually	27,468; on average 6,867 annually
1838/39	6,259	1,057 (incl. criminal cases)	574 (incl. criminal cases)	146	8,036
1843/44	9,020	2,091 (of which 1,242 as First Instance and 849 as Second Instance)	138 (as the Higher Court)	x	11,249

TABLE 1 Number of civil cases adjudicated (*cont.*)

a Data for the period 8 June 1816–30 September 1817.
b Data for the period 1 October 1817–30 September 1818.
c Data for the period 1 June 1818–28 February 1819.

SOURCE: AUTHOR'S OWN COMPILATION BASED ON: *ZDANIE SPRAWY ... W DNIU 3 GRUDNIA 1817 ROKU*, 23–25; *ZDANIE SPRAWY ... W DNIU 10 GRUDNIA 1818 ROKU*, 60–63; *ZDANIE SPRAWY ... 9 GRUDNIA 1819 ROKU*, 46–48; *STAN KRAJU RZECZYPOSPOLITEJ*, 16–17; *OBRAZ KRAJU 1822 ROKU*, 48; *ZDANIE SPRAWY ... 1823*, 40–41; *ZDANIE SPRAWY ... 1824 ROKU*, 32–33; *ZDANIE SPRAWY ... 1825 ROKU*, 13–14; *ZDANIE SPRAWY ... 1826 ROKU*, ANK, 29/200/407 (WMK V-196), 444–446; *ZDANIE SPRAWY ... 1827 R.*, 24–27; *ZDANIE SPRAWY ... NA DZIEŃ 21 SIERPNIA 1833 ROKU ZWOŁANYM*, ANK, 29/200/407 (WMK V-196), 1265–1266; DPR.WMK OF 1833, 6–8; *ZDANIE SPRAWY ... R. 1837*, ANK, 29/200/863 (WMK VI-65), 560–563; *ZDANIE SPRAWY ... W R. 1844 PRZEDŁOŻONE PRZEZ SENATORA DO TEGOŻ ZGROMADZENIA DELEGOWANEGO*, DPR.WMK OF 1844, 77–81; ANK, 29/200/407 (WMK V-196), 811–816.

and the court statutes determined that they headed court offices, which were expanded according to the size of the court. They assisted the judges in many activities, including, *inter alia*, editing judgments. They also kept records of civil and commercial cases, as well as appeals and cassation cases, which they placed on the docket on the orders of the court chairmen, generally according to the date of receipt. This was important because the order of the docket determined the order in which the cases were heard; the scribes monitored compliance with the time limits for the filing of pleadings, as well as the payment of court fees.[78] Scribes were required to have legal qualifications and experience, as evidenced by the case of Wincenty Janicki, who, when applying for this post, submitted documents confirming several years of "unpaid public service" to the Sejm Qualification Commission.[79]

The court archive at the Tribunal was also very active, and as time passed it was also responsible for collecting and storing the files of the other courts. In terms of the filing system, it used a subject-based filing system, which showed the influence of French solutions and those in force in the central offices of the

78 *Statut Urządzający Sądownictwo* of 27 August 1833, Chapter VI "On the Court of Third Instance" (Articles 27, 32–33, 35); *Statut Organiczny dla Władz Sądowych* of 27 January 1842, Chapter V "On the Tribunal". Chapter II "On the Organisation of the Tribunal with Regard to Civil and Commercial Cases" (Articles 43–47).

79 Letter from W. Janicki to the Ruling Senate of 7 September 1833, ANK, 29/200/188 (WMK III-7 B), 1715. His professional career before becoming a scribe had the following course: one and a half years as an apprentice at the Tribunal, two and a half years at a Court of the Peace, including acting as deputy scribe of the same court; two and a half years as an honorary (unpaid) assessor at the Tribunal; and finally as deputy scribe of the Tribunal for one year.

Kingdom of Poland; according to this system, files were arranged according to an archival key, introducing subject groups.[80] A Court Cashier's Office was set up to handle cash, staffed by a cashier and a controller. In their work they were guided by the accounting regulations of 1818 and 1838. Their duties included the collection of fees constituting the income of the Public Treasury (stamp and registration fees, court fines, "posthumous taxes"), the management of the court depository, the care of the equipment of the court offices, and the taking of funds from the General Cashier's Office to pay the salaries of judges and other officials; they also submitted accounts of the activities of the cashier's office.[81]

Court ushers were also officials indispensable to the daily functioning of the judiciary. Following the model of the Duchy of Warsaw, they were divided into two categories: a) delivery ushers, who delivered letters, above all lawsuits and other summonses, to the parties, collecting fees from them; b) audience ushers, who performed an internal and policing service in the court premises. They were all guided by the provisions of the Code of Civil Procedure (Book II, Title II "On lawsuits"; Book V "On the enforcement of judgments"), the decree of 14 October 1811, the Act on Courts of the Peace and the "Fee for Officials" of 1825.[82] As the qualifications of ushers often left much to be desired, in 1842 they were covered by the Judicial Apprenticeship Act. They were henceforth examined on "subjects concerning theory and practice". In the written examination, candidates also had to demonstrate their ability to "write fluently" and write "a specimen of some judicial act".[83]

---

80 Pańków 1954, 113–115; *Urządzenie wewnętrzne Senatu WMK i Jego Okręgu*, dated 15 July 1816, promulgated by the letter of the Ruling Senate, No. 2104 DGS, DRRz.WMK of 1816. Chapter VII "On the Archivist" (Articles 59–66).

81 *Urządzenie tymczasowe dla Władz Sądowniczych Wolnego Miasta Krakowa ...*, of 1816. (Article 7(a–e)); Statute of the Organising Commission of 2 June 1818 (to No. 1656 DGS), *O urządzeniu Rachunkowości w Wolnym Mieście Krakowie*, DRRz.WMK of 1818; Regulation of the Ruling Senate of 28 June 1838 No. 2863 DGS, *Urządzenie Rachunkowości*, ANK, 29/200/302 (WMK V-102 B), 1049–1106. For more, see Mataniak 2019a, 221–231.

82 Decree of 14 October 1811, *Powierzający funkcje burgrabiów woźnym i komornikom i ustalający związane z ich działalnością przepisy organizacyjne oraz należne opłaty*, DPKW, vol. 3, 407–413; Act of the Extraordinary Legislative Assembly of 17 June 1825, *Prawo oznaczające postępowanie przed Sądami Pokoju w kraju Rzeczypospolitey Krakowskiey*, announced by a letter of the Ruling Senate No. 3647 DGS, Dz.Pr.RK of 1825 r. Title XI "On the Enforcement of Judgments of a Justice of the Peace" (Articles 73–74); Regulation of the Ruling Senate of 5 May 1826 No. 849 DGS, *Ustanowienie tax dla urzędników sądowych*, Dz.Pr.RK of 1826. Chapter VI "Regulations and the List of Fees for Court Ushers" (Articles 37–40). For more, see Mataniak 2019b, 83–87.

83 Regulation of the Ruling Senate No. 2124 DGS, *O applikacji i examinach sądowych*, DPr. WMK of 1842 (Article 42 (A)(a); Article 45). The ushers were required to be familiar with

The officials appointed to enforce final court judgments, settlements reached before the Courts of the Peace, as well as official acts testified before scribes, were bailiffs ("civil justice executive officers"). Until the mid-1840s, they functioned under the provisions of the Code of Civil Procedure, the Decree of 14 October 1811, the Enforcement Act of 1823 and the Regulation of 1826.[84] It was not until 1845 that the Government detailed the rules of their activities.[85] Each bailiff ran a separate office, and they performed official activities in a uniform. It is worth mentioning that bailiffs were not allowed to carry out enforcement on public holidays, i.e. Sundays, "all solemn holidays" as well as on 11 September, which was a public holiday to commemorate the anniversary of the granting of the Constitution to the Free City of Cracow. In 1842, bailiffs were required to take an examination before a Government commission. The duration of the apprenticeship of a bailiff was two years, and appointments were granted by the Ruling Senate. Before taking up the post, a deposit had to be paid and an oath taken. In 1823, there were six bailiffs in Cracow and one in Chrzanów.[86]

Government prosecutors were also an institution introduced following the model of the Duchy of Warsaw.[87] No doubts were expressed by the members of the Extraordinary Legislative Assembly as to the legitimacy of their continuation under the new political conditions, who agreed to establish prosecutors both before the Tribunal and the Court of Appeal. In contrast, a proposal by one of the priest-deputies of the Sejm, providing for the existence of clerical procurators, who would be appointed by the Holy See and then by diocesan synods, did not meet with approval. Their main task would be to oversee the interests of the Catholic Church, especially the succession of deceased priests, and to participate in the auctioning off of Church property or landed assets encumbered with obligations to ecclesiastical institutes; in addition, they would act as "protectors of the marriage bond" among parishioners.[88]

---

the following acts: on Courts of the Peace, on enforcement, and on fees, as well as the Code of Civil Procedure, as regards enforcement and how to serve summonses and other letters.

84 Decree of 14 October 1811, *powierzający funkcje burgrabiów woźnym i komornikom ...*; Act of the Extraordinary Legislative Sejm of 17 June 1823, *O egzekucji sądowej*, announced by a letter of the Ruling Senate of 6 August 1823 No. 2116 DGS, Dz.Pr.RK of 1823 (Articles 1, 13). Regulation of the Ruling Senate of 5 May1826 No. 1755 DGS, *Postępowanie przy licytacjach, inwentacji itp.*, Dz.Pr.RK of 1826.

85 Regulation of the Ruling Senate of 9 September 1845 No. 4515 DGS, *Instrukcja dla Komorników Sądowych*, DPr.WMK of 1845.

86 For more, see Mataniak 2019b, 87–92.

87 On the office of prosecutor in France, see Hube 1828, 1–32.

88 Minutes of the meeting of the Extraordinary Legislative Assembly of 6 February 1818, *Gazeta Krakowska* No. 19 of 8 March 1818, 217.

Government prosecutors were obliged to take part in civil proceedings whenever the public interest or the welfare of minors required it, as well as in criminal trials. In this case, they were to conduct investigations, draw up indictments and then support them at trial. From 1818, prosecutors were appointed by the Government from among candidates proposed by the Chairman of the Court of Appeal.[89] In 1833, the requirement for a candidate to be supported by the judicial authorities was abolished. Under the 1826 instruction of the Ruling Senate, prosecutors began to be considered part of the Government apparatus, with the rank of commissioners. They were primarily to supervise the observance of the law by judicial officials, including the prevention of acts constituting an abuse of judicial independence. Thus, the supervision did not concern the judge's utterance of a "particular opinion in the adjudication of a case", but only such reprehensible behaviour as partiality ("apparent partiality"), bribery, dilatoriness harmful to the parties ("delay of interests, by marking time limits where such is not known to the law itself"; "withholding the enforcement of final judgments and bringing them, to the detriment of the parties, to a new audience"), or unlawful "refusal of military assistance in enforcements or withholding enforcement steps for the delay of time", etc. Therefore, the prosecutors submitted opinions ("lists of conduct") on judicial officials, including judges, to the head of Government. On specific matters, we can still describe the representation of the interests of the Public Treasury, beside one of the senators and a Government assessor, and the participation in trials concerning minors, as well as public institutes, municipalities and any corporations which"the Government considered to be moral persons".[90]

Since an acute economic problem for the Senate was a lack of sufficient investment necessary to stimulate economic growth ("keeping credit in the Country"),[91] the prosecutor was also supposed to investigate the correctness of the establishment of mortgage deeds, the legitimacy of the announcement of so-called 'mortgage moratoria' or the distribution of debts in instalments. An acute and unresolved problem remained so-called 'merchant bankruptcies',

---

89 *Urządzenie tymczasowe dla Władz Sądowniczych ...*, (Article 2a–d); Bartel 1981, 821–822; Sobociński 1964, 252–253.

90 Regulation of the Ruling Senate of 14 June 1826 No. 1137 DGS, *Instrukcja dla Prokuratora Rządowego przy Sądach i Sądownictwie w ogólności*, ANK, 29/200/219 (WMK V-20 B), 1149–1156. The provisions concerning the duties of prosecutors were scattered over numerous regulations (NC, Commercial Code, Criminal Code of 1803, Code of Civil Procedure, decrees from the time of the Duchy of Warsaw, Provisional Organisation of the Judiciary of 1816).

91 On the economic situation, see Meus 2016, 29–37, 40–54; Mataniak 2018, 267–298. See also Malec 2004, 79–95.

which the Commercial Code divided into simple cases (prosecuted by means of so-called 'correctional police measures'), and deceitful ones, considered to be acts of a criminal nature. The prosecutor could demand the declaration of bankruptcy of an untrustworthy merchant and then investigate the factual causes. He could also apply to the court for the penalties provided for in the Commercial Code and the Criminal Code of 1803 (the *Franciscana*).[92]

Persons applying for the office of prosecutor at the tribunal had to demonstrate, *inter alia*, a completed law degree, the passing of a judicial examination and at least three years' service in the judiciary.[93] Yet, after 1839, prosecutors could only take part in civil trials.[94] It may be added that the tribunal's prosecutor was also involved (by way of monthly "prison reviews") in the supervision of the Criminal Prisons Building; both prosecutors sat on the management of the House of Forced Labour.[95]

In terms of the organisation of the notary profession, the French system was in force in the Free City of Cracow. It consisted of notaries who were public officials, appointed to prepare deeds and contracts to which the parties should, or hoped to, receive "the characteristic of officialdom", which entitled them to "acts of public solemnity". They also dated documents, stored them and issued main extracts and copies of them. The legal basis for the activities of notaries was the Notarial Act of 16 March 1803.[96]

Information on typical notarial activities is provided by the 1826 list of court fees. It indicates, *inter alia*: (1) the drawing up of protocols for the issuance of extracts and copies of records, including by way of enforcement of a tribunal's

92 Regulation of the Ruling Senate of 14 June 1826 No. 1137 DGS, *Instrukcja dla Prokuratora Rządowego przy Sądach i Sądownictwie w ogólności*, ANK, 29/200/219 (WMK V-20 B), 1152–1153 (Article 14). In consultation with the Senate, a prosecutor could also determine the admissibility of "restoring the bankrupt to honour and being able to trade again".

93 *Statut Organiczny dla Władz Sądowych*, of 27 January 1842. Chapter V "On the Tribunal", Section I "On the Composition and Organisation of the Tribunal" (Article 26).

94 Bartel 1981, 821–822. At that time, the criminal judiciary saw the removal of vestiges from the Duchy of Warsaw. On the prosecution in the Duchy of Warsaw, see Sobociński 1964, 252–253; Sobociński 1993.

95 Regulation of the Ruling Senate of 18 June 1834 No. 3387 DGS, *Instrukcja Więzień Kryminalnych*, DPr.WMK of 1834 (Title VII "On the inspection of prisons", Article 75); Regulation of the Ruling Senate of 27 October 1841 No. 5804 DGS, *Zmiany w zasadach Domu Pracy*, DPr.WMK of 1841 r. (Articles 1–2). For more, see Mataniak 2017c, 213–249.

96 *Wyciąg z Ustawy Francuskiej o Organizacji Notaryatu z stosownymi zmianami*, ANK, 29/200/204 (WMK V-5), 401–414. The Act consisted of five chapters: "On the Office and Duties of Notaries", "On Deeds, their Form, Original Deeds, Official Extracts, Certified Copies and Registers", "On the Authorisation of Notaries to Hold Office", "On the Transfer of the Notary's Archives and the Return of the Due", and "General Arrangements". For more on the Notarial Act of 1803, see Halperin 1996, 69–70.

FIGURE 11 *Seal of the public notary Marcin Strzelbicki,* (seal matrix, brass, 1st half of the 19th century)
SOURCE: NATIONAL ARCHIVES IN CRACOW, ANK, 29/661/75; PHOTO & PERMISSION BY NATIONAL ARCHIVES IN CRACOW

judgment (Article 849 of the Code of Civil Procedure); (2) accepting so-called “deeds of respect” from persons entering into marriage (Articles 151–154 of the NC); (3) the drawing up of inventories after the appraisal of the immovable and movable property of the spouses, in the event of a request for divorce “by mutual consent” (Article 279 of the NC); (4) the drawing up of protocols for “court instructions”, in the event of divorces “by mutual consent” (Articles 284–285 of the NC); (5) the drawing up of inheritance inventories (Articles 941–943 of the Code of Civil Procedure); (6) submitting proposals to the Chairman of the Tribunal in the event of disputes between inheritors concerning the designation of “administration of the common property”, succession or other items (Article 944 of the Code of Civil Procedure); (7) the drawing up of protocols of partition (Articles 977–978 of the Code of Civil Procedure) and depositing them in court archives; (8) and the drawing up of contracts and other “acts of goodwill" (partitions, powers of attorney, wills, receipts, "obligations and any transactions").[97]

Notarial fees increased if the preparation of a deed took more than one day (notaries in Cracow were entitled to nine Polish zlotys and in Chrzanów six zlotys). If the action was performed outside the notary's office and the parties did not provide the notary with means of transport, he was entitled to reimbursement of travel costs and an additional fee (six and four zlotys); if the "expeditions and extracts" prepared by the notary had a length of more than 28 lines and 18 syllables on each page, an additional fee in Cracow was three zlotys for each sheet (two zlotys in Chrzanów). Notaries also had to comply with the so-called 'Law of the Poor', which consisted of drawing up deeds free of charge; this usually referred to the so-called 'deeds of respect', widely used among the peasant population.[98]

Before taking office, a notary paid a deposit, which acted as security for any claims arising from his activities. Notaries were appointed for an indefinite period by the Ruling Senate, at the request of the Chairman of the Court of Appeal (later the Chairman of the Court of Third Instance). The qualifications of notaries were specified by the Act of 1803 and by the Decree of 11 July 1809, and later by the Act on Apprenticeships; the supervision of notaries was exercised by the Chairman of the Tribunal. It should be added that there was no notarial self-government in the Free City of Cracow, like a notarial chamber. Between 1816 and 1846 there were a total of 14 notaries in Cracow (three in Chrzanów).[99]

Court officials also included the so-called Regent of Mortgage Deeds (conservator of mortgages), whose powers included: (1) making entries and deletions of mortgage rights, including entries in the so-called "*księga ingrosacyjna*" (the subject of the entry could be a contract, a court judgment and a receipt); (2) preparing mortgage extracts; (3) issuing certificates on the absence of mortgage encumbrances on real estate; (4) issuing copies from mortgage documents; (5) announcing property auctions and assessments; and (6) supervising the mortgage archive. The regent charged a stamp duty for the deeds drawn

97 *Ustanowienie tax dla urzędników sądowych*, Chapter II "Regulations and a List of Fees for Deed Scribes, i.e. Notaries" (Aricles 13). For these activities notaries charged 6 zlotys in Cracow and 4 zlotys in Chrzanów.

98 Ibidem (Articles 14–15, 17–19). Disputes over notary fees were settled by the Tribunal of First Instance.

99 For a detailed description, see Malec 2001, 185–202; Malec 2007, 88–95.

up.[100] In 1844, the so-called Mortgage Authority was established, consisting of the Regent of Mortgage Deeds and two judges of the tribunal.[101]

We cannot omit a discussion on professional legal representatives either, i.e. advocates (patrons).[102] The distinction in the Duchy of Warsaw between patrons, advocates and attorneys, depending on the type of court at which they were appointed, was abandoned in the Free City of Cracow.[103] The rights and duties of advocates were set out, *inter alia*, in the Code of Civil Procedure and the 1842 Court Statute. The code indicated numerous situations in which a party was obliged to appoint an advocate, which had to be communicated to the court and to the opposing party's advocate. In general, the participation of advocates was mandatory in cases before courts of second instance.[104]

The Statute of 1816 only temporarily allowed advocates with the right to appear in the Tribunal for the Cracow Department to continue to serve "in both tribunals, as well as in the third instance, and even in the Supreme Court".[105] In 1818, the Organising Commission expressed the view that it would be necessary to determine at last the number of advocates in the Free City of Cracow, and to decide whether they should enjoy the right to appear before all judicial instances.[106] At the same time, the Commission recommended reducing

100 *Ustanowienie tax dla urzędników sądowych.* Title III "Regulations and a List of Fees for the Conservator of Mortgages, or the Regent of Deeds" (Article 20).

101 Act of 1 July 1844, *Zaprowadzenie Zwierzchności Hipotecznej,* announced by a letter of the Ruling Senate No. 3002 DGS, DPr.WMK of 1844 (Article 2); Letter from the Chairman of the Higher Court to the Administrative Council of 31 March 1846 No. 509, ANK, 29/200/220 (WMK V-21), 749; Malec 2004, 84–85. On the mortgage law of the Free City see below, Chapter 6.

102 It is worth mentioning that in France, the activities of professional representatives were dealt with by the Act of 13 March 1804 re-establishing the Bar, the Decree of 14 December 1810 tightening state supervision, and the Act of 27 February 1822 introducing their division according to their ability to appear before the Tribunal or the Court of Cassation. Halperin 1996, 44–45, 69–70, 172–173. For more on Cracow's advocates, see Mataniak 2019b, 98–100.

103 Sobociński 1964, 253–254; Cichoń 2012, 48–49.

104 *Kodex Postępowania Sądowego Cywilnego ...,* Title III "On the Establishment of Patrons and the Reciprocal Presentation of Writs and Defences" (Articles 75–76); *Statut Organiczny dla Władz Sądowych ...,* of 27 January 1842. Chapter V. Section II. "On the Arrangement of the Court in Respect of Civil and Commercial Matters" (Articles 52–54); Chapter VII. Section II. "On the Arrangement of the Higher Court with Respect to Civil and Commercial Cases" (Articles 82–83).

105 *Urządzenie tymczasowe dla Władz Sądowniczych Wolnego Miasta Krakowa ...,* of 1816 (Article 4). The Chairman of the Court of Third Instance could only increase their number "if absolutely necessary".

106 Interestingly, during the work of the extraordinary session of the Legislative Assembly in 1818, there was a proposal, by deputy Feliks Jaroński, that it would be appropriate to

the number of advocates in Cracow. On 28 July 1818, an *ad hoc* committee (comprising judges, prosecutors and members of the Legislative Committee) resolved that it would be sufficient to set the number at just ten advocates who could appear before all courts, in all categories of cases. This was intended to guarantee a more thorough knowledge of the case file, useful especially in the later stages of proceedings, and to limit expenses for litigants, who did not thus have to appoint another representative as a result of the case going to the higher instance.[107]

The issue was problematic in that, according to the Chairman of the Court of Appeal, as many as 17 lawyers were providing their services at Cracow's courts. They were therefore called upon to make immediate declarations as to whether they wished to continue to appear before the local courts. In an attempt to reach a compromise, the committee proposed a provisional solution, i.e. to keep all 16 advocates (one had not made a declaration), while maintaining the opinion that their number should eventually be reduced to ten.[108]

In subsequent years, the list of advocates was increased sporadically. For example, in 1821, the Court of Appeal presented for nomination to the Senate a Jan Bąkowski, who, having completed his legal studies at Jagiellonian University, took the judicial examination and then "honourably passed" the advocate's examination before the same court (still under the terms of the Decree of 11 July 1809). In addition to the flattering opinion of the president of the court of his "excellent conduct and moral integrity", a clerk of the Department of Internal Affairs also spoke favourably of the candidate. Accordingly, the Senate appointed Bąkowski, calling on him to pay the stamp duty and to collect the "certificate authorising him to perform his duties".[109] It may be added that

"repeal the privileges of advocates, patrons, etc., and return the former Bar". Due to the different subject matter of the debate, the proposal was not discussed. *Gazeta Krakowska* No. 15 of 22 February 1818, 172–173.

107 Letter from the Chairman of the Court of Appeal to the Ruling Senate, 1 February 1819 No. 324, ANK, 29/200/221 (WMK V-22 A), 517–520. The Committee pointed out that due to the poverty of the residents, patrons often have to appear for free, especially in civil cases.

108 Ibidem, 520–523. The advocates at the time were: Augustyn Boduszyński, Józef Borzykowski, Adam Ekielski, Jan Kanty Fachinetty, Józef Jankowski, Teodor Kawecki, Michał Karaszewicz, Wojciech Kowalski, Józef Kalasanty Kozłowski, Adam Krzyżanowski, Hilary Kudlicki, Onufry Męciński, Aleksander Niesiołowski, Feliks Słotwiński, Franciszek Urbański, Maciej Wojewódzki and Piotr Wiktorowicz. Only F. Urbański did not submit a declaration. Following the resignation of A. Boduszyński, who became a senator, Tadeusz Krzyżanowski was authorised to perform the duties of patron on a temporary basis.

109 Letter from the Court of Appeal to the Ruling Senate, 26 July 1821 No. 2072, ANK, 29/200/221 (WMK V-22 A), 471–472; Opinion of the Department of the Internal Affairs of 5 August 1821, ibidem; Letter from the Ruling Senate to the Chairman of the Court of Appeal and

nearly 20 years later, disciplinary proceedings were initiated against Bąkowski, the reason being his disregard for his official duties and the instructions of the judicial authorities. The tribunal notified the Ruling Senate of Bąkowski's behaviour, and the President of the Tribunal stated that, since "milder measures of punishment" had not been successful, it was inevitable that Bąkowski should be deprived of his right to practise his profession. After examining the investigation file, this reasoning was shared by the Senate.[110]

The insufficient number of advocates in Cracow was repeatedly brought to the attention of the Senate by the judicial authorities. In 1833, the Chairman of the Court of Third Instance asked the chairmen of the courts whether it would not be beneficial, from the point of view of the efficiency of adjudication and the interests of the parties, to appoint additional advocates, in the persons of Adam Gołemberski and Józef Stróżecki. The answer was in the affirmative, because, due to a very large number of trials before the courts, at least eight advocates were needed at any one time, and the perceived difficulties of the parties in finding an advocate resulted in "delays and postponement of cases"; this was also contrary to the requirement of "haste in the administration of justice".[111]

Advocates and notaries were considered to be employees of the judiciary, even though they did not draw a salary from the Public Treasury. This is evidenced by the Senate's response to a question from the Directorate of Police on the requirement for them to obtain the permission of the Chairman of the Tribunal to be "away from their duties" before applying to the Directorate for a "foreign passport" when they intended to take their leave of absence.[112]

In the Free City of Cracow, the principle of *incompatibilitas* was in force, prohibiting the combination of professorial dignity with legal professions, above all that of an advocate, notary and judge, but also with other public positions

---

Bąkowski of 7 August 1821, No. 2672, ibidem, 473; Decree of 11 July 1809, *w sprawie kwalifikacji zawodowych pracowników wymiaru sprawiedliwości*, DPKW, vol. 1, 298–312.

110 Letter from the Ruling Senate to the Presidium of the Ruling Senate, the Higher Court, the Directorate of Police and the "Government Journal of the Free City of Cracow" of 30 September 1842 No. 5145, ANK, 29/200/139 (WMK III-28 A), 7. "Removal from Office" took place on the basis of Article 121 of the Statute of 1842.

111 Letter of the Court of Third Instance to the Ruling Senate of 31 October 1833, No. 214, ANK, 29/200/221 (WMK V-22 A), 405–408; Opinion of the Department of Internal Affairs of 7 November 1833, No. 7313, ibidem, 406. The need for additional appointments also resulted in the transformation of the Court of Third Instance into a "permanent *magistratura*".

112 Letter of the Ruling Senate to the Presidium of the Ruling Senate, the Higher Court, the Police Directorate and the Department of Internal Affairs of 27 October 1843 No. 5641, ANK, 29/200/142 (WMK III-31 B), 2211.

FIGURE 12 *Józef Brodowski, portrait of Adam Krzyżanowski,* (painting, oil on canvas, 1st half of the 19th century)
SOURCE: JAGIELLONIAN UNIVERSITY MUSEUM, MUJ-135-M, PHOTO BY JANUSZ KOZINA; PERMISSION BY JAGIELLONIAN UNIVERSITY MUSEUM

(senator, deputy). This was determined by the university statutes of 1821, 1828 and 1833. It should be added though that these provisions were not respected in practice, due to the constant protests of those concerned. At one point, a complaint was made to Chancellor Metternich, claiming that at the universities of Prague, Budapest and Lviv, professors could also be lawyers, etc. However, Stanisław Wodzicki, the long-standing Chairman of the Ruling Senate, was in favour of absolute enforcement of the principle of incompatibility of offices at all costs, as he wanted to undermine the position of Jagiellonian University as a hotbed of anti-Senate opposition. The professors speaking out against his actions were defending not only university autonomy, but also their own additional livelihood. The fact is that, in the early 1820s, all were doing such extra work: Adam Krzyżanowski, Feliks Słotwiński and Augustyn Boduszyński were advocates; Walenty Litwiński and Mikołaj Hoszowski were judges.[113]

Among the advocates who were particularly active in the first period of the Free City of Cracow, and who are still remembered well from the old, pre-partition times, one should mention Józef Kalasanty Kozłowski. He was a graduate in law and philosophy from Cracow Academy, then a bailiff at the Commercial Court, and from 1814 a patron at the Tribunal, and an established member of the Sejm (1819–23).[114] There was also Onufry Męciński; a patron at Cracow's courts as early as 1789, a lawyer at the Crown Tribunal in Lublin, and then an advocate at the Cracow Court of Nobility, at the Civil Tribunal of the Cracow Department and in the Republic of Cracow.[115]

Among Cracow's lawyers, Adam Krzyżanowski (1785–1847) certainly stood out in his effectiveness. He graduated in philosophy and law from Cracow Academy (doctorate in 1804), after which he taught bills of exchange law, and then the NC. In 1812, he took over the Department of the Civil and Commercial Code, which he headed until 1847. In the years 1814–16 and 1826–33 he was the Dean of the Faculty of Law, and in the years 1845–47 the rector of Jagiellonian University. During his lectures, Krzyżanowski most likely confined himself to interpreting code provisions, and although during the 37 years of his professorship, Krzyżanowski published only one dissertation on the NC, he was rightly considered the foremost expert on this codification in Cracow.[116] Thanks to his effective representation of his clients' interests, Krzyżanowski became the owner of two tenement houses in Cracow, as well as manors at Czulice and Cudzynowice (in the Kingdom of Poland).[117]

Another professor of Jagiellonian University, Feliks Słotwiński (1788–1863), was also very active as an advocate, was for several decades (1812–28, 1833–60) the head of the Department of Natural and Church Law, and frequently the Dean of the Faculty of Law. In his case, however, his activity as an advocate did

113 Patkaniowski 1964, 162–166; Mataniak 2022a, 296–297. Although the Academic Statute of 1833 upheld the prohibition on combining dignities, the Reorganisation Commission relaxed these restrictions, limiting them to future states of affairs.

114 Letter from J. Kozłowski to the Qualification Commission of 11 December 1823, ANK, 29/200/50 (WMK II-30), 495–496; *Gazeta Krakowska* No. 99 of 12 December 1819, 1091; No. 99 of 10 December 1820, 1181; No. 97 of 5 December 1821, 1177; "Dyariusz Czynności Seymu Rzeczypospolitey Krakowskiey roku 1822", ANK, 29/200/46 (WMK II-26), 10.

115 Letter from O. Męciński to the Qualification Commission of 11 December 1823, ANK, 29/200/50 (WMK II-30), 497–499; Letter from O. Męciński to the Residents of 6 May 1828, ANK, 29/200/117 (WMK III-3), 255–259. Męciński practised as an advocate for 34 years.

116 See P. Michalik below, Chapter 3.

117 Patkaniowski 1964, 206–207; Żukowski 2014, 262–263; PSB, Vol. XV, 587–588.

not prevent him from publishing numerous, and indeed high-quality, academic studies.[118] Other advocates associated with Jagiellonian University were also outstanding, such as Wincenty Szpor (1796–1856) and Józef Jankowski (1781–1847).[119] Antoni Matakiewicz (1784–1844), a popular Cracow notary, became a professor, who used the works of leading humanists of the Enlightenment during his lectures on criminal law (he headed the Department of Criminal Law and Judicial Procedure).[120]

118 Patkaniowski 1964, 188–190, 205–205; Szlachta 2000, 129–134. In his works, Słotwiński became known as an advocate of the law of nature school. For the most recent studies devoted to Słotwiński, see Mostowik 2023, 25–48.

119 Szpor headed the Department of Political Skills for a short time, while Jankowski, also for a short time, headed the Department of Natural Law and Canon Law (he was a professor in the Department of Philosophy at the Faculty of Philosophy of Jagiellonian University in the years 1818–29 and 1831–47). Żukowski 2014, 199–200; PSB, Vol. X, 541–542; Malec, Malec 2010, 103–104.

120 Patkaniowski 1964, 193–196; Żukowski 2014, 331–332, 522–523; PSB, Vol. XX, 169–170. From 1835 to 1837 Matakiewicz was the Dean of the Faculty of Law, and from 1837 to 1839 the Rector of Jagiellonian University.

FIGURE 13 *Portrait of Antoni Matakiewicz* (*unknown author*), (painting, oil on canvas, 1st half of the 19th century)
SOURCE: JAGIELLONIAN UNIVERSITY MUSEUM, MUJ-136-M, PHOTO BY JANUSZ KOZINA; PERMISSION BY JAGIELLONIAN UNIVERSITY MUSEUM

CHAPTER 3

Attempts to Codify Civil Law and the Enactment of Legal Principles

Piotr Michalik

1 Codification Work in the Free City of Cracow between 1816 and 1818[1]

When establishing on 3 May 1815 the Free, Independent and Strictly Neutral City of Cracow, Austria, Russia and Prussia did not decide what judicial law would apply there.[2] At the same time, they made it clear that they did not accept the status quo left behind by the Duchy of Warsaw in Cracow, at least in terms of the French civil law in force from 1810.[3] This was expressed explicitly by the Prussian Resident in Cracow, Baron Ernest Reibnitz, when he described the French codes as a "shocking memory of Bonaparte's usurpation".[4] According to Article XII of the Constitution of the Republic of Cracow of 3 May 1815, it was the Assembly of Representatives that was to deal with the establishment of the civil and criminal code and the shape of procedure. To this end, the Assembly was to appoint a special committee which, in its preparatory work, was to take into account "the local character of the country and the spirit of its inhabitants" (*aux localités du pays et à l'esprit des habitants*).[5] Until new laws are enacted, the existing codes remained in force,[6] namely the

1 This chapter is a modified and expanded version of the author's article on the principles of succession law in the Free City of Cracow: Michalik 2022.

2 *Traktat tzw. dodatkowy, dotyczący Krakowa zawarty przez Austrię, Prusy i Rosję*, Tokarz ed. 1932, 3–9.

3 The applicability of the NC was extended to the territories taken from Austria in 1809 from 15 August 1810. See *Dekret z 9 kwietnia 1810 r.*, DPKW, vol. 2, 220–221.

4 Tokarz ed. 1932, 161; Uruszczak 1997, 94. The quote by Reibnitz about the "shocking memory of Bonaparte's usurpation", was introduced into the study of the subject by Franciszek Xawery Fierich. As early as more than a century ago, he postulated a comprehensive analysis of "the history of the attempts to reform civil and criminal legislation in the Republic of Cracow, the Duchy of Warsaw and the Kingdom of Poland": Fierich 1917, 170. This chapter is another contribution to such an ambitious synthesis.

5 Tokarz ed. 1932, 12; Uruszczak 1997, 93.

6 *Urządzenia tymczasowego dla władz sądowniczych Wolnego Miasta Krakowa z 5 grudnia 1815 r.*, Nos. 1904 and 1796 DGS, DRRz.WMK of 1816, 91–104.

 | DOI:10.1163/9789004688742_005

French Civil Code of 1804, the Civil Procedure Code of 1806, the Commercial Code of 1807 and the Austrian Criminal Code and Criminal Procedure Code of 1803 (*Franciscana*), amended in the Duchy of Warsaw by the Royal Decree of 1810.[7]

By a decision of the Organising Commission,[8] whose task it was to bring the provisions of the Constitution into effect, the implementation of Article XII of the Constitution had already begun at the first extraordinary session of the Assembly of Representatives,[9] solemnly inaugurated on 22 January 1816.[10] "The Committee for the laying down of laws for the inhabitants of the Free City of Cracow and its District" (the Legislative Committee) was established by the Assembly a day later. It consisted of seven members elected by the Assembly "by silent vote" and, in accordance with the Constitution, two delegated members of the Senate. The elected members were professors of the Faculty of Law of the Academy: Father Bonifacy Garycki, Adam Krzyżanowski, Walenty Litwiński, Mikołaj Hoszowski; professional judges[11] Józef Nikorowicz and Józef Januszewicz; and the justice of the peace, and owner of the estate of Mysłowice, Stanisław Mieroszewski. The Senate was represented by Kajetan Florkiewicz and Stanisław Kostka Zarzecki.[12] Having completed its task, i.e. the establishment of the Committee, the Assembly was postponed "until an indefinite

---

7 *Dekret z 26 lipca 1810 r.*, DPKW, vol. 2, 291–303; Pauli 1968, 21–23.

8 The Commission, established under Article VII of the Treaty of 3 May 1815, consisted of the three Residents of the Protective Powers: Austria (Count Joseph Sweerts-Spork), Russia (Count Ignacy Miączyński) and Prussia (the aforementioned Baron Ernest Reibnitz), and three representatives of the citizens of the Free City of Cracow selected by them at the first session on 12 October 1815: Count Feliks Grodzicki (representing the nobility), Father Wincenty Łańcucki (representing the clergy) and Walenty Bartsch (representing the burghers). The latter three, however, had a "decisive vote" only in the event of a complete divergence of the Residents' votes: Tokarz ed. 1932, 31–36; Wachholz 1957, 133–135.

9 Tokarz ed. 1932, 76–77. The literature refers to extraordinary sessions of the Assembly of Representatives convened to implement Article XII of the Constitution as "extraordinary Legislative Sejms" (see, for example, Bartel 1976, 63–64; Pauli 1968, 27). The minutes of the Organising Commission of 22 October 1817 refer to an "extraordinary session" (*séance extraordinaire*), and the minutes of 30 December 1817 refer to an "assembly convened extraordinarily (*l'assemblée convoquée extraordinairement*)": Tokarz ed. 1932, 395 and 455. The latter phrase in the letter from the Organising Commission to the Senate of 30 December 1817, is translated as the "extraordinarily convened Sejm", and the term "Legislative Sejm" is used in *Gazeta Krakowska*'s account of the extraordinary session of the Assembly of Representatives in 1818: see below, footnotes 54 and 55.

10 *Gazeta Krakowska* No. 9 of 31 January 1816, 107–108.

11 Professional judges were also Litwiński and Hoszowski; Krzyżanowski and Florkiewicz were advocates.

12 *Gazeta Krakowska* No. 10 of 4 February 1816, 119–120; Pauli 1968, 27.

period of time", understood as a period necessary for the Committee to carry out the codification work entrusted to it.[13]

As the Assembly of Representatives had not enacted a procedure for the work of the Legislative Committee, on 16 February 1816, the Organising Commission imposed a special instruction.[14] It was prepared by Reibnitz, who, on behalf of the Commission, oversaw the codification work from the beginning.[15] In addition to an introduction of a historical-legal nature, the instruction contained specific guidelines in the form of four sets of questions, dealing successively with the matter of: the Civil Code, the Criminal Code, civil procedure and criminal procedure.[16] Furthermore, "in order to expedite the work", Committee members were required to meet three times a week, and to report their progress at a meeting with the Organising Commission every week. The Committee was also to elect its chairman and deputy members.[17] Judges Jakub Mąkolski, Franciszek Piekarski and Bernard Dwernicki were also appointed to support the work of the Committee "on behalf of the Commission", and thus contrary to Article XII of the Constitution.[18]

The Commission's guidance on civil law largely concerned the law of succession, which was the subject of one in three of the 23 questions to the Civil Code.[19] In these, the commissioners asked about: the allowance of the statutory succession of ascendants (question six);[20] the extent of the right of representation in the lateral line (question seven);[21] the distinction between the origins of the property to be inherited (question eight);[22] the distinction

13 *Gazeta Krakowska* No. 10 of 4 February 1816, 121.

14 Tokarz ed. 1932, 103.

15 Already in the instruction to the Organising Commission of 4 July 1815, it was recommended to the future legislative committee to read Reibnitz's work *Versuch über das Ideal einer Gerichtsordnung*. This recommendation was implemented in an instruction of 16 February 1816, Tokarz ed. 1932, 18 and 108. The special role of Reibnitz in the codification work in the Free City of Cracow was already pointed out by Fierich 1917, 170–173.

16 Tokarz ed. 1932, 104–108.

17 Mieroszewski became the chairman.

18 Tokarz ed. 1932, 108.

19 A full catalogue of them in Polish translation is presented by Uruszczak 1997, 94–95.

20 See Articles 731 and 746 of the NC. The *Code Napoléon* did not provide for restrictions on the succession of ascendants who came into the succession in the absence of the testator's descendants (parents concurrently with siblings).

21 See Article 742 of the NC, which limited the principle of representation to the descendants of the testator's siblings.

22 See Article 732 of the NC, which rejected the customary law's fundamental differentiation of the order of succession on the basis of the nature and origin of property.

between inheritance of further relatives by birth (*parents germains*) and step relatives by mother or father (*parents utérins ou consanguins*) (question nine);[23] the mutual succession of spouses (question ten);[24] the amount of a compulsory portion (*portion légitime*) for necessary heirs (*héritiers nécessaires*) (question 11);[25] and the need for life annuities (*advitalité*) (question 12).[26] These issues were addressed by the Committee and were taken into account in the legal principles prepared jointly with the Commission.[27]

Soon after, the Organising Commission's interference in the codification work led to satisfactory results. But Reibnitz's recommendations were ignored by the Committee, which continued its work on the drafts of the individual codes on its own.[28] As a result, on 13 July 1816, again on the initiative of a Prussian colleague, the Residents explicitly decided to change the subject matter of the work of the Legislative Committee. Its role as a drafting body was limited to the preparation of specific assumptions (principles) for individual codes in the form of legal questions to be discussed and decided upon at an extraordinary session of the Assembly of Representatives. Only the principles thus enacted, were to become the basis for the preparation of the final draft acts. However, this would now be entrusted to a newly elected committee and to individual codifiers, which clearly expressed the Commission's dissatisfaction with the interference of the Committee up to that time.[29]

---

23 See Articles 733 and 752 of the NC, which provided for the succession of ascendants and collateral relatives (*parents collatéraux*), divided into paternal (*ligne paternelle*) and maternal (*ligne maternelle*) lines, each of which was entitled to half the inheritance. They all inherited within their line. This rule applied to all the aforementioned relatives with the exception of siblings from the same bed (*germains*). Indeed, according to Article 752 NC, the testator's brother or sister by birth inherited in both lines at the same time.

24 See articles 723 and 767 of the NC. The NC included the spouse, together with the natural children and the State (in the original text "the Republic") among the irregular heirs (*successeurs irrégulières*). The spouse only inherited by statute in the absence of relatives and natural children.

25 The *Code Napoléon,* as a safeguard for the rights of necessary heirs (*héritiers réservataires*), provided for a reserve (*réserve héréditaire*): see Articles 913–919 of the NC. The terms used in question 11, i.e. *portion légitime* and *héritiers nécessaires*, are more general and include both the institution of a reserve and a legitime.

26 Tokarz ed. 1932, 105.

27 See below, pp. 78–79.

28 Wachholz 1957, 268. On 5 April 1816 Mieroszewski informed the Commission that, due to the other duties of its members, the Committee was able to meet not thrice, but only once a week. However, he would endeavour to increase the number of meetings to two, the clear implication being that there would no longer be enough time to meet together with the Commission: Tokarz ed. 1932, 128–129.

29 Tokarz ed. 1932., 161; Uruszczak 1997, 94.

Despite this unequivocal position of the Commission, the Committee continued for the next few months with the task entrusted to it by the Assembly of Representatives. It completed it on 22 November 1816, submitting to the Commission for approval "its draft [as to] the foundations of the Civil and Criminal Code in 115 pages".[30] In the light of both, Tokarz's published protocols of the Organising Commission, and the hitherto unpublished manuscripts of the protocols of the joint deliberations of the Commission and the Committee, the so-called Legislative Protocols (*Prothocoles législatifs*),[31] it can be assumed that the Committee did in fact prepare and submit draft codes to the Commission, and not merely their assumptions (principles), as Reibnitz wished them to do.[32] However, the latter got his way, and at the first legislative meeting of the Commission and the Committee on 13 December 1816, it was decided that the draft civil code (*Code rédigé par le Comité législatif*) prepared by the Committee would merely be the basis for formulating the principles of future civil codification in the form of legal questions for the Assembly of Representatives.[33] The work of the Commission and the Committee on these questions, as well as those for the other codes, continued for a further five months, during which 24 joint legislative meetings were held.[34]

The forced nature of the Committee's cooperation with the Commission was reflected in the actions of the ordinary Assembly of Representatives in February 1817. At that time, anticipating the Committee's expected complaints, the Commission refused to allow the Committee to report on its codification work to date, unambiguously informing the Legislature that it had not yet been

30 Tokarz ed. 1932, 211 presents the text: "*Le comité législatif présente son projet des bases des codes: civil et criminel en 115 feuilles*", omitting an illegible word. It may be read as "*quant*", which would suggest that the recording clerk originally wanted to write: "*Le comité législatif présente son projet quant á des bases des codes*", ANK, 29/200/3 (WMK I-3), 185. Unfortunately, this draft could not be found in the files of the Organising Commission and the Senate (Wacław Tokarz had not found it there). The protocol of 22 November 1816 only shows that the Commission commissioned its translation into French and German. Its further history is unknown.

31 ANK, 29/200/8 (WMK I-8).

32 The idea that there was an advanced codification draft is confirmed both by Mieroszewski's request to the Legislative Sejm on 8 January 1818 (see below, pp. 80–81) and by Reibnitz's note of 12 January 1818 arguing against it. He notes that accepting Mieroszewski's request would be a retreat to the state of 1816, when the draft codes had already been presented to the representatives for discussion: Tokarz ed. 1932, 465–466.

33 ANK, 29/200/8 (WMK I-8), 1–2. Unfortunately, we learn virtually nothing from the protocol about the content of the Committee's draft, other than concluding that its draft code consisted of three parts "according to the order adopted in the Austrian Code", i.e. the ABGB.

34 Tokarz ed. 1932, 217; Wachholz 1957, 268; ANK, 29/200/8 (WMK I-8), 1–92.

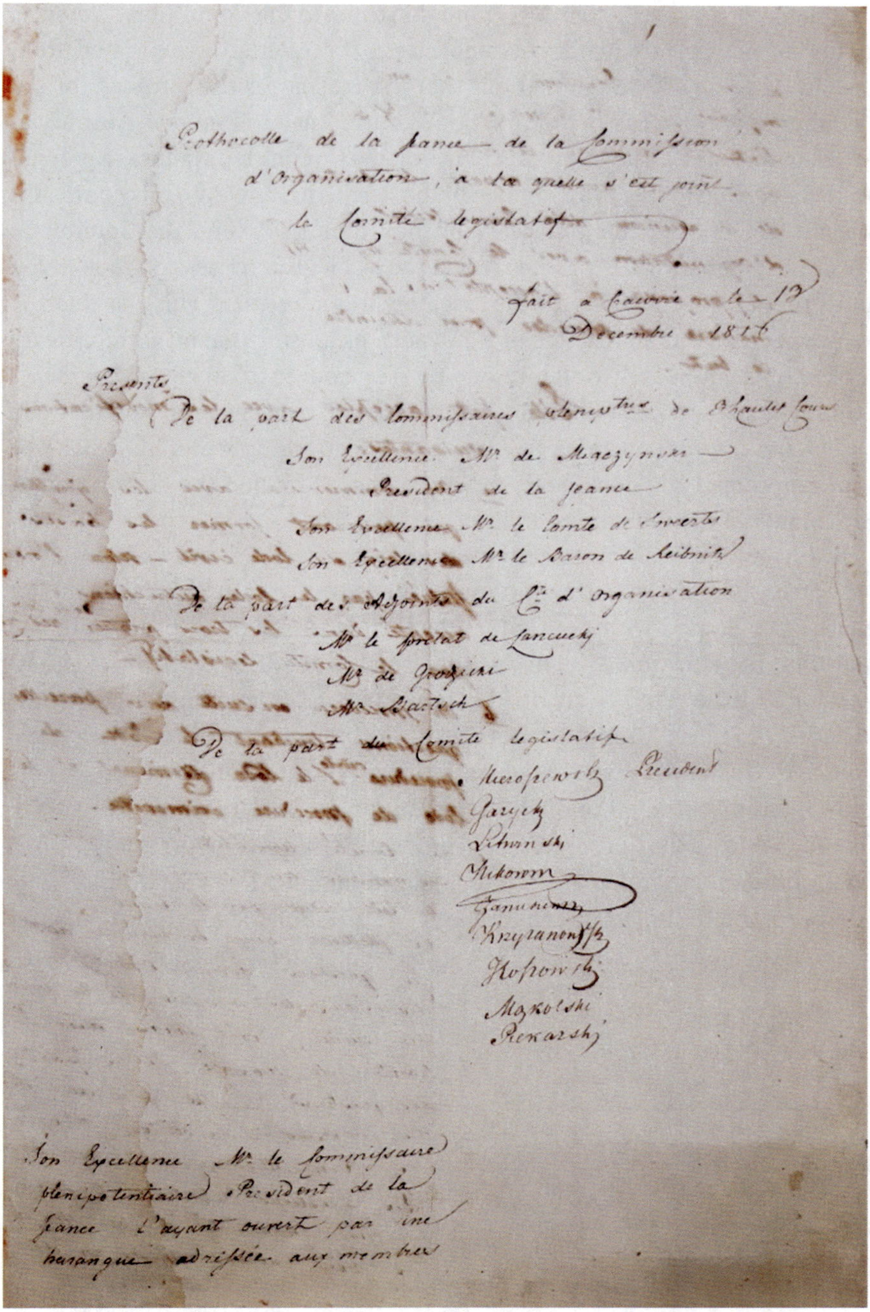

FIGURE 14 *Prothocole législatif of 13 December 1816*, (manuscript, paper, 1816)
SOURCE: NATIONAL ARCHIVES IN CRACOW, ANK, 29/200/8, 1; PHOTO & PERMISSION BY NATIONAL ARCHIVES IN CRACOW

completed.[35] However, Adam Krzyżanowski came to the Committee's defence, taking an active part in the Assembly as a representative delegated from Cracow Academy.[36] He pointed out that the reason for the tardiness of the Committee's work was the Commission's continuing interference, contrary to Article XII of the Constitution, and above all the Committee's failure to prepare draft codes. Due to the omnipotence of the Residents, however, this complaint did not bear fruit.[37] The joint work of the Commission and the Committee thus continued until 24 April 1817, when the last legislative session took place, and a set of legal questions for the assembly was adopted.[38] This was referred to by Sweerts-Spork in his note of 11 July 1817, proposing that an extraordinary session of the Assembly of Representatives be convened on 26 August 1817.[39] Eventually, however, the Commission's decision to convene representatives on 20 October 1817 was taken on 30 August 1817, as it was only then that Sweerts-Spork presented the documents in which Austria ratified the elaboration of Article XIII of the Constitution.[40]

Following the decision to convene the Assembly, the Commission sent to the Senate "for official use" a printout of the legal questions for the Sejm that had been prepared with the Committee.[41] It consisted of 40 pages with 297 questions in Latin and Polish in two columns. It was followed first by 130 questions on civil law. These were divided into parts and titles. "Part I. on Persons" included the titles: "I. On the Laws concerning personal qualities" (nine questions); "II. On Marital Rights" (eight questions); "III. On Rights between Parents and Children" (seven questions); "IV. On Adoption" (one question); and "V. On Guardianship" (four questions). In "Part II" the titles were: "VI. On Matters" (four questions); "VII. On Pledges" (six questions); "VIII. On Servitudes" (one question); "IX. On Wills and Inheritances" (24 questions); "X. On Joint Property of Spouses" (one question); "XI. On Contracts in General" (six questions); "XII.

35 Tokarz ed. 1932, 238.

36 *Gazeta Krakowska* No. 14 of 16 February 1817, 158.

37 *Gazeta Krakowska* No. 17 of 26 February 1817, 197; Meciszewski 1849, 16–18.

38 ANK, 29/200/8 (WMK I-8), 89 and 92.

39 Tokarz ed. 1932, 341.

40 Ibidem, 370–371; ANK, 29/200/1 (WMK V-1), 663. It is clear from both the protocol of the Commission and its letter to the Senate of 30 August 1817, that the reason for the delay in convening the Legislative Assembly was that the residents were waiting for Vienna to ratify the amendments to the text of Article XIII of the Constitution, which had already been adopted by the Residents on 17 February 1817, and not the prolongation of the work of the Legislative Committee. See ANK, 29/200/7 (WMK I-7), 32.

41 Letter from the Organising Commission to the Senate of 25 September 1817, ANK, 29/200/200 (WMK V-1), 669.

On Donations". (eight questions); "XIII. On Lending" (13 questions); "XIV. On Powers of Attorney" (seven questions); "XV. On Sale and Purchase, and on a Contract of Lease" (13 questions); and "XVI. On the Contract of Company and Fate" (four questions); "XVII. On the Statute of Limitations" (14 questions).[42] These were followed by 44 questions "concerning Judicial Proceedings",[43] 83 questions "on the Criminal Code",[44] seven questions "on Embezzlement and Contraband",[45] and 33 "Questions on the Code of Criminal Procedure".[46]

Convened on 20 October 1817, the Legislative Assembly did not, however, proceed to answer the questions prepared for it, as for formal reasons it "did not come into effect".[47] The representatives assembled at the inauguration objected to its formation, pointing out that they had been elected/delegated to the Ordinary Assembly, which had been held and dissolved in February 1817. Consequently, their mandates expired because "the High Organising Commission itself, in its rescript stated that the character and office of a representative lasts only until the end of the Sejm".[48] In these circumstances, the Commission had to admit its mistake and, by a decision of 22 October, ordered the dissolution of the Assembly.[49] At the same time, it instructed the Ruling Senate to hold elections and to convene another extraordinary session of the Assembly on 7 January 1818.[50] This took place with a proclamation of 13 December 1817, in which the Senate summoned to the Sejm representatives elected in the individual communes and delegated by the corporations (Chapter and Academy). In addition, those members of the Legislative Committee who did not sit in the new Assembly as representatives were also allowed to attend "in an advisory capacity".[51]

---

42 ANK, 29/200/200 (WMK V-1), 671–696.

43 Ibidem, 697–711.

44 Ibidem, 713–724.

45 Ibidem, 725.

46 Ibidem, 727–730.

47 Meciszewski 1849, 21.

48 The Senate Report for the Commission of 20 October 1817, ANK, 29/200/200 (WMK V-1), 893–894; in addition, the question of whether the representatives elected to the Extraordinary Assembly in January 1816 should sit in the Assembly, remained unresolved, as it was only postponed (see above, pp. 73–74). For more details, see Meciszewski 1849, 19–27.

49 Ibidem, 25.

50 Senate Order of 24 October 1817, ANK, 29/200/200 (WMK V-1), 945–947.

51 *Uniwersał zwołujący nadzwyczajne Zgromadzenie Reprezentantów* of 13 December 1817, ANK, 29/200/200 (WMK V-1), 949.

At its meeting on 22 October 1817, the Organising Commission also approved the procedure to be followed in extraordinary sessions of the Assembly.[52] Following this, Reibnitz prepared a detailed work plan for the Legislative Assembly on the principles for future codifications, which was approved by the Commission on 30 December 2017.[53] Taking into account the events that had already occurred, it provided a five point programme where: (1) the Assembly would elect a Legislative Committee in January 1816; (2) the Committee, together with the Organising Commission, would

> arrange the questions in a disjunctive form as to the most serious matters with regard to both civil and criminal legislation and procedure, and particularly as to the subjects in respect of which the codes of the civilised nations differ most widely.

which would take place between 1816 and 1817; (3) "A representation convened on an *ad hoc* basis shall decide these questions by a majority of votes and with unrestricted freedom by the choice of one alternative or the other of the questions"; (4) the Assembly shall elect a new committee (the Editorial Committee) "to which the editing of the codes shall be entrusted"; (5) the Legislative Committee "shall guard" that in the codes prepared by the Editorial Committee "nothing contrary" to the principles passed by the Assembly "shall be adopted".[54]

After such careful preparations, on 7 January 1818 the opening of the Legislative Assembly was ceremonial and undisturbed by unexpected events.[55] However, the very next day a dispute arose between the Organising Commission and the Legislative Committee. Contrary to Reibnitz's policy of *fait accompli*, he continued to demand that he be allowed to complete its task to the end, that is, to prepare draft codes and put them to the vote of the Sejm. Mieroszewski, as the Chairman of the Committee, therefore proposed a resolution of the Assembly to this effect. Despite the motion being supported by other representatives, the chairman of the session, Senator Mikołaj Hoszowski, refused to put Mieroszewski's motion to a vote. Instead, he agreed to turn it into a request

52 Tokarz ed. 1932, 395.

53 Ibidem, 452.

54 Ibidem, 455–457; letter from the Organising Commission to the Senate of 30 December 1817, ANK, 29/200/201 (WMK V-2), 1–7.

55 *Gazeta Krakowska* No. 5 of 18 January 1818, 49–51. As the minutes of the Sejm meetings have not been preserved, the course of the debate and the votes on the individual principles can only be presented on the basis of the reports in *Gazeta Krakowska*.

FIGURE 15 *Meeting place of the Legislative Assembly of 1818 (Collegium Novodvorscianum) – current view*
PHOTO BY ZYGMUNT PUT FROM 2022 IN PUBLIC DOMAIN (WIKIMEDIA COMMONS) – GNU FREE DOCUMENTATION LICENSE (CC BY-SA 4.0)

from the Assembly to the Organising Commission.[56] The latter's answer, given at the meeting of 12 January 1818, was amicable. It ordered the rules to be enacted, but at the same time allowed Reibnitz's plan to be amended and the Legislative Committee to be entrusted with the completion of the draft codes it was preparing. The Sejm was to "receive the drafted codes, and see to it that laws contrary to the principles adopted by the decision of the question [resolving the questions – P.M.] are not pressed into it".[57]

The extraordinary session of the Assembly, which lasted until 3 March 1818, deserves to be called the Legislative Assembly, as during the 23 days of its work[58] its Representatives responded to the 297 legal questions presented

56 *Gazeta Krakowska* No. 6 of 21 January 1818, 61–63; Letter from the President of the Assembly of Representatives to the Senate of 8 January 1818, ANK, 29/200/201 (WMK V-2), 11–13; Tokarz ed. 1932, 462–465 (French translation for the Commission).

57 Tokarz ed. 1932, 460; *Gazeta Krakowska* No. 6 of 21 January 1818, 64.

58 13–15, 19–20, 22–23, 26–27 January; 5–6, 9–10, 12, 16–17, 19–20, 24, 26–27 February; 2–3 March 1818.

to them, adopting 297 principles[59] "for the Codes of Civil Law, Criminal Law and Procedure from Article XII of the Constitution given to this country, to be arranged".[60] After the completion of the work on the principles of law, Marshal Hoszowski reminded the Chamber of the guidelines of the Organising Commission for further codification work. In accordance with these, the Sejm obliged the Legislative Committee (renamed the Editorial Committee) to prepare the individual codes in accordance with the adopted principles of law. In order to facilitate the work, Count Antoni Stadnicki, Father Mateusz Dubiecki, Józef Sołtykowicz, Feliks Słotwiński and Leon Chwalibogowski were added to the Committee. The completed drafts of the codes were to be presented by the Committee to the Assembly for adoption at the next session, which was postponed "indefinitely", and the adopted principles were sent to the Ruling Senate.[61]

The Legislative Sejm of 1818 seemed to be an important step towards the introduction of the Republic of Cracow's own codifications. The adopted principles were approved in June by the Organising Commission, which made only one remark,[62] and, at the Assembly of Representatives in December, the Senate expressed the expectation that the Editorial Committee would soon complete its work.[63] In reality, however, neither in 1818 nor in the following years were the codifications in preparation completed, and the Committee confined itself to submitting drafts of a few special acts.[64] It was not until 1826 that Mieroszewski's successor as chairman, Józef Nikorowicz, officially acknowledged that the Editorial Committee was unable to perform the task entrusted to it, and proposed its reform.[65] This did not, however, improve the situation, and the Committee was eventually dissolved in 1833; and in the Free

59 *Odpowiedzi przez Nadzwyczajne prawodawcze Zgromadzenie Reprezentantów roku 1818. na pytania przez Rządzący Senat przy Reskrypcie de dato 13. Grudnia 1817. do Nr 3732 przysłane – Uchwalone*, ANK, 29/200/201 (WMK V-2), 63–95 (manuscript). Studies to date (Pauli 1968, 27; Bartel 1976, 101; Uruszczak 1997, 96) erroneously give a total number of 295 principles, including 128 principles of civil law, when in fact 130 were enacted. The footnotes in these works indicate that the source of this information was the findings of H. Meciszewski (Meciszewski 1849, 28).

60 *Gazeta Krakowska* No. 5 of 18 January 1818, 49.

61 *Gazeta Krakowska* No. 44 of 3 June 1818, 521–522; Letter from the President of the Assembly of Representatives to the Senate of 3 March 1818, ANK, 29/200/201 (WMK V-2), 61–62.

62 Tokarz ed. 1932, 532.

63 Pauli 1968, 34.

64 Wachholz 1957, 271. For more, see Chapter 4.

65 Wachholz 1957, 271–272.

City of Cracow, until the end of its existence, the codes inherited from the Duchy of Warsaw were used.[66]

2 The Enactment of the Principles of Personal and Family Law in the Civil Code of the Free City of Cracow in 1818

Of the 130 principles of civil law enacted by the Legislative Sejm of 1818, it is worth taking a closer look at the principles of personal and family law, and the law of succession, the enactment of which in many cases was preceded by a heated debate related to key social issues for the inhabitants of the Free City of Cracow.[67] The debate in the Assembly of Representatives on the questions as to the principles of civil law, began at the sitting of 13 January 1818 with nine questions on personal law, and were collected under Title I: "On the rights attached to personal qualities".[68] The representatives answered these questions in unison, leaning towards the opinion of the Legislative Committee. Only in the case of the question of the continuation of civil registry records was an objection raised, by Father Professor Feliks Jaroński, who "in a long speech argued that they were unnecessary".[69] However, he was decisively voted down (34 against three) and the Parliament passed the several principles of law.

These were: "A foreigner shall enjoy the same rights in the country of the Republic of Cracow as local citizens enjoy in the foreigner's country" (principle one);[70] "The domicile of a person is to be considered as to personal obligations where he lives, but as to obligations *in rem* where he has immovable property" (principle two);[71] "The domicile of a public official is to be considered where he holds office" (principle three); "There shall be no difference between life and elected officials" (principle four);[72] "The wife's domicile as regards the exercise

66 Pauli 1968, 35–36.

67 These principles are also the point of reference for the analysis of the application of personal and family law in Chapter 5 and of succession law in Chapter 8.

68 ANK, 29/200/200 (WMK V-1), 671.

69 *Gazeta Krakowska* No. 6 of 21 January 1818, 64.

70 See Article 11 of the NC; § 33 of the ABGB.

71 See Articles 102–103 of the NC. In the NC, a "domicile" (*un domicile*) was a legal relationship between a person and the place where the person has his or her principal dwelling (*un principal établissement*) and may or may not correspond to a "residence" (*une habitation; une résidence*), which is the actual stay of a person in a given place: Burzyński 1852, 177. Principles 2–5 do not take this distinction into account.

72 See Articles 106–107 of the NC. Determining the exclusive domicile according to the place of holding office was important due to the fact that many officials of the Free City of Cracow lived and owned immovable property outside its borders.

of her civil rights is normally to be deemed to be the place where the husband has his permanent residence, except in special cases to be determined by law" (principle five);[73] "A second marriage is not dissolved by the mere return of the first spouse – but it is permissible for a person, having been legally declared dead when he or she returns, to apply to the court for dissolution of the new marriage" (principle six);[74] "Civil registry records will be received by officials deliberately appointed to do so" (principle seven); "Civil registrars shall in general be clergymen, except in special cases to be determined by law laymen" (principle eight);[75] and "The age of majority regardless of gender shall begin after reaching the age of 21"[76] (principle nine).[77]

A day later, on 14 January, a meeting was held to address the questions within Title II: "On Marital Rights".[78] It is clear from the report in *Gazeta Krakowska* that the debate on this topic was particularly long, heated and attracted a great deal of interest.[79] In the first place, the Assembly was to decide which model of marital law (Austrian,[80] Prussian, Polish or

73 See Article 108 of the NC. Article 214 of the NC obliged a wife to actually live together with her husband, so the wife could not have a separate residence and domicile from her husband. According to French legal scholarship and case law, the exceptions to this rule were the separation of the spouses as to persons (*une séparation de corps*: Article 306 of the NC). The wife could also have her own domicile when she was appointed guardian of her incapacitated husband (Article 507 of the NC), but then it was the husband who shared her domicile (Article 108 of the NC).

74 In contrast to the ABGB (§ 24 in conjunction with § 278 of the ABGB), the NC did not have the institution of declaration of death, but instead provided for the complex institution of "unconsciousness" (*une absence*). This meant that a marriage concluded by an absent spouse always suffered from the defect of nullity resulting from an obstacle of bigamy (see Article 147 in conjunction with Article 184 of the NC): Burzyński 1852, 209. However, the position of those commentators who – on the basis of Article 139 of the NC, understood as *lex specialis* in relation to the rules on marriage – grant the right to revoke such a marriage only to the returning absentee, seems to be correct.

75 Principles seven and eight reflected the factual and legal situation introduced in Cracow after its incorporation into the Duchy of Warsaw, and which was an adaptation of the provisions of the NC on civil registry records to Polish realities: see below, Chapter 5.

76 See Article 488 of the NC *a contrario* to § 21 of the ABGB.

77 *Gazeta Krakowska* No. 6 of 21 January 1818, 64; ANK, 29/200/201 (WMKV-2), 63–64.

78 In accordance with the classification of the NC, this title covered only personal matrimonial law.

79 *Gazeta Krakowska* No. 7 of 25 January 1818, 73–77, No. 8 of 28 January 1818, 85–88, No. 9 of 1 February 1818, 97–101, No. 10 of 4 February 1818, 109–110. A presentation of the debate, due to its length, is beyond the scope of this chapter.

80 "So, are the principles of the Austrian code to be preserved in Cracow's legislation as regards the principles of marriage, obstacles and divorce?", ANK, 29/200/200 (WMK V-1), 673.

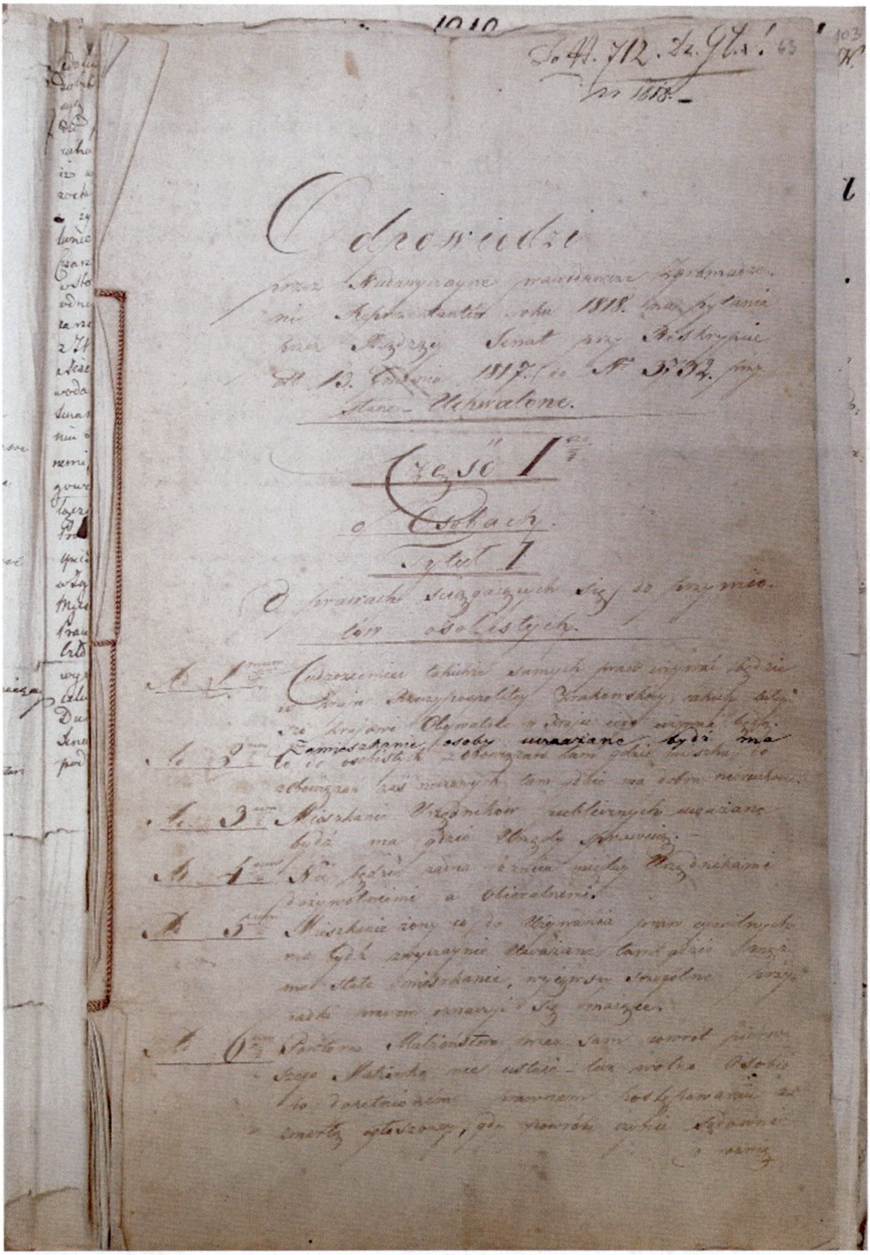

FIGURE 16 *Principles of law enacted by the Legislative Assembly of 1818*, (manuscript, paper, 1818)
SOURCE: NATIONAL ARCHIVES IN CRACOW, ANK, 29/200/201, 63; PHOTO & PERMISSION BY NATIONAL ARCHIVES IN CRACOW

French)[81] would be used in the Civil Code of the Free City under preparation. In spite of strong objections from both clergy and secular representatives, who pointed out that the provisions of the NC were incompatible with the doctrine and law of the Catholic Church, in a secret ballot, the Sejm, by an overwhelming majority (30 to eight), resolved that "The principles of the code hitherto in force shall be maintained with regard to the rules governing the conclusion of marriages, as well as obstacles and divorce in the Cracovian legislation" (principle four).[82] Thus, the Assembly was unequivocally in favour of the secular model of marriage, which was introduced in Cracow by the French Civil Code in 1810,[83] rejecting the mixed model adopted in the Austrian West Galician Code of 1797 and the ABGB of 1811[84] and the Prussian *Landrecht* of 1794.[85] The proposal to rely on the solutions to be adopted in the proposed Civil Code of the Kingdom of Poland, was also rejected because, as rightly noted, it did not yet exist.[86]

On the same day, the Legislative Assembly enacted four more principles of marriage law. In the first: "A man before the age of 18 and a woman before the age of 15 may not marry" (principle five), thus the age of matrimonial capacity adopted in Article 144 of the NC was confirmed. In the second: "The Senate may grant exemption from this provision for important reasons, as long as the physical capacity to marry is present" (principle six), thus exemption for its absence was allowed.[87] In the third principle, the canonical principle of the legitimation of illegitimate children *ipso jure* by the subsequent marriage of the parents (*legitimatio per subsequens matrimonium*), was maintained, stipulating that "Children begotten before marriage become legitimate through the marriage subsequently contracted of the father and mother when they legally recognise it before their marriage or in the very act of marriage" (principle

81 The question did not explicitly state this, referring to the "code hitherto in force in Cracow's legislation", ANK, 29/200/200 (WMK V-1), 673.

82 ANK, 29/200/201 (WMKV-2), 64.

83 For more, see Chapter 5.

84 "The principles of the Austrian code will not be preserved in Cracow's legislation as far as the rules on marriage, obstacles and divorce are concerned" (principle one), ANK, 29/200/201 (WMKV-2), 64.

85 "The principles of the Prussian code regarding the rules on marriage, obstacles and divorce shall not be adopted". (principle two), ANK, 29/200/201 (WMKV-2), 64.

86 "When the Polish Code does not exist you have no place to adopt the rules of this" (principle three), ANK, 29/200/201 (WMKV-2), 64.

87 Following Article 145 of the NC.

seven).[88] It is significant that this principle was also adopted on the basis of the provisions of the NC, which required, for effective legitimation, the legal recognition of the child (Article 331 of the NC),[89] and not the West Galician Code, previously in force in Cracow, or the Austrian Civil Code (ABGB), then in force in Galicia, which adopted a more favourable construction for the illegitimate child of *legitimatio per subsequens matrimonium* without the requirement of prior recognition (§ 161 of the ABGB). Similarly, principle eight, the last with the title "On Matrimonial Rights", rejected the possibility, provided for in Article 162 of the ABGB, to legitimate an illegitimate child by a royal rescript.[90]

The following day, 15 January 1818, the Assembly answered seven further questions, this time relating to Title III: "Of the Rights between Parents and Children".[91] A vote on the question of the religious upbringing of children of parents of different faiths, preceded the debate. Professor Feliks Słotwiński argued that according to Article 1 of the Constitution of the Free City of Cracow, which established the Catholic religion as the State religion,[92] if one parent is of this confession, the common children must be brought up in the Roman religion. On the other hand, in the case of other Christian denominations, as well as non-Christian religions, the principle of tolerance should apply, i.e. sons should be brought up in the religion of their father and daughters in the religion of their mother. He made the reservation, however, that the above positions do not apply to situations in which parents have concluded an agreement on the religious upbringing of their children. The former position was supported by Father Professor Jaroński, and the latter by Senator Karol Hube, who referred in this respect to Article 2 of the Constitution, which equates Christian denominations in civil rights.[93] In contrast, Father Mateusz Dubiecki took the opposite view, demanding the right for a father, who exercises parental authority, to decide on the religious upbringing of his children.[94]

---

88 ANK, 29/200/201 (WMKV-2), 64. The manuscript erroneously repeats "legitimate" instead of "legally". The correct word, i.e. in accordance with Article 331 of the NC, is given by: *Gazeta Krakowska* No. 10 of 4 February 1818, 110.

89 It could take place through a voluntary official act of the father or mother (Article 334 of the NC), a judicial recognition of paternity or maternity (Articles 340 and 341 of the NC) or a recognition in a marriage certificate (Article 331 of the NC), see Burzyński 1852, 309.

90 "The legitimation of children by a Senate's rescript may not take place", ANK, 29/200/201 (WMKV-2), 64.

91 ANK, 29/200/200 (WMK V-1), 675.

92 "The Apostolic Roman Catholic religion (professed by the majority of the inhabitants of the Free City of Cracow and its district) is maintained as the religion of the country".

93 "All Christian denominations make no difference as to social rights".

94 *Gazeta Krakowska* No. 10 of 4 February 1818, 110–111.

After the debate, the vast majority of representatives (25 against six) voted in favour of the principle that "If the parents are of different Christian denominations and there is no agreement between them in which religion the children are to be brought up, then the sons are to be of the same denomination as the father and the daughters of the same denomination as the mother" (principle one).[95] This time it was in accordance with Austrian law on which the solution, unanimously adopted in the next two rules, was based, the first one stipulating that "The age of discretion concerning the conversion from a non-Christian to a Christian religion begins with the sixteenth year of life" (principle two), and the second one deciding that "After reaching the age of discretion, children can choose their own state, and if their parents do not allow them to, they can go to court" (principle three).[96] It is significant, however, that the age of discretion (*annos discretionis*), was defined in these principles not following the ABGB (which assumed an age of maturity in these cases of 14 years (§ 148 in conjunction with § 21 of the ABGB)), but apparently 16, adopted as the limit for the full exercise of paternal authority in the NC (Article 377). The regulations of the Austrian Code[97] were also rejected in a further principle, proclaiming that "Parents cannot be judicially enslaved during their lifetime to give their daughter a dowry" (principle four).[98]

As might be expected, there was also no controversy among the representatives on the question of consent as to the search for paternity by illegitimate children and the means of proof admissible in these proceedings.[99] It was decided in accordance with the then generally accepted rule that "A child born out of wedlock is not allowed to seek paternity" (principle five), which made it unnecessary to address the question of evidence, which "Because of the answer to five [was] negatively settled" (principle six). The real split in the Assembly, however, was caused by the question of the obligation to provide alimony to an illegitimate child, but recognised by the father, once the child had reached the age of 14. In the debate, Father Dominik Markiewicz and Professor Słotwinski encouraged the adoption of such a solution. The former proposed alimony "until the age of 30, or at least until the age when the child will be able to earn his or her own living", and the latter until the age of majority, i.e. 21. In the end, in a secret ballot, the Sejm decided by a majority of one vote (16 to 15) that "An acknowledged child from an illegitimate childbed shall be

95 Ibidem; ANK, 29/200/201 (WMKV-2), 65.
96 See § 140 and 148 of the ABGB.
97 See § 1220 and 1221 of the ABGB.
98 *Gazeta Krakowska* No. 10 of 4 February 1818, 111; ANK, 29/200/201 (WMKV-2), 65.
99 ANK, 29/200/200 (WMK V-1), 675.

entitled to alimony from his or her father for a longer than fourteen years of age" (principle seven). At its session on 15 January, the Assembly also gave a concurring answer to the last legal question on family law, and the only one from Title IV: "On Adoption", by enacting that "A minor may be adopted with the prior permission of the parents, and in the absence of the parents with the permission of the guardians".[100] Thus, the Legislative Assembly enacted a total of 25 principles of personal and family law, which accounted for one-fifth of all the principles that formed the basis of the Civil Code.

3 The Enactment of the Principles of Succession Law into the Civil Code of the Free City of Cracow in 1818

The Legislative Assembly's debate on the questions relating to the principles of succession law, collected under Title IX: "On Wills and Inheritances", began its session on 19 January 1818 with the question of whether the oral form of a will should be allowed.[101] Father Dubiecki was in favour of its introduction, arguing that it was necessary due to the illiteracy of the majority of the Free City's inhabitants. Judge Mąkolski took the opposite view, arguing that allowing oral wills opened the way to "considerable litigation", "and peasants who cannot read and write can make wills before a Court of the Peace". In a secret ballot, a majority of representatives supported Dubiecki (17 against 14) and the House passed a resolution that "In addition to written wills, verbal wills will also be allowed" (principle one).[102] The Sejm unanimously also agreed that "Monastic persons in special cases, such as the abolition of a monastic order, a foundation or a monastery, or when they have benefices or income attached to a secular office, may dispose of their property by will" (principle two).[103]

The subject of a wider debate was the question of limiting the testamentary capacity of a judicially recognised prodigal, which the Committee advised to be limited to half of the estate. Professor Litwiński, contrary to this opinion,

---

100 *Gazeta Krakowska* No. 10 of 4 February 1818, 111; ANK, 29/200/201 (WMKV-2), 65.

101 Absent in the NC (Article 969), but adopted from the *Codex Theresianus* in the Austrian codes (§ 577 and 585 of the ABGB). For more, see Dziadzio 2022a, 463.

102 *Gazeta Krakowska* No. 11 of 8 February 1818, 122; ANK, 29/200/201 (WMKV-2), 67.

103 Ibidem. See Article 902 of the NC. The *Code Napoléon*, in accordance with the principle of universality of law (Articles 6 and 7 of the NC), did not limit the testamentary capacity of the clergy, unlike the Austrian West Galician Code, which granted it only in exceptional situations (§ 367 Part II of the West Galician Code).

and in line with the *Code Napoléon*,[104] was in favour of leaving a prodigal with full capacity, pointing out that "guardianship cannot extend beyond the lifetime of a person ... and it cannot be to the detriment of children and necessary heirs, for these are secured by law with a necessary part". On the other hand, the Committee's position was defended by Judge Mąkolski, who referred to the protection of the interests of the family potentially in conflict with the prodigal, and Professor Feliks Słotwiński, who pointed out that "the public interest requires that every citizen and inhabitant should dispose of his property in the most rational manner possible, and a person judicially considered a prodigal should be understood as one who cannot dispose of his property rationally". In the end, the Chamber rejected the Committee's opinion by a majority of four votes and resolved that "A person judicially declared a prodigal may testamentarily dispose of all his property" (principle three).[105]

At the meeting on 19 January, four more principles were adopted, unanimously without debate. Three concerned 'substitution', which, being a 'model' institution of the *ancien régime*, in the NC was threatened with the sanction of absolute nullity.[106] In the first of these, the Sejm decided that "Fideicommissary substitution has no further place above the second degree of substitution" (principle five);[107] in the second that "Parents may make a pupillary substitution in the event of their child's death before the age of 14 or in the event that they are unable to make a will" (principle six); and in the third that "Such a substitution may not take place as regards property which would otherwise have been vested in the child" (principle seven).[108] The last principle adopted on this first day of the work on the law of succession, was a principle establishing that "An inheritance without a preceding judicial attribution may not be taken into possession, but a legacy may" (principle eight).[109] This principle, too, was contrary to the system of succession adopted in the NC, where the institution of the seising (*saisine*) of legal heirs (*héritiers légitimes*) in the succession was

---

104 See Article 513 of the NC, which, while enumerating the scope of the limitation of the capacity for legal acts of a prodigal (*prodigue*), does not mention testation.

105 *Gazeta Krakowska* No. 11 of 8 February 1818, 122–123; ANK, 29/200/201 (WMK V-2), 67.

106 See Article 896 of the NC. The exceptions were substitutions of the first degree between the closest relatives provided for in Articles 1048 and 1049 NC, the so-called permitted substitutions (*substitution permises*). Article 898 of the NC also allowed for common substitution (*substitution vulgaire*), which did not limit the testamentary freedom of the heir.

107 Principle four of the title "On Wills and Inheritances" was not adopted until 5 February, see below, p. 95.

108 The NC also did not allow pupillary substitutions.

109 *Gazeta Krakowska* No. 11 of 8 February 1818, 122–123; ANK, 29/200/201 (WMKV-2), 67. See § 797 of the ABGB.

fundamental, occurring by virtue of the law itself on the death of the testator.[110] In contrast, legatees could only take possession of legacies after they had been brought into possession by the heirs or a court.[111]

On 20 January, the deliberations began with the question of the limitation of the freedom to testate due to the rights of the necessary heirs. First of all, in accordance with the Committee's opinion, the House resolved that "A will does not become invalid if the testator omits one necessary or all of the children, but the necessary heirs, whether one or more, have the right to apply to the court for the compulsory portion" (principle nine), and that "If, of several children, a share of one is omitted in the will, the will shall not become invalid, but the omitted heir is allowed to apply to the court for the compulsory portion" (principle ten).[112] Both of these principles, in terms of testamentary freedom itself, were compatible with the provisions of the NC, which left the testator full freedom to shape the content of his or her last will.[113] However, as was already the case with principle eight, they indicated a departure from the reserve system adopted in the NC in favour of the legitime system in force under Austrian law. During the debate on securing the rights of the necessary heirs, Professor Słotwiński spoke actively. *Inter alia,* he opposed the Committee's opinion equating the amount of the compulsory portion of minors with that of adults, as in the NC.[114] He argued that "the legal duties of parents towards their children end when the children comes of age, and it cannot be denied that a minor needs more than an adult in order to be brought up and prepared for civil life and all higher purposes". Professor Litwiński, his colleague from the Faculty of Law, agreed, adding that "parents should give their children an equal share of the estate: this would not be the case if such a compulsory share was assigned to a minor as well as to an adult, because an adult has had more through education".[115] However, the view of the academics did not convince the Assembly, which stood by the Committee's position and, by a majority of 19 votes against 11, resolved that "Such a compulsory portion shall be due to an adult as well as to a minor" (principle 11). Furthermore, also following the NC, the Chamber

110 See Articles 724 and 1004 of the NC.

111 See Articles 1004, 1011 and 1014 of the NC.

112 *Gazeta Krakowska* No. 11 of 8 February 1818, 123; ANK, 29/200/201 (WMKV-2), 68.

113 See Articles 967, 1002 and 1003 of the NC.

114 See Article 914 of the NC.

115 The *Code Napoléon*, taking the position of equal shares of the inheritance (reserve) of all children, provided in Article 843 for the obligation to restore to the inheritance before its division generosities (gifts and legacies) received from a parent. However, funds received for education were exempted from this obligation (Article 852 of the NC).

unanimously agreed that "In the size of the compulsory portion, there will be a difference due to the number of children" (principle 12).[116]

Later in the session on 20 January, the Sejm resolved the important question of the succession of the spouse, whom the NC did not include at all among the reserved heirs (*héritiers réservataires*) and allowed his or her succession *ab intestato* only in the absence of any relatives of the testator up to the twelfth degree of the Roman computation.[117] This regulation was, however, rejected by the representatives, as the Assembly unanimously resolved that "The compulsory part, is due to the spouse in half of what he or she would have taken if there had been no will made by the deceased spouse" (principle 13), and that:

> The surviving spouse of a deceased testator, whether he or she has his own property or not, is entitled to an equal share of the estate with each child, if there are three or more children; if there are fewer than three children, then a fourth part of the succession is due, for lifetime use, the ownership of this part remains with the children, if there is no child but another heir according to the law, then the surviving spouse receives a fourth part of the succession estate in unrestricted ownership, however, in both cases everything should be included in the succession estate which is due to the surviving spouse from the estate of the other spouse by virtue of the marriage contract, the agreement of succession, or the last will (principle 14).[118]

In a subsequent speech, Słotwiński tried to persuade the Chamber to establish an original order of statutory succession, dividing the heirs into nine classes that should successively come into the estate. These were: (1) descendants, (2) parents, (3) siblings and their descendants (by right of representation), (4) grandparents and their descendants (third degree of kinship), (5) great-grandparents and their descendants (fourth degree of kinship), (6) spouse, (7) in-laws, (8) benefactors and, finally, (9) "the community of which the deceased was a member" i.e. the *fiscus*.[119] However, this proposal did not

116 *Gazeta Krakowska* No. 11 of 8 February 1818, 123–124; ANK, 29/200/201 (WMKV-2), 68. See Article 913 of the NC.

117 See Article 755 in conjunction with Article 738 of the NC and above, footnote 24.

118 Principle 14 reiterates the content of § 757 and 758 of the ABGB. Rule 13, however, provides for a legitime for a spouse, which was absent in the ABGB, by granting the spouse in § 796 only "decent livelihood which he or she does not have", *Gazeta Krakowska* No. 12 of 11 February 1818, 133–134; ANK, 29/200/201 (WMKV-2), 68–69.

119 *Gazeta Krakowska* 1818, No. 12 of 11 February 1818, 133–134.

become a subject of debate. The Chamber unanimously passed only two principles on the matter, both taken directly from the NC. The first stipulated that:

> The rights of a natural child for the estate of his dead father or mother shall be arranged as follows: if the father or mother has left legitimate descendants, such right shall count for one third of the hereditary portion which the natural child would have had if he or she were legitimate, and for one half if the father or mother has left no descendants but only ascendants or brothers or sisters; and for three-quarters if neither the father nor mother has left any descendants, ascendants, brothers or sisters (principle 15).[120]

The second principle stipulated that "In the case of a person who dies without issue, the brothers and sisters with their surviving parents shall take the inheritance in this order: half the parents and the other half the brothers and sisters" (principle 16).[121]

A further part of the debate that day was devoted to the inheritance of estates from the clergy and to testation for the benefit of the Church, which, given the social and property structure of the Republic of Cracow, was an important issue. In the end, the Sejm passed as many as five principles regulating this issue.[122] The first principle whereby "After a lay clergyman of the Catholic religion without a will dies, the inheritance is divided into three parts – one for the successors, one for the Church, one for the poor" (principle 17); the second whereby "Such a clergyman, when he has made a will, is not obliged to leave a compulsory part" (principle 18); the third stipulating that "Where the inheritance is without a will, it does not matter where the property of the deceased came from"[123] (principle 19). The fourth principle that was agreed was "With the exception of academic institutes, it shall not be permitted to dispose of real estate by will for the benefit of the clergy, or pious institutes"[124] (principle 20); and the fifth principle, already passed at the beginning of the session on 22 January, was that the Chamber agreed that "With the exception of academic institutes, it shall be permissible, but with a limitation, to make bequests of capital sums for the benefit of clergy or pious institutes" (principle 21).[125]

---

120 Ibidem; ANK, 29/200/201 (WMKV-2), 69. This was the content of Article 757 of the NC.

121 *Gazeta Krakowska* No. 12 of 11 February 1818, 134; ANK, 29/200/201 (WMKV-2), 69. This was the content of Article 748 of the NC.

122 See also above, p. 89.

123 See above, footnote 22.

124 *Gazeta Krakowska* No. 12 of 11 February 1818, 134–136; ANK, 29/200/201 (WMK V-2), 69.

125 *Gazeta Krakowska* No. 13 of 15 February 1818, 145; ANK, 29/200/201 (WMKV-2), 70.

The session of 22 January opened with a debate on the institution of disinheritance, to which the Chamber unanimously "gave place for valid reasons which the law shall designate" (principle 22).[126] This decision was another expression of the Assembly's wish to move away from the succession system adopted in the NC. Indeed, the latter made no provision at all for the institution of disinheritance, limiting the forms of exclusion from an inheritance to only unworthiness (*indignité*).[127] However, a dispute arose over the admissibility of *exheredatio bona mente facta*, of which the Committee gave a negative opinion. Litwiński argued in favour of its adoption, arguing that:

> in this case, where there is an evident fear that what they [the parents – P.M.] leave from their estate to their son or daughter will be of no benefit to them [the children – P.M.], but will be immediately swallowed up by their creditors, who have often, through their favours, contributed considerably to the prodigality of the children and the distress of the parents, and in the meantime the children and grandchildren must remain in poverty and deprivation ... Roman and Austrian legislation[128] allows ... to disinherit them [the children – P.M.] with a good thought.[129]

The opposite view was expressed by Judge Mąkolski, who referred to Litwiński's deprecation of creditors' rights, and warned against a "conspiracy to damage a third party". This position was supported by Professor Słotwiński, who furthermore made a telling speech about the risks involved in assessing the will of the testator:

> the law cannot and is not even capable of looking into a person's thought, because this thought, being internal, cannot be judged by an external judgment; who would be able to prove the good thought of the testator, supposing that disinheritance by a good thought takes place, thus the rule laid down above, that such a thing only takes place for legal and valid reasons [principle 22 – P.M.], would be abolished.

In the end, the Sejm, by a majority of 18 votes against 15, followed the Committee's opinion and adopted the rule that "A disinheritance done by a good thought should not take place" (principle 23). After this discourse, the

126 Ibidem.
127 See Article 727 of the NC.
128 See § 773 of the ABGB.
129 *Gazeta Krakowska* No. 13 of 15 February 1818, 146.

Assembly, by unanimously adopting the principle that "An heir who receives an inheritance up to the level of net assets may not privately, without losing the benefit of the same, transfer the ownership of the property belonging to the inheritance to someone else" (principle 24), formally concluded the debate "On Wills and Inheritances".[130]

Over the course of further deliberations on the principles of civil law, however, the Sejm returned several times to the law of succession. As late as 22 January, during the debate on the law of obligations, further rules directly concerning inheritance were passed. One was included in Title XI: "On Contracts in general", stating that "The inheritance of a person who is still alive must not be ceded to anyone else"[131] (principle four).[132] The next four rules were included in Title XII: "On Donations". The first stipulating that "An heir who is entitled to the compulsory part, and who is harmed by donations, may demand the fulfilment of the compulsory part, starting from the latest beneficiary and proceeding backwards towards the eldest beneficiaries"[133] (principle three). The second stated that "A donation to a child born later falls, as to the obligatory part" (principle five). The third stipulating that "Health officials and religious ministers attending the last illness of the deceased, from which the death occurred, may not take what was a donation between the living, or from a will made at the time of that illness" (principle six). The fourth rule that was agreed stated that "Such a disposition of property to persons unable to benefit from it, is invalid when it is covered by a contract of any name, or by other substituted persons, such as parents, ascendants or the spouse" (principle seven).[134]

At the sitting of 27 January, when the Sejm debated the rules of Title XVII: "On Statutes of Limitations", it was further decided that "The five-year statute of limitations is against the power to challenge a will for invalidity" (principle seven), and that "A similar length of time shall remit the right to claim a compulsory part and the fulfilment thereof" (principle eight).[135] At the end of the debate on civil law principles, at its 5 February sitting, the Chamber returned to the "question in Title IX on wills and successions left in deliberation", and resolved that "A minor from 14 to 18 years of age may dispose of half of the estate by will" (principle four).[136] In this way, the Legislative Sejm

130 Ibidem, 147; ANK, 29/200/201 (WMKV-2), 70.

131 See Articles 1130 and 1600 of the NC, which expressly prohibit inheritance contracts.

132 ANK, 29/200/201 (WMKV-2), 70.

133 See Article 923 of the NC.

134 *Gazeta Krakowska* No. 13 of 15 February 1818, 148–149; ANK, 29/200/201 (WMKV-2), 71.

135 *Gazeta Krakowska* No. 18 of 4 March 1818, 205; ANK, 29/200/201 (WMK V-2), 75.

136 *Gazeta Krakowska* No. 18 of 4 March 1818, 206; ANK, 29/200/201 (WMKV-2), 67.

adopted a total of 31 principles of inheritance law, which constituted almost one-quarter of all the principles that were to form the basis of the Civil Code.

4 Conclusion

When the Free City of Cracow began to function in the autumn of 1815, the French codes – the Civil Code, the Code of Civil Procedure and Commercial Code – had been binding on its inhabitants for five years. This period was definitely too short for the legal institutions adopted in the NC to take root in society. These few years, however, were enough for Cracovian lawyers, educated mainly in Austrian law, to begin to appreciate the advantages of Napoleonic codification.[137] Other representatives of the elite and ordinary inhabitants of the city also more or less consciously associated the new law with a period of relative freedom and independence, not only in the political and social dimension, but also in the personal one.[138] These circumstances undoubtedly influenced the course of the codification work between 1816 and 1818, and the content of the principles of law enacted at the Legislative Assembly of 1818. Determining the extent of this Napoleonic influence is one of the subjects of this monograph, pursued in this chapter in terms of the legislative process itself.

It is clear from the surviving source material analysed in the first subchapter above that the *spiritus movens* behind the introduction of new legal codifications in the Free City of Cracow, and in particular a new civil code to replace the NC, were the Protective Powers. As Szczęsny Wachholz and Wacław Uruszczak[139] rightly pointed out, the Residents representing the interests of Austria, Russia and Prussia (Joseph Sweerts-Spork, Ignacy Miączyński and Ernest Reibnitz), acting through the Organising Commission, consistently pursued this objective throughout their entire tenure in Cracow. This aspiration was mainly politically motivated, as the victorious powers wanted to eliminate the remnants of the French empire on the territory they controlled, as Reibnitz unequivocally expressed in his statement about "Bonaparte's usurpation". To a lesser extent, this aspiration was also supported by legal argumentation, which was an important element of the codification work of the Organising Commission.

137 Dziadzio 2020a, 270.
138 Cichoń 2021, 44.
139 Wachholz 1957, 271; Uruszczak 1997, 93–94.

Granting the initiative to the Commission for this work on the legislative process of 1816–1818, raises the question of the attitude of the Legislative Committee. Wojciech Bartel, on the basis of the statement by Reibnitz of 13 July 1816, assumed the thesis of the Committee's desire to preserve French codifications, which was to become a seedbed of its conflict with the Commission, and consequently led to the protraction of the legislative process.[140] This thesis is difficult to verify though, as the materials from the Committee's work have not been preserved. The fact is, however, that from January 1816 onwards, the Committee worked independently and, until the submission of the drafts of the Civil and Criminal Codes in November 1816, consistently ignored successive attempts by the Commission to interfere in its activities. It seems, therefore, that Reibnitz's invoking of the threat of a continuation of Bonaparte's "usurpation" was rather intended to discipline the other Residents in a joint effort to speed up the Committee's work. Indeed, the Prussian Resident, as he indicated in his note of 12 January 1818, believed that the procedure followed by the Committee, i.e. the preparation of draft codifications and their submission to the Assembly of Representatives for debate, was too protracted and should be replaced by a procedure of legal questions developed by him for the enactment of the principles of future codifications.

Contrary to expectations, the above friction continued to remain unresolved. An analysis of the legislative minutes of the joint meetings of the Commission and the Committee from December 1816 to April 1817, show that the Commission rejected the Committee's draft civil code and forced it to cooperate in the preparation of legal questions for the Assembly, but these questions were prepared by Committee members based on this very draft. From the material in the minutes, however, we do not learn how the discussion on the individual questions proceeded, as the minutes only report on the scope of the subject matter of the meeting and the list of questions adopted.[141] Consequently, all we know about the content of the draft civil code prepared by the Committee is that it replicated the structure of the three parts of the Austrian Code (ABGB), which were divided into titles adopted in the list of legal questions submitted to the Assembly of Representatives.[142] This is certainly not enough evidence to put forward the thesis that the solutions adopted in the *Code Napoléon* were applied in the Committee's draft. The fact is, however, that Reibnitz's aim of accelerating the codification work by drafting legal

140 Bartel 1976, 100–101; Uruszczak 1997, 93–95.

141 The exceptions are a few written positions of members of the Commission or Committee on certain legal questions attached to the protocols.

142 See above, pp. 78–79.

questions was achieved, and that the almost one-year wait (April 1817–March 1818) for the enactment of legal principles was due to circumstances beyond the Committee's control.

We learn much more about the assessment of the NC by the Cracovian legislators from the reports in *Gazeta Krakowska* on the debate and resolutions of the Legislative Sejm of 1818, than from the legislative minutes. Both the discussion held by the representatives and the content of the principles adopted, leave no doubt that the Assembly had no intention to replicate French law *en masse* into the Civil Code of the Free City of Cracow. The principles of law adopted by the Sejm are in fact an original selection of solutions adopted from Austrian law – known to Cracovians from the West Galician Code and the ABGB, and French law (i.e. the *Code Napoléon* still in force in Cracow and the neighbouring Kingdom of Poland). It is evident from the catalogue of legal questions and the Committee's opinions on some of them, cited in the reports, that it was the Committee's aim to make such a selection from the outset. The representatives themselves were also aware of this, as evidenced by their statements during the debate and the resolutions adopted.

These conclusions are supported in detail by the analysis presented in subchapters two and three above. It shows that only in the area of personal and matrimonial law were the legal principles enacted generally based on the provisions of the NC. For example, in the Civil Code of the Free City of Cracow under preparation, majority was set at 21 years of age according to Article 488 of the NC (rule nine of Title I), and matrimonial capacity according to Article 144 of the NC, at 18 years for men and 15 for women (rule five of Title II). Slight modifications, as in the case of the rules regulating the place of residence of an official (rules three and four of Title I) or the exercise of the functions of civil registrars by clergy (rule eight of Title I), obviously resulted from the political and administrative characteristics of the Republic of Cracow. Particularly noteworthy is the fact that the Legislative Assembly fully accepted the French model for the registration of civil registry records[143] (principle seven of Title I) and a secular model of marriage (rule four of Title II), with civil marriage[144] as well as the admissibility of divorce for all regardless of their religion.[145] The wording of principle seven of Title II also implies the adoption of the French model of *legitimatio per subsequens matrimonium*, the condition of which, according to Article 331 of the NC, was the official recognition of a child.

143 For more see below, Chapter 5.

144 Ibidem.

145 On the issue of the application of divorce law by Cracow's courts, see above, Chapter 1.

However, in this latter aspect, i.e. as regards the status of a child out of wedlock, the acceptance of French solutions was equivocal. Neither the content of any legal questions posed, nor the debates, nor the rules passed by the Assembly in response to them, can determine the attitude of Cracow's legislators towards the category of adulterous and incestuous children distinguished in the NC but absent in the Austrian codes. This term does not appear in any of the principles concerning "children begotten before marriage" (principles seven and eight of Title II), or "illegitimate children" (principle five and seven of Title III) or "natural children" (principle 15 of Title IX). However, this absence does seem to indicate a conscious rejection of the French division of illegitimate children. This is indicated by Article 331 of the NC in juxtaposition with Rule seven of Title II, which reproduces its content, as well as by Article 762 of the NC in the context of Rule 15 of Title IX, which reproduces Article 757 of the NC. The words contained in Article 331 of the NC "other than such as are the fruit of an incestuous or adulterous intercourse" were not rewritten into principle seven, nor was the reservation in Article 762 of the NC that "the regulations of Articles 757 and 758 are not applicable to children who are the fruit of adulterous or incestuous intercourse" added to principle 15. This *argumentum ex silentio* allows for the assumption that the Legislative Assembly, in this respect, adopted the solution of Austrian law, which was also indirectly confirmed in the course of the application of these provisions of the NC by the Cracovian courts.[146]

In the field of family and inheritance law, only part of the principles enacted reproduced specific provisions of the NC. For example, principle five of Title III prohibited the search for paternity in accordance with Article 340 of the NC, and principle three of Title XII concerning the reduction of donations to complete the compulsory part, repeated the regulation of Article 923 of the NC. However, a similar situation existed as regards the Austrian Code; for example, principles one and two of Title III, defining the religion of children, adopted the solutions arising from § 140 of the ABGB; and principle 14 of Title IX regulating the statutory succession of a spouse, copied § 757 and 758 of the ABGB. Some of the principles adopted were a compromise between the Austrian and French solutions, as in principle three of Title III modifying the age of discretion of a child in § 140 ABGB from 14 to 16 years, following Article 377 of the NC and in principles 22 and 23 of Title IX, which, according to the Committee's opinion, allowed disinheritance unknown to the *Code Napoléon*, but rejected *exheredatio bona mente facta* adopted in the ABGB.

---

146 See Chapters 1 and 8.

The analysis presented in the third of this chapter, shows the adoption, in the enacted rules of succession law, of a number of specific solutions of the NC, while rejecting the basic assumptions of succession in French law. This latter tendency is best illustrated by principle eight of Title IX, which refers to the judicial introduction of the possession of an estate, as well as principles nine and ten, which, under Austrian (Roman) law, give precedence to testamentary succession over non-testamentary (statutory) succession, while guaranteeing the necessary heirs the right to a *legitime*. By contrast, in the NC, the necessary heirs came into possession of the entire inheritance by virtue of law, and the reserve due to them could not be affected by testamentary dispositions, which only affect the disposable portion.[147] It was also characteristic of the principles of succession law in Cracow to adopt solutions that were blatantly incompatible with French law, such as: the admission in principle five of Title IX of a fiduciary substitution; in principle 17 of a special order of succession after a Catholic clergyman; and in principle 13 of a spouse's right to a compulsory portion, *nota bene* absent also in the Austrian codes.

In the light of the arguments presented, the thesis that the Cracovian legislators aimed to preserve the validity of French civil law in the Free City *en masse* is untenable. Prepared on the basis of the legal principles enacted, the new civil code, although essentially faithful to French solutions in the field of personal and matrimonial law, was closer to the Austrian ABGB in the field of family and inheritance law. However, in spite of the enactment of such legal principles, after the Residents left Cracow, the Legislative Committee abandoned work not only on the Civil Code but also on more extensive changes in the field of private law. The result was that the provisions of the NC, which some of the representatives and most of the members of the Committee applied in their daily legal practice, remained in force.

This situation is difficult to understand and explain, and *prima facie* suggests the illusory nature of the legislative work of both the Committee and the Legislative Sejm, which may provide a weighty argument in favour of the thesis of a methodical obstruction against the efforts of the Protective Courts to eliminate Napoleonic codifications from Cracow's legal system. However, such a conclusion is too far-fetched, as it ignores the results of this contradiction, apparent from the research carried out on the application of the *Code Napoléon* by the courts of the Free City of Cracow. As it turns out, Cracovian lawyers, in a situation of incompatibility between the provisions of French law and the solutions established in their legal consciousness, were ready to

147 Michalik 2021, 319 and 322.

deviate grossly from the legal principles adopted in the NC.[148] It is likely that a similar mechanism worked in the case of discrepancies between the content of the rules passed at the Legislative Sejm of 1818 and the fact that *Code Napoléon* inheritance law remained in force in the Free City of Cracow.

To sum up the discussion in this chapter, it has to be assumed that over the course of the codification work of 1816–18, the intention of the Committee and the Legislative Sejm was to introduce, in place of the personal, family and inheritance law provisions of the NC, a regulation modified by the solutions adopted in the Austrian ABGB. At the same time, however, at the formal level, this codification work took place under pressure from the Organising Commission, which ultimately failed to realise the goal of the Protecting Powers to eradicate the Napoleonic codifications from the legal system of the Free City of Cracow. It seems that it was the cessation of this pressure in the autumn of 1818 that changed the situation, so much so that work on enacting a new civil code was abandoned. This did not, however, mean that Cracovian lawyers automatically accepted the entirety of French civil law, which was largely rejected in the principles enacted by the Legislative Sejm of 1818. They simply opted for the easier route, that is, selectively, the modification of that law by special acts,[149] and for the rest the application of the NC by Cracow's courts.

---

148 For more, see the remaining chapters.

149 See below, Chapter 4.

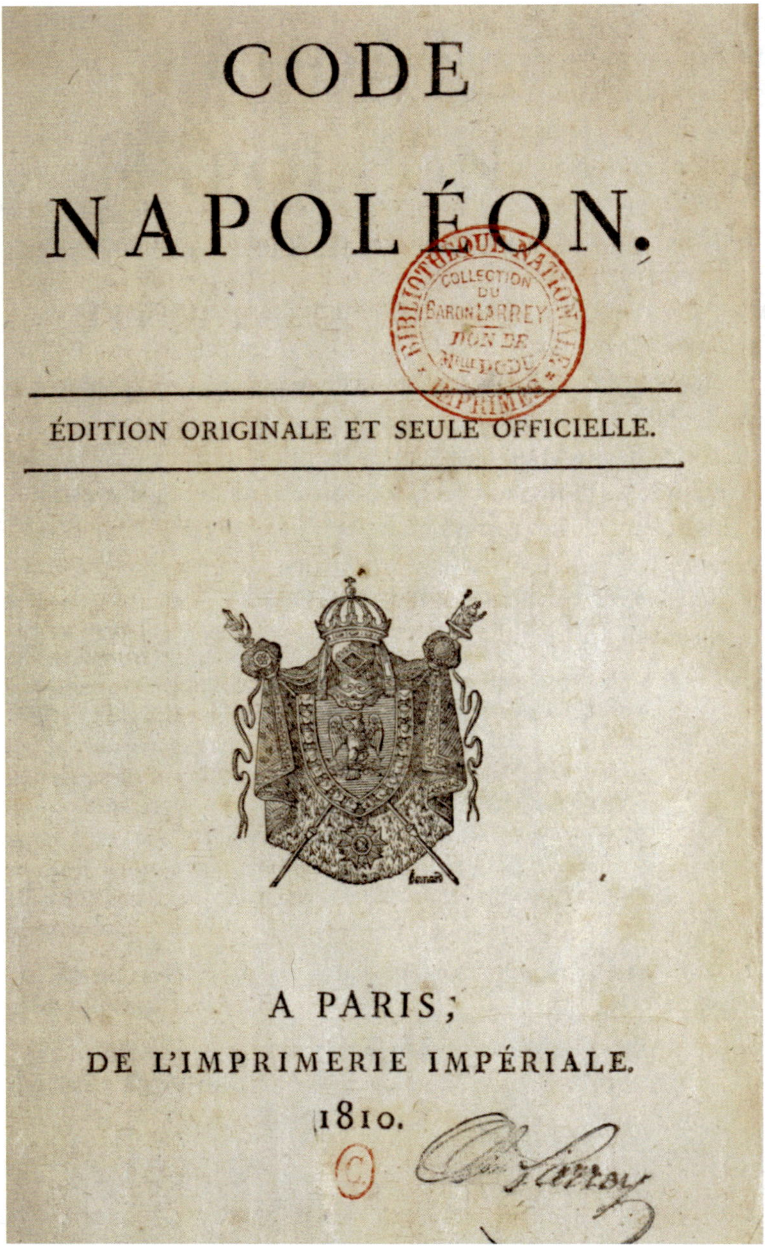

CODE NAPOLÉON.

ÉDITION ORIGINALE ET SEULE OFFICIELLE.

A PARIS;

DE L'IMPRIMERIE IMPÉRIALE.

1810.

FIGURE 17 *Napoleonic Code of 1807*, (print, paper, 1810)
SOURCE: NATIONAL LIBRARY OF FRANCE, 8-Z LARREY-248; SCAN BY GALLICA DIGITAL LIBRARY IN PUBLIC DOMAIN (WIKIMEDIA COMMONS)

CHAPTER 4

Modifications of the Napoleonic Code in the Free City of Cracow

Mateusz Mataniak

1 Mortgage Law

In addition to the servitudes discussed above, other types of rights *in rem* also appeared widely in the legal theory and practice of the Free City of Cracow, including those of key importance in economic transactions: the pledge and the mortgage. The former was the subject of questions formulated during the work of the Legislative Committee (Title VII: "On the Pledge"). In particular, the first question raised serious doubts as to whether a private, and therefore non-official ("non-judicial and non-authentic") document could be the basis for an entry in a mortgage book. Contrary to the Committee's opinion, Feliks Słotwiński took the view that there should not be any restrictions in this respect, as, from the creditor's point of view, it is, after all, crucial to be able to obtain reliable information on "whether he will be satisfied in his receivables". It was precisely mortgage books, which Słotwiński referred to as "security books", that could provide such information. A debtor, whose property becomes a "pledge for his creditors" can, after all, always apply for the debt to be removed from the mortgage if the obligation is paid. Słotwiński also pointed out that the prohibition would reduce the level of mortgage security, as the debtor could then incur further debts at the expense of the interests of the first creditor, which would not be recorded in any way. Despite this rather rational argumentation, the Chamber resolved that: "A document not judicially, not authentically, but privately drawn up cannot be entered in the mortgage books" (principle one).[1]

Greater doubt was apparently not raised by the subsequent questions on this subject, since the Members unanimously resolved that: "A note of the right of first eviction should take place in public books" (principle two);[2] "The

1 *Gazeta Krakowska* No. 10 of 4 February 1818, 112–113. Also very important to Słotwiński was the facilitation of credit, of which "private debentures" were an important source. This was supposed to have a positive effect on an "increase in the circulation of money". However, he seems to have overlooked the dangers of usury.

2 It should be noted that the translation of this question from Latin submitted to the deputies is not very clear: "*Prenotacja prawa dopiero mającego być ewinkowanego ma miejsce w*

 | DOI:10.1163/9789004688742_006

extension of a mortgage without the debtor's consent shall not take place" (principle three); "A contractual mortgage may not be extended to an unlisted property. A judicial mortgage, i.e. from a judgment, may be extended" (principle four); "The sums entered into mortgage books constitute the subject matter of the mortgage, so that on them the recording of the mortgage (*super intabulatio*) takes place" (principle five); "Secret mortgages entered without any title shall not be legal" (principle six).[3]

Some of the questions posed within Title XVI: "On the Limitation Period" also dealt with pledge rights *in rem*. These concerned in particular the theses passed by the Legislative Assembly: "By the incorporation of the title of ownership into a mortgage, all rights of a third party are cancelled by the statute of limitations of more than three years" (principle one); "After an entry into mortgage books, title to property and other rights *in rem* shall be acquired by a limitation period of more than three years" (principle two).[4] In contrast to the aforementioned issues, the question of doubling the length of the period of usucapion, compulsory against the property of the Public Treasury or the Catholic Church, raised considerable doubts. Contrary to the unsurprising opinion of Father Feliks Jaroński, who referred to the 60-year period of usucapion in canon law, it was decided (by a vote of 23 to seven) that "For barring by limitation against the Public Treasury or any moral body not twice as much time is needed as against anyone else" (principle four).[5]

The debate outlined above was only a prelude to a much more serious task facing the legal elite of the Free City of Cracow. Namely, it concerned a deeper revision of French mortgage law, which had been in force in the area from 1810.[6] It was the subject of widespread criticism, especially with regard to the difficult control of the transfer of ownership of real estate and the taking of

księgach hipotecznych". In the original, it read as follows: "*An praenotatio iuris primum evincendi in libris publicis locum habeat*", booklet with questions to the Extraordinary Legislative Assembly of 1816, ANK, 29/200/200 (WMK V-1), 679.

3 *Gazeta Krakowska* No.10 of 4 February 1818, 13.

4 And principle three, indicated above in relation to servitudes: "In the absence of written evidence, the right of servitude shall be acquired after thirty years".

5 *Gazeta Krakowska* No. 17 of 1 March 1818, 196–197. The remaining issues arising from Title XVII: "On the Statute of Limitations" did not concern rights *in rem*. See *Gazeta Krakowska* No.18 of 4 March 1818, 205–206.

6 The previously applicable West Galician Civil Code of 13 February 1797, contained only substantive provisions, saying nothing about the form in which mortgage books were to be kept. The rules for keeping mortgage books in the Duchy of Warsaw were set out in the Saxon King's Decree of 31 August 1809 and the Mortgage Instruction of 21 September 1809. They were in force in Cracow on the basis of transitional provisions of 16 January 1811 (DPKW, vol. 3, 157–173). Fierich 1888, 492–493.

credit against it, the admission of secret mortgages, and the need to renew entries; far more favourable were the solutions of the Old Polish mortgage, which, precisely because of its general principles, became very popular among the nobility. The law "On Records" of 1588, which constituted it, introduced the principles of: the priority of entry in the books (*prior tempore, potior iure*), the public nature of entries, and detail and material openness (the principle of good faith).[7] It thus differed favourably from Roman mortgage, followed by German and French mortgages, in which the security for the loan was personal rather than real. Other negative features of a German and French mortgages were their secrecy (a mortgage was created as a result of the contract itself, without the need for an entry) and its general nature (it covered all the debtor's assets, regardless of the amount of the debt), which essentially reduced the credibility of the entire institution.[8]

The first problem that the authorities of the Republic of Cracow had to face was the necessity to extend several times the time limit for renewal of entries, resulting from Article 2154 of the NC, in order to enable the validity of mortgages and privileges to be maintained. The Court of Appeal also drew attention to the need to establish a cadastre of immovable properties located in the Free City of Cracow; appropriate instructions were issued to the *wójtowie* (commune heads) in 1822. Above all, work began on regulating property relations for the purposes of the future law, a task entrusted to the Mortgage Commission.[9]

A major success of the Cracovian legislator was undoubtedly the Act "On Establishing the Ownership of Immovable Property, Privileges and Mortgages", passed by the Extraordinary Legislative Assembly on 17 June 1822. It showed considerable similarity to the mortgage law of the Kingdom of Poland.[10] This was the case in terms of the structure of the two acts, although the Cracovian

---

7 Płaza 2002, 289–290; Wójcikiewicz 1967, 25–30. The last-mentioned principle determined that the entries and the facts were deemed to be consistent with each other, so that a party acting in reliance on the contents of the entries could be certain that he would not suffer any damage to his property.

8 Płaza 2002, 290–291. Modern solutions appeared in Prussia, in the form of the Mortgage Ordinance of 1722, amended by the Ordinance of 1783 and supplemented by the Prussian Landrecht of 1794. See also Górnicki 2002, 169–171.

9 Malec 2004, 79–81. It was headed by Franciszek B. Piekarski, a judge of the Court of Appeal. The Commission's main task was to establish the ownership of properties and mortgage rights, and then prepare drafts of new mortgage lists. In principle, the time limit for implementing this intention expired on 31 May 1826, but it was extended several times. For a detailed account of the work of the Commission, see Malec 2004, 85–96.

10 Act of 14 (26) April 1818. A detailed description of the Polish Mortgage Act is included in: Wójcikiewicz 1967, 63–72. See also Górnicki 2002, 174–175.

Act was somewhat less comprehensive, consisting of ten sections, divided into divisions.[11] Its authors also clearly retained many of the solutions of the NC.[12]

In terms of content, the 1822 Act mandated the compulsory entry of all mortgages in the mortgage books, as well as any deeds of disposal of real estate. The old Polish principle of openness and detail in mortgages was also given full force. This openness was not limited by anything; a mortgage was public and open to the public, while its inspection was possible in the presence of the Mortgage Regent, regardless of the legal interest. In order to establish the priority of a mortgage, it was necessary to indicate the number of its registration in the correspondence log (rule of priority of entry). Pursuant to Article 1 of the Act, all *inter vivos* acts which related to real estate (transfer of ownership, limitation of ownership, as well as encumbrance or release from encumbrance) required for their validity the form of a notarial deed, drawn up by a notary (scribe of deeds), with the participation of two witnesses. Secret mortgages that had been created before the Act came into force and had not been submitted for entry within the time limit set for a given property, could only be enforced in court; thus, entry could only take place as a result of a final judgment (Article 84). The creators of the Act essentially restricted its effects to urban and district immovable property, registered in the cadastre and belonging to private and legal persons, but excluding peasant properties. Numerous privileges taken from the NC were also retained, which became a cause for criticism. The so-called 'main mortgage books' took the form of lists kept for the individual municipal and district communes. They covered in one volume all the properties located in their area; no separate books were kept for them.[13]

11 These were: Section I: "General Regulations". Division I. "On Titles" (Articles 1–3). Division II: "On Mortgage Books" (Articles 4–24); Division II: "On Privileges" (Articles 25–28). Division I: "On Privileges on Movable Property" (Articles 29–30). Division II: "'On Privileges on Immovable Property'" (Articles 31–34); Division III: "On Mortgages" (Articles 35–49). Division I: "On Judicial Mortgages" (Article 50). Division II: "On Contractual Mortgages" (Articles 51–57); Division IV: "On the Abolition of Privileges and Mortgages" (Articles 58–66); Section V: "On Giving Effect to Entries on Immovable Property or Mortgaged Capital Belonging to the Estate" (Articles 67–69); Section VI: "On Warnings"". (Articles 70–78); Section VIII: "On the Gradual Establishment of a New Mortgage Order" (Articles 79–93); Section VIII: "On the Publicity of Acts, and the Responsibility of the Regent" (Articles 94–99); Section IX: "On the Commission Arranging the Mortgage" (Articles 100–103); Section X: "On the Rules of Application of this Law" (art. 104).

12 Fierich 1888, 495 points out the substantial similarity between the provisions of the Act in relation to Articles 2092–2105, 2115–2117, 2124, 2131, 2157–2165 of the NC.

13 Malec 2004, 83–84. The books were to be kept by the Regent of Mortgage Deeds, from 1844 onwards in cooperation with the mortgage authority. Mortgage books were in use until 1871, when the Austrian General Act on Land Books came into force.

Procedural issues concerning the regulation of mortgages were further clarified in the Senate Instruction of 1826.[14] The proceedings had two stages: administrative and judicial. In general, draft mortgage lists were to be drawn up in the communes; once these were received by the Mortgage Commission it set time limits for the preparation of the mortgage list. Ongoing work on the mortgage lists was announced in the press and by individual summonses. They were received by property owners, persons claiming to have a superior or equal right to the property, creditors, persons entitled by virtue of mortgage rights and persons claiming debts and mortgage encumbrances.[15]

An objection could be lodged against the contents of the list before the Mortgage Commissioner (an official of the Mortgage Commission), within the prescribed period. The Commissioner presented the objection at a meeting of the Commission, together with his proposal for regulating the mortgage. The Commission ruled in the first instance on the items on the list to which the objection had been lodged; if there was no objection from a party, it issued a resolution to accept the draft. The Commission could resolve disputes over the order of mortgage and listing title or right *in rem*. The Commission's decisions were delivered to the parties.[16]

Pursuant to Article 101 of the Mortgage Act, its decision could be appealed by the parties to the Court of Appeal, under the terms of the 1826 Instruction. The appeal had to be filed within 14 days. At the same time, it was incumbent upon the appellant to acquaint the claimants with the rights *in rem* covered by the list, as well as to strictly identify the disputed items in the mortgage list. The parties were bound by a compulsory representation by an advocate. Disputes were resolved by summary proceedings, in a public hearing. Judgments of the Court of Appeal were to be submitted to the Mortgage Commissioner to record changes in the mortgage list; a simple rectification could also be made

14 Regulation of the Ruling Senate of 10 November 1826, No. 4788 DGS, DRz.WMK No. 2–3 of 26 January 1827, 5–10. The instruction consisted of 18 articles.

15 The failure of a duly summoned person to appear resulted in his or her being deemed not to have objected to the draft mortgage list. In the absence of an objection to the draft list, it was signed by the parties.

16 Regulation of the Ruling Senate of 10 November 1826. Some of the provisions were enacted with a view to safeguarding the interests of the Public Treasury. In the event of an intention to waive a claim owed to the Treasury or a property right of the Public Treasury, the attorney for the Government party was obliged to consult with the senator overseeing the institute's affairs. If, on the other hand, the Commission's decision was unfavourable to the institute or the Public Treasury, then the attorney could not withdraw from the appeal without the consent of the Senate. The legal basis for this was the Saxon King's decree of 12 February 1812, published in the DRz.WMK of 1816, No. 20, 77–80.

FIGURE 18 *Seal of the President of the Court of Third Instance of the Free City of Cracow*, (seal matrix, brass, 1st half of the 19th century)
SOURCE: NATIONAL ARCHIVES IN CRACOW, ANK, 29/661/455; PHOTO & PERMISSION BY NATIONAL ARCHIVES IN CRACOW

by the Regent of Mortgage Deeds. Significantly, the conflicting decision of the Mortgage Commission and the judgment of the Court of Appeal could be appealed to the Court of Third Instance. In the event of a concurrence of these rulings, the parties could apply to the Faculty of Law of Jagiellonian University for an opinion as to whether there had been a violation of substantive or formal law. If the opinion of the Faculty was positive, then it was possible for the parties to appeal to the Court of Third Instance.[17]

The course of the regulation of mortgages revealed numerous discrepancies in the interpretation of mortgage law between the Mortgage Commission, the Court of Appeal and the Ruling Senate. Between 1 May 1827 and 19 May 1828, during 34 sessions, the Commission heard objections to entries in mortgage lists arranged by it, and also approved items not contested by the parties. In total, the Commission examined 877 cases, mostly approving entries to which

17 Regulation of the Ruling Senate of 10 November 1826. A separate register of appealable cases was also to be kept; in proceedings before the Court of Appeal the parties were exempt from the stamp duty (entry fee). See also Malec 2004, 88–92.

no objections had been lodged. It ceased its activities on 11 June 1830. The fruit of its efforts was the establishment of the status of ownership of properties covered by mortgage law, as well as the settlement of 2,050 disputed cases in Cracow and its district.[18]

The mortgage judgments of the Court of Appeal, issued between 16 January 1828 and 17 July 1833, mostly upheld the Commission's decisions. On the basis of the completely preserved mortgage files of that court, it may be stated that the entities whose rights were in dispute included not only private individuals and the Public Treasury of the Free City of Cracow, but also Jagiellonian University, Cracow's charitable organisations (the Charitable Society, the Archbrotherhood of Mercy and the Pious Bank), churches and monasteries, and even the General Counsel's Office of the Kingdom of Poland.[19] The results of the research on the archival material are presented in the table below.

However, a few words of commentary are needed to the above results of adjudication, which are generally not highly controversial. First, cases terminated due to non-appearance also include the cases specified in Article 153 of the Code of Civil Procedure (joint judgment).[20] Furthermore, a case was also classified as having been decided in favour of a given party if the Court of Appeal upheld even a part of its petition (claim). A separate mention should also be made of atypical cases, which do not fall within the limits of the above list. Here, one may mention cases in which the postponement (suspension) of the judgment or rejection of the petition was due to the failure to submit the required documentation,[21] or the failure of the Mortgage Commission to complete its work with respect to the disputed real estate.[22]

---

18 Malec 2004, 92–95. See the Proclamation of the Ruling Senate of 8 July 1830, No. 3101 DGS, DRz.WMK No. 23 of 17 July 1830, 90: information on the termination of the activities of the Mortgage Commission.

19 On its activities, see Wąsowicz 1977, 143–164; Wąsowicz 1979, 109–147; Wąsowicz 2017, 41–54.

20 "If, of two or more parties summoned, one fails to appear and the other appears, a firm decision shall be suspended, and the judgment so suspended shall be handed to the party failing to appear, appointed by the Burgrave. The handing over will contain a summons for the day on which the case is to be called; there will be only one judgment, against which no objection can be raised".

21 Judgments of the Court of Appeal of: 27 February 1828, 7 May 1828, 4 June 1828, 27 January 1830, 23 February 1831, ANK, 29/200/1769 (WM 296), 113–115, 173–176, 207–209, 497–499, 687–689; of 23 November 1831, 29 February 1832, ANK, 29/200/1770 (WM 297), 411–413, 783–785; of 19 June 1833, ANK, 29/200/1772 (WM 299), 49–52. The reason was sometimes also the ineffectiveness of delivery.

22 Judgment of the Court of Appeal of 4 June 1828, ANK, 29/200/1769 (WM 296), 221–224.

TABLE 2 Mortgage cases before the Court of Appeal between 1828 and 1833

Plaintiff/ defendant	Private person	Public treasury	Ecclesiastical or secular institute	General Counsel's Office of the Kingdom of Poland
Private person: victory	16 (2)	23 (0)	5 (0)	1 (0)
Private person: loss	36 (20)	31 (19)	4 (0)	3 (1)
Public Treasury: victory	13 (1)	x	10 (0)	1 (0)
Public Treasury: victory	42 (11)	x	3 (0)	3 (0)
Institute: victory	1 (0)	2 (0)	1 (0)	0
Institute: loss	6 (1)	1 (0)	0	0
General Counsel's Office: victory	1 (0)	x	0	x
General Counsel's Office: loss	6 (3)	0	0	x

SOURCE: AUTHOR'S OWN CALCULATIONS BASED ON ANK, 29/200/1769 (WM 296) – 29/200/1772 (WM 299). NUMBERS IN BRACKETS INDICATE THE NUMBER OF JUDGMENTS RENDERED AS A RESULT OF A PARTY'S FAILURE TO APPEAR. THEY ADD UP TO THE VALUE GIVEN BEFORE THE PARENTHESIS

It is worth noting that in one judgment, the court explicitly stated that the Commission only has jurisdiction to settle disputes relating to the "mortgage order".[23] Equally important, between 1 September 1831 and 24 April 1834 there were also 20 appeals heard by the Court of Third Instance against decisions of

23 Judgment of the Court of Appeal of 1 July 1829: ANK, 29/200/1769 (WM 296), 303–305. In one case there was a reference to the "ordinary way of law": Judgment of the Court of Appeal of 2 March 1831, ibidem, 707–710.

the Mortgage Commission and judgments of the Court of Appeal.[24] In addition, two more Acts introducing significant amendments to the Mortgage Law of 1822 should be noted.[25]

2 Guardianship Law

Due to its unquestionable social role, guardianship law certainly deserved close attention from the legal community of the Free City of Cracow.[26] The Cracovian lawmaker, however, did not venture to make any profound changes to the French system, despite numerous criticisms of it. These criticisms were, after all, quite serious and related primarily to its excessive complexity, resulting from the overdevelopment of certain institutions. High costs and its relatively low effectiveness were also cited as drawbacks. Nevertheless, the French system also had numerous advantages. In matters of guardianship, the family was to have the final say, and there was an extensive system for supervising decisions concerning the pupil's property; in the absence of both parents, the guardian was to be a person appointed by them, then the ascendants of the pupil, and finally a person appointed by a family council. The latter was also responsible for appointing a so-called "awarded guardian" (in Polish: *opiekun przydany*), who was to look after the interests of the minor in the event of a conflict of interests between him or her and the guardian. The council also exercised general supervision over the guardianship. It was to be composed of an equal number of three relatives from the paternal and maternal line. At the same time, the role of women in the exercise of guardianship was expressly

---

24 *Wyroki hypoteczne Sądu Najwyższej Instancji od dn. 1 września 1831 r. do dn. 24 kwietnia 1834 r. zapadłe*, ANK, 29/200/1690 (WM 217). Of the cases where the parties were private persons, only in one case was the decision in favour of the plaintiff, and in four in favour of the defendant. In cases where the plaintiff was a private person against the Public Treasury, the latter won twice and lost once (due to failure to appear). Interestingly, when the plaintiff was the Public Treasury, the cases always ended unfavourably for it (nine times). In addition, in two cases a private person as the plaintiff obtained a favourable settlement in a dispute with an institute; the latter was victorious once, also as a plaintiff.

25 These were: the Act of 26 January 1838, *Zmiany w Ustawie hypotecznej z roku 1822*, promulgated by the letter of the Ruling Senate of 8 March 1838, No. 466 DGS, DPr.WMK of 1838, whereby document books were introduced; and the Act of 27 June 1844 *Zaprowadzenie Zwierzchności Hipotecznej*, promulgated by the letter of the Ruling Senate of 1 July 1844 No. 3002 DGS, DPr.WMK of 1844.

26 The only available work from the first half of the 19th century devoted entirely to guardianship law is an interesting and competent work by Antoni Malinowski, a notary in Poznań during the period of the Duchy of Warsaw: Malinowski 1811.

limited: they could not be guardians (except for mothers and ascendants, Articles 442 of the NC); if the mother became a guardian, the father could appoint a special advisor for her (Article 391 of the NC). In the event of remarriage, the family council decided whether the mother could continue to exercise guardianship (Article 395 of the NC).[27] These solutions differed significantly from Old Polish guardianship law, in which there were as many as three types of guardianship: testamentary, statutory and official guardianship.[28]

A debate on the principles of law governing the care of minors began as early as 1818. It resulted in the following resolutions, taken under Title V: "On Guardianships": "There shall be family councils to manage the interests of minors under the chairmanship of a justice of the peace" (principle one); "The guardian shall be obliged to give an account every year" (principle two). Unanimity was lacking on the question of the priority of guardianship. Should it go to the mother, as indicated by natural rights (which, after all, "civil acts may not violate"), or to the grandfather on the father's side, to whom, as a rule, *patria potestas* passed?[29] It comes as no surprise that almost identical questions arose during the "postponed" debate of 1825. It should be made clear that the main work at that time revolved around two drafts, the proposals from which were finally embodied in the form of an act.[30]

27 Sójka-Zielińska 2008, 97–98. On family councils under the NC, see Tkaczuk 2012, 179–185; Machut-Kowalczyk 2014, 49–200.

28 Especially from the 15th century onwards, there was a clear limitation of women's parental authority when it came to the management of children's property, with the result that guardians had to be appointed in the event of the father's death, absence or illness. It was not until the 18th century that women's rights were improved in this respect. It was very common for guardians to be appointed in the wills of the nobility; they then had priority over other guardians. After that, relatives were entitled to guardianship, with closer relatives excluding further relatives. In early land law, *lotunk* was popular, i.e. the auction-based appointment of the guardian who offered the most favourable financial terms to the pupil. In the 16th to 18th centuries, the principle of priority of relatives for guardianship gained predominance. Official guardianship, known as awarded guardianship, was also common: Uruszczak 2013, 307–308; Machut-Kowalczyk 2010, 57–65; Maciejewski 2003, 133–134; Maciejewski 2016, 79–80.

29 *Gazeta Krakowska* No. 10 of 4 February 1818, 111–112; booklet with questions to the Extraordinary Legislative Assembly of 1816, ANK, 29/200/200 (WMK V-1), 677. The principles of natural law were indicated by Feliks Słotwiński, his adversary was Father Mateusz Dubiecki. By a majority of 29 to two, it was resolved that "A mother is closer to legal guardianship than a paternal grandfather" (principle three). It was also decided, this time unanimously, that "A prodigal is subject to custody with the strictest limitation" (principle four).

30 *Gazeta Krakowska* No. 20 of 9 March 1825, 268–269. There was a discussion at that time on the effective exercise of control over the property of minors, the obligation to submit annual accounts of guardianship, time limits for the approval of family councils

The Act of 31 October 1825 formally repealed the validity of Titles X and XI Book I of the NC.[31] The modifications introduced at the behest of Cracow's deputies included, firstly, the classifications. Thus, the sections of Title X: "On Minors, Guardianship and Emancipation" of the NC were merged into a common Title I: "On Minors, Guardianship and Emancipation".[32] Title XI: "On Majority, Interdiction, and the Judicial Adviser" of the NC was in turn renamed into Title II: "On Interdiction and the Judicial Adviser" and divided into two sections (I: "On Interdiction"; II: "On the Judicial Advisor").

On substantive matters, Article 25 of the Act explicitly stated that family councils should be attended by at least five of its members, including a justice of the peace; the minor's guardians had only an advisory vote, "not constituting a set".[33] The Act also imposed an obligation, not explicitly resulting from the NC, that an awarded guardian, i.e. a person who supervised the main guardian, informed the family council of any of his actions that could negatively affect the situation of the pupil (Article 30). The time limit for filing an appeal against the decision of the family council to appoint a guardian was also slightly extended, from three days to one week (Article 49 of the Act; Article 439 of the NC). The catalogue of persons who, by law, could not be guardians or members of a family council or were "unfit" for this role, was also expanded. Thus, in addition to minors (with the exception of the father or mother), women (with the exception of the mother and grandmother), incapacitated persons and those who have a conflict of interest with the pupil, as well as those who were unreliable or had an indecent lifestyle, the law also included, *inter alia*: senators, judges, prosecutors and other court officials, foreigners residing permanently outside the borders of the Free City of Cracow,

resolutions by the Court, and the safeguarding of orphan property. Both drafts were reviewed by a five-member Sejm committee.

31 Act of the Extraordinary Legislative Sejm, *Prawo o Opiekach* of 31 October 1825 promulgated by the letter of the Ruling Senate of 7 April 1826 No. 1068 DGS, DPr.WMK of 1826.

32 Title I consisted of the following sections: I: "On the Various Types of Care"; II: "On an Awarded Guardian"; III: "On Causes Relieving from Guardianship"; IV: "On the Impossibility, Unfitness and Withdrawal of Guardianship"; V: "On the Establishment of a Guardian"; VI: "On Accounts and Liability Arising from Guardianship"; VII: "On the Emancipation of Legitimate Children"; VIII: "On the Guardianship of Illegitimate Children and the Emancipation of Such Children".

33 The NC only stipulated that at least three-quarters of the members of the family council had to be present at meetings concerning the appointment of guardianship for them to be valid (Article 415).

monks, persons of a non-Christian faith, as well as persons expressly excluded by the child's father or mother from exercising care.[34]

The list of conditions that were required for the acceptance or rejection of an inheritance by the guardian, on behalf of the pupil (the former could only take place up to the level of net assets) was also expanded. Namely, in addition to requiring the prior consent of the family council, the Act added the obligation to review the assets and also to obtain court confirmation (Article 75 of the Act; Article 461 of the NC). The Act also loosened the strictness as regards the conclusion of agreements on behalf of a minor. When its source was to be a settlement ("conciliatory agreement") and the value of the subject matter did not exceed 500 Polish zlotys, the consent of the Tribunal was not required, but only that of the family council (Article 82 of the Act; Article 467 of the NC). The creators of the Act also introduced solutions alien to the NC, e.g.: the exclusion of a member of the family council or a guardian from participation in meetings of the family council if there was a conflict of interests with the pupil's interests; control of accounts from the management of the pupil's property by the awarded guardian; the guardian's liability for any damage and lost benefits resulting from negligent management of the minor's property, which could involve joint and several liability with the awarded guardian; mortgage security of any possible claims by the ward on the guardian's property (Articles 83, 87–88, 93–96 of the Act). They also imposed a duty on justices of the peace to report to the Court of Appeal, as well as to the senator appointed to oversee the affairs of minors, on the care given within their jurisdiction (Article 99 of the Act).[35]

A complete novelty was all of Section VIII: "On the Care and Emancipation of Illegitimate Children", within Title I of the Act. It provided for the transfer of illegitimate children to "competent guardianship institutes", to which the care of their person and property thus passed. In principle, guardianship was to last until the child came of age or was emancipated; however, it was permissible for the pupil to leave the institution earlier. As far as emancipation was concerned, the authorities of the institute had the rights of parents. Children outside the institute and those who left the institute were to be cared for by the parent who had legally recognised them; if both parents had recognised them, the mother was to be the guardian, and only after her death or loss of guardianship was the

34 The Act omitted those sentenced to corporal punishment (but not to 'infamous punishment'), a category which was present in the NC (Articles 442–444). See Articles 52–53 of the Act.

35 Article 98 of the Act also explicitly imposed liability on family council members for any negligence and intentional harm ("deceit") caused to a minor.

child's father to be the guardian. A guardian for an illegitimate child could be appointed by a guardianship council, consisting of six persons "known to be charitable", if the child was without parents or a guardian appointed by them. The provisions on the guardianship and release of legitimate children were to be applied to illegitimate children (Articles 113–120 of the Act).

Minor changes were also made to Title II: "On the Deprivation of One's Own Will and on Judicial Counsel". For example, Article 128 clarified the content of Article 498 of the NC dedicated to judgments of incapacitation issued on request. In addition to requiring the parties to be heard (in the Act also *in absentia*, in case of failure to appear), in a public audience, the Act provided for the Court to appoint a special custodian if the minor's incapacitation was requested by his or her guardian (Article 128 of the Act; Article 498 of the NC).

An amendment to the Act adopted in 1844 proves that the Cracovian legislator was not indifferent to the fate of the estates of minors. In order to increase the level of their security, the threshold of the value of the property set out in Article 73 of the NC, in relation to which a family council could decide to sell "without an auction", was then significantly increased: from 1,000 to 6,000 Polish zlotys. At the same time, the requirement of court approval of the resolution was maintained.[36]

Even a brief discussion of court practice in the field of guardianship law cannot fail to mention the very frequent convening of family councils, which showed genuine concern for the property of those under their care. Thus, they authorised the investment of money left to children by deceased parents; the sale of a tenement house to pay off mortgage debts; or movable property to cover funeral expenses. Their decisions also concerned the designation of a trousseau in the event of marriage or the settlement with creditors of the inheritance estate.[37] It should be borne in mind that in more serious matters, such as leaving all property in the hands of the guardian mother, the confirmation of a family council resolution by the Tribunal was required.[38]

36 Act of 21 June 1844 *O zmianie artykułu 73 ustawy o Opiekach z 1825 roku*, promulgated by the letter of the Ruling Senate of 1 August 1844, No. 2895 DGS, DPr.WMK of 1844, Article 73. If the value of an immovable property did not exceed 1,000 Polish zlotys, the family council was allowed to sell it without an auction, which, however, had to be approved by a resolution of the Tribunal. Auction sales entailed additional costs for the owner.

37 Minutes of family council meetings: of 4 October 1816, ANK, 29/200/2334 (Tryb 137), 99–101; of 25 July 1825, ibidem, 79–80; of 22 February 1828, ibidem, 55–56, 61; of 27 January 1842, ibidem, 1027–1029.

38 Letter from the Tribunal of First Instance to the Court of the Peace of District II of 23 March 1842, ANK, 29/200/2334 (Tryb 137), 1163–1164; minutes of the Family Council meeting of 12 March 1842, ibidem, 1215–1216, 1221.

The courts ensured that the competence of the family councils was respected, e.g. when a request was made to remove the previous guardian from guardianship and appoint a new guardian, for which a resolution of a council was required (Article 446 of the NC).[39] At the same time, they strictly guarded their competences when it was a matter of, for example, declaring joint and several liability of guardians or resolving a dispute over accounts arising from guardianship.[40] Based on the statistical data, it can be concluded that the activity of the courts in guardianship cases was very high. In the period from 1 October 1817 to 30 September 1818 alone, 111 guardianships were established and 146 family councils were convened; not surprisingly, the largest number of family councils were convened in Cracow.[41] This high number of cases remained stable in the following years.[42]

Guardianship issues arose in various, often quite surprising situational contexts. These included divorces, as evidenced by the case of Franciszek and Antonina (née Gloger) Giełgów. In the case in question, although the Court of Appeal approved the Tribunal's judgment granting the Giełgłóws a divorce, at the same time it modified its decision as to the further fate of the minor child, in such a way that custody of the child was entrusted to the father, respecting all the rights of the child's mother under Article 303 of the NC.[43] It also applied,

39 Judgment of the Court of First Instance of 3 October 1816, ANK, 29/200/1960 (Tryb 157), 87–90.

40 Judgment of the Court of First Instance of 18 October 18, 1816, ANK, 29/200/1960 (Tryb 157), 291–298. The necessity of civil proceedings was indicated in this case by Article 473 of the NC.

41 For example, between 1 June 1819 and 31 May 1820, 156 in Cracow's Courts of the Peace in districts I and II, 156 guardians (97 + 59) were appointed, and 178 family councils (116 + 62) were established. In District III (Mogiła), there were only 16 guardianships and 12 family councils, in District IV (Chrzanów) eight guardianships and family councils each, in District V (Krzeszowice) 13. A total of 266 guardianships and 284 family councils were established. Letter of the Court of Appeal to the Ruling Senate of 21 November 1820, ANK, 29/200/407 (WMK V-196), 229–232.

42 In the period from 1 June 1818 to 28 February 1819, there were a total of 141 guardianships and 152 family councils. In the reporting year 1821/22 there were 321 family councils, in 1823/24: 324, in 1824/25: 288, in 1825/26: 438 (of which 275 in Cracow), in 1826/27: 475 (and 392 guardians). In the four-year period 1833–37 there were a total of 2,466 family councils (an average of 616 per year) and 1,967 guardianships (an average of 491 per year). In 1839 there were 617 family councils and 527 guardianships, and in 1843: 798 and 607 respectively. Source: data under Table 1.

43 "Whichever person holds the custody of the children, the father and mother shall not lose the right to take part in the maintenance and upbringing of the children, and they shall be obliged to do so, in proportion to their ability".

as permitted by Article 302 of the NC,[44] an exception to the rule that the custody of minor children should be placed in the hands of the spouse "who has obtained the divorce".[45]

In the case of Ignacy Ulrych versus his daughter Romualda and Adam Biron, her uncle and at the same time her "awarded" guardian, the Court of Appeal approved the resolutions of the family council authorising the removal of Romualda Ulrych from paternal authority, as well as her taking of benefits from the family property. The court, analysing the provision of Article 477 of the NC[46] rejected the interpretation by Mr Ulrych's advocate, that it was possible to impose conditions on the father's act of emancipation of a minor child, as well as on its revocation, at any time, in particular when the emancipated person failed to comply with any of the conditions imposed.[47]

In another judgment, the Court of the Third Instance ruled that in relation to an awarded guardian, the application provisions of Articles 29–30 of the Guardianship Law,[48] regarding the scope of his duties, may be excluded if only the main guardian had a separate authorisation from the family council.[49]

---

44 "The children shall be entrusted to the spouse receiving the divorce, unless the Tribunal, at the request of the family or the Imperial Prosecutor, orders for the greater good of the children that all or some of them be given to the other spouse".

45 Judgment of the Court of Appeal, 28 February 1822, ANK, 29/200/1720 (WM 247), 235–236. The court agreed with the father's view that "the boy needs an education very soon", which his mother could not provide him with ("so he does not need female firmness as much as the father's supervision and management"). The court's decision was also influenced by other circumstances. Giełgowa was a single mother raising daughters from her first marriage,"whom she could not manage".

46 "A minor, even if unmarried, may be emancipated by his father, or in the absence of a father, by his mother, when he or she has reached the age of 15 years. Such emancipation shall be effected by the mere declaration of the father, or of the mother, accepted by a justice of the peace, in the presence of his scribe".

47 Judgment of the Court of Appeal of 1 June 1837, ANK, 29/200/1758 (WM 285), 1945–1947; resolutions of the family council of 30 April and 18 November 1836, ibidem. In the discussed case, the condition was that the father would not demand that his daughter return home to assist with the running of the farm. The estate due to Romualda Ulrych was estimated at the serious sum of 17,115 Polish zlotys, which, at an interest rate of 5 per cent, gave an annual sum of 855 zlotys.

48 Article 29: "In each care, an awarded guardian will be appointed by the Family Council. It will be his duty to act for the good of the minor, in any case when the interests of the minor conflict or contradict the interests of the guardian". Article 30: "The awarded guardian must also report to the family council about any actions of the guardian which could be seen or predicted as having harmful consequences for the minor".

49 Judgment of the Court of the Highest Instance of 8 January 1841, ANK, 29/200/1687 (WM 214), no card number. In connection with the above, the Court also ruled the exclusion of the provisions of Articles 96–97 of the Guardianship Law regarding the financial liability

Finally, it is worth adding that in the initial period of the Free City of Cracow, the courts also applied the guardianship provisions contained in the West Galician Code.[50]

3 The Law on Courts of the Peace

Among the institutions constituting the legacy of the Duchy of Warsaw, which were particularly well adapted to the socio-political conditions of the Free City of Cracow, one should without hesitation include justices of the peace. Characteristically, their presence in the justice system was not controversial; the disputes concerned only the scope of their competences. Both the constitutions of the Free City of Cracow and the Code of Civil Procedure obliged them to reconcile parties in minor civil cases, recognise property disputes, and represent the property interests of the Public Treasury and clerical as well secular institutes. Justices of the peace also *ex officio* chaired family councils, i.e. meetings of family members of a minor, which decided on the most important matters for them, especially property matters.[51]

Questions about the permissible scope of the powers of justices of the peace appeared for the first time during the debate on the principles of law in 1818. As part of the discussion on the principles of civil procedure (Section: "Concerning Judicial Proceedings"), five theses regarding justices of the peace were adopted at that time. Namely, by a majority vote of 26 to five, it was resolved that "a justice of the peace will be granted the power to adjudicate disputes up to 200 Polish zlotys" (principle one). This was a result of the position that extending their powers was particularly necessary in this area, even in disputes up to 500 Polish zlotys. This concept, according to its proponents, was consistent with the "good of the country and the convenience of its citizens", as it could

of the awarded guardian, including his joint and several liability with the main guardian, provided that the law obliged them to act together.

50 See e.g. judgment of the Court of Appeal of 14 October 1818, ANK, 29/200/1713 (WM 240), 843–845. It concerned the provisions of Chapter V "About Care and Guardianship", Articles 164–265 of the same code.

51 As mentioned, justices of the peace were appointed by the Assembly of Representatives for a three-year term from among candidates presented by municipal assemblies. In practice, they were representatives of local elites: landowners, parish priests, officials and retired soldiers. They were not covered by the increasingly common principle of nomination, because it was citizens who chose candidates for vacant positions, who were then appointed by a designated state authority. Pomianowski 2022, 323–324.

significantly contribute to reducing the costs of disputes.[52] However, there were also opposing voices at the meeting. It was argued that the intended action would be inconsistent with Article XIV of the Constitution, which said nothing about this. Moreover, it could result in an excessive workload for justices of the peace. Hence, there was a proposal to partially assign arbitration judiciary powers to parish priests, as well as unspecified "brotherhoods in cities".[53]

Later in the debate, solutions regarding the above-mentioned *in possesorio* disputes were adopted. By a majority of 21 to nine, it was decided that "*in possesorio* cases will be adjudicated in the Courts of the Peace" (principle two). It was then unanimously agreed that: "The matters expressed above shall be judged entered into the judge's records" (principle three).[54] In accordance with the wishes of the Legislative Committee, it was also resolved, by a majority of 25 to five, that: "Cases of up to 30 Polish zloty may be judged by a justice of the peace as the last instance" (principle four). Finally, it was unanimously resolved that "settlements concluded in a Court of the Peace between the parties are enforceable" (principle five).[55]

The principles discussed above set the direction for the modifications introduced by Cracow's deputies in the Code of Civil Procedure (Part I: "Proceedings

52 *Gazeta Krakowska* No.18 of 4 March 1818, 207–208. The relatively small cost of the functioning of the Courts of the Peace was pointed out by Szczepan Lubowiecki, Rev. Jan Dzianotty and Franciszek B. Piekarski. They added that hitherto in cases involving up to 20 Polish zlotys, i.e. relatively minor cases, rural residents had to go to courts in Cracow, which required considerable expenses. Court fees (entry fees) and advocatess' fees were also significant costs. The applicants also wanted to relieve the Tribunal, which was "overwhelmed with cases", especially criminal ones.

53 *Gazeta Krakowska* No. 18 of 4 March 1818, 208–209. Father F. Jaroński's claim was inaccurate because, as the Marshal of the Sejm noted, "parsons were elected as justices of the peace". The Marshal also strongly opposed the idea of having justices of the peace hear appeals against the judgments of *wójtowie* (commune heads) "the Constitution designates only one Court of Appeal for all disputes".

54 *Gazeta Krakowska* No. 18 of 4 March 1818, 209. Judge Jakub Mąkolski was convinced that *in possesorio* cases should fall within the jurisdiction of the Tribunal. The Marshal of the Sejm pointed out that "in frequent evictions from properties and inns, for which an authority must be established, and this is most convenient in the Courts of the Peace". This was particularly about the need to "see the disputed item". F. Słotwiński was convinced that the Courts of the Peace can adjudicate *in possesorio* cases only if the value of the subject matter of the dispute determined for them is not exceeded.

55 *Gazeta Krakowska* No.18 of 4 March 1818, 209–210. With reference to principle No. 3, F. Słotwiński argued that in view of the principle of equality of all citizens before the law (Article III of the Constitution), it is unacceptable to exclude the possibility of filing an appeal to the Court of Appeal. In such a case, "the lower classes would have to submit to the arbitrariness of conciliation officials".

before Courts of the Peace and Tribunals", Book I: "Courts of the Peace"), by means of the Act of 1 June 1825.[56] In addition to the above-discussed, still quite cosmetic, modifications in relation to the examination of *in possesorio* cases, as well as the significant possibility of adjudicating civil disputes of up to 200 Polish zlotys, the emergence of the possibility of filing an appeal against a judgment of a Court of the Peace directly to the Court of Appeal within 14 days from the date of its delivery, was certainly very important. This option could be used not only in the case of decisive judgments, but also in preparatory and pre-decisive ones, e.g. regarding evidentiary issues; in this case, the obligation to have an advocate applied. Interestingly, it was also permissible to present new circumstances and evidence in relation to those reported during the proceedings before a Court of the Peace.[57]

A major achievement of the Cracovian legislator was also the introduction of an appeal to the Court of Third Instance, which was a solution unknown in French regulations. It concerned two different judgments of a Court of Peace and the Court of Appeal, if the value of the subject of the dispute exceeded 30 Polish zlotys. Somewhat surprisingly, it was also possible to lodge an appeal against a judgment of a justice of the peace in cases up to 30 Polish zlotys directly to the Court of Third Instance if a party claimed that substantive or formal law had been violated.[58] What is more, following the proposals formulated as early as 1818, the enforcement by bailiffs of judgments of Courts of the Peace in cases worth between 30 and 200 zlotys was also introduced.[59]

In organisational terms, the division of the Courts of the Peace into five districts, introduced in 1816, was maintained in subsequent legislation, including

56 Act of the Extraordinary Legislative Sejm of 1 June 1825, *Prawo oznaczające postępowanie przed Sądami Pokoju w kraju Rzeczypospolitej Krakowskiey,* promulgated by the letter of the Ruling Senate of 31 August 1825, No. 3647 DGS, DPr.WMK of 1826. The Act came into force on 1 December 1825.

57 Ibidem. Title IX "On the Appeal", Articles 58–67. The Act provided for the exchange of letters between the parties' representatives. In order to prevent barratry, the requirement to pay a sum of money by the appellant who loses the dispute was introduced.

58 As with the two concurring judgments of a Court of the Peace and the Court of Appeal, a favourable opinion from the Faculty of Law was then required: Title X. "On the Appeal to the Court of Last Instance", Articles 68–72. Interestingly, the Court of Third Instance, when examining a judgment of the Court of Peace up to 30 zlotys, ruled on the merits and not as an instance of cassation. Fierich 1917, 233–234.

59 Title XI: "On the Enforcement of the Judgments of a Justice of the Peace", Articles 73–84. In cases up to 30 Polish zlotys, enforcement took place with the participation of lower officials of these courts, i.e. ushers, paid from the Public Treasury; the justices of the peace performed their duties without payments; the professional factor was represented in the justices of the peace by scribes, who kept, *inter alia*, the entry book.

the 1833 Court Statute.[60] The above solutions clearly extended the range of possibilities for protecting residents' interests in court cases.[61] The importance of the Courts of Peace for the legal life of the Free City of Cracow is best illustrated by the statistics on the number of cases dealt with by them in Table 1.[62] It shows a clear increase in the number of cases from the 1825/26 reporting year onwards, which was due to the exemption of disputes of up to 30 Polish zlotys from stamp duties and registration fees.[63]

4 The Law on Judicial Enforcement

Crucial to the effectiveness of the execution of the law, is certainly the proper shaping of enforcement law. In the Free City of Cracow, the French Code of Civil Procedure, which contains numerous provisions on enforcement law (Book v: "On the Enforcement of Judgments"), played a decisive role in this regard.[64] In the questionnaire of the Legislative Committee, among the questions intended to guide further legislative work, there was a question on the permissibility of an enforcement sale of real estate below two-thirds of its value, as determined by an estimate.[65] The question was important because it concerned the sale of seized property by way of auction. This was an institution which caused heated disputes, both in the Duchy of Warsaw and the Kingdom of Poland, as well as in the Free City of Cracow, the main reason

60 *Statut Urządzający Sądownictwo* of 27 August 1833, Chapter II "On Courts of the Peace" (Articles 2–3). Their seats were located in Cracow (two court districts), Mogiła, Krzeszowice and Chrzanów.

61 However, due to the entry into force of the new Constitution of 1833 (Article XVIII), appeals could not be brought to the Court of Third Instance in cases below 600 Polish zlotys. In disputes *in possesorio* brought before a Court of the Peace, if the value of the dispute was less than this amount, the parties were required to specify the exact value. This was aimed at preventing barratry and inundating justices of the peace with trivial cases.

62 Similarly, the Courts of Peace of the Duchy of Warsaw were very active, settling (in the conciliation departments) an impressive number of around 95,000 cases between 1807 and 1812. The equivalent courts in the Kingdom of Poland dealt with 25,312 cases, and that only in the years 1816–21. Rosner 1988, 661.

63 *Zdanie sprawy o Stanie i Położeniu Kraju Wolnego, Niepodległego i ściśle Neutralnego Miasta Krakowa i Jego Okręgu dla Zgromadzenia Reprezentantów 1826 roku,* promulgated by the letter of the Ruling Senate No. 4925 DGS, ANK, 29/200/407 (WMK V-196), 444–446. This was done on the basis of Article 20 of the Act on the Courts of the Peace.

64 On the aplication of the French Code of Civil Procedure, see: Broniewicz 1993, 217–221.

65 "Can immovable property below two-thirds of the estimate resulting from be sold by way of enforcement or not?". Booklet with questions to the Extraordinary Legislative Assembly of 1816, ANK, 29/200/200 (WMK V-1), 709.

being that it was absent in old Polish law.[66] It should be added that the Sejm unanimously resolved at the time that a sale for less than two-thirds of the value of real estate was not permissible.[67]

As regards enforcement law, the unanimously adopted resolutions were as follows: (1) in order for a creditor to present a enforcement claim to court of a debtor's movable property which is in the possession of a third party, a resolution of the judge is necessary in addition to a document; (2) in the absence of the document, a deposit is necessary for the validity of the announcement; (3) sequestration of proceeds (*sequestratio proventuum*) and tradition (*traditio*) cannot be considered as a step of enforcement, unlike a lease by way of public auction; (4) disputes by way of enforcement between the persuading law (*iure vincentem*) and the persuaded law (*iurevictum controversae*) are to be resolved in a public audience of the Court, upon summons of a patron by a patron, by way of judgment; (5) the adjudication (by way of enforcement) to the creditors of the salary of an official may not exceed one-quarter of his salary.[68]

The question of the admissibility of personal enforcement on the debtor certainly became the subject of an interesting discussion. Father Mateusz Dubiecki, Józef Nikorowicz (President of the Court of Appeal) and Józef Sołtykowicz spoke in unison against such a possibility, suggested by the Legislative Committee. They all pointed to the constitutional guarantees of personal freedom, the need to protect inalienable human dignity, and the clear incompatibility of this institution with modern civilised times.[69] The

66 It was clearly contrary to the Old Polish institution of so-called *potioritas*, or "contest to the estate", Królasik 2019, 39–54.

67 *Gazeta Krakowska* No. 20 of 11 March 1818, 230.

68 *Gazeta Krakowska* No. 20 of 11 March 1818, 230. This calculation gives us an idea of the broad perspective of Ernest Reibnitz, highly likely to be the author of the questions on the issue of enforcement.

69 *Gazeta Krakowska* No. 20 of 11 March 1818, 230–235. J. Nikorowicz discussed at length the state of legislation in other European countries in this respect. In Austria, one year's personal arrest was allowed, except when "the debtor, through unfortunate circumstances through no fault of his own, is brought to insolvency, anticipating the commencement of an overlap of creditors, voluntarily and judicially surrenders all his assets". French law generally did not allow personal arrest "in the civil line", except for commercial debts, "misconduct of a debtor caused by the attitude of the creditor" and "maladministration of the public penny". Sołtykowicz, meanwhile, asked: "Or is it that we live at the time when a debtor could turn into our property, and having become our slave, pay us by forced labour?". He also pointed to an example from Roman law, which, in the Laws of the Twelve Tables, allowed "to chop into quarters their debtors and to divide among themselves their ragged flesh!".

above argumentation proved sufficiently successful, as the deputies passed by 19 to nine that "Enforcement against the person of the debtor in the civil line has no place"; at the same time, however, it was allowed for commercial cases.[70] Two resolutions were also unanimously passed: "The detention of a debtor suspected of escape at the request of the creditor may be allowed"; and "The arrest of a person in commercial matters shall constitute the last stage of enforcement".[71]

Before turning to a discussion of the most important changes introduced in the enforcement law of the Free City of Cracow, it should be stated beforehand that the French model of judicial enforcement in force was very complicated. Described in Part I of Book V: Code of Civil Procedure, the system provided for several types of enforcement. These were: (a) a bailiff's notice, consisting of the seizure of the debtor's claims and movable property in the possession of third parties; b) the seizure of standing crops, i.e. *de facto* uncut grain; c) a notice of the debtor's claim against his tenant for rent; d) enforcement against movable property, combined with the possibility of an auction sale by the bailiff; and e) enforcement against real estate.[72] The provisions from other Titles (XIII–XVI) were combined with the seizure of immovable property as the most important institution.[73] A separate title was devoted to general provisions.[74] It should be added that Book V of the Code of Civil Procedure described other issues of enforcement law in detail.[75]

---

70 Ibidem, 235. Adopted by 16 votes against 12, the Sejm resolution read as follows: "In commercial matters there shall be enforcement against the person of the debtor". The deputies thus agreed with the proposal of the Legislative Committee, although the equal treatment of merchants with other citizens of the Free City of Cracow was demanded by a representative of the Merchants' Congregation, Antoni Morbitzer. Father M. Dubiecki retorted that in this type of case personal arrest "should take place both by common custom and by the nature of the contract under which [the merchant] submitted to this law".

71 *Gazeta Krakowska* No. 21 of 15 March 1818, 241.

72 Code of Civil Procedure, Titles: VII: "On Notice or Opposition", Articles 557–582; IX: "On the Seizure of Standing Crops", Articles 626–635; X: "On the Notice of Items Placed at Rent with Private Persons", Articles 636–655; VIII: "On the Seizure of Movable Property", Articles 583–625; XII: "On the Seizure of Immovable Property", Articles 673–717.

73 Code of Civil Procedure, Titles: XIII: "On Incidental Disputes in Support of Seizure of Immovable Property", Articles 718–748; XIV: "On Classification", Articles 749–779; XV: "On Imprisonment", Articles 780–805; XVI : "On Prompt Decision", Articles 806–811.

74 Title VI: "General Provisions on the Violent Enforcement of Judgments and Deeds", Articles 545–556 of the Code of Civil Procedure.

75 Code of Civil Procedure, Titles: I: "On the Acceptance of Deposits", Articles 517–522; II: "On the Settlement of Damages and Lost Profits", Articles 523–525; III: "On the Accounting of Products", Article 526; IV: "On the Passing of Accounts", Articles 527–542; V: "On the Accounting of Expenses and Costs", Articles 543–544.

The classification of the Enforcement Act passed in 1823 was similar to the French prototype.[76] The Cracovian regulation thus consisted of a general part and ten titles.[77] A comparison between the prototype and the text adopted in 1823 makes it possible to conclude that from Book V Code of Civil Procedure, its Titles I–V were left in force.[78] A serious effort had already been made by the Cracovian legislator when working on the general part of the law, the equivalent of which is not to be found in the Code of Civil Procedure. It specified that, as a general rule, judicial enforcement could only be carried out on the basis of a final court judgment; under certain circumstances, it was also permissible to submit a settlement concluded before a justice of the peace or a deed drawn up by a court scribe. In addition to final judgments of the Court of Third Instance, validity was also granted to judgments of courts of second instance, i.e. the Tribunal and the Court of Appeal. These were not appealed before the Court of Third Instance, and differed from the judgments of courts of first instance (i.e. a Court of Peace or the Tribunal of First Instance) and to judgments of courts of first and second instance (i.e. of a Court of the Peace or the Tribunal of First Instance and the Court of Appeal), which were identical, and for which no cassation appeal had been lodged with the Court of Third Instance.[79] The Act also allowed for the enforcement of judgments issued in foreign countries, under the terms of international treaties and agreements, after they had been verified by a Cracow court. Only bailiffs under the supervision of the prosecutors at the Tribunal and the chairmen of the courts were authorised to carry out enforcement actions.[80]

The Act contained numerous provisions, which were guarantees by their nature. These certainly included the aforementioned: the prohibition of

---

76 Act of the Extraordinary Legislative Assembly of 17 June 1823, *Prawo o egzekucji sądowej*, DRRz.WMK of 1823.

77 These were the following titles: I: "On Notice"; II: "On the Seizure of Movable Property"; III: "On Proportional Partition"; IV: "On Leasing"; V: "On the Attachment of Immovable Property"; VI: "On Incidental Disputes in Support of the Seizure of Immovable Property"; VII: "On Classification"; VIII: "On Imprisonment"; IX: "On Prompt Decision"; X: "On the Rules of Application of this Law".

78 These were the following titles: I: "On the Acceptance of Deposits", Articles 517–522; II: "On the Settlement of Damages and Lost Profits", Articles 523–525; III: "On the Accounting of Products", Article 526; IV: "On the Passing of Accounts", Articles 527–542; V: "On the Accounting of Expenses and Costs", Articles 543–544.

79 Enforcement Act, Article 3. See Fierich 1917, 191–192. As already mentioned, until 1833, in the case of unanimous judgments, a cassation appeal was possible after obtaining a favourable opinion from the Faculty of Law of Jagiellonian University. This requirement was not provided for judgments differing in content.

80 See above, M. Mataniak. Chapter 2.

auction sales of real estate below two-thirds of its value, as well as the admissibility of debtors' satisfaction from the salaries of officials payable from the Public Treasury only up to one-quarter of their salaries. A default judgment could be enforced no later than six months from the date of its issuance; after that date it became ineffective (Articles 13–14, 16). The Act also indicated the permissible types of enforcement, however the number of these was smaller than in the Code of Civil Procedure.[81]

In the section on the bailiff's notice, among the changes introduced were: (a) the extension of the possibility of making it also with the consent of a justice of the peace, in cases falling under his jurisdiction (the Code of Civil Procedure always required the consent of the Chairman of the Tribunal), but this resolution had to be stated in the act of notice; (b) a slight extension – from seven to eight days – of the time limit for the creditor to notify the debtor of the notice made; (c) the omission of the provision on the sale of the matter in the notice and the partition of the amount obtained from its sale, if the notice was deemed valid; at the same time, the catalogue of items excluded from notice was left.[82] The sections of the Act relating to the attachment of movable property were also affected by significant changes. The party supporting the enforcement was allowed to participate in the seizure (this was excluded under the Code of Civil Procedure), either in person or by a representative, who could thus participate on an equal footing with two witnesses who could read and write (this requirement was not present in the Code of Civil Procedure), and citizens of the Free City of Cracow, of full age and who were not at the same time relatives or in-laws of the parties or their cohabitants. The course of the enforcement itself remained basically unchanged (drawing up a protocol, sealing the items and depositing them, participation of a caretaker: a person of trust), as did the catalogue of items excluded from enforcement.[83]

Although a person claiming to be the owner of the seized objects could file an objection, which was examined by the court under an expedited procedure, he or she had to expect to have to pay damages to the seizing party if the claim

81 Bailiff's notice, seizure of movable property, lease by public auction, seizure of immovable property and personal arrest were left out (Article 17 of the Act). However, the seizure of standing crops and the notice of the debt owed by the debtor from his tenant for rent were omitted (Articles 626–655 of the Code of Civil Procedure).

82 These were: items excluded by virtue of law; alimony and temporary court-ordered alimony; and sums and items expressly excluded from seizure in a will or donation (Articles 28–29 of the Act).

83 These were: bedding, clothing, books and workbench items necessary for the practice of the occupation, including craft tools, flour, etc. food products, for one month, one cow or three sheep together with fodder, grain and straw (Article 36 of the Act).

was not proven; the Act specified that this was to be one-tenth of the value of the item in dispute. The period that should elapse between the notification of the seizure to the debtor and the auction was extended from seven to eight days. It was also explicitly indicated that the estimate was to be carried out by two sworn experts, in the presence of the debtor and the creditor or their representatives. The legislator deleted the auction sale on Sunday, which, following the model of the Code of Civil Procedure, was to take place at the "nearest public market, on the day and time of the ordinary market"; only in an exceptional case could the Chairman of the Tribunal order a different, more convenient place. Valuables could only be auctioned in Cracow. The announcement of the auction was also extended to three days, which was to take place at the place where the item was to be auctioned, as well as at the office of the *wójt* (commune head) or a justice of the peace, and in the local press. A note of the correctness of the announcement was to be included in the minutes of the auction. The Act also introduced the stipulation that the debtor's personal data (name and surname) must not be given; also, the description of the object of the auction was to be devoid of unnecessary details. The content of the provision of Article 622 of the Code of Civil Procedure remained unchanged. This stated that when the value of the seized objects exceeds the amount of the claim, the sale may include objects only up to the value of the "claims and costs", at the choice of the debtor.[84]

The provisions of Title III: "On Proportional Partition" dealt primarily with the situation in which the amount obtained from the auction was insufficient to satisfy the claims of all creditors. This part in relation to the Code of Civil Procedure underwent only minor changes. Of the more significant issues, the obligation to attempt an amicable partition of sums among the creditors was deleted (Articles 656–657 Code of Civil Procedure). Instead, a requirement for the placement of the amount obtained by the bailiff to be put in a court deposit and for the preparation of a report by the bailiff to the court, together with a need to compile a list of claims made, were introduced. The dispute was decided by a delegated judge appointed by the President of the Tribunal, after reviewing the requests of the prosecutor.[85]

What was new compared to the Code of Civil Procedure, was all of Title IV: "On Leasing Out" (Articles 73–79). Indeed, the institution of enforcement of

84 Articles 46, 49–52, 55–56 of the Enforcement Act.

85 Articles 58–59, 69–72 of the Enforcement Act. The parties were entitled to appeal against the judgment within ten days of its delivery.

immovable property by way of lease was unknown in French law.[86] In Cracow it was carried out by a bailiff, with prior seizure and assessment of the immovable property. The lease of district villages required going to the Tribunal. It lasted from one to three years, with the possibility of extension at the request of the unsatisfied creditor. The seizure of immovable property by the bailiff was accompanied by a description of the condition of the buildings and land inventories and any other burdens (taxes, *corvée*); an estimate of the annual income was to be made by experts. The creditor supporting the execution was obliged to lodge a deed of seizure and evaluation in the office of the scribe of the Tribunal, and then to lay down the terms of the auction, a copy of which he was to deliver to the debtor. Once approved by the Court, these were advertised in the press by the delegated judge, four weeks before the scheduled auction. The winner of the auction, who was also the tenant, was required to pay the annual rent in advance ("anticipative") on St John's Day (23/24 June), on pain of losing possession of the property.

Due to its great practical importance, the enforcement of real estate, usually ending in an auction sale, deserves a wider discussion. Although this procedure was lengthy and quite expensive, the parties had the possibility to avoid it, and this was done by paying the obligation voluntarily. The law shortened the time limit for this, from 30 to 14 days, which was counted from the date of the delivery of the demand for payment. After the time limit expired, the bailiff could proceed with the seizure of the real estate, the purpose of which was to protect the real estate from the owner's actions that could lead to the depletion of the substance of the property and thus to the detriment of the creditors. The order for payment was valid for three months. Following the model of the Code of Civil Procedure, the Act specified in detail the subsequent actions of the bailiff, including the preparation of a seizure report, which was to contain the most important information about the property (location, legal status, tax burden, etc.), and to indicate the legal basis for enforcement. Those claiming seizure had to be represented by an advocate.

The list of persons to whom the bailiff was to deliver a copy of the "seizure protocol" was expanded to include the debtor-owner of the estate (he was listed there alongside the *wójt* (commune head) as a representative of the local administration; the scribe of the justice of the peace was omitted). The seizure of the property was to be recorded by the Mortgage Regent in the mortgage books, at the request of the "auction supporter". Cracow's legislator also

86 Interestingly, it was introduced almost simultaneously in the neighbouring Kingdom of Poland by means of the Prince Governor's decisions of 8 July and 2 September 1823, which remained in force there provisionally until 1876, Królasik 2019, 48–51.

gave a creditor the possibility to apply to the Tribunal for a judicial determination of the price of the seized property and the appointment of a caretaker to look after it. The creditor could also propose his own estimate of the property ("give an estimated price"), but if this was not accepted by the debtor, the court commissioned an estimate by experts. In addition to a justice of the peace, creditors were allowed to participate without restriction, with the possibility of submitting motions and comments. The debtor was not allowed to sell the property on pain of nullity of the legal act (Article 92; equivalent to Article 692 of the Code of Civil Procedure), unless the purchaser offered an amount sufficient to satisfy the mortgage claims.

The creators of the Act omitted the solution in Article 688 of the Code of Civil Procedure, which allowed the debtor to remain in possession of the property if it could not be leased or rented and the creditors did not object; he then acquired the status of a person subject to judicial sequestration. In the Enforcement Act (Article 90), as was the case in the Code of Civil Procedure, the debtor was forbidden to undertake actions that could cause damage to the occupied property (e.g. cutting down trees), with the obligation to compensate for damages and lost profits; in extreme cases, criminal liability could be imposed for this. It was also very important that Article 698 of the Code of Civil Procedure was omitted, which allowed the property to be adjudicated to the creditor if there were no other bidders.[87]

Following the model of the Code of Civil Procedure, the law also distinguished between a preparatory and a final adjudication, between which at least six weeks had to elapse. Auctions took place in Tribunal sessions, with the participation of patrons (advocates) and with the use of candles burning for about one minute (as this was the amount of time given to the bidders to make a decision, with each call). It was necessary on this occasion to call three times to purchase the auctioned property. The Act provided for three auction dates, of which the public was informed by means of announcements by the scribe of the Tribunal of First Instance. In addition to detailed information about the property (location, value), the reasons for initiating the procedure and the conditions of the auction, they included a summons to mortgage creditors and other persons with rights *in rem* to submit documents to the Tribunal confirming these claims. The auction could be considered completed when the estimated price, or, obviously, a higher price, had been offered on the

87 This was likely to prevent the undervaluation of property by creditors wishing to acquire goods at the lowest possible price. In the Duchy of Warsaw, this was to be remedied by a decree of the Saxon King of 1811 prohibiting the award of immovable property put up for forced public sale for less than two-thirds of its value.

first date. There was then a "firm adjudication". A sale below the asking price was possible, but only at the third auction and for an amount of not less than two-thirds of the "established price"; the adjudication could also take place in favour of the sole bidder.

In another part of the Act one can notice solutions referring to the institution of so-called 'overbidding', regulated in Articles 710–711 of the Code of Civil Procedure. Article 105 of the Act indicated that within one week from the day of the auction anyone could offer for the auctioned property, personally or by a representative, an amount higher by at least one-quarter than the amount obtained through the auction. It was necessary to go to the office of the Tribunal of First Instance with this proposal and to inform the advocate of the person supporting the auction, the debtor and the person in whose favour the "original" adjudication took place (Article 106). In this case, the final adjudication of the property, either to the winner of the auction or to the "extraordinary bidder", was to take place on a date separately determined by the Tribunal (Article 107; equivalent to Article 712 of the Code of Civil Procedure).

The following persons were excluded from participating in an auction, on pain of nullity: court employees (judges, prosecutors, assessors, scribes), advocates representing creditors, and also debtors and insolvent persons. As mentioned, all claims against the property subject to seizure had to be filed before the auction; failure to do so resulted in the inability to assert claims during or after the auction. Failure to pay the bid amount in time could result, at the request of the debtor or creditor, in the auction being repeated at the risk ("at the expense and peril") of the late purchaser of the property, but with the asking price preserved. It was then possible to auction the property even below two-thirds of its value. The acquisition of rights to the property was established by the Tribunal of First Instance in the form of a so-called Heritage Decree.

Linked to the issue of auction sales of real estate was the issue of so-called incidental disputes (Articles 114–124 of the Act), which affected real estate owners and third parties, and could adversely affect the effectiveness of an auction sale. They were resolved in an expedited procedure; in the Cracovian Act the provisions of Articles 719–725 of the Code of Civil Procedure were also affected, which dealt with the so-called 'concurrence of enforcements' directed to the property of the same debtor or to the same real estate.[88] The protection of the interests of mortgage creditors was provided for by Article 115, a variation of the provisions of Article 719 of the Code of Civil Procedure. They

88 The division of incidental disputes was introduced by Thomine-Desmazures 1833, 120, cited by Królasik 2018, 137–138.

could claim authorisation to act for a seizer who did not support the seizure of the property. An identical authorisation could also be granted in the event of negative acts of the occupier, such as conspiracy, deceit or negligence (Article 116; equivalent to Article 722 of the Code of Civil Procedure).[89] The person to whom the power to act as a person "supporting the seizure" had been ceded could demand from the person who had hitherto acted in such a capacity and who had given up his or her power to do so, the surrender of the documents necessary for the continuation of the dispute (Article 118; the equivalent of Article 724 of the Code of Civil Procedure). A firm judgment rendered in an incidental dispute could be appealed, within a period of ten days, which was calculated from the date of delivery of the judgment to the advocate (Article 117; equivalent to Article 723 of the Code of Civil Procedure).[90]

The Enforcement Act omitted some of the detailed solutions of Article 719 of the Code of Civil Procedure. These concerned actions taken when two different seizers applied to the same Court for the seizure of different immovable properties, but belonging to the same person. The provisions concerning appeals against a judgment on the basis of which the property was seized (Articles 726–730 of the Code of Civil Procedure) were shredded, while the solutions giving the possibility to exclude the seized property from an auction were repeated without major changes (Articles 119–122; equivalents of Articles 727–730 of the Code of Civil Procedure). The Enforcement Act also contains provisions concerning pleas of nullity directed against the proceedings preceding the preliminary adjudication (Articles 733–736 of the Code of Civil Procedure). The drafters of the Enforcement Act omitted a number of other important provisions of the Code of Civil Procedure, including those on the debtor's action for a declaration of invalidity of proceedings conducted after a 'provisional adjudication',[91] as well as those concerning the so-called 're-auction'[92] and the conclusion of agreements between creditors and debtors to conduct a voluntary sale instead of a forced sale.[93]

---

89 Negligence was understood in the Act to mean the failure to comply with formalities, or the failure to carry out "any act of conduct", within the prescribed period. Proof of conspiracy or deceit resulted in compensation for damages and lost profits.

90 Article 723 of the Code of Civil Procedure provided for a two week time limit.

91 It was governed by the provisions of Articles 735–736 of the Code of Civil Procedure; the complaint had to be filed at least 20 days before the scheduled "firm adjudication"; the judges were given a period of ten days to examine the objections; an appeal against the judgment thus rendered had to be lodged within one week from the date of its delivery.

92 It was governed by the provisions of Articles 737–745 of the Code of Civil Procedure.

93 It was governed by the provisions of Articles 746–748 of the Code of Civil Procedure. In addition, the Enforcement Act omitted quite important general provisions, including those proclaiming that a "firm adjudication transfers to the purchaser only those rights to

From the point of view of Cracow's court practice, the important provisions were those of Title VII: "On Classification" (Articles 125–132 of the Act). They concerned the formulation of objections against the so-called 'classification of creditors', i.e. the division of the amount obtained from the auction sale in a situation where it turned out to be insufficient to satisfy the claims of all mortgage creditors. The Chairman of the Tribunal would then appoint a 'classification judge', whose task was to draw up a classification plan. This was to be done on the basis of the documentation produced during the auction, within a period of 14 days. On the basis of the classification plan, the Tribunal of First Instance would issue a so-called 'classification judgment', resolving the mortgage priority dispute; this could be appealed to the Court of Appeal within ten days. Only after it had become final, the purchaser had satisfied the creditors and paid the 'estimated sum', did the court order the deletion of all mortgage entries encumbering the auctioned property. Fragmentary source research convinces us that the procedure described above was generally followed by the judiciary of the Free City of Cracow.[94]

Finally, it is worth looking at the final form of the provisions concerning the already mentioned enforcement against the debtor, i.e. the so-called 'personal enforcement'. The issue of personal enforcement was dealt with in Title XV: "On Imprisonment" (Articles 780–805 of the Code of Civil Procedure), whose counterpart in the Act was the identically named Title VIII. Under the Act, personal coercion in civil cases ("arrest") was only permissible for fraud, i.e., in this case, the act of selling real estate of which the perpetrator of the act knew that it was not his property, but also the making of a mortgage entry on such real estate. Misleading the other party as to the alleged absence of a mortgage burden or as to its actual amount was also treated as fraud.[95]

Personal coercion could also be used, and in principle without limitation, for promissory note and commercial debts (Article 136). Another form was the detention of an insolvent debtor, in the event of suspected escape (Article 137).

---

property which the expropriated debtor was entitled to" (Article 731 of the Code of Civil Procedure); as well as a provision on the effects of delaying the announcement of the auction, which required a new suspension of announcements and publication of notices in the press (Article 732 of the Code of Civil Procedure). See Królasik 2018, 137–138.

94 For a discussion of several cases in this area, see Mataniak 2022a, 258–265.

95 The use of personal coercion (arrest) was also possible when it came to the return of: a) revenues collected during unlawful possession, as well as compensation for damages and lost profits when a court ordered the return of unlawfully taken land; b) money entrusted to a public person in connection with the performance of official duties; c) money and "titles" entrusted to the Regent of Mortgage Deeds, notaries, advocates, bailiffs and ushers (Articles 133–134 of the Act).

The demand for arrest or detention had to be brought before the Tribunal; it was dealt with by the court on an expedited basis, no later than 24 hours after the suit was brought. Personal coercion could not be used against minors, the elderly (over 70 years of age), women (unless it was a case of fraud) and also if the value of the subject matter of the dispute did not exceed 300 Polish zloty. Personal coercion could only be applied on the basis of a court sentence; a bailiff was responsible for bringing the convicted person to prison (Articles 138–143).[96] Interestingly, the rules for conducting "personal coercion in civil and commercial matters" were still the subject of correspondence between Government authorities, the judiciary and the Merchants' Congregation as late as in the 1840s.[97] It may be also pointed out that both the Code of Civil Procedure and the Act forbade the arrest of debtors: a) before sunrise and after sunset; b) on public holidays; c) in places of religious worship ('houses dedicated to the Divine Service'); d) in places where public authorities met, during their work; and e) at home ("even in one's own dwelling"), unless the justice of the peace decided otherwise (Article 146).

In conclusion, it should be noted that the provisions of enforcement law became the subject of work in the last Sejm of the Free City of Cracow in 1844. Although the members of the Sejm's legislative commission complained about the alleged incompatibility of the Act with the economic realities of the time, the final modifications introduced did not turn out to be too far-reaching. First and foremost, the division of permissible types of enforcement was maintained, although "all other types of enforcement" were allowed, provided they had been ordered by a final judgment (Article 25). The content of the protocol drawn up by the bailiff in the case of enforcement against movable property was specified (Article 41). The categories of items excluded from seizure were maintained (Article 49). The title "On Leasing", which does not appear in the Code of Civil Procedure, was left in place (Articles 88–94). The catalogue of duties of the caretaker, upon seizure of immovable property, was clarified (Article 111). The penalisation of secret agreements on the occasion of an auction sale of real estate (conspiracy) was introduced, treated as an act of fraud and punished according to the rules laid down for this type of offence in the

96 The drafters of the Act left without major changes (in the form of Articles 146–151) the provisions of Articles 780–788 of the Code of Civil Procedure concerning arrest and imprisonment procedures, as well as (in the form of Articles 152–161) Articles 789–805 of the Code of Civil Procedure, detailing the rules for the serving of custodial sentences (the latter provisions approximating in their substance to the penitentiary regulations).

97 See, for example, letter of the Administrative Council to the Higher Court of 16 July 1846, ANK, 29/200/221 (WMK V-22 B), 1295.

Criminal Code (Article 133). An entire Title VI was also introduced. "On the Arrangement of Mortgage Creditors" (Articles 142–150).[98]

98 Act of 5 July 1844, *Prawo o Exekucyi Sądowej*, promulgated by the letter of the Ruling Senate No. 3108 DGS, DPr.WMK of 1844. The Sejm commission also appeared in the sources under the rather pompous name of "Committee for the revision of legislation". It should be added that minor modifications submitted by the commission were taken into account during the votes. See the letters of the Sejm Committee for Legislative Revision to the Ruling Senate: of 9 May 1844, ANK, 29/200/221 (WMK V-22 B), 1399–1401; of 26 June 1844, ibidem, 1501–1512; *Projekt do zmian w Ustawie Exekucyjnej*, ibidem, 1515–1615.

CHAPTER 5

Civil Weddings and Marriage Certificates of the Jewish Population

Piotr Michalik

1 The Legal Status of Jews in the Free City of Cracow[1]

Following the incorporation of Cracow and its environs into Austria as part of the Third Partition of Poland in 1795, the Jews living there became subject to the regulations of Austrian law. This meant bringing the hitherto autonomous Jewish community[2] under the emancipatory reforms of Maria Theresa and Joseph II.[3] Among the numerous regulations issued by Vienna for the territory partitioned in the first partition of Poland in 1772 (Galicia, from 1795 onwards Eastern Galicia), there were also provisions for the conclusion of Jewish marriages. *Inter alia*, in 1773, the conclusion of such a marriage was made conditional on obtaining a special permission from the State authorities and the payment of a wedding fee.[4] However, these injunctions were not respected, and Jews married in a religious form without complying with the administrative requirements.[5] After subsequent legislative changes, Joseph II's Edict of Toleration of 1789 finally lifted the earlier restrictions and brought Jewish marriages under the regime of universal civil law,[6] i.e. the *Codex Josephinus* of 1786.[7] At the same time, it was made compulsory for all heads of families to adopt a permanent surname, and for commune heads, together with rabbis, to keep records of Jewish births, marriages and deaths.[8] These changes were also

1 This chapter is a modified and expanded version of the author's article on the consent to marry for Jews in the Free City of Cracow: Michalik 2020, 102–109. Due to the fact that the marriage law of the NC was in force in Cracow from 1810 to 1852, the timeframe of the analysis presented here extends slightly beyond the period of the Republic of Cracow.

2 Until 1795, the structure of the autonomous Cracow municipality was regulated by a statute of 1595. See Jakimyszyn 2005, 41–49.

3 See Grodziski 2007, 73–85; Eisenbach 1983, 615–629.

4 Piller 1794, No. I, 4.

5 Grodziski 2007, 77.

6 Piller 1789, No. XLIV, 105.

7 Which was introduced in Galicia as of 1 May 1787. See Płaza 1993, 45.

8 Piller 1789, No. XLIV, 106. Records were to be kept in German. The records of Jews in the Kazimietrz district of Cracow from 1798 to 1809, kept in Latin and German, have survived

 | DOI:10.1163/9789004688742_007

met with resistance, which led to further concessions in the form of adapting the obstacle of consanguinity to Jewish law and limiting Jewish divorces to the letter of the divorce procedure in the Circular of 1791.[9]

This legislation was gradually introduced in the territories seized by Austria in 1795, known as Western (New) Galicia. It remained unchanged even after the introduction of the Austrian West Galician Code of 1797 in Cracow on 1 January 1798,[10] which, like Joseph II's earlier civil code, did not contain separate regulations on Jewish marriages.[11] This did not change until the Napoleonic Wars, which, by virtue of the Peace of Schönbrunn of 14 October 1809, led to Western Galicia being incorporated into the Duchy of Warsaw. This meant that the Jewish population was also covered by a new legal regime, the framework of which was set by the Duchy's constitution of 22 July 1807, imposed by Napoleon. Formally, in Article IV, it introduced equality before the law of all citizens.[12] In practice, however, by the Decrees of Frederick Augustus, King of Saxony and Duke of Warsaw, dated 7 September and 17 October 1808, this provision of political rights was suspended for the Jews for ten years, "in the hope that during this time they would destroy in themselves the distinctive marks which distinguish them so much from other inhabitants".[13] The above restriction, however, did not apply to civil law, which, from 1 May 1808, was regulated in the Duchy by the NC on a universal basis (Articles 7 and 8 of the NC).[14] Formally, therefore, in 1810, the *Code Napoléon* was also implemented for the Jews of Cracow.

Although the Government of the Duchy of Warsaw was working on a comprehensive regulation of the legal status of Jews, which was to be based on solutions already adopted in the Prussian partition,[15] by the end of the existence of the Duchy it had not been introduced.[16] Instead, a number of partial administrative and legal regulations were introduced, limiting the rights of the Jewish population. These included: decrees limiting civil rights, such as the Decree of

to this day. See, for example: *Geburtsbuch für der kasimirer Judengem 1798. ANNO-1809*, ANK 29/1472/1.

9 Piller 1791, No. XIII, 29–30.

10 By the Imperial Patent of Francis II of 13 February 1797.

11 The latter, including the institution of a divorce letter, were finally introduced into the Austrian Civil Code (ABGB) of 1811. See Dziadzio 2022a, 462.

12 *Ustawa Konstytucyjna Księstwa Warszawskiego*, DPKW, vol. 1, II.

13 Bartel, Kosim, Rostocki eds. 1964–69, vol. 1, 142 and 148.

14 *Dekret z 27 stycznia 1808 r.*, DPKW, vol. 1, 46–47.

15 More specifically, based on *Generalne Urządzenie Żydów w prowincjach Prus Południowych i Nowo-Wschodnich* of 17 April 1797 r.

16 Filipiak 2016, 147–149.

19 November 1808 temporarily depriving Jews of the right to acquire landed property,[17] decrees restricting the freedom of residence, such as the Decree of 16 March 1809 prohibiting the Jewish population from living in certain streets in Warsaw,[18] or decrees imposing special taxes on the Jewish population, such as the Decree of 25 March 1809 on the Kosher Tax.[19] With the incorporation of Cracow into the Duchy, the 'Jewish' regulations in force there took the place of the previous Austrian regulations,[20] although some of the latter were retained, such as the Jewish family tax, established by the Patent of 20 August 1806.[21] In addition, the Decree of 19 March 1812, regulated the rules of Jewish residence in Cracow and Kazimierz.[22]

The fall of Napoleon in 1815 also ended the existence of the Duchy of Warsaw, and as a consequence Cracow changed its political affiliation for the third time in a generation, becoming a Free City by the will of the victorious powers. This also meant that Cracow's Jews were subject to a new legal regime based on the successive constitutions of the Republic of Cracow.[23] Following the model of the constitution of the Duchy of Warsaw, Article III of the 1815 Constitution guaranteed the equality of all citizens and the legal protection of tolerated religions.[24] This norm was confirmed by Article III of the 1818 Constitution,[25] as well as Articles III and VI of the 1833 Constitution.[26] The former granted *expressis verbis* legal protection to the Judaic religion.[27] At the same time, however, the constitutions of the Free City of Cracow excluded Jews from equality in the "use of civil and political rights" that only Christians were entitled to.[28] Consequently, the 1818 Constitution, in Article VII, deprived Jews of the active

17 Bartel, Kosim, Rostocki eds. 1964–69, vol. 1, 159.

18 Ibidem, vol. 2, 26–30.

19 DPKW, vol. 2, 34–36.

20 *Dekret z 22 maja 1810 r. wprowadzający podatek od mięsa koszernego w departamentach „galicyjskich" i dotyczący środków na umorzenie długów kahalnych*, DPKW, vol. 2, 189–192.

21 Ibidem; *Dekret z 14 czerwca 1810 r. ustalający na rok 1810 zasady uiszczania rozmaitych podatków w nowo do Księstwa Warszawskiego wcielonych departamentach galicyjskich*, Bartel, Kosim, Rostocki eds. 1964–69, vol. 4, 179–181.

22 *Dekret zezwalającym Żydom krakowskim na zamieszkanie zarówno na Kazimierzu żydowskim, jak i katolickim*, Bartel, Kosim, Rostocki eds. 1964–69, vol. 3, 235–237.

23 See above, Chapter 1 and Jakimyszyn 2008, 23–67.

24 *Konstytucja Wolnego Miasta Krakowa*, Tokarz ed. 1932, 10–15.

25 *Konstytucja Wolnego Miasta Krakowa i Jego Okręgu*, Kallas and Krzymkowski eds. 2006, 183–190.

26 *Konstytucja Wolnego Miasta Krakowa i Jego Okręgu*, No. 4711 DGS, DPr.WMK of 1833.

27 "La loi protège les Cultes tolérés, au nombre desquels est compris celui des Israëlites".

28 Article IV of the 1833 Constitution: "La différence des Cultes Chrétiens n'en établit aucune dans la jouissance des droits civils et politiques". Article II of the 1815 and 1833 Constitutions refers to social rights (*les droits sociaux*).

right to vote "until they acquire political rights", and the 1833 Constitution, maintained this exclusion in Article X.[29] Furthermore, in Articles XII and XXI, it explicitly excluded the "Followers of the Old Testament"[30] from holding the offices of a senator, judge, representative (deputy) and *wójt* (commune head). This meant that by virtue of the constitution itself, and not, as in the Duchy of Warsaw, by a decree of the ruler, Jews remained second-class citizens in the Free City.

The above constitutional regulations only provided a framework for the formation of the legal status of Jews in Cracow, especially as they did not establish the extent to which they enjoyed civil rights. Based on the Austrian models and the legacy of the Duchy of Warsaw, there was a conviction among the political elite of Cracow that such a determination was necessary as part of the continuation of the process of emancipation of the "Followers of the Old Testament". To this end, as early as late 1815, the Senate of the Free City began work on preparing a comprehensive regulation of the rights and obligations of the Jewish community under its authority. The result of this work was the preparation of a draft which, after approval by the Senate, was forwarded in July 1816 to the Organising Commission.[31] On the basis of this, a final draft regulation was drawn up by the Austrian Resident Joseph Sweerts-Spork and presented to the Commission on 12 September 1816, under the name *Rapport sur le système futur de juifs*.[32] Discussions on the report, to which reservations were raised by the Prussian Resident Ernest Reibnitz,[33] continued at meetings of the Commission until 7 December 1816, when its contents were agreed in French.[34] However, it was not until 14 April 1817 that it was finally accepted by Reibnitz, and formally by the whole Commission, and forwarded to the Senate for translation into Polish.[35] The official content of the regulation was promulgated by the Senate in the Journal of Governmental Regulations as the *Statute Organising the Followers of the Old Testament in the Free City of Cracow and its District*, with effect from 1 June 1817.[36]

---

29 "Ne jouissent pas du droit politique d'élection, même lorsqu'ils possèderaient d'ailleurs les qualités prescrites … Les individus professant des religions seulément tolerées, tells que les Juifs et autres non-chrétiens, avant d'avoir acquis les droits politiques".

30 The term "Follower of the Old Testament" (in Polish, *Starozakonny*) was used to refer to a Jew in the official documents of the Free City of Cracow.

31 Wachholz 1957, 364.

32 Tokarz ed. 1932, 197.

33 Ibidem, 201–202. For more, see Wachholz 1957, 365.

34 Tokarz ed. 1932, 218–219. The manuscript is located in ANK, 29/200/3 (WMK I-3), 195–203.

35 Tokarz ed. 1932, 283.

36 *Statut Urządzający Starozakonnych w Wolnym Mieście Krakowie i Jego Okręgu*, No. 1358 DGS, DRRz.WMK of 1817, 287–320 (henceforth cited as the *Statute*). The date on which

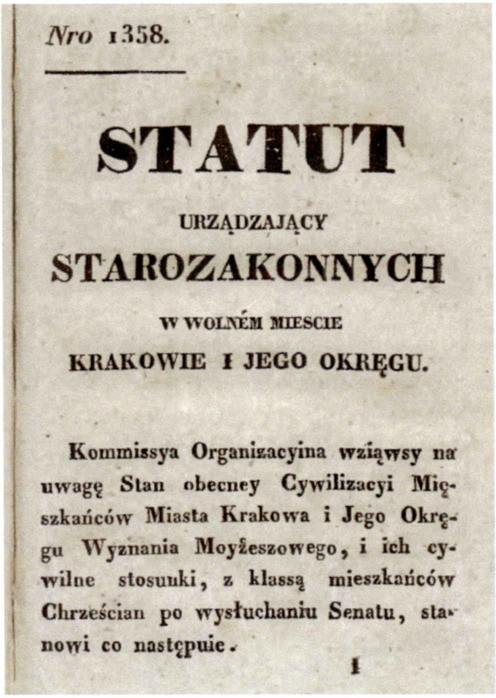

Nro 1358.

STATUT

URZĄDZAJĄCY

STAROZAKONNYCH

W WOLNÉM MIESCIE

KRAKOWIE I JEGO OKRĘGU.

Kommissya Organizacyina wziąwsy na uwagę Stan obecney Cywilizacyi Mięszkańców Miasta Krakowa i Jego Okręgu Wyznania Moyżeszowego, i ich cywilne stosunki, z klassą mieszkańców Chrześcian po wysłuchaniu Senatu, stanowi co następuie.

1

FIGURE 19 *First page of the Statute Organising the Followers of the Old Testament of 1817*, (print, paper, 1817)
SOURCE: JAGIELLONIAN LIBRARY, BJ 10979 I; SCAN BY JAGIELLONIAN DIGITAL LIBRARY IN PUBLIC DOMAIN

In line with the emancipatory aspirations inherited from the Austrian authorities, the implementation of the Statute's provisions was to lead to the gradual "civilising" of the Jewish population, which was to take place through their adoption of "universal customs".[37] In the long term, this was to lead to granting them full civil and political rights. The latter were *de lege lata* enjoyed only by a group of the most 'useful' individuals to society. This included, among others, outstanding artists and significant merchants, provided,

---

the provisions of the Act came into force was established by the Senate in its decision of 28 May 1817, DRz.WMK of 1817, No. 20, 87.

37 *Statute*, preamble; § 23.

however, that they had already assimilated into Christian society.[38] In order to accelerate the assimilation process, the Statute abolished a number of civil-administrative distinctions to which the Jewish population had hitherto been subject. First of all, it abolished the *Kahal* organisation that had been restored in the period of the Duchy of Warsaw, bringing the Jews under the "authority and supervision" of the *wójts* (heads of the communes).[39] Only "strictly religious" matters were excluded from the competence of the commune heads, which continued to be under the authority of the rabbis. Among them, the right and duty of the rabbis to keep minutes of "all religious acts held in the community on the occasions of birth, marriage, divorce or death",[40] and to issue religious rulings, was retained. This was with the proviso, however, that they should also be recorded in Polish (as authentic) and sent monthly to the Senate.[41]

As in the case of *Kahal*s, the Statute also reinstated the obligation for every Jew to have "a permanent family name, from father to son to pass hereditarily".[42] In order to fulfil this obligation, the law prescribed a census of the Jewish population, in which each family was to be assigned a specific surname *ex officio*, while families with surnames given in Austrian times retained them. The possession of such a surname was the basis for the head of a family or an unmarried person to receive a certificate of "local-nationality", containing "a description of the person, age, profession, condition, or employment". According to the Act, the certificate was the holder's primary identity document, certifying the holder's status as a resident of the Free City of Cracow and entitling the holder to deal with all official matters. The lack of a certificate, on the other hand, constituted a misdemeanour punishable by up to 15 days' imprisonment and, in the case of persistence, was even a crime.[43]

38 Ibidem, § 28. Assimilation was to be confirmed by living (with prior consent) in the Christian part of Cracow, speaking Polish or German, wearing Christian clothes and sending children to public schools (under § 13 Jewish public schools in the Free City of Cracow were abolished).

39 Ibidem, § 1.

40 Ibidem, § 3.

41 Ibidem, § 7.

42 Ibidem, § 16.

43 Ibidem, § 16 and 20.

2 The Introduction of Civil Status Registry Records and Civil Weddings in Cracow

As of 15 August 1810, by the Royal Decree of 9 June 1810, the NC came into force in the Cracow Department of the Duchy of Warsaw, which was part of Western Galicia, incorporated into the Duchy of Warsaw on 14 October 1809.[44] This meant the introduction in Cracow of French civil registry records for all its inhabitants, the majority of whom were Catholics. Until then, they were covered by the registration of the Catholic Church, i.e. baptisms, marriages and deaths kept in parish books by parish priests from the 16th century onwards.[45] In 1797, the Austrians standardised this registration by making it compulsory to keep it on printed forms according to Latin-Polish instructions, in separate books for baptisms, marriages and deaths.[46] Parish books in the Austrian partition also were kept exclusively by the clergy and stored in parishes.[47] The other Christian denominations also kept their own records, as did the Jews, who were subject to the provisions of Joseph II's Edict of Tolerance of 1789 in this regard.[48] In principle, therefore, the registration of civil status was not something new in the administrative and legal order of Cracow. Only its form was to be changed, with a reservation regarding civil registry records kept by secular civil registrars.[49]

The situation was different with the introduction of civil weddings in Cracow. This institution was unknown in Polish-Lithuanian Commonwealth law, in which, by virtue of the Constitution of the Piotrków Sejm of 1577, the canonical religious form of marriage was obligatory for Catholics according to the *Tametsi* Decree of 1563, and for other denominations and religions.[50] Nor was the civil wedding known in Austrian law, which, from the time of Joseph II's *Ehepatent* of 1783, had recognised marriage as a civil contract, but could be concluded only in a religious form. This was also provided for by the regulations of the West Galician Code of 1797 in force in Cracow at the time of its incorporation into the Duchy of Warsaw.[51] Also, according to Joseph II's Edict

44 DPKW, vol. 2, 220–221.

45 Szpak 1973, 55. Weddings began to be recorded in St Mary's Parish from 1548, births from 1568 (St Anne's and St Stephen's Parishes), deaths from 1712 (Parish of Corpus Christi).

46 In most parishes, separate registers for baptisms, marriages and deaths were kept from the beginning.

47 Ibidem, 54–58.

48 See above, footnote 8.

49 See below, Chapter 5, Section 4.

50 Karabowicz 2004, 175.

51 Dziadzio 2020c, 159.

of Tolerance of 1789 and earlier Austrian regulations, Jewish marriages were to be concluded exclusively in a religious form. Formally, therefore, the introduction of civil marriage in Cracow in 1810 was revolutionary, but in practice its real meaning depended on government policy and the attitude of the society towards it.[52]

At the time of the introduction of French regulations in Cracow, the Government of the Duchy of Warsaw had already worked out legal and administrative solutions for the application of the new regulations. First of all, this entailed the appointment of civil registrars who were authorised to draw up the civil registry records required by the NC and to make announcements and perform civil weddings. Following the French model, these should be secular persons. Administrative and social realities only allowed this solution in large cities, where there was a qualified civil staff of mayors or their deputies. In smaller places, it was necessary to entrust this function mainly to clergymen, who had the relevant education and experience both from the times of the Polish-Lithuanian Commonwealth and the Prussian partition.[53] This was done by a Council of Ministers' Regulation of 21 April 1808, which ordered Catholic parish priests to temporarily act as civil registrars in villages "where there are parishes and there is not a considerable number of Jews".[54] In the case of villages "where there are many dissenters and where a fit organist can be found, he may substitute for a civil registrar".[55]

The provisional nature of the Regulation was already perpetuated by § 24 of the Decree of 9 May 1808, in which the obligation to "maintain records" was placed *expressis verbis* on "parish priests and their vicars, priests of the Greek rite, pastors of Evangelical denominations, rabbis and all those who by then … had [this] instructed to themselves".[56] This principle was finally confirmed by Article 1 of the Decree of 23 February 1809 on fees for civil registrars, stating that "civil registrars are to be clergymen performing parish duties". The

52 See Michalik 2023.

53 The territory of the Duchy of Warsaw was created from the lands taken from Poland by Prussia in the Second and Third Partitions in 1792 and 1795. From 1 June 1794 and 1 September 1797 respectively, the Prussian Landrecht of 1794 was in force on them. However, the ecclesiastical marriage law and jurisdiction in force in the Republic was maintained. See Płaza 1993, 47. This jurisdiction was, however, limited, *inter alia* by the possibility for Catholics to obtain a divorce before a State court. See Karabowicz 2004, 175–176; Pomianowski 2018, 63–65.

54 Obviously with the cooperation of the ecclesiastical authorities, which is confirmed by the Government's correspondence with the Catholic bishops and consistories. See Jemielity 1995, 165–166.

55 *Urządzenie urzędników aktów cywilnych w Księstwie Warszawskim*, Pomianowski 2015, 104.

56 DPKW, vol. 1, 54.

same Decree, in Article 2, also regulated the order of a clergyman's activities by ordering him to "perform first the civil act, then the religious rite attached to that act". It stipulated, however, that Catholic clergy were exempted from the obligation to pronounce "civil divorces[57] … to announce divorces only civilly, nor [were they required] to perform such civil weddings", a duty to be performed by "mayors" (Article 4).[58] However, due to the suspension of Jews from political rights, the provisions of this Decree no longer applied to Jewish rabbis.[59] Consequently, civil registry records, announcements and weddings for Jews were conducted either by clergymen of other faiths or by secular civil registrars or their substitutes, such as organists, mentioned in the 1808 Council of Ministers' Regulation.[60]

With regard to the legal regulations themselves, i.e. the provisions of Title II of Book 1 of the NC of Acts before the Civil Authorities (Articles 34–101), the Government of the Duchy of Warsaw found it necessary to adapt them to local administrative conditions. This was done by a resolution of the Chamber of Deputies promulgated by the Royal Decree of 18 March 1809, which amended Articles 41, 43–45, 49, 53, 70–72 of the NC, with effect from 18 March 1809.[61] The amended provisions dealt with the general organisation of civil registry records (Articles 34–53 of the NC), including particularly important obligations for the functioning of the whole system: the keeping of civil registry records in two copies (Article 40 of the NC); the numbering (Article 41 of the NC) and continuity of the registers (Article 42 of the NC); the obligation to close them annually and transfer them to the competent archives (Article 43 of the NC), together with appendices attached to the records (Article 44 of the NC); and, linked to the establishment of the marriage record (Articles 63–76 of the NC), the institution of the act of notoriety (*l'acte de notoriété*), which was a substitute for the birth certificates that were missing for persons about to be married (Articles 70–72 of the NC).

In all the amended provisions, the relevant civil registry authorities were replaced by the *Code Napoléon*. This was not due to the lack of Polish equivalents of the French bodies, since the administration of justice of the Duchy

57 Based on Article 258 of the NC. The announcement of a divorce, from which a civil record was drawn up under the general rules (Articles 34–54 of the NC), was constitutive in the sense that the plaintiff's failure to announce the divorce judgment within two months of it becoming final, resulted in the loss of its legal force (Articles 264–266 of the NC).

58 Ibidem, 195–196.

59 See above, footnote 13.

60 Pomianowski 2015, 98.

61 *Dekret z 18 marca 1809 r.*, DPKW, vol. 1, 231–236.

duplicated their structure, but mainly due to the need to "bring closer" the civil status administration to the inhabitants. Thus, the place of the President of the Tribunal of First Instance, his deputy or the scribe of the Tribunal, was taken by a justice of the peace, his deputy or the scribe of the court (Articles 41, 45 and 49 of the NC); the place of the archives of the Tribunal of First Instance was taken by the archives of a Court of the Peace (Articles 43 and 44 of the NC); the place of the Imperial Prosecutor at the Tribunal of First Instance by a justice of the peace or a scribe (Articles 49, 53 and 72 of the NC), and the place of a justice of the peace by a head or mayor of the commune (Articles 70 and 71 of the NC). Of a more substantive nature was the additional change introduced in the prerequisites for the admissibility of an act of notoriety. It consisted of reducing the number of seven witnesses, required by the original wording of Article 71 of the NC, to two and, in the absence of such witnesses and an ineffective investigation of a justice of the peace, allowing for a substitute oath with respect to "foreign persons" (Article 71 of the NC).[62]

The remaining provisions of Title II of the *Code Napoléon* remained in force in their original wording. Doubts in this respect, at least formally, were finally resolved by the Royal Decree of 10 October 1809, which was a transitional law to the NC, already in force in the Duchy for more than a year. According to the law, all the provisions of the new Code – of which the French text remained the authentic text, with the Polish text published in 1808 in the Printing House of the Piarist Fathers in Warsaw (Article 2) – had "full force of law", subject to the amendments already introduced (Article 3), for all "actions and incidents which have occurred" from 1 May 1808 (Article 2 in conjunction with Article 5).[63] This meant that from that date both civil marriages concluded and marriage certificates drawn, as well as all the legal effects of these acts (Article 10), were exclusively governed by the NC in the wording established by a resolution of the Chamber of Deputies promulgated by the Royal Decree of 18 March 1809. *A contrario*, these acts, and in fact the corresponding legal acts occurring before 1 May 1808, were subject to prior law and could not be rescinded "under the guise of the Napoleonic Code" (Article 9).[64] Obviously, in the case of Cracow, the *terminus a quo* for the application of the *Code Napoléon* was 15 August 1810.[65]

The regulations developed between 1808 and 1809 were implemented in full in Cracow. Pursuant to Article 1 of the Royal Decree of 23 February 1809, from

62 *Dekret z 18 marca 1809 r.*, DPKW, vol. 1, 234–235.

63 DPKW, vol. 2, 84–86.

64 Ibidem, 90.

65 See above, footnote 44.

mid-August 1810, the clergy of 11 of Cracow's Catholic parishes (St Mary's, Corpus Christi, St Salvatore, St Cross, St Anne, St Florian, St Nicholas, St Stanislaus (*Skałka*), St Wenceslaus (*Wawel*), St Stephen and All Saints) began registering civil records, announcing weddings and conducting civil weddings.[66] As early as 19 August 1810, i.e. the first Sunday after the entry into force of the NC, the first civil announcements in the parish of St Mary were made "loud and clear" by the vicar, Walenty Grabowski, "performing the duties of a civil registrar". In accordance with Articles 63 and 64 of the NC, Father Grabowski drew up a record of the announcement and "nailed" it on the door of the "clerk's house".[67] After eight days, i.e. on the following Sunday, 26 August, in accordance with Article 64 of the NC, the newly appointed registrar announced and posted the second announcement.[68] The first civil wedding in St Mary's parish also took place before Vicar Grabowski on 5 September 1810, i.e. on a Wednesday, after two announcements had been made on 26 August and 2 September, i.e. again in accordance with Article 64 of the NC, allowing the marriage to take place on the third day after the second announcement at the earliest.[69]

According to the marriage certificate drawn up at the time, the ceremony itself proceeded properly, as evidenced by the diligence of the "acting registrar" in fulfilling the requirements of the *Code Napoléon*. Following Article 75 of the NC, Father Grabowski, after presenting the birth certificates (i.e. baptismal certificates) of Joachim Wocicki and Agnieszka Karwacka, as required by Article 70 of the NC, and confirming that they were 29 and 28 years old respectively and, as declared by them, residing with relatives present at the ceremony in Cracow, proceeded to confirm the consent of these relatives to the marriage (Article 73 of the NC)[70] and the absence of acts of opposition (Article 69 of the NC). Then, according to the further guidelines of Article 75 of the NC:

---

66 Fonds from the individual parishes are in: ANK, 29/328/0, 29/324/0, 29/334/0, 29/327/0, 29/323/0, 29/326/0, 29/329/0, 29/330/0, 29/333/0, 29/331/0, 29/332/0. Records kept by the clergy of the Evangelical Augsburg parish of St Martin's have also been preserved, but only from 1818 onwards, ANK, 29/325/0.

67 According to the literal wording of Article 63 of the NC, it should be the door of the "town-hall" (*maison commune*). The vicar also used this term, ANK, 29/328/2, 1 and 8.

68 Ibidem, 2–3.

69 Ibidem, 7–8.

70 This was a *superfluum*, as according to Article 76(4) of the NC, permission was required "when necessary", i.e. when the prospective spouse were minors. The age of majority for marriage, i.e. the possibility to marry independently, was, according to Article 148 of the NC, for persons who had reached the age of 25 (male) and 21 (female) respectively. On the

> "having read all the above-mentioned papers and Six of the Title of the Napoleonic Code on Marriage, we asked the future husband and wife whether they wished to be united in marriage. To which, when each of them separately answered that it is their will, we declare in the name of the law that Joachim Wocicki, bachelor, and Miss Agnieszka Karwacka are joined to each other by the bond of marriage. We have drawn up the act in the presence of" four witnesses whose names, age, state and place of residence as well as relationship to the parties have also been specified in the marriage certificate [Article 76(9) of the NC] by the vicar.[71]

The records of the civil registry of Cracow's parishes show that Catholic clergy generally performed their duties as civil registrars correctly.[72] Secular registrars were even more diligent,[73] initially acting directly on the basis of Article 4 of the Decree of 23 February 1809,[74] and then on the basis of an implementing rescript issued to by the Minister of Justice on 6 September 1811.[75] According to these regulations, in Cracow, each "municipal president" or his deputy was "the civil officer of the County and City of Cracow, [required – P.M.] to declare and record according to the law, civil divorces, also to make announcements, and to receive marriage certificates between civilly divorced persons".[76] The first such secular civil registrars were, in the years 1810–15, the mayor of the city, Stanisław Kostka Zarzecki, and his deputy and first juror, Walenty Bartsch, who drew up the first 'secular' civil registry record in Cracow, which was the announcement of the divorce of Kajetan Wytyszkiewicz and Józefa Wytyszkiewiczowa, née Sobieniowska, on 13 December 1810.[77] The first 'secular' civil wedding was conducted, and the marriage certificate drawn up, by Stanisław Zarzecki on 6 October 1811.[78]

At the turn of 1815 and 1816, i.e. at the time of the constitution of the authorities of the Free City of Cracow, regulations from the time of the Duchy of

---

other hand, the certificate rightly does not mention respectful acts (Article 76(5) of the NC), as the parents and grandparents of the bride and groom were no longer alive.

71 ANK, 29/328/2, 7–8.

72 See above, footnote 66.

73 See a fond of certificates drawn up by secular civil registrars of the city of Cracow from the period when the NC was in force in the city, i.e. from 1810–52, entitled *Akta rozwodowe z terenu gmin, powiatu i miasta Krakowa*, ANK, 29/336/0.

74 ANK, 29/336/2, 1.

75 ANK, 29/336/17, 1.

76 ANK, 29/336/2, 1.

77 ANK, 29/336/1, 1.

78 ANK, 29/336/2, 1. The spouses were Kajetan Wytyszkiewicz, a divorcee, and Marianna Toryani, a widow.

Warsaw were still in force there.[79] Directly on the basis of these, the functions of civil registrars were performed by both clergy and secular civil registrars.[80] The latter were, successively, Deputy Mayor Juror Kajetan Wytyszkiewicz (20 November 1815–10 April 1816) and Deputy Mayor Senator Feliks Grodzicki (11 April–31 July 1816).[81] As of 1 August 1816, with the abolition of the office of "municipal president" in Cracow, the related office of secular civil registrar, established by a rescript of 6 September 1811, was also abolished.[82] Therefore, by a resolution of 21 August 1816, the Ruling Senate appointed Wojciech Kucieński, *wójt* of the second commune to this post, henceforth titled "civil registrar of the City of Free Cracow".[83] The Royal Decree of 23 February 1809 remained in force in the Republic of Cracow until 1826. It was only on 1 June 1826 that it was replaced by the provisions of Articles 1–12 of the Senate Resolution of 5 May 1826. These regulated the status and duties of clerical (Articles 1–2) and secular (Article 10) registrars, and introduced new fees for the latter's activities in the Free City of Cracow.[84]

3 Consent for the Marriages of Jews from Cracow

As already indicated, the provisions introducing civil marriages and marriage certificates of the NC in Cracow also applied to the Jewish population. However, irrespective of the Code regulations, marriages of Jews, following the solutions of the Theresian era, were subjected to the regulations of the Statute of 1817. Formally, these regulations, although incompatible with the

---

79 *Urządzenie tymczasowego dla władz sądowniczych Wolnego Miasta Krakowa z 5 grudnia 1815 r.* placed civil registrars under the supervision of the Tribunal of First Instance, DRRz. WMK of 1816, 93.

80 By the decision of the Organising Commission of 10 June 1816, only the fee charged by the former was changed, DRRz.WMK of 1816, 127–140.

81 ANK, 29/336/16, 1–32. At that time, executive power in the Free City of Cracow was already exercised by the Ruling Senate, whose chairman, Stanisław Wodzicki, took over the powers of mayor.

82 DRz.WMK of 1816, No. 5, 20.

83 Ibidem; ANK, 29/336/16, 32–33. This Resolution also appointed Karol Spandel, Head of the Chrzanów Commune, as the secular civil registrar for the District, i.e. the remainder of the territory of the Republic of Cracow.

84 No. 849 DGS, Dz.Pr.RK of 1826. The validity of these provisions was confirmed by the Decree of the Ruling Senate of 30 November 1841 *Rygor na urzędników stanu cywilnego za udzielanie ślubów małżeńskich, bez poprzedniego spisania aktu cywilnego*, No. 638 DGS, DPr.WMK of 1842. It introduced a fine of 100 to 1,000 zlotys for both clerical registrars and prospective spouses for attending a church wedding "without a previous civil act".

letter and spirit of the *Code Napoléon*, had a legal basis in the constitutions of the Republic of Cracow limiting the civil rights of Jews until their full assimilation. In pursuance of these assumptions, § 17 of the Statute introduced the obligation for Jewish fiancées wishing to marry to obtain a special permit from the *wójt* (commune head).[85] This permission could be granted subject to the combined fulfilment of three conditions. The first was the possession of marital capacity according to the NC[86] and the fulfilment of the other conditions of civil law. The second was "that the future husband demonstrate a secure way of life, i.e. that he owns mortgaged land, is engaged in a craft, is a merchant, the son of a wealthy capitalist, or makes his living as a farmer or handicraftsman". The third, deferred for six years from the promulgation of the Statute, required every "young man" to be able to read and write in Polish or German and to know "the first beginnings of arithmetic", which had to be confirmed "by a certificate from superiors over schools".[87]

Formally, the consent of a *wójt* was required not for the marriage itself, but for the conclusion of the prenuptial agreement (engagement). However, the sanction of the dismissal of an official, "allowing unlawful marriages", introduced in the same provision, clearly indicates that it functionally concerned the marriage itself.[88] The aim of introducing the permission[89] was not only to control the Jews' compliance with the law, but above all to stimulate their assimilation. However, it soon became apparent that this objective would not be achieved. In the preamble to the Act of 20 December 1821, which developed the Statute, it was already pointed out that:

> the Followers of the Old Testament, by entering into religious marriages in secret,[90] and by frequently abusing the benefit of the law, which allows them to substitute proof of their age by means of witness statements, are attempting in this way to undermine the aim pursued by the provisions of

85 *Statute*, § 17.

86 According to Article 144 of the NC, 15 years for women and 18 years for men respectively.

87 Ibidem.

88 Ibidem, *in fine*.

89 The name was officially introduced in the Act of 20 December 1821 *Prawo o zapobieżeniu nadużyciom Starozakonnych*, promulgated by the Senate on 28 December 1821, No. 4831 DGS, DRRz.WMK of 1822, 5–12 (hereinafter referred to as the Act of 1821).

90 "The Followers of the Old Testament after an engagement, in the town of Kazimierz, in the suburbs, or in the District in the villages, religiously unite in secret, and there celebrate the wedding feast", DRz.WMK of 1818, No. 24, 99.

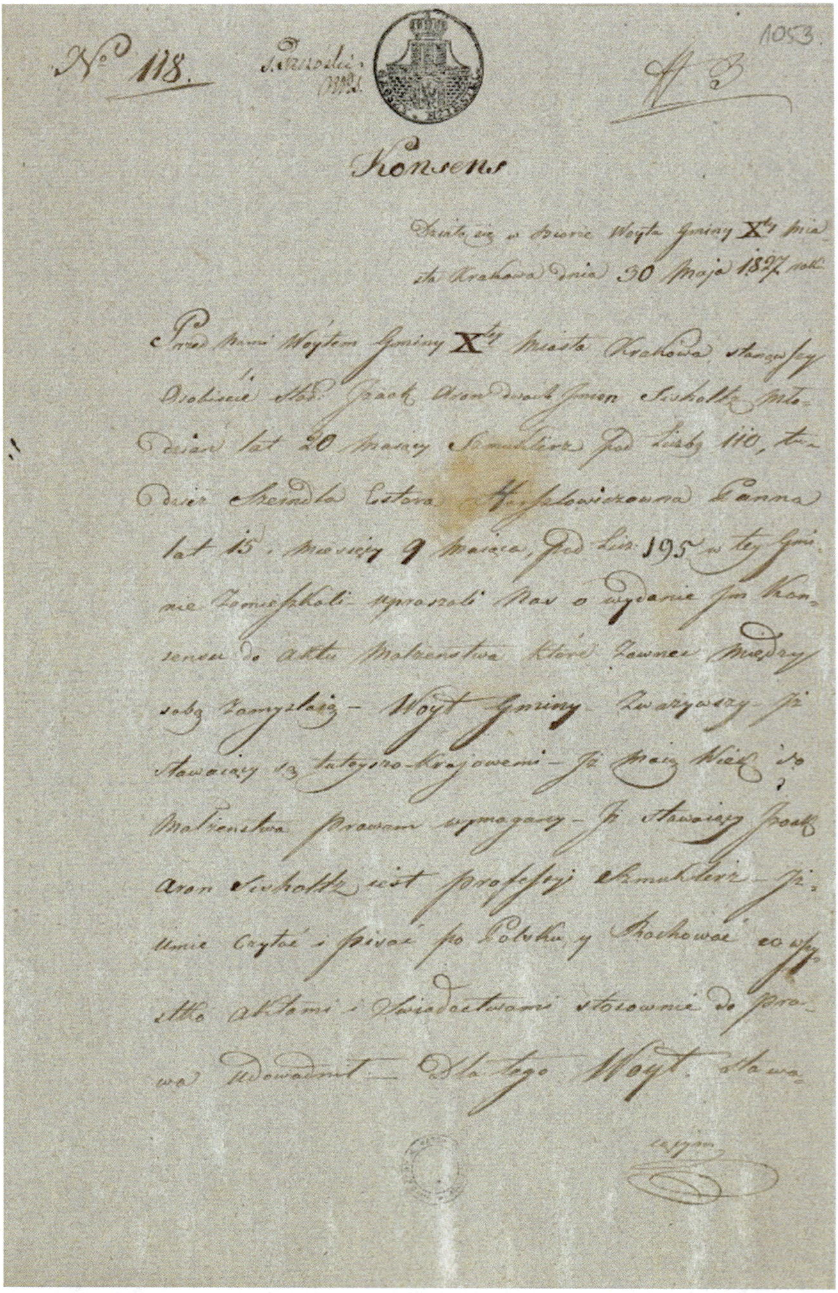
No 118.

Konsens

Działo się w biórze Woyta Gminy Xtej Miasta Krakowa dnia 30 Maja 1827 roku

FIGURE 20 *Consent for Jewish marriage* (*konsens*) *from 1827*, (manuscript, paper, 1827)
SOURCE: NATIONAL ARCHIVES IN CRACOW, ANK, 29/1472/119, 1053
PHOTO & PERMISSION BY NATIONAL ARCHIVES IN CRACOW

> the civil laws and the statute governing the organisation of the Followers of the Old Testament.[91]

The provisions of the Statute were therefore not respected, as Jews either did not enter into civil marriages at all or circumvented the law by relying on the dubious testimony of relatives and acquaintances. Furthermore, due to the fact that the provisions of the Statute were not specific enough, permissions were issued to unauthorised persons.[92]

In order to counteract "similar abuse", the Act of 1821, in force from 1 February 1822, provided for a number of sanctions for breaching the rules governing the civil marriages of Jews. First of all, it modified, with regard to the "Followers of the Old Testament", the institution of a witness statement. This was to rule out the circumvention of civil conditions, in particular the age of marital capacity. According to the amendment, the testimony of witnesses given for the purpose of drawing up a witness statement, was to be given under oath and in the presence of the prospective spouse in whose favour the testimony was given. In addition, giving or seeking to give a false testimony was qualified as the crime of fraud under § 178, Part I of the Criminal Code (*Franciscana*), and in the case where "if it turns out that in place of the right person, another person has been substituted to circumvent the law" this will be seen as judicial perjury under § 183 of the Criminal Code.[93] The scope of sanctions provided for these offences was very broad, as it ranged from six months to one year in prison in the basic type (§ 178 in conjunction with § 181 of the Criminal Code), up to a severe sentence of life imprisonment in the qualified type (§ 183 of the Criminal Code).

Not on the basis of the Criminal Code, but on the basis of Article 5 of the 1821 Act, "The Followers of the Old Testament marrying religiously, openly or secretly, without having first concluded a civil marriage contract before a competent civil registrar are to be punished".[94] The fine of 1,000 zlotys, half of which was paid to the informer, was to be imposed by the court not only on the prospective spouses, but also on the clergy and witnesses assisting at the religious ceremony. In the event of an inability to pay it, which, due to the amount of the fine, would affect the majority of prospective spouses,[95] the court converted it into a correctional arrest penalty of five days for every 30 zlotys of the fine not paid. An additional sanction provided by Article 5 was the inadmissibility of

91 The Act of 1821, preamble.

92 The Act of 1821, preamble.

93 Act of 1821, Article 3.

94 Ibidem, Article 5.

95 Cichoń 2016, 182.

legitimising illegitimate children from an exclusively religious marriage, either *per subsequens matrimonium* or by adoption. Consequently, a civil registrar who would enter legitimacy of illegitimate origin on the birth certificate of such a child would also be liable to a fine of 500 zlotys and, in case of recidivism, to dismissal.[96] Moreover, Article 2 of the Act provided for similar sanctions for a *wójt* for the issuing of an unlawful permission.[97]

The changes introduced by the 1821 Act to the regulation of § 17 of the Statute finally constituted the institution of permission for marriage of the Followers of the Old Testament in the Free City of Cracow. According to the Act, permission was formally issued no longer for the purpose of concluding a prenuptial agreement, but directly for the purpose of concluding a marriage. Moreover, obtaining a permission was a civil prerequisite for the validity of a marriage, and consequently its absence constituted its nullity. This was stated *expressis verbis* in Article 5, which refers to children born of a "civilly invalid marriage",[98] and Article 4 introducing the sanction of "nullity of the certificate" for the drawing up of a marriage certificate earlier than 30 days after the issuing of the permission for this marriage by a *wójt*.[99] The importance of the changes introduced by the Act of 1821 was confirmed by the tightening of the legal prerequisites for obtaining a permission and, in particular, by the criminal sanctions it laid down, the severity of which clearly demonstrated its deterrent function. The additional formal requirements for drawing up a marriage certificate and the sanctions protecting them, had a similar objective, especially since, in practice, a witness statement was the basic document certifying the matrimonial capacity of the prospective spouses.[100]

Like the provisions of the Statute, the regulations of 1821 also failed to produce the expected results. For the most part, Jewish marriages continued to be conducted exclusively in a religious form. In spite of this, the authorities of the Free City of Cracow maintained the existing legislation.[101] The Assembly of Representatives did not decide to amend the legislation until more than 16 years later, on 30 January 1838.[102] The preamble to the new Act acknowledged that the 1821 Act "is not sufficient to restrain the Followers of the Old

96 Act of 1821, Article 5.

97 Ibidem, Article 2.

98 Ibidem, Article 5.

99 Ibidem, Article 4.

100 See below, Chapter 5, Section 4.

101 DRz.WMK of 1824, Nos. 41–42 and of 1830, Nos. 36–37.

102 *Ustawa o karach na Starozakonnych zawierających związki małżeńskie bez poprzedniego spisania przed urzędnikiem stanu cywilnego kontraktu,* No. 539 DGS, DPr.WMK of 1838 (hereinafter referred to as the Act of 1838).

Testament from marrying religiously in secret, without a previous civil registry record". However, it also stated that the reason for this state of affairs was the lack of "certain rules for establishing evidence for the marriage secretly entered into", and that "the rigour of punishment prescribed by this Act … is not adequate".[103] Consequently, Article 1 of the new Act provided that the penalty for concluding an open or secret religious wedding without first concluding a "marriage contract" before a civil registrar would remain a fine, but the amount was doubled to 1,000 zlotys from each of the prospective spouses, clergymen and witnesses.[104] Similarly, the length of substitute correctional arrest was also increased, to six months for each of the prospective spouses, clergymen and witnesses.[105]

In addition, in Article 2, the Act introduced a new legal-procedural measure, which was, in its essence, legal proof of the fact of an illegal religious marriage. The Act provided that:

> legal proof of this kind of transgression, in the absence of the defendants' own admission, or the evidence of witnesses or accomplices, shall be the coincidence of the following two circumstances in addition to cohabitation: a) the raising of offspring, b) the cutting of the hair by the woman, and c) the use of a tallit by the man.[106]

In accordance with the will of the legislator, the provisions of the new Act, in force from 1 April 1838, were entered in place of Article 5 of the 1821 Act, which had been repealed in its entirety. This meant that the authorities of the Free City of Cracow did not intend to change the remaining regulations of the institution of the permission, and thus their previous policy towards Jewish marriages. However, the preamble of the 1838 law itself indicated that the repeal of Article 5 of the 1821 law brought about a significant change in the status of children from religious marriages contracted without a permission. This is because the "undeserved consequence" that was the prohibition of legitimation of these children both *per subsequens matrimonium* and by adoption, was abolished. The sanctions imposed on civil registrars for registering such children as legitimate on the birth certificate had also been derogated.[107]

103 Ibidem, preamble.

104 The repeal of the provision for half of the fine to be passed on to the informer probably indicates the ineffectiveness of this measure due the cohesion of the Jewish community.

105 Act of 1838, Article 1.

106 Ibidem, Article 2.

107 Ibidem, preamble *in fine*.

Subsequent amendments to the provisions on the permission occurred quite frequently, the main reason being that Jews effectively bypassed the formal requirements allowing them to enter into a civil marriage. Therefore, the subsequent Senate Regulations of 9 April 1839,[108] 28 December 1839,[109] 10 December 1841,[110] and 23 June1843,[111] successively tightened the eligibility prerequisites for fiancées, under § 17 letter b of the Statute. In particular, the Regulation of 9 April 1839 ordered the prospective spouses to submit a certificate of "local-nationality" and allowed the birth certificate to be replaced by a witness statement only on presentation of a certificate from a civil registrar stating that the former was missing,[112] while the Regulation of 10 December 1841 refused "admission to this country" to the wife of a citizen of the Free City of Cracow who had married her abroad without first obtaining the permission.[113] At the same time, the Decree of 9 April 1839 transferred the competence to issue permissions to the Department of Internal Affairs and Police in the Ruling Senate,[114] which was the consequence of the abolition of the office of *wójt* on 1 December 1838.[115]

In the assessment of the authorities of the Republic of Cracow, the numerous amendments to the regulations in the late 1830s and early 1840s also failed to produce the expected results. According to the preamble to the Act of the Assembly of Representatives of 3 July 1844, the problem was to be solved by a new comprehensive regulation of the institution of the permission, replacing the qualifying conditions for betrotheds in § 17 letter b of the Statute, and in the entirety of the Acts of 1821 and 1838.[116] In the former respect, the comprehensive Article 1 of the law detailed all the existing conditions necessary for obtaining a permission.[117] In addition, Article 1 also contained new conditions, which, depending on the age of the bridegroom, either tightened or softened the rigour of the old conditions accordingly. On the one hand, according to the Act, any "Follower of the Old Testament wishing to marry before the 30th

108 DRz.WMK of 1839, No. 25.

109 DRz.WMK of 1840, No. 6.

110 DRz.WMK of 1841, No. 13.

111 DRz.WMK of 1843, No. 93–94.

112 DRz.WMK of 1839, No. 25, point 2.

113 DRz.WMK of 1841, No. 13, point 2.

114 To which applications were to be submitted through the Police Directorate in Cracow or the district commissioners in the District.

115 DRz.WMK of 1839, No. 25, point 1.

116 *Prawo co do zawierania małżeństw przez Starozakonnych*, No. 3106 DGS, DPr.WMK of 1844 (hereinafter referred to as the Act of 1844), preamble and Article 5.

117 Ibidem. Article 1 points I–III.

year of age", irrespective of the fulfilment of all other requirements of the Act, was obliged to prove that "since the date of promulgation of this Act, has not differed in any way in his attire from Christians".[118] On the other hand, a permission could be obtained by "a Follower of the Old Testament" over 30 years of age, despite not having certificates of elementary Christian education, if he proved "that he had any way to live".[119] In the latter case, however, it was a condition that he had not previously entered into a religious marriage and that he was not cohabiting with his future wife.[120]

The repeal of the 1821 and 1838 Acts did not mean, however, that the 1844 Act abandoned the criminal law protection of the institution of the permission. According to its Article 2, the conclusion of a religious marriage by Jews openly or secretly, but without a prior civil marriage, continued to constitute a criminal offence. Unlike under previous laws, however, the 1844 law referred in this respect to the grave police offences of § 252 and § 253 of Part II of the Criminal Code.[121] Consequently, prospective spouses and "all persons giving aid and facilitation in this kind of marriages" were liable for their act as "entering into a marriage contrary to the law without a dispensation" (§ 252 of the Criminal Code), and parents or guardians for "forcing their children into a legally invalid marriage" (§ 253 of the Criminal Code). In both cases, the sanction provided for by the Code was 'strict arrest' for three to six months. This punishment, although temporally similar to the substitute punishment of correctional detention provided for by Article 1 of the 1838 Act, was nevertheless a more severe punishment, as 'strict arrest' as a qualified form was exercised with a number of restrictions, in particular the shackling of the legs and the prohibition of uncontrolled prison visits (§ 12 of Part II of the Criminal Code).[122] By analogy with the substantive law, the 1844 Act also referred to the provisions of § 360 of Part II of the Criminal Code with respect to the proceedings concerning the offence of entering into a religious marriage. Consequently, the circumstantial evidence enumerated in Article 2 of the 1838 Act indicating the conclusion of such a marriage,[123] was qualified as "circumstances", the

118 Ibidem, Article 1 *in fine*.

119 A farmer "who has been personally engaged in agricultural work for three years and who owns or leases a house and five *morgens* of land" was not subject to the requirement of elementary Christian education, but he too was subject to the requirement of Christian attire until the age of 30.

120 Act of 1844, Article 1, points IV–V.

121 Ibidem, Article 2.

122 At the same time, the problem of the unenforceability of the financial penalty sanction provided for by the previous provisions was resolved – see above, footnote 95.

123 Act of 1838, Article 2.

"confluence" of which already constituted full proof of the offence under § 252 and § 253, Part II of the Criminal Code.[124]

The provisions of the Act of 1844, the last in the history of regulation of the permission for marriage by Followers of the Old Testament in the Free City of Cracow, indicate that its aim was primarily to unify the legislation. Indeed, despite the repeal of § 17 letter b of the Statute and the Acts of 1821 and 1838, the fundamental shape of the institution of the permission was not changed. From a civilian point of view, it remained an extra-Code condition for the validity of a marriage, as is clearly evidenced by the penal provisions of the 1844 Act, treating its absence as a marital obstacle. Furthermore, Article 4 of the Act required parents wishing to register the birth of a child to submit a marriage certificate, which the registrar was obliged to mention in the birth certificate, under penalty of a fine of 500 zlotys. If a marriage certificate was not produced, the child would be registered as natural, which, as in the Act of 1838, did not, however, close the way to his or her legitimisation *per subsequens matrimonium* or through adoption.[125] Similarly, from an administrative law perspective, the permission remained a means of stimulating the assimilation of the Jewish community. At the same time, it was a measure that was far from effective, as evidenced by the small number of civil marriages concluded by Jews,[126] despite the dynamic increase in their number in the Free City of Cracow.[127]

4 The Civil Weddings and Marriage Certificates of Jews from Cracow

In the National Archives in Cracow, in the fonds *Akta stanu cywilnego Izraelickiego Okręgu Metrykalnego w Krakowie* (*Civil Registry Records of the Israeli District in Cracow*),[128] there are preserved civil registry records of the marital status of Cracovian Jews, prepared on the basis of the provisions of the NC, in force in Cracow from 15 August 1810 to 19 April 1852, i.e. until the

124 Act of 1844, Article 3.

125 Idem, Article 4. According to the same provision, it was also punishable to fail to report the birth of a child to a registrar for the purpose of drawing up a birth certificate. The sanction for this act was a fine of 20 to 200 zlotys or detention from three to 20 days.

126 See below, next subchapter.

127 Between 1818 and 1843, the number of Jewish residents in the Free City of Cracow increased twofold, from 8,522 to 16,746 people. See *Zdanie sprawy o stanie i położeniu Kraju W.M. Krakowa i Jego Okręgu w Zgromadzeniu Reprezentantów w r. 1844 przedłożone przez Senatora do tegoż Zgromadzenia delegowanego*, DPr.WMK 1844, 27–28.

128 ANK, 29/1472/0.

introduction of the marital law of the Austrian Civil Code (ABGB) in the then Grand Duchy of Cracow.[129] The first marriage certificate of Jews comes from 17 January 1811 and confirms that the civil wedding before Stanisław Dudzicz of Habdank coat of arms,[130] "a civil registrar in the commune of the city of Kazimierz near Cracow for people of the Judaic faith, established in the Cracow County and Department", was concluded by "Chaim Mojżesz Glasshut, soap maker, 25, and Miss Gitel Weiskerz, 18".[131] As was the case with Christian marriage certificates, the certificate drawn up by Dudzicz met the requirements of the *Code Napoléon*, in particular it contained the statement "in the name of the law" that the prospective spouses "are united to each other by the knot of marriage".[132] The Act also included annexes submitted by the engaged couple in the form of two witness statements, confirming their "age and status" and a certificate of the previous death of Chaim Glasshut's father, issued by the Kahal of Kazimierz, which was mentioned in the margin of the certificate.[133]

Stanisław Dudzicz, being one of two secular civil registry officials in Cracow,[134] remained a civil registrar for the Jewish community for the first 12 years, i.e. until 1822.[135] From October 1815, Dudzicz titled himself "a civil registry official in the Free City of Cracow established for persons of the Jewish faith",[136] and later also "the civil status official of the sixth, tenth and 11th commune of the Free City of Cracow established for the Followers of the Old Testament".[137] His jurisdiction in the Republic of Cracow, however, extended to all " Followers of the Old Testament residing within the city of Cracow", which was confirmed by the Senate in 1823.[138] The marriage certificates prepared by Stanisław Dudzicz in the years 1811–22 show that he duly fulfilled his obligations, both in terms of the marriage certificates themselves (Articles 63–76 of the NC) and the general requirements of keeping files and registers, i.e. civil registry books (Articles of the 34–54 of the NC).[139] Interestingly, Dudzicz also

129 In force from 20 April 1852, under the Imperial Patent of Francis Joseph I of 23 March 1852.

130 Dudzicz signed the documents he prepared as either "Stanisław Dudzicz" or "Stanisław Habdank Dudzicz". See e.g.ANK, 29/1472/20, 38–39.

131 ANK, 29/1472/6, 3.

132 Ibidem.

133 Ibidem; ANK, 29/1472/7, 3–14.

134 See above, pp. 145–146.

135 See below, Table 3.

136 ANK, 29/1472/48, 2.

137 ANK, 29/1472/68, 43.

138 DRz.WMK of 1823, No. 4, 13–14. Jews living outside Cracow, i.e. in the District, were subject to the jurisdiction of the civil registrar in Chrzanów.

139 This is confirmed by an analysis of the individual volumes of the files: ANK: 29/1472/6 [1811]; 29/1472/12 [1812]; 29/1472/20 [1813]; 29/1472/27 [1814]; 29/1472/36 and 29/1472/37

dealt with exceptional situations, such as the refusal of the parties and witnesses to sign marriage certificates due to the wedding taking place on a holy day, i.e. Saturday. Pursuant to Article 39 of the NC, he only signed the Act himself, along with the annotation that "those appearing, the parties and witnesses could not sign due to Shabbat".[140]

It is also worth emphasising that the entries in each book are continuous, "leaving no white paper" (Article 42 of the NC), and in the event of rare mistakes, a blank page is crossed out and sometimes also described.[141] Immediately after the last marriage certificate in a given year, entries are closed with an appropriate annotation dated 31 December, prepared and signed by Dudzicz in accordance with Article 43 of the NC. Moreover, on the last page of each book there is an annotation signed by the justice of the peace competent for the seat of the civil registrar (Kazimierz). Pursuant to Article 41 of the NC, he confirmed that "I numbered the book for acts of announcements, marriages and divorces for the Jewish community in Kazimierz near Cracow for the year ... covering pages ... and put initials".[142] In some of the books there is also an annotation confirming that the scribes of the Courts of the Peace have fulfilled their control duties with regard to the records and registry books (Article 53 of the NC),[143] and only in one book there is annotation by Dudzicz stating that it is a copy in accordance with "the original book deposited in the Court of the Peace".[144] The books were drawn up in two copies, one of which was transferred to the archives of a Court of the Peace and the other remained in the archives of the civil registrar, in accordance with Articles 40 and 43 of the NC.[145]

Among the duties properly performed by Stanisław Dudzicz was also the keeping of a collection of appendices to the marriage certificates, in a separate book for a given calendar year. They were described and numbered in chronological order in accordance with Article 44 of the NC.[146] For the first

---

[1815]; 29/1472/48 [1816]; 29/1472/52 [1817]; 29/1472/58 [1818]; 29/1472/63 [1819]; 29/1472/68 [1820]; 29/1472/75 [1821]; 29/1472/82 [1822], on the basis of which Table 3 was prepared.

140 ANK, 29/1472/52, 23.

141 See e.g. ANK, 29/1472/38, 1; 29/1472/75, 42–43.

142 ANK, 29/1472/48, 91.

143 See ANK, 29/1472/13, 38; 29/1472/21, 38; 29/1472/28, 43; 29/1472/47, 12.

144 ANK, 29/1472/64, 47.

145 Individual volumes of copies of the books: ANK, [lack for 1811]; 29/1472/13 [1812]; 29/1472/21 [1813]; 29/1472/28 [1814]; 29/1472/38 and 29/1472/39 [1815]; 29/1472/47 [1816]; 29/1472/53 [1817]; 29/1472/59 [1818]; 29/1472/64 [1819]; 29/1472/69 [1820]; 29/1472/76 [1821]; 29/1472/83 [1822].

146 Individual volumes: ANK, 29/1472/7 [1811]; 29/1472/14 [1812]; 29/1472/22 [1813]; 29/1472/29 [1814]; 29/1472/40 [1815]; 29/1472/49 [1816]; 29/1472/54 [1817]; 29/1472/60 [1818]; 29/1472/65 [1819]; 29/1472/70 [1820]; 29/1472/77 [1821]; 9/1472/84 [1822].

TABLE 3 Civil registry for Jewish population in Cracow (1811–22)

Year	Civil registrar	Number of civil marriages	Requirements of articles 34–54 and articles 63–76 of the NC	Requirements of the 1817 Statute and the 1821 Act – permission	Justice of the peace	Remarks
1811	Stanisław [Habdank] Dudzicz	23	fulfilled	not required	Konstanty Chościak-Popiel	lack of the second copy of the book
1812	Stanisław [Habdank] Dudzicz	36	fulfilled	not required	Mikołaj Gostkowski	lack of one entry on card 71
1813	Stanisław [Habdank] Dudzicz	35	fulfilled	not required	Stanisław Mieroszewski	
1814	Stanisław [Habdank] Dudzicz	41	fulfilled	not required	Stanisław Mieroszewski	
1815	Stanisław [Habdank] Dudzicz	16	fulfilled	not required	Mikołaj Gostkowski	records till August
	Erazm Bieniecki [deputy]	2	fulfilled	not required	Jan Rudnicki	records of November; no index

TABLE 3 Civil registry for Jewish population in Cracow (1811–22) (*cont.*)

Year	Civil registrar	Number of civil marriages	Requirements of articles 34–54 and articles 63–76 of the NC	Requirements of the 1817 Statute and the 1821 Act – permission	Justice of the peace	Remarks
1816	Stanisław [Habdank] Dudzicz	11	fulfilled	not required	Stanisław Mieroszewski	records from October to December
1817	Stanisław [Habdank] Dudzicz	23	fulfilled	not required for ten weddings; lack of mention and appendix for 13 weddings	Jan Nepomucen Gaspary	
1818	Stanisław [Habdank] Dudzicz	28	fulfilled	lack of mention and appendix for all weddings	Jan Nepomucen Gaspary	mistake in page numbering from card 21
1819	Stanisław [Habdank] Dudzicz	44	fulfilled	lack of mention and appendix for all weddings	Szczepan Lubowiecki	in record no.1 on card three, December was erroneously entered instead of January
1820	Stanisław [Habdank] Dudzicz	42	fulfilled	lack of mention and appendix for all weddings	Szymon Białecki	

TABLE 3 Civil registry for Jewish population in Cracow (1811–22) (*cont.*)

Year	Civil registrar	Number of civil marriages	Requirements of articles 34–54 and articles 63–76 of the NC	Requirements of the 1817 Statute and the 1821 Act – permission	Justice of the peace	Remarks
1821	Stanisław [Habdank] Dudzicz	53	fulfilled	lack of mention and appendix for all weddings	Wojciech Like	
1822	Stanisław [Habdank] Dudzicz	23	fulfilled	lack of mention for all weddings but there are permissions in the appendices	Wojciech Like	records January (18) and February 1822 (5); (the latter formally invalid!)
	Wojciech Kucieński	24	fulfilled	mentions (19) and appendices (18) for all weddings, except non-local-nationals (five)	Wojciech Like	records from April to December; no appendices for the marriage certificate of 16 June 1822

SOURCE – SEE ABOVE, FOOTNOTE 139.

eight years of Dudzicz's time in office, the vast majority of documents filed in appendices were birth witness statements drawn up "to replace a birth certificate".[147] They were the almost exclusive proof of the parties' marital capacity, as well as of their majority, conditioning the possibility of marriage without the consent of their parents or relatives.[148] Only exceptionally were these prerequisites established on the basis of excerpts or certificates from records kept outside Cracow.[149] Due to the minority of most prospective spouses, parental consent was necessary for the validity of the marriage, and this condition was meticulously verified by Dudzicz, certainly also in view of the sanctions provided for in Article 156 of the NC. As a rule, the parents or, in the event of their prior death, the grandparents, present at the wedding gave their consent orally before the registrar, who recorded this fact in the marriage certificate in accordance with Article 76(4) of the NC.[150] A document containing parental consent to marriage was therefore attached relatively rarely in the appendices,[151] the exception being the minutes of family councils meetings giving their consent to marriage pursuant to Article 160 of the NC.[152]

A partial change in the composition of the appendices took place in 1819, when birth certificates began to be replaced by extracts drawn up by Dudzicz himself from Jewish birth records kept by the Austrian authorities between 1798 and 1809.[153] This was made possible by the finding and putting in order in 1818 of the records in question, and handing them over to Dudzicz for "official use",[154] which *nota bene* coincided with the entry of the persons covered by them into the age of marital capacity. This state of affairs continued between 1820 and 1822, but the majority of the records still consisted of witness statements.[155] It is worth emphasising that, contrary to the literal wording of the

147 ANK, 29/1472/49, 5.

148 An interesting practice, not explicitly resulting from the law, was the insertion of remarks on the appearance of the persons included in the record, i.e. the future spouses, by the sub-judges or scribes of the Courts of the Peace. As a rule, they express their acceptance of the age given by the witnesses. However, doubts do occur, as in the certficate of 30 April 1811: "Although it is difficult to determine that the Jewish woman Drobne Adelung on Saint Michael's Day of the current year will be 16 years old, as the witnesses testify, nevertheless it seems to the undersigned that Drobne Adelung according to her sex and body arrangement may be those years old, the more so that the Jews morally maintaining themselves, even if they are older, seem to be younger"., ANK, 29/1472/7, 83.

149 See e.g. ANK, 29/1472/7, 29.

150 See above, footnote 139.

151 See e.g. ANK, 29/1472/60, 37 and 39; 29/1472/77, 179.

152 See e.g. ANK, 29/1472/77, 309–312.

153 ANK, 29/1472/65, 1 and 3.

154 ANK, 29/200/407, 118–119; ANK, 29/1472/65, 197.

155 See e.g. ANK, 29/1472/70, 117 i 119; 29/1472/77, 93 and 95.

amended Articles 70 and 71 of the NC, promulgated by the Royal Decree of 18 March 1809, witness statements were drawn up in Cracow not by the locally competent mayor or *wójt*, but by the sub-judge of the county and city at the time of the Duchy of Warsaw, or by the scribe of a Court of the Peace at the time of the Free City. However, according to the letter of Article 72 of the NC, these statements were approved by a justice of the peace "at the request of a public office", i.e. a sub-judge or scribe acting as a prosecutor at that time.[156]

The second half of Stanisław Dudzicz's years in office coincides with the entry into force of the Statute of 1817. In § 17, it obliged civil registrars to keep separate books of births, marriages and divorces and the deaths of Jews. These books were to be kept according to general principles, i.e. in accordance with the modified provisions of the NC.[157] As already indicated, this issue did not pose any major difficulties, as these requirements had already been implemented in practice from 1811 onwards. What was new, however, was the introduction of the institution of the permission and the regulations associated with it. Formally, these regulations entered into force on 30 June 1817, meaning that a Jewish wedding concluded after that date should be preceded by obtaining a permission from the *wójt*. However, in the marriage certificates drawn up by Dudzicz between 1817 and 1821, we do not find a mention of the permission.[158] Also, in the attached appendices, there are no documents concerning the requirements of § 17 of the Statute, in particular the permissions themselves.[159] In the light of the above, it may be presumed that Stanisław Dudzicz was of the opinion that the Statute did not impose any additional obligations on him as a civil registrar, and that obtaining or not obtaining a permission was irrelevant from the point of view of the validity of the wedding and the marriage certificate itself.

---

156 See e.g. ANK, 29/1472/22, 9–12; 29/1472/49, 9–12. It can therefore be concluded that the assessment of the state of civil status registration inherited from the Duchy of Warsaw, presented by Senator Wojciech Kucieński to the Assembly of Representatives on 10 December 1818, was too harsh, at least as far as Jewish records were concerned. In it, Kucieński pointed out that "The introduction into the order of civil registry records, which have a beneficial influence on almost the entire course of the lives of the inhabitants, was the subject of the efforts of the Government and the judicial authorities, whose task it is by law to watch over their maintenance. When our Government found them in disorder, it detected numerous shortcomings in the form of books and records and inadequacies in the administration, it punished those responsible and saw to it that the shortcomings were rectified", ANK, 29/200/407, 118–119. It is likely that Kucieński, who was also a secular civil registrar, wished to emphasise his contribution in this field.

157 *Statute*, § 17.

158 See above, footnote 139 and Table 3.

159 See above, footnote 146.

However, the situation changed radically in late 1821 and early 1822, undeniably due to the enactment and promulgation of the 1821 Act amending the regulations of the Statute. Although the new law did not come into force until 1 February 1822, at a wedding concluded on 3 January 1822, Dudzicz included the permission by the *wójt* of Commune X of the City of Cracow, Maciej Mączeński, in the appendices. It stated that:

> the Followers of the Old Testament, Dawid Früciuf and Gitla Treibitz ... proved their age as prescribed by law ... and being of a tailor's profession from which they can make a living, and for this being authorised by a rescript of the Ruling Senate ... for these reasons we have issued a permission for them to enter into marriage, sending them back to the competent registrar for the performance of what the law requires.[160]

The same was the case with a further 22 weddings concluded before Stanisław Dudzicz in 1822.[161] However, until the end of his *de facto* term of office, i.e. 24 February 1822, Dudzicz did not mention in the marriage certificates that the prospective spouses had submitted a permission from the competent *wójti*.[162] It seems that his sudden recall of the requirement for the prospective spouses to obtain permissions, was forced upon Dudzicz by the Senate, and that he himself was opposed to the radicalism of the 1821 Act. This is evidenced not only by his resignation on 19 February 1822,[163] but it also turns out that the last five marriage certificates drawn up by him in February 1822 were technically invalid under Article 4 of the 1821 Act. This was because they occurred earlier "than within 30 days" of the issue of permissions for the conclusion of these marriages by the *wójt*.[164]

In such circumstances, Dudzicz's duties were taken over by Wojciech Kucieński, who had been responsible for the civil status records of divorced Christians from 1816, thus combining in one person both functions of a secular

160 ANK, 29/1472/84, 1.

161 Ibidem, 17, 29, 41, 53, 65, 77, 93, 109, 121, 133, 145, 157, 177, 193, 205, 221, 233, 245, 257, 269, 281 and 293.

162 ANK, 29/1472/82, 3–25.

163 DRz.WMK of 1822, No. 6, 21. The resignation was accepted on 22 February 1822. After his resignation, Dudzicz drew up three more marriage certificates: on 20, 22 and 24 February 1822, ANK, 29/1472/82, 23–25.

164 Ibidem, 21–25; ANK, 29/1472/84, 245, 257, 269, 281 and 293. This fact has not been officially established. Had this occurred, Dudzicz would have been fined 1,000 zlotys, as he could no longer be dismissed: Act of 1821, Article 4.

civil registrar in Cracow.[165] Although it is not apparent from the act of his appointment, there is no doubt that Kucieński's main task was to finally implement the legislation on the permission. The new "civil registrar of the Jewish communes" did not disappoint the Senate, and meticulously verified the legality of the marriages entered into by Jews.[166] This is evidenced by references to the submission of permissions by prospective spouses contained in subsequent marriage records from 1822.[167] They appear not only in those records where the fiancé was a foreigner, and so was not required to obtain a permission.[168] At the same time, the issuing dates of the permissions in the appendices confirm that Kucieński also observed the 30-day time limit in Article 4 of the 1821 Act.[169] This state of affairs continued in the subsequent years of the service of Wojciech Kucieński, who remained in his position as registrar until 1838,[170] but in the years 1825–28 he was temporarily replaced by Szymon Białecki, the *wójt* of Commune I of the City of Cracow.[171]

It is worth noting that the small number of civil marriages contracted by Jews during the tenure of Stanisław Dudzicz,[172] only slightly increased during the term of office of Wojciech Kucieński. In the 1820s, it still amounted to only several dozen marriages per year, and in the 1830s it approached 100. The lowest annual number of civil weddings in that period concluded by Jews was in 1823 (only 43), and the highest (117), ten years later in 1833.[173] These statistics remained at a similar level during the last decade of the existence of the Republic of Cracow. At that time, from 1 June 1838, the registrar for the Jewish residents of the city of Cracow was Franciszek Salezy Gawroński.[174] During his

165 DRz.WMK of 1822, nr 6, 21. See also above, footnote 156.

166 See above, Table 3.

167 ANK, 29/1472/82, 26–56.

168 Ibidem, 32–33, 49–54. Three were from the Kingdom of Poland, one from Galicia and one from Hungary.

169 ANK, 29/1472/84, 309, 325, 337, 361, 393, 409, 421, 437, 453, 465, 485, 505, 521, 533, 549, 567, 647, 667.

170 See individual volumes of marriage certificates: ANK, 29/1472/89 [1823]; 29/1472/96 [1824]; 29/1472/103 [1825 – substituted by Białecki]; 29/1472/110 [1826 – substituted by Białecki]; 29/1472/117 [1827 – substituted by Białecki]; 29/1472/124 [1828 – substituted by Białecki]; 29/1472/132 [1829]; 29/1472/139 [1830]; 29/1472/146 [1831]; 29/1472/153 [1832]; 29/1472/160 [1833]; 29/1472/165 [1834]; 29/1472/172 [1835]; 29/1472/179 [1836]; 29/1472/185 [1837]; 29/1472/192 [1838].

171 In December 1824, Kucieński was elected by the Assembly of Representatives to the Ruling Senate. See DRz.WMK 1825, nr 3–4, 15.

172 See above, Table 3.

173 See footnote 170.

174 DRz.WMK of 1838, Nos. 38–39, 149.

term of office, most weddings, 102, were celebrated in 1844, the fewest (only 27) in 1848. Formally, Gawroński retained his position even after the annexation of the Free City by Austria in 1846, until the introduction of the ABGB in 1852. However, the Jewish marriage records were kept then by his deputy Filip Etgens.[175]

5 Conclusion

Undoubtedly, the introduction of the French marriage law of the *Code Napoléon* in Cracow in 1810 was a landmark event for its inhabitants. The Code provisions regulating the registration of a marriage by a State official and, in particular, the entry into marriage in the form of civil wedding, were complete novelties in the Polish legal culture of the time. Therefore, it is particularly noteworthy that these provisions were actually applied, and generally very meticulously. This was certainly facilitated by their technical nature and their clarity and precision, which did not hinder the work of officials. At the same time, the new system of civil status registration very quickly revealed its advantages for the functioning and development of the State administration, and was therefore strongly supported by it. It is worth noting, however, that both the authorities of the Duchy of Warsaw and of the Free City of Cracow decided not to create a civil service corps, entrusting the keeping of civil status records to the clergy of individual denominations, mainly Catholic. This meant that for the Christian majority of Cracow's inhabitants, the new system of civil status registration was introduced in its old form and thus was not revolutionary in nature.

The situation was different for the community of Cracow's Jews however, who were not Christian and were subject to the rigours of the Government's assimilation policy. As Jewish clergy were excluded from acting as civil registrars of their religion, this position was entrusted to secular officials. Consequently, for the Jews, not only the letter, but also the spirit of the post-revolutionary NC, was fully applied in this regard. Yet, since the Constitution of the Free City of Cracow allowed for a restriction of the civil rights of the 'Followers of the Old

175 See individual volumes of marriage records: ANK, 29/1472/192 [1838]; 29/1472/199 [1839 –partly substituted by Etgens]; 29/1472/207 [1840 – substituted by Etgens]; 29/1472/213 [1841 – partly substituted by Etgens]; 29/1472/221 [1842]; 29/1472/227 [1843]; 29/1472/235 [1844]; 29/1472/241 [1845]; 29/1472/248 [1846 – partly replacing Etgens]; 29/1472/255 [1847 – partly substituted for Etgens]; 29/1472/262 [1848 – substituted by Etgens]; 29/1472/270 [1849 – substituted by Etgens]; 29/1472/276 [1850 – substituted by Etgens]; 29/1472/283 [1851 – substituted by Etgens]; 29/1472/290 [1852 – substituted by Etgens].

Testament', the provisions of the *Code Napoléon* were modified with regard to them by the Statute of 1817 and its subsequent amendments. In particular, this was by the Act of 1821, which constituted, unknown to the NC, a marital obstacle in the form of the lack of the *wójt*'s permission to marry. The rigorism of this regulation, backed up at the same time by severe criminal sanctions for Jews entering into exclusively religious marriages, was contrary not only to the letter but also to the spirit of the *Code Napoléon*, which departed from the original radicalism of the French secular model of marriage.

An analysis of the application of the provisions of the NC by Cracow's civil officials and judges, shows that they were competent and committed to the process of building a new legal and administrative system. However, in the social perspective, their work did not have much direct effect, as the resistance of the Jewish population to the assimilation policy of the Government proved to be extremely effective. This is evidenced both by the small number of civil marriages concluded by 'Followers of the Old Testament' during the entire period under discussion, and by the powerlessness of the authorities of the Free City of Cracow in their efforts

to force Jews to enter into such marriages. Irrespective of the above, the fact remains that the French marriage laws, with the secular registration of marriage certificates and civil weddings, which are today the basic institutions of Polish marriage law, were first applied for an extended period of time, from 1810 to 1852, in Cracow.

CHAPTER 6

Servitudes, Expropriations and Possessory Protection

Mateusz Mataniak

1 Servitudes

1.1 *General Remarks*

In the books of court judgments from the period of the Free City of Cracow, one can find numerous traces of proceedings concerning two land servitudes: party walls and view rights.[1] These were servitudes of an "urban" nature, and the drafters of the NC devoted the whole of Title IV: "Of Servitudes or Manorial Services" (Articles 637–710), within Book II ("Of Property, and the Different Modifications of Property") to the issue. Under the Code, servitudes were, of course, in addition to the right of ownership, the main right *in rem*; at the same time, they were the most important limited right *in rem*, alongside usufruct. They were of Roman origin and, as perceived by ancient jurists, belonged to so-called 'rights in foreign affairs' (*iura in re aliena*).[2] Personal servitudes disappeared from the NC, while land servitudes, called, depending on their location, rural or urban, remained. The latter include the right: a) to drain rainwater onto a neighbour's land; b) to build a beam from one's own building into the wall of a neighbour's building; c) to lean a building against the wall of a neighbour's building; and d) to open a window over a neighbour's land. Land servitudes can consist of abandonment (*non facere*), as in the case of urban servitudes, or of abolition (*pati*) (rural servitudes). This was expressed by the principle: *servitus in faciendo consistere nequit*. The servient land also had be useful to its each owner at any time.[3]

1 The discussion presented in this subchapter is an abridged and modified version of the author's article: Mataniak 2021, 11–65.

2 The definition proposed by Hube 1877, 333, states that a servitude is a right encumbering another person's land, which consists in increasing the utility or multiplying the benefits of the owner of the land to whom the servitude is granted.

3 Litewski 1999, 222–223. Of contemporary studies on servitudes in general, see Picard 1952, 866–879.

 | DOI:10.1163/9789004688742_008

On the basis of the archival material examined, it can be concluded that the inhabitants of Cracow litigated in cases concerning such servitudes as party walls (Articles 653–673 of the NC), the view rights (Articles 675–680 of the NC) and the right of drainage from roofs (Article 681 of the NC).[4] The first of these institutions is based on the fact that neighbours share a wall or other fence separating two buildings, up to the roof line ("up to the top of the lower building"). A wall can also separate courtyards, gardens, etc. The co-ownership of the wall refers to the entire thickness of the wall, with further consequences for the co-owners, including the obligation to repair and alter it, if necessary. Relief from these obligations was only possible through a "waiver of the right of middleness"; however, this right is not available to the owner of a building supported by the party wall. The issue of "middleness" entails a number of advantages, including the ability to make additions, to let in beams and to raise the wall at one's own expense and with due regard for the interests of one's neighbour; in doing so, one must take into account the need to compensate for any damage caused to the wall (Articles 653, 655–659 of the NC). The erection of a party wall or the making of an existing wall into a party wall – by means of the acquisition of a "middleness" (Articles 660–661 of the NC) – is usually associated with the exercise of a servitude of view or light. A kind of opposite of a party wall is the so-called 'non-middle wall', which is the exclusive property of one of the neighbours.[5]

1.2 *An Analysis of Cases Concerning Servitudes*

The discussion of some of the most interesting cases in this area will allow the identification of the most important juridical problems faced by Cracow's judges and advocates, as well as the ways in which they were resolved under the NC.

In the case of Stefan and Salomea Borkowscy versus Isaac Wermuth, concerning a tenement house in Kazimierz in Żydowska Street, its purchaser (Wermuth) wished to obtain a view of the neighbouring property belonging to the Borkowscy. This could only be done by removing bricks from two

4 French authors point out that the institutions of the servitude of the right of view and drainage were taken from the Coutume de Paris and not from Roman law. See Ourliac and Malafosse 1971, 404; Halperin 2004b, 48–49. On the legal sources of the NC, see Basdevant-Gaudemet and Gaudemet 2000, 375–377.

5 Also in the practice of the Paris courts, the question of the party wall raised many doubts. Hence, on the basis of, *inter alia*, the Coutume de Paris, there was a presumption that a wall was a party wall unless the circumstances clearly indicated otherwise. In addition, an enumeration of signs of non-middleness followed: Ourliac, Malafosse 1971, 404–405.

FIGURE 21 *Seal of the Tribunal of the Free City of Cracow and its District*, (seal matrix, brass, 1st half of the 19th century)
SOURCE: NATIONAL ARCHIVES IN CRACOW, ANK, 29/661/213; PHOTO & PERMISSION BY NATIONAL ARCHIVES IN CRACOW

formerly bricked-up windows of his house. Following an inspection of the building, Wermuth's idea was approved by a police and building committee, which included engineers from the Building Authority and an officer from the Intermediate Police Office. Administrative approval was given by the Police Department of the Ruling Senate. The Borkowscy protested against these decisions by applying to the Court of the Peace with a demand to grant them possessory protection, which was to keep them in peaceful possession of the immovable property.[6] Accordingly, Wermuth requested that the exclusive ownership of the wall separating the two properties be adjudicated in his favour. It would thus become a 'non-middle' wall, which would enable Wermuth to enjoy the privileges of Article 676 of the NC, i.e. the ability to "make openings

6 *Notta Oppozycyjna ze strony Starozakonnego Izaaka Wermuth przeciwko Stefanowi i Salomei Borkowskim małżonkom*, ANK, 29/200/1723 (WM 250), 445–446. In this case, peaceful possession of the immovable property consisted of Wermuth having to refrain from interfering with his own property (making a window), as the owner of the servient land.

for a view, or a window with an iron lattice, and with a glazing which does not open".[7] The Borkowscy therefore then began to claim that they had acquired joint ownership of the wall by usucaption, as the time of use by the previous owners of the house should be added to their period of possession. The resulting middleness of the wall prevented Wermuth from making windows without their consent as neighbours (Article 675 of the NC). His claim was ultimately nullified by his failure to exercise the servitude for 30 years, resulting in its loss (Article 706 of the NC).[8]

The justice of the peace examining the possessory claim ordered Wermuth to immediately brick up the recently made windows, due to the content of the aforementioned Article 675 of the NC. This did not cause any objection of the Court of Appeal hearing the appeal, which also strongly objected to the examination by the Court of the Peace of petitory issues.[9] However, Wermuth did not give up and, through his advocate, pointed out further circumstances in favour of his right of view in relation to the neighbouring property. He thus argued that the right of view was a land servitude and therefore vested in each successive owner of the property. He argued that it had been exercised throughout the years 1787–1819, and that, since the Borkowscy had tolerated servitude on the property for so long, they could not now deny it to him (prohibiting "the opening of new windows, in an equal or superior line with the former ones"). Wermuth's representative also argued that the servitude of the party wall should be considered "continuous and visible" (Articles 688–689 of the NC),[10] and therefore such which, pursuant to Article 690 of the NC, may be acquired by usucaption.[11] He also questioned the evidentiary force of the

---

7 Ibidem, 446–447.

8 This non-exercise of the servitude consisted of "not using the right of opening". *Obrona ze strony Borkowskiej pko Wermuthowi*, ANK, 29/200/1660 (WM 187), 179–181. The window servitude can be viewed in two ways: as an opportunity to look onto the neighbour's property, which the neighbour must endure; or, alternatively, as prohibiting the neighbour from erecting structures above a certain height that would prevent that view.

9 *Notta Oppozycyjna ze strony Starozakonnego Izaaka Wermuth przeciwko Stefanowi i Salomei Borkowskim małżonkom*, ANK, 29/200/1723 (WM 250), 448–450.

10 Article 688 (1): "Servitudes are either continual or interrupted. Continual servitudes are those whose use is or may be continual without having a necessity for the positive act of man: such are water-pipes, house-eaves, windows, and other things of that description". Article 689 (1): "Apparent servitudes are those which are manifested by external works, such as a gate, a window, or aqueduct".

11 Article 690: "Continual and apparent servitudes are acquired by deed, or by possession for 30 years". Article 707: "The 30 years begin to run according to the different species of servitudes, either from the day on which they have ceased to be enjoyed, when the case regards interrupted servitudes, or from the day on which an act has been made contrary to the servitude, in the case of continual servitudes".

documents submitted by his opponents, which were supposed to support the co-ownership of the wall (an expert opinion; a protocol of the court "window revision" of 1783; a verdict of the Magistrate of Kazimierz of 1784). However, the only useful document, in the form of a decree of the Magistrate of Cracow, was dated 1793, and thus did not confirm the lapse of 30 years of peaceful possession, as of 1819. The middleness of the wall, "from the foundations to the present height", was also supposed to be contradicted by the fact that the co-ownership of the wall was not declared at the successive auctions of the house.[12]

Wermuth's arguments were rebutted by the Borkowscy in a reply read out to the Court of Appeal. They pointed to the presumption of Article 653 of the NC that any neighbourhood wall is in principle 'common' (this is supported e.g. by the public interest), and it is precisely on the party claiming otherwise, i.e. Wermuth, to prove to the contrary (*ei incumbit probatio qui dicit, non qui negat*). Wermuth could have done so by citing any legal title, e.g. a contract, or "signs to the contrary" proving that the wall was non-middle, however he failed to do so. The Borkowscy also defended the credibility of the documents they presented: the protocol of the judicial inspection (1783) was officially approved, and thus functioned as a fully-fledged official document and thus as fully-fledged evidence, the credibility of which could only be challenged with a suspicion of forgery, which, however, Wermuth did not do; acting "against the wording" of the document, on the other hand, was inadmissible. The allegation that the Magistrate's judgment (1784) had been overturned by the Governor's judgment (1793) was at least partly inaccurate, as it actually concerned two separate issues: peaceful possession and the reimbursement of the costs of reparation of the building. With regard to the allegation of failure to notify the co-ownership of the wall, they replied that only possible mortgage creditors had been summoned at the auction of the house; there was no need to do so in relation to the co-owners of the wall, as no threat to the durability of its structure had been identified.[13]

---

12 *Notta Oppozycyjna ze strony Starozakonnego Izaaka Wermuth przeciwko Stefanowi i Salomei Borkowskim małżonkom*, ANK, 29/200/1723 (WM 250), 449–455. He also submitted evidence to the court in the form of a receipt issued by one of the monasteries, proving that the Borkowscy's predecessors had "acquired only an empty square, but not the co-ownership of the wall".

13 The prosecutor's receipt could not be counter-evidence to the inspection protocol and the Magistrate's verdict, as evidence which was too trivial: *Odpowiedź ze strony Borkowskich pko Wermuthom*, ANK, 29/200/1723 (WM 250), 457–458; *Obrona ze strony Borkowskiej pko Wermuthowi*, ANK, 29/200/1660 (WM 187), 179–181. There were also doubts as to whether the findings of the "committee in political line" could be evidence of the co-ownership of

The Court essentially accepted the Borkowscy's arguments, finding that they had demonstrated their rights with documentation from 1783–84 and, as a result of 30 years of use, had acquired by usucaption the co-ownership of the wall from the previous owners. At the same time, Wermuth did not use the right of view ("the opening of the bricked-up windows"), as a result of which he lost it under Article 706 of the NC.[14] He also undertook "changes that would increase the burden on the servient land" prohibited by Article 702 of the NC, in contravention of the Roman maxim *servitutibus civiliter utendum est*.[15] The Tribunal's judgment was upheld in its entirety by the Court of Appeal.[16] Wermuth therefore exercised his right to appeal to the Faculty of Professors and Doctors of Law of Jagiellonian University.[17] The Faculty found that the proper resolution of the case depended on answering the following questions. First, whether the documents submitted by the Borkowscy indeed constitute evidence of the co-ownership of the wall; and second, whether the servitude of the wall had been acquired by usucaption as a result of 30 years of possession? The Law Faculty held that the judicial review (1783), as "unilaterally effected", did not constitute evidence of co-ownership of the wall. The same was true of the Magistrate's judgment (1784), which was overturned by a decree of the Governor (1793). A serious negligence on the part of the Borkowscy was the failure to notify the co-ownership of the wall, on the occasion of the auction. And since other provisions of the NC were also violated (Articles 544, 690, 1315, 2240, 2229, 2268), to which the adjudicating courts paid no attention, the Faculty of Law concluded that the Borkowscy had "neither by title nor by 30-year possession acquired the right to the co-ownership of the wall", and thus gave place to an appeal to

---

the wall, as the law provided for "forms under nullity" in this case, in the form of expert testimony and "eyewitness opinion".

14 Article 706: "Servitude is extinguished by non-usage during 30 years". In this context, the court also pointed to Article 2229 of the NC ("In order to be able to prescribe, there is required possession continual and uninterrupted, peaceable, public, unequivocal, and under the title of proprietor") and Article 2262 of the NC ("All actions, as well real as personal, are prescribed by 30 years, without compelling the party who alleges it to produce a document thereon, or without permitting an objection to be opposed to him derived from bad faith").

15 *Notta Oppozycyjna ze strony Starozakonnego Izaaka Wermuth przeciwko Stefanowi i Salomei Borkowskim małżonkom*, ANK, 29/200/1723 (WM 250), 449–450, containing a description of the judgment of the Tribunal of the First Instance of 26 January 1821. Due to the "indecency of the act", the court sentenced Wermuth to court costs.

16 Court of Appeal judgments: of 7 October 1823; of 10 October 1822 (in default), ANK, 29/200/1723 (WM 250), 441–442.

17 See above, A. Dziadzio. Chapter 1, Section 2.

the Court of Cassation.[18] However, the Third Instance Court did not share the Law Faculty's position, twice upholding the lower courts' decisions.[19] During the course of the cassation proceedings, the parties consistently reiterated the arguments used in the lower instances.[20]

Similar legal doubts arose in the case of Ignacy and Klara Raab, owners of a tenement house at No. 46 Stolarska Street, versus Franciszek Wysocki, owner of a house at No. 30 Grodzka Street. The possessory protection for the exercise of the view servitude was granted by a justice of the peace on the basis of witness testimony and expert opinions. In their rulings, the courts confirmed that the right of view was a continuous and visible servitude, and could therefore be acquired by way of usucaption (*per prescriptione longissimi temporis*; Articles 688–689 of the NC). The parties proved the usucaption by means of official documents and witness testimony. In doing so, the Court was assisted by expert opinions ("expert reports"). The consequences of declaring a wall to be either co-owned or 'not middle' were examined, as well as the party's observance of the appropriate distance of a window made in the wall from the neighbouring property (Articles 676–680 of the NC), etc.[21]

The reporting of servitudes also appeared in the case, in connection with the regulation of mortgages then underway in the Free City of Cracow (see above).[22] On the latter issue, the Raabs argued, citing a decision of the

18 The opinion of the Faculty of Law of Jagiellonian University of 19 November 1823, Dziadzio and Mataniak eds. 2022, 131–132. In general, the Faculty agreed with Wermuth's argumentation; the exception was the recognition that the prosecutor's receipt only proves the acquisition of an empty square. The opinion was issued by: Mikołaj Hoszowski, Augustyn Boduszyński, Feliks Słotwiński, Father Mateusz Dubiecki and Antoni Matakiewicz.

19 Judgment of the Court of Third Instance of 4 March 1824, ANK, 29/200/1660 (WM 187), 69–70; Judgment of the Court of Third Instance of 22 April 1824, ibidem, 171–172. In general, the Court of Third Instance accepted the Borkowscy's arguments.

20 *Nota Oppozycyjna ze strony Starozak. Jakuba Wermuth pko Salomei Borkowskiej wdowie*, ANK, 29/200/1660 (WM 187), 175–176; *Obrona ze strony Borkowskiej pko Wermuthowi*, ibidem, 179–181.

21 An account by the reporting judge of 12 April 1839, ANK, 29/200/1683 (WM 210), 991–992; *Odpowiedź Wysockiego na Uciążliwości Raabów*, ANK, 29/200/1670 (WM 197), 1383–1386; judgement of the Tribunal of First instance of 24 February 1832, ANK, 29/200/2007 (Tryb 204), no pagination; *Odpowiedź Raabów na Punkt Incydentalny Wysockiego*, ANK, 29/200/2007 (Tryb 204), no pagination; *Pozew rekurrujących Raabów* of 12 June 1833, ANK, 29/200/1670 (WM 197), 1022–1028.

22 From 1822 onwards, owners of immovable property, persons claiming to have a superior or equal right as to the property, as well as persons entitled to rights *in rem* and claiming debts and encumbrances on mortgages, were summoned by the Mortgage Commission to submit evidence on which their right was based. See Malec 2004, 88–89. The question of whether it was necessary for a servitude to be entered in the mortgage books in order to establish a servitude on an immovable property, was discussed during the extraordinary

Mortgage Commission, that the reporting had been neglected by one of the previous owners of the house at No. 30.[23] Feliks Słotwiński, Wysocki's attorney, incorrectly argued that this allegedly belonged to the person who derived the legal consequences from it.[24]

The issue of the reconstruction of a party wall (Articles 658–660 of the NC) was reflected in the case of Wermuth versus Józef and Katarzyna Gajdzińscy, residents of a Cracovian tenement house at No. 99. A wall was erected between the two buildings, which, according to Article 653 of the NC, up to the top of the lower building (in this case, the Wermuths' house) was to be used in the form of joint ownership.[25] Above this level, it was the property of the Gajdzińscys, who agreed to make it available to the Wermuths, "when necessary" and for a fee of half its value. The conflict arose over renovation and construction work carried out by the Gajdzińscys on the basis of an agreement with Wermuth, concluded in the form of a notarial deed. It is worth adding that, taking advantage of the NC's flagship principle of freedom of contract (Article 1134: "Agreements legally formed have the force of law over those who are the makers of them"),[26] the parties significantly modified the code's provisions, in terms of liability for damage caused.[27]

In the discussed case, the courts applied further provisions of the NC devoted to servitudes, namely: Article 658, allowing for the rebuilding of a party wall by one of the owners, at his own expense and with the concomitant obligation to maintain the elevated part and compensate the neighbour for

---

sessions of the Assembly of Representatives. A unanimous resolution was passed at the time that it was necessary, *Gazeta Krakowska* No. 10 of 4 February 1818, 113.

23 *Wywód Uciążliwości ze strony Raabów* of 23 March 1833, ANK, 29/200/1749 (WM 276), 545–547; Raabs' petition delivered by the usher, ANK, 29/200/2007 (Tryb 204), no pagination; decision of the Mortgage Commission of 19 May 1828, No. 343, stating that the owner of No. 30 "did not raise objections within the limitation period and six months".

24 That is to say, the Raabs, as invoking the right to demand that their neighbour brick up their windows: *Odpowiedź Wysockiego na Uciążliwości Raabów*, ANK, 29/200/1670 (WM 197), 1385–1386. Słotwiński also argued that if the right to make a window in one's own wall were to be treated as a servitude, the fact of not declaring it could not result in the loss of the servitude anyway.

25 Article 653: "In towns and fields every wall which serves as a boundary between buildings, even to its base, or between courts and gardens, or even between enclosures in the fields, is presumed party, if there be no title or mark to the contrary".

26 The importance of Article 1134 as an article-symbol, affirming and even sanctifying the freedom of contract, was pointed out by Carbonnier 2004, 34–35. On its doctrinal basis, see Arnaud 1969, 197–214. See also Basdevant-Gaudemet and Gaudemet 2000, 391–393; Jean and Royer 2003–04, 131; Catala 2005, 20.

27 Notarial deed drawn up by Notary Wojciech Olearski dated 11 December 1835; Sójka-Zielińska 2008, 114–118.

any inconvenience; and Article 659, which imposed an obligation on the co-owner committing damage to a party wall to repair it or, in extreme cases, to re-brick it. The latter provision was applied because of the serious damage caused by the Gajdzińscys' building of superstructures.[28] In contrast, the parties gave up the possibilities offered to the neighbours by Article 660 of the NC. They agreed that, once the works had been completed, the co-ownership of the wall would apply only to its original height, but not to the increase in height.[29] In addition, the parties also confirmed the applicability of another provision of the NC, namely Article 681,[30] concerning the prohibition of directing rainwater onto the land of a neighbour.[31] Advocate Stanisław Boguński, the Gajdzińscys' attorney, also attempted to convince the court that alterations, including thickening of walls, were allowed not only if agreed by the parties by contract, but also because of the flexible provisions of Articles 1135 and 1156 of the NC.[32] Ultimately, the Tribunal ruled that the use of an expert opinion to determine whether the Gajdzińscys had complied with the construction work plan in the performance of the notarial contract, was reasonable. This position was shared by the Court of Appeal.[33]

In another of the cases (Andrzej Wielopolski v. Anastazy Siemoński), the Faculty of Professors of Jagiellonian University drew attention to the misinterpretation by the courts of the rather obvious provision of Article 654 of the NC. It pointed to one of the prerequisites (presumptions) allowing a wall to be considered the property of only one of the neighbours. Namely, this was the case if only on the side of his property the wall "showed a slope", had

---

28 Article 659: "If the party-wall is not in condition to support the additional building, he who desires to elevate it must cause it to be entirely rebuilt at his own expense, and the excess in thickness must be taken from his own side".

29 Article 660: "The neighbour who has not contributed to the elevation may acquire right of partition by paying half of the expense it has cost, and the value of one moiety of the soil furnished for the excess of thickness, if there be any".

30 Article 681: "Every proprietor must so form his roofs, that the rain-water shall drop upon his own land or the public way; he must not suffer it to flow upon his neighbor's land".

31 *Odpowiedź Józefa i Katarzyny Gajdzińskich*, ANK, 29/200/1758 (WM 285), 2279–2281. The parties explicitly stated that "any eaves on the Wermuths' part" was prohibited.

32 Article 1135: "Agreements bind not only as to what is expressed therein, but further as regards all the consequences which equity, usage, or law attribute to an obligation by its nature". Article 1156: "In agreements it is necessary to search into the mutual intention of the contracting parties, rather than to stop at the literal sense of terms".

33 Judgment of the Court of Appeal of 28 August 1838; Judgment of the Court of First Instance of 18 May 1838, ANK, 29/200/1761 (WM 288), 911–913. As experts, the court appointed architects (Karol Kremer, Tomasz Majewski, Jan Bogumił Trenner), from whom the oath was taken by the deputy judge Eustachy Ekielski.

ledges, "protruding parts" or "hollows (of stones) made during the brickwork". Meanwhile, in the wall under expert assessment "starting from the rear facade up to the corner of the outbuilding of the house at No. 194, there were canopies and frames on both sides". Given the facts, therefore, it had to be assumed, *a contrario*, that the wall was jointly owned.[34] The entire juridical problem was viewed in the same way by the Court of Third Instance, which considered it necessary for the experts to look at the wall again.[35] It should be added that the solution in Article 654 of the NC was linked to Article 681 of the NC, which directed that the drainage from roofs (eaves) should only be directed onto one's own land.[36]

The issue of the definitions of 'non-middleness', which allowed the presumption that, *inter alia*, due to the expenses made by only one of the neighbours, the wall is his exclusive property, was also examined by the courts in their other judgments. Antoni Matakiewicz, Professor of Law at Jagiellonian University and attorney for one of the parties, and also in the Tribunal of First Instance, assumed that such a definition could be considered to be, *inter alia*: "the foundation walls of the house, to which the staircase and the vault used to be attached"; the cellar near the wall, which was used only by one of the neighbours; the beams recessed into the wall, "through the entire thickness", above the level of the window, "up to the neighbour's rooms"; the fact that one of the neighbours, who did not own the wall, lowered a gutter located on the wall, on the side of the building belonging to the owner of the wall; and the beams "going through the entire thickness" on the side of the house owned by the owner of the wall.[37] The case in question (successors of Józef Zwierzyna versus Samuel Rozenfeld) was also used as a basis for considering the question of whether, for the purposes of the acquisition of a servitude by usucaption (Articles 688–690 of the NC), it is permissible to sum up the

34 The opinion of the Faculty of Law of Jagiellonian University of 5 May 1829, Dziadzio and Mataniak eds. 2022, 387–388. The opinion was issued by Antoni Matakiewicz, Józef Jankowski, Ferdynand Kojsiewicz, Mikołaj Hoszowski and Józef Słoniński.

35 Judgment of the Court of Third Instance of 15 October 1829, ANK, 29/200/1666 (WM 193), 335–338. The court delegated judge Józef Pareński and expert architects, Franciszek Sapalski and Jakub Czerniński, who were to "lay out the drawing of the wall" and determine whether the framing and ledges had the physical properties in question.

36 Delsol 1873, 480. For the author, moreover, the right of drainage was not a servitude, but merely a "simple sanctification of any property".

37 *Uciążliwości Sukcesorów Józefa Zwierzyny przeciwko Starozakonnemu Samuelowi Rozenfeld*, ANK, 29/200/1742 (WM 269), 789–792; Judgment of the Court of Appeal of 22 September 1835, ANK, 29/200/1742 (WM 269), 785–788; judgments of the Court of First Instance: of 7 July 1832; of 28 June 1833, ibidem.

periods during which there was first an "opening with a lattice" (Article 675 of the NC) and only then a traditional window? On the basis of Article 676 of the NC, the courts adopted the interpretation that a "window with lattices [that are] grated and not opening" is a kind of equivalent to an "opening for light". Thus, functionally speaking, it can be assumed that the servitude of light is something separate from the servitude of view.[38]

The permissibility of summing up – this time the periods of the usucaption of a servitude, and on the basis of different legal regimes – was addressed in the case of Berl Luxemberg versus the heirs of Kazimierz Maydrowicz. The case concerned the exercise of servitudes of view, passage and carriage of goods, and as a result of its examination by the courts, it turned out that the party claiming the usucaption of the servitude had not, in fact, fulfilled the necessary conditions for it to take place.[39] This applied to the requirements of both Article 608 Part III of the West Galician Code (lapse of three years and six weeks) and Article 2281 of the NC.[40] The court also analysed the validity of the argumentation of Luxemberg's attorney (Advocate Józef Kozłowski), who referred to Article 266 Part II of the West Galician Code, concerning the termination of a servitude as soon as the reason for its creation ceased to exist.[41]

Finally, the Court of Third Instance rejected Luxemberg's assertion that all laws had identical requirements for the "establishment, acquisition and abolition of rights". The court pointed out that, for example, in French law, if there was a contractual mortgage, the party had to be notified and its permission obtained at the time of making an entry (identical for abolition); in Austrian law, on the other hand, there was an obligation to notify mortgage rights at an auction, on pain of losing them.[42] The Court of Third Instance, therefore,

38 Delsol 1873, 489–490. However, what is more important in the case of an usupcation is the nuisance which the owner of the encumbered property does not oppose, which he permits, allowing to look over his property.

39 Judgment of the Tribunal of 30 December 1818, ANK, 29/200/1967 (Tryb 164), 2235–2238, 2241–2243.

40 Article 2281: "Prescriptions commenced at the period of the publication of the present title shall be regulated conformably to the ancient laws. Nevertheless, prescriptions at that time commenced, and for which there was still requisite, according to the ancient laws, more than 30 years computing from the same date, shall be accomplished by such lapse of 30 years".

41 *Wywód i Konkluzja ze strony Starozakonnego Berla Luxemberga*, ANK, 29/200/1967 (Tryb 164), 2245–2247; *Obrona ze strony Sukcessorów śp. Kazimierza Majdrowicza pozostałych, pozwanych, przeciwko Starozakonnemu Berl Luxembergowi powodowi*, ibidem, 2249–2251.

42 *Wywód Uciążliwości ze strony Luxemberga*, ANK, 29/200/1656 (WM 183), 103–105. Luxemberg said that he had used the servitude, which he could prove by an "inquisition from witnesses". Among the allegations, he also indicated: he had not been summoned; the mortgage entry had not been deleted; and the easement was not time-barred. He asked whether it was permissible to extend the effects of an action between two parties to a third party. He argued that the judgment of the Court of Appeal was supported by "neither law nor equity".

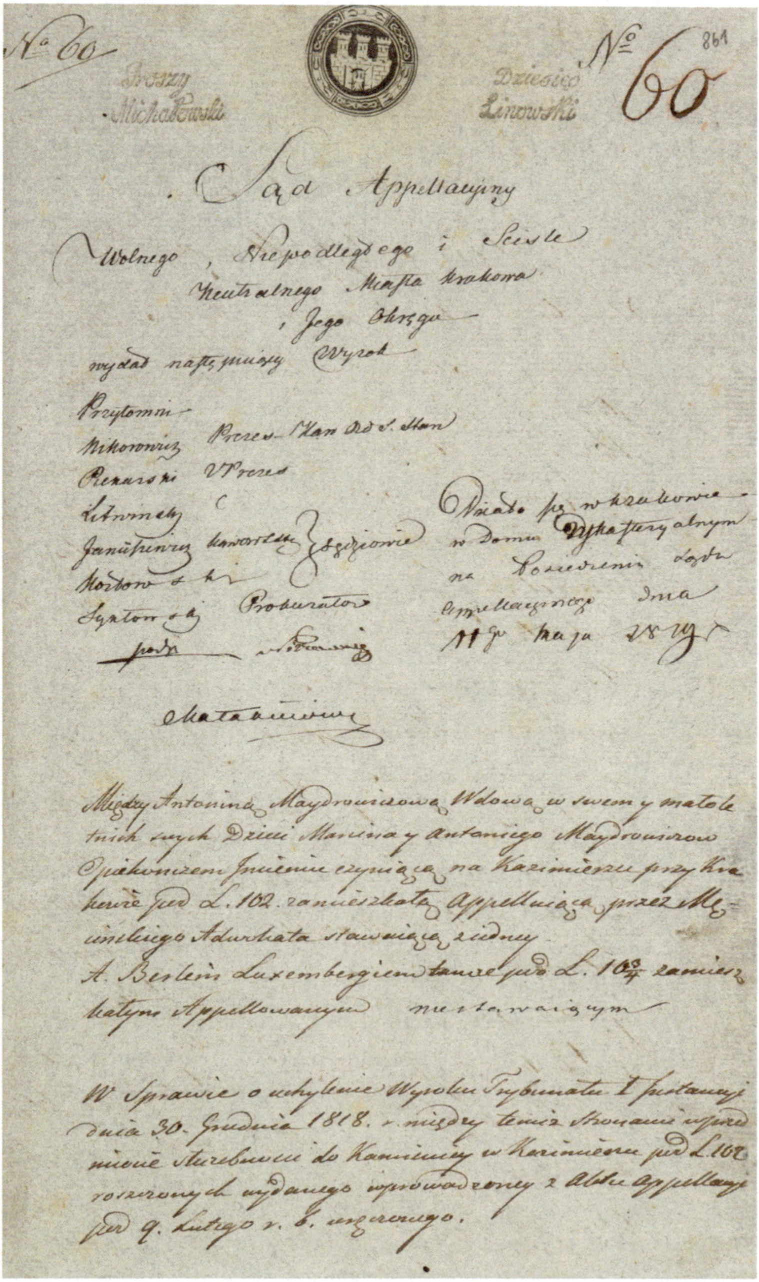

FIGURE 22 *Judgment of the Court of Appeal of 11 May 1819 in case of A. Maydrowiczowa*, (manuscript, paper, 1819)
SOURCE: NATIONAL ARCHIVES IN CRACOW, ANK, 29/200/1714, 861; PHOTO & PERMISSION BY NATIONAL ARCHIVES IN CRACOW

approved in full the judgment of the Court of Appeal,[43] which had already ruled much earlier in one of its judgements that, according to Austrian law, any auction sale of real estate should be preceded by a public summons to mortgage creditors and other persons with any claims, on pain of their loss. Since Luxemberg, despite being duly summoned, had not declared his servitude, he could no longer claim the right to: "access" the wall of the Maydrowicz tenement house; to introduce onto their land "windows that have an unobstructed view"; the right of passage for him and the workers involved in the construction work; the right to transport belongings and to draw water from the well belonging to the No. 102 tenement house, "for domestic necessity and for the factory" (construction work).[44]

A party wall in its various aspects was also involved in the case of Feliks Słotwiński versus Julianna Schwartz. Her attorney, advocate Józef Jankowski, tried to convince the courts that a servitude consisting in the person encumbered with it refraining from building a wall above a certain height, was a continuous invisible servitude (Articles 688–689 of the NC) and could therefore only be established by contract (Article 691 of the NC). As Słotwiński did not present any contract, he lost the case, in view of the denial of the other party. Jankowski also referred to Article 657 of the NC, that a co-owner of a party wall has the right to place beams up to half of its thickness. In addition, he referred to Article 662 of the NC, which stipulates that any attachment to the middle wall is permissible with the co-owner's consent, and in the absence of such consent, an expert opinion should be decisive; an expert opinion was obtained by Schwartz, as evidenced by the minutes of an expert committee and the permission of the Building Office. Jankowski also formulated reservations about the insufficient distance between an annexe built by Słotwiński and the Schwartz's tenement house. This allegedly amounted to seven ells, while Articles 678–679 of the NC stated a minimum distance of 6 decimetres (2 feet) from the structure, which the owner looked at "from the side or diagonally".[45] Based on the opinion of the Judge-Rapporteur, the Court of Appeal held that, in view of the wording of Articles 657–660 of the NC, each co-owner could not

43 Judgment of the Court of Third Instance of February 1820, ANK, 29/200/1656 (WM 183), 99–100. The court also decided to waive costs.

44 The court also found that the Maydrowiczes had properly acquired ownership of the tenement house under the terms of the deed of auction. Judgment of the Court of Appeal of 11 May 1819, ANK, 29/200/1714 (WM 241), 861–864.

45 Letter from J. Schwartz to the Court of Appeal, ANK, 29/200/1717 (WM 244), 85–87. In the case of "straight views" the distance was 19 decimetres, or 6 feet. The letter also mentions seven committees and "as many super-reviews" in which the appellee had to participate.

only heighten a wall, but also – within the limits of their right of ownership – attach building elements to it. It also accepted Jankowski's argument that his client was not restricted by any servitude to build only up to a certain height for the benefit of Słotwiński's house; the aforementioned Article 691 of the NC was applicable here (Słotwiński had not proven title, etc.). The Court of Appeal also fully endorsed the experts' findings on the technical parameters of the annexe.[46]

Compliance with the technical requirements of Articles 676–680 of the NC was also addressed in the judgments of the courts in the case of the congregation of Mansionary Priests at the Church of the Blessed Virgin Mary in Cracow against Maurycy Samelson.[47] In the context of the party wall, Wincenty Szpor, as an advocate for the Mansionary Priests, wishing to make it easier for the courts to resolve the dispute, posed some basic questions. Is a window open to another's property a servitude: yes, but should it be considered a statutory or contractual servitude? Szpor argued that a servitude of view could not be considered to arise by operation of law, and therefore the Court in its judgments erroneously referred to Articles 675–677 of the NC, whereas the restrictions in Articles 678–680 of the NC were applicable. Szpor also emphasised the differences between statutory and contractual servitudes, because it was only within the framework of the latter that the owner, burdened with the servitude, had to refrain from actions that could impede the use of the servitude (Article 701 of the NC). But as there was no agreement between the parties establishing a servitude, there was also no servitude by usucaption (Article 690 of the NC). Hence, it was crucial to determine whether the window had a straight view ("without any distance") of the property of the Mansionary Priests and, if so, whether the provisions of Articles 678 and 680 of the NC had been complied with.[48]

---

46 Judgment of the Court of Appeal of 27 July 1820, ANK, 29/200/1717 (WM 244), 221–224. The height of the wall of the annexe erected by Schwartz was not to exceed 6 fathoms of Viennese measurement, counting "from the surface of the ground up to the top of the roof". The height of the second wall erected in Schwartz's yard, "at the point where it meets the wall co-owned with Słotwiński", could not exceed 4.5 Viennese fathoms and 2 feet.

47 Judgment of the Court of Third Instance of 13 October 1836, ANK, 29/200/1677 (WM 204), 491–493; Judgment of the Tribunal of First Instance of 4 April 1834, ibidem; Judgment of the Court of Appeal of 28 November 1834, ibidem. The courts read the code requirements on these parameters literally.

48 *Odpowiedź XX. Mansyonarzy kościoła P. Maryi pko Samelsohnowi*, ANK, 29/200/1677 (WM 204), 501–504. A separate question concerned the proper organisation of the drainage, in accordance with Article 681 of the NC.

Doubts about the closed nature of the catalogue ("*numerus clausus*") of the servitude arose in the case of Franciszek Hatzfeld versus Jadwiga Wilczyńska. Her attorney, Advocate Stanisław Boguński, tried to convince the court of the existence of a "*cloacae non aedificandi*" servitude; according to F. Słotwiński (Hatzfeld's representative), it was unknown to the substantive law, and "servitudes cannot be presumed". This point of view was adhered to by the Tribunal when it ruled that the prohibition on the erection of the *cloacae* was a manifestation of the exercise by the owner of the real estate: a servitude of view, a form of use, and not a separate institution.[49] The Tribunal's position was upheld by the Court of Appeal, which, at the same time, ordered Hatzfeld to dismantle the *cloacae* that had been put up under the party wall (and "against the plan") and to move them "to the place indicated by the plan", on the grounds that they obstructed the neighbour's view.[50]

In the case of Franciszek Chachulski versus Wincenty Goliński, the Court of Appeal, analysing the Tribunal's judgment, saw a violation of the provisions of the NC, including Articles 688–689. The Code introduced a division into servitudes existing continually, i.e. without the need for human action (water-pipes, house-eaves, windows), and interrupted servitudes, where human action was required (rights of way, of drawing water, of pasture). Article 689 of the NC further distinguished between apparent servitudes, "manifested by external works" (a gate, a window, or aqueduct) and non-apparent servitudes, "having no external sign" (a prohibition to build upon a field, or against a building beyond a determinate height). The Tribunal concluded that a servitude over a window is a continual and apparent servitude, capable of being acquired by 30 years' possession (usucaption), or alternatively "by title" (Article 690 of the NC).[51] However, during the trial, witnesses testified that the hole in the wall had been made seven years before; Goliński also failed to produce documents granting the title. Moreover, Article 675 of the NC forbade a neighbour, without the consent of the other, to make a window or other opening in the party wall, "in any way or manner". And under Article 678 of the NC, it was forbidden to make "direct views" of "the estate of his neighbour" if the distance

49 *Uciążliwości Franciszka Hatzfeld przeciwko Jadwidze Wilczyńskiej*, ANK, 29/200/1742 (WM 269), 885–890. On this servitude see, however, Ourliac and Malafosse, 1971, 382.

50 Judgment of the Court of Appeal of 29 September 1835, ANK, 29/200/1742 (WM 269), 881–883; Judgment of the Tribunal of First Instance of 18 June 1834, ibidem.

51 It ruled identically in the case of Adler versus Gajdziński, Judgment of the Court of Appeal of 9 March 1837, ANK, 29/200/1758 (WM 285), 873–874. By title, legal scholarship meant "any legal act capable of transferring property or one of its detached parts", e.g. an agreement of donation, exchange or, as in Gajdziński's case, sale. Delsol 1873, 488–489.

to the wall in which they were to be made was less than six feet. Overturning the Tribunal's judgment, the Court of Appeal ordered Goliński to brick up the window facing the back of the house at No. 20, awarding the opponent legal costs (30 Polish zlotys).[52]

To conclude the discussion of servitudes, it may be added that the courts also sometimes examined the validity of contracts for the establishment of servitudes.[53] In one of the cases (Jakub Adler versus Józef Gajdziński), the Court of Appeal analysed the admissibility of evidence from oaths (of witnesses or experts) against the wording of a notarial deed. In doing so, the court found a violation of Article 1341 of the NC,[54] because Gajdziński did not produce a written deed proving a modification or limitation of the content of the servitude established by Adler by means of a written agreement and "the beginning of the proof was by a writ".[55] In an earlier judgment, the Tribunal had allowed an "eyewitness inspection of the subject matter of the dispute" by expert jurors, in the presence of a judge. Their role was to determine the actual content of the servitude, in terms of circumstances "beyond the wording of the contract".[56]

1.3 *Conclusions*

The analysis of the archival material allows us to draw several conclusions of a very general nature.[57] Above all, it is noteworthy that there is an absence in the court books examined of certain servitudes that seem obvious in the conditions of a large city. These are, namely, the servitudes of: a) the obligation to receive water flowing from higher land (Articles 640–645 of the NC); b) a common ditch (Articles 666–669 of the NC) and a common hedge (Articles 670–673 of the NC); and c) a common house (Articles 664–665 of the NC).[58] The

52 Judgment of the Court of Appeal of 31 March 1828, ANK, 29/200/1730 (WM 257), 993–996; *Wywód Uciążliwości ze strony Franciszka Chachulskiego pko Wincentemu Golińskiemu*, ibidem, 997–1004; Judgment of the Tribunal of the First Instance of 4 October 1827; rescript of the Police Department of 26 July 1820, No. 2787.

53 See below, Chapter 7.

54 Article 1341: "An act must be made before notaries or under private signature, respecting all things exceeding the sum or value of 150 francs, even in the case of voluntary deposits; and no proof can be received by witnesses against or beyond what is contained in such acts, nor touching what shall be alleged to have been said before, at the time of or subsequently to such acts, although there may be question of a sum or value less than 150 francs. The whole without prejudice to what is prescribed in the laws relative to commerce".

55 Judgment of the Court of Appeal of 9 March 1837, ANK, 29/200/1758 (WM 285), 874–875. See Dziadzio 2020c, 269–277.

56 Judgment of the Court of Appeal of 9 March 1837, ANK, 29/200/1758 (WM 285), 873–874; Judgment of the Tribunal of First Instance of 14 January 1837, ibidem.

57 For a detailed discussion of the cases, see Mataniak 2021, 16–60.

58 On the subject of a common home, see Weill, Terré, Simler 1985, 525–526.

latter concerns the rules for carrying out repairs and alterations to the main walls, roofs and floors of houses jointly owned by several persons.[59]

Records of trials concerning the determining of the boundaries of immovable properties (Articles 646–648 of the NC) were also not found in the files of the Court of Appeal and higher instances.[60] The same is true of the regulations setting out the rules for rebuilding burnt houses, which could have been successfully applied on the occasion of the great fire of 1850 in Cracow.[61] Nor were any documents found to show the establishment of statutory servitudes for "public benefit".[62] A servitude of the right of way (Articles 681–685 of the NC) appeared in only one case (Maydrowicz's successors). Of the 14 cases examined, as many as nine concern the use of view rights, and eight concern the middleness of a wall. In nine cases, the judges used a variety of evidence (expert opinions, witness statements, official documents); in five cases, the case was brought before a Court of the Peace, although this was not always correct (possessory issues). The Faculty of Professors and Doctors of Law of Jagiellonian University issued opinions in four cases, one of which proved unnecessary, for formal reasons. When it comes to the assessment of how the NC was interpreted by lawyers of the Free City of Cracow, it seems reasonable to say that a literal interpretation prevailed, with only a few elements of a functional or systemic nature. Some advocates were also quite well versed in the code provisions: A. Krzyżanowski, F. Słotwiński, W. Szpor, S. Boguński and J. Jankowski certainly deserve a mention. To sum up, it seems that the provisions of the NC fulfilled their role quite well, allowing for at least partial alleviation of disputes and conflicts between neighbours in Cracow at that time.

---

59 Article 664: "When the different stories of a house belong to different proprietors, if the titles to the property do not regulate the mode of reparations and reconstructions, they must be made in the manner following: the main walls and the roof are at the charge of all the proprietors, each in proportion to the value of the story belonging to him. The proprietor of each story makes the floor belonging thereto. The proprietor of the first storey erects the staircase which conducts to it; the proprietor of the second storey carries the stairs from where the former ends to his apartments; and so of the rest".

60 An exception to this is the case of the courtyards of Dominican houses, which lasted for more than ten years. See, for example, the Judgment of the Court of Appeal of 19 November 1839, ANK, 29/200/1763 (WM 290), 1837–1840.

61 The consent of all co-owners was then required. If one of them objected, a judicial partition had to be carried out or the land had to be sold by auction and the amount obtained divided in proportion to the shares of ownership; co-ownership of the house could be established "indivisibly or divided by floors". Delsol 1873, 470.

62 In the case of the Free City of Cracow, those would only concern the benefit of the Public Treasury.

2 Expropriations

2.1 *General Remarks*

A discussion of the content of the Cracovian Expropriation Act and its application must be preceded by some introductory remarks.[63] The institution of expropriation, after all, has a centuries-old tradition. By means of it, the State acquires rights belonging to other entities, if they are necessary for the achievement of important public objectives. It may be added that history knows more radical forms of State interference in the sphere of property relations, in the form of, for example nationalisation (e.g. of basic branches of the economy), land reform or taking away individual rights without compensation (confiscation).[64]

The institution of expropriation dates back to antiquity, but its expansion can only be seen with the development of the commodity-money economy in Europe (13th–14th centuries), including the expansion of the urban network. Expropriations were particularly popular in France, where the basic condition for their use was that they were for the benefit of the general population or the State, while the size was limited by the limits necessary to achieve the objective (e.g. building roads, churches, fortresses). In the German States, expropriations were used on a smaller scale, as was the case in Poland, where rulings on the subject were issued first by the King and then by the Sejm. In the modern era, European rulers ceded their powers to various entities, such as commissaries (France). In the era of the police state, where the will of the ruler was the law and the highest good was the interest of the State, expropriation became the domain of the administration.[65] The theories of the leading thinkers of the Enlightenment had a decisive influence on the formation of the modern notion of expropriation: of Ch. Wolff, S. Puffendorf, J. Locke and J.J. Rousseau, and especially Hugo Grotius and also Montesquieu. The war on the arbitrary intrusion of absolute monarchs into the domain of private property was declared during the French Revolution. It was crowned with success, as can be seen, for example, in Article XVII of the Declaration of the Rights of Man and of the Citizen (1789) or in the French Constitution of 1791.[66]

63 The discussion presented in this section is an abridged and modified version of the article: Mataniak 2020a, 71–98.

64 Woś 2011, 13, 20–21.

65 Zimmermann 1933, 132–138, 142–147, 152–157; Sójka-Zielińska 1998, 207.

66 Zimmermann 1933, 163–169; Sójka-Zielińska 1998, 207–209; Sójka-Zielińska 2008, 31–42. Montesquieu created the construction of expropriation as a civil contract of forced sale.

The ways of thinking about property rights that particularly influenced the 19th century codifications, including the NC, were the law of nature and the theory of the social contract. The French codification introduced maximum guarantees for the owner, while at the same time minimising the restraint on him in the exercise of his right to property. The absolute nature of this right meant that it was permissible to do almost anything with a 'thing'; the restrictions in this respect were exceptional.[67] However, it is undeniable that in Napoleonic-era France, the administration's omnipotence in the matter of expropriation was very clear. The curbing of the overly-powerful position of the prefects was attempted with the law of 8 March 1810. A two-stage expropriation model then emerged, according to which it was up to the administration to issue so-called "declarations of public utility" (stage I), while it was up to the judicial authority to determine the amount of compensation, as well as to pronounce judgments awarding ownership (stage II). These expropriation proceedings were widely imitated in other countries, especially those in the French sphere of influence. Because of the lengthiness of court proceedings, the procedure was gradually simplified, entrusting the issue of compensation adjudication to committees of mixed civil-judicial composition. It was up to the civil courts to oversee appeal proceedings.[68] In the Duchy of Warsaw – which temporarily (in the form of a separate department) included Cracow with its environs – in addition to the provisions of the NC, only the Decree of 14 February 1811 was in force, in which the Duke of Warsaw explained that it was up to him to decide on expropriation under Article 545 of the NC.[69]

2.2 *The Expropriation Act of the Free City of Cracow of 1821*

Moving on to a discussion of Cracovian expropriation law, it can be said in general terms that the initiative for its enactment came from the Ruling Senate, which not only exercised governmental authority in Cracow, but also enjoyed the exclusive right of legislative initiative. In 1820, the draft was submitted to the Fifth Ordinary Sejm, which sat from 1 December 1820 to 9 January 1821, and although most of the Government's proposals eventually found their way into the Act, a lively debate heated up around several provisions. It concerned key issues not only from the point of view of protecting property rights, but

67 For more, see Sójka-Zielińska 2009, 115–119, 209–211, 323–325; Dziadzio 2020c, 343–344. See also Weill, Terré, Simler 1985, 77–83; Martin 1993, 233–244; Van Erp 2019, 1042–1043.

68 Zimmermann 1933, 197–201, 206–208, 211–213, 219–221; Sójka-Zielińska 1998, 211. In the German states, Hungary and Switzerland, yet another solution was adopted: for expropriation a statutory authorisation was necessary.

69 Sójka-Zielińska 1998, 211; Sobociński 1964, 219.

also civil rights in the broadest sense. Deputies first considered the very permissibility of expropriation in the light of the Constitution of the Free City of Cracow of 11 September 1818.[70] Its Article 23 stated that "the law may never provide for the seizure of the property of a citizen for the Treasury, with the exception of contraband items taken by the Treasury". According to some deputies (Feliks Słotwiński, Adam Siemoński and Kryspin Żeleński), this provision ruled out any discussion of expropriation from the outset, as it explicitly forbade the "seizure of private property". From their point of view, the key issue was "the security of private property guaranteed by the Constitution".[71]

However, important arguments were also put forward by supporters of expropriation. The crowning argument was the provisions of the NC, which, in Article 545, guaranteed that "No one can be compelled to give up his property, except for the public good, and for a just and previous indemnity". And it was this exception that Leon Chwalibogowski referred to, further pointing out that the regulation under discussion should secure not only the rights of the expropriated landowners, but also of the Public Treasury. There was also a view that the aforementioned Article 23 of the Constitution prohibited the "seizure of property" only in general, and the draft also referred to "specific forms of conduct in the seizure of property". Still another of the participants in the debate pointed out that it was in fact not a matter of "taking property", but of conversion, in connection with the principle that substitute land was to be given to the expropriated person in exchange for the land taken by the Public Treasury. Another important point was made by another deputy, namely the vagueness of the provisions of the NC on the issue of expropriations, which could be clarified by means of an act. There was also the most radical argument: expropriations are a matter of civil law, so in this case the provisions of the Constitution do not apply at all (justice of the peace Jakub Mąkolski). It is worth adding that a kind of "lobbying" took place in the Sejm: one of the deputies, representing a rural commune, demanded special guarantees for perpetual leaseholders when land was seized; while a delegate of the Cracow Chapter demanded that the interests of "spiritual institutes" be protected by using land exchange in their case, instead of compensation in cash.[72]

70 Text of the Constitution of 1818: Kallas and Krzymkowski 2006, 186–187.

71 Minutes of the fourth meeting of the Assembly of Representatives of 7 December 1820, "Dyaryusz Czynności Seymu Rzeczypospolitey Krakowskiey R. 1820", ANK, 29/200/38 (WMK II-18), 44–45; *Gazeta Krakowska* No. 101 of 17 December 1820, 1208.

72 Minutes of the 14th meeting of the Assembly of Representatives of 20 December 1820, ANK, 29/200/38 (WMK II-18), 208–212; *Gazeta Krakowska* No. 5 of 17 January 1821, 49–50.

Numerous shortcomings of the draft were also pointed out by the Sejm Legislative Commission. These included, in particular, the omission of the condition of public utility in the seizure of property, as well as the lack of the possibility for a party to appeal against a decision issued by the administration to the judicial authorities.[73] As a result of the insufficient support given by the deputies, the Senate draft did not become law until the next, Sixth, Ordinary Sejm, which sat from 3 December 1821 to 7 January 1822. During its deliberations, some comments were added to the arguments presented at the previous Sejm. The objections this time concerned the lack of a catalogue of public investments for which seizures could be made. Also, the proposed size of the compensation was said to be inadequate to the actual value of the property. The legal status of expropriated real estate had to be demonstrated by means of extracts from the mortgage books, which, in view of the unregulated mortgage in the Free City of Cracow, was highly problematic. Feliks Słotwiński reiterated his thesis on the supremacy of the Constitution over the NC, which, as a later act, derogated provisions contrary to it, according to the principle of *lex posteriori derogat legi priori*. He also indicated that the NC was also in force in the Kingdom of Poland, which, after all, did not prevent the Constitution from prohibiting the seizure of private property. However, the crowning argument against expropriation for public use was the poor financial situation of the Free City of Cracow, manifested in the lack of funds for major investments (construction of sewage and water supply systems, damming of rivers, etc.). Supporters of the project pointed out that the contradiction between the NC and the Constitution was apparent, as its Article XXIII in fact prohibited confiscation, while Article 545 of the NC prohibited expropriation with compensation. One of the deputies demanded that the seizure of land for road construction should be based on the opinion of not one but two experts, meeting with the retort that for many years "instructions to experts" had been used in evaluation, which thus took into account the local conditions of the property's location in their estimates. Attention was also drawn to the compatibility of the draft with the "principles of civil law" enacted by the Extraordinary Legislative Sejm.[74]

73 Minutes of the meeting of the Sejm Legislative Commission of 13 December 1820, ANK, "Księga I. Postanowienia Seymu Rzeczypospolitey Krakowskiey R. 1820", ANK, 29/200/39 (WMK II-19), 109–112. The omission of the right of devolution was a violation of Article XV of the 1818 Constitution. The Commission also demanded the introduction of control of the Faculty of Professors and Doctors of Law of Jagiellonian University, in the form of opinions stating the admissibility of cassation appeals to the Court of Third Instance.

74 Minutes of the sittings of the Assembly of Representatives: the fifth of 7 December 1821, ANK, "Dyaryusz Czynności Seymu Rzeczypospolitey Krakowskiey R. 1821", ANK, 29/200/

As regards the content of the Expropriation Act, first of all, it is important to note the significant similarity between its general principles and those of Article 545 of the NC. Thus, expropriation could only be carried out against fair and prior compensation, for strictly defined reasons, among which were: the need to delineate or widen municipal streets and squares, the construction of sewers and waterworks, the straightening of rivers and making them navigable, as well as "other public needs and conveniences". It should be added that the NC, in Article 538, considered all "minor and major" roads maintained by Government authorities, navigable rivers, ports, bays, etc. to be public property. The primary method of seizure was to be by agreements (settlements) between the Government and landowners, based on estimates by experts, once the need for seizure had been established. In the absence of an agreement, the estimate was to be made by the Tribunal of First Instance. The same was true in the event of the expropriated person's failure to appear and in the seizure of land belonging to institutes, corporations and communes and to minors, the incapacitated and absentees (preamble; Articles 1–3). The Act introduced the requirement to announce three times, in the *Gazeta Krakowska* and *Dziennik Rządowy*, the planned seizure of real estate in order to inform absentee owners and possible mortgage creditors. Representation of the financial interests of the Public Treasury belonged to the legal assessor "or another patron appointed on the part of the Government". Persons not permanently resident in the Free City of Cracow and absentees were to be appointed a curator from among local advocates, who was to be delivered "all summonses, petitions and judgments", together with information on the date of court hearings (Articles 4–6).[75]

From the point of view of the rule of law, an important guarantee was the possibility for a party to lodge an appeal against a ruling (judgment) of the Tribunal of First Instance, both on the appointment of experts or their exclusion, and on the determination of the amount of compensation, within eight days of its delivery. An analogous right was available against a judgment awarding ownership of the expropriated property. Thereafter, an appeal was available, which had to be filed within 14 days of delivery of the judgment (Article 7). On general principles, it was also possible to apply to the Faculty of Professors and Doctors of Law for a declaration of violation of substantive or

---

43 (WMK II-23), 48–49, 69–70; the 13th of 19 December 1821, ibidem, 275–288; *Gazeta Krakowska* No. 100 of 16 December 1821, 1214–1216; No. 7 of 23 January 1822, 75–78; No. 8 of 27 January 1822, 85. See also above, Chapter 3.

75 The Act of 19 December 1821, *O zajęciu własności prywatnych na użytek publiczny*, promulgated by the letter of the Ruling Senate dated 24 December 1821 No. 4801 DGS, DRRz.WMK of 1822.

formal law, with the possibility of cassation before the Court of Last Instance (see A. Dziadzio, above). As a condition for the payment of remuneration for the occupied land, the owner had to obtain an estimate judgment from the Tribunal. It was also necessary to prove, by means of an extract from the mortgage books, that the real estate was not encumbered by a mortgage; the decision to pay the fee was made by the Senate. If it was found to the contrary, however, the Government ordered that the amount due be deposited with the court. The latter action was also provided for in the case of the seizure of property belonging to institutes, communes and other corporations or minors and absentees (Articles 8–9). The final stage of the expropriation procedure was the Tribunal's judgment awarding the property to the Public Treasury. This had to be preceded by the presentation, by the assessor applying for expropriation, of a receipt for payment of the assessment sum to the owner of the property. It was also incumbent on the Tribunal to mention in the judgment the circumstances of its issuance, the judicial assessment and the payment of compensation; once it became final, the judgment was entered in the mortgage file. The costs of the expropriation proceedings and the assessment were borne by the Public Treasury (Articles 10–11).[76]

2.3 *Construction of the Cracow-Silesia Railway Line*[77]

The usefulness of the statutory solutions can be analysed on the basis of the surviving Senate records concerning road, bridge and railway investments carried out in the Republic of Cracow in the late 1840s and early 1850s. These primarily concerned the construction of a railway line connecting Cracow with Silesia and the Warsaw–Vienna Railway.[78] In order to delineate it, the Iron Railway Society was established in 1844; this was a joint-stock company whose main shareholders were Prussian entrepreneurs, with a smaller number of Cracovians (one-third of the shares). In its contract with the Society, the Government of the Free City of Cracow undertook to provide land in the treasury estates, as well as to act as an intermediary in negotiations with private entities regarding the acquisition of land for the railway route, stations, stops and viaducts, and if necessary to compulsorily expropriate it.[79]

In connection with the work on the Cracow-Krzeszowice section, which initiated the entire investment, the first expropriations of Church-owned

76 For a detailed discussion of the content of the Act, see Mataniak 2020a, 73–77.

77 For a thorough discussion of the case, see Mataniak 2020a, 79–84.

78 Among recent works, see Meus 2016, 34–35; Bieniarzówna and Małecki 1979, 180–184.

79 *Statut Kolei Żelaznej Krakowsko-Górno-Szląskiej*, promulgated by the letter of the Ruling Senate of 1 March 1844, No. 922 DGS, DPr.WMK of 1844 (art. 6, point b).

properties took place (the land was owned by, among others, the Marian Church of the Blessed Virgin Mary in Cracow, the Cracow Cathedral Chapter and St Lazarus Hospital). This was land in Krowodrza, Bronowice Małe and Rząska Duchowna, as well as in Zabierzów, Siedlec and Żbik, Kobylany, Rudawa and Brzezinka.[80] Due to the urgency of the matter, the Society's Board of Directors insisted that the transfer of the land be done at lightning speed. Since the estimate was to be made by experts appointed by the Tribunal, the Senate authorised the institutes to make the appropriate requests before the court, at the same time authorising the defender of Government affairs (assessor) to take part in the trials for remuneration; during these trials, he was also to represent the interests of the peasants holding the land in perpetual lease. The case involved negotiations with the villagers; the judgements were made after an analysis of the technical documentation prepared by officials of the Building Department, expert surveyors, etc. (plans, measuring tables, calculations, expert reports). Other statutory requirements were also complied with, that is: three announcements in the press about the seizures, a deposit of compensation in the court depository, and the proper wording of the operative parts of the judgments by the Tribunal[81]

Because of the need to mark the legal status of the immovable properties, the "situational plans", "measurement tables", etc. were subject to the approval of the Government authorities. They ordered their attorney to apply to the Mortgage Authority to record in the mortgage books the fact that the land had changed ownership. They also called on the Society's management to pay the amounts set by the Court into the General Fund. Compensation was then paid to the peasants, in proportion to the area of the property and its value.[82] The provisions devoted to the distribution of sums of money for occupied land raised numerous doubts, hence the Government authorities had to interpret them.[83]

80 Proclamation of the Ruling Senate of 18 April 1845, No. 1825 DGS, DRz.WMK of 1845, Nos. 56–57 of 23 April 1845, 224–225; Nos. 60–61 of 30 April 1845, 241–242.

81 Letter of the Ruling Senate to the Department of Internal Affairs, the Society's Directorate and the Government Commissioner to the Society of 18 April 1845, No. 1826, ANK, 29/200/301 (WMK V-101 A), 950, 955.

82 Letter from the Administrative Council to the Department of Internal Affairs, the Department of Public Revenue and the Accounts Office, 29 March 1847, No. 1636, ANK, 29/200/301 (WMK V-101 B), 2229.

83 As regards land in Krowodrza, see the letter from the Administrative Council to the Department of Internal Affairs, the Department of Public Revenues, the General Directorate of Hospitals and the Krowodrza community of 7 October 1847, ANK, 29/200/301 (WMK V-101 B), 1987–1988.

It should be added that, in a separate act, expropriated perpetual lessees were guaranteed the possibility of receiving replacement land for the land subject to seizure, or, alternatively, of deducting the rent paid by them.[84] They were applied in the case of expropriations from land in Łobzów, which belonged to Jagiellonian University.[85] A contract for the sale of peasant land was concluded in the form of a notarial deed, which included a detailed list of the rights and obligations of the purchaser of the land.[86] The deductions were sometimes made with tax liabilities.[87]

Numerous differences can be seen in the proceedings. For example, on the occasion of the acquisition of land in Niegoszowice and Pisary, the Society declared its intention to do so directly, excluding the intermediation of the Senate.[88] A major problem was the protection of the mortgage claims of various institutes, mostly ecclesiastical, in the context of the need to isolate new mortgage items (*corpus tabulare*).[89] It should be explained that Article 19 of the Mortgage Act of 1822 expressly provided that properties having a separate card in the mortgage list were to be considered as a separate *corpus tabulare*

---

84 Act of 9 July 1844, *Przepisy regulujące stosunki dzierżaw wieczystych w Dobrach Rządowych, tudzież wieczysty czynsz z gruntów włościańskich w Dobrach Rządowych i do Duchowieństwa należących*, promulgated by the letter of the Ruling Senate dated 1 October 1844, No. 3219 DGS, DPr.WMK of 1844 (Article 14). The Act listed the land subject to seizure for public use and for the mining of minerals.

85 Letter from the Court Commissioner to the Government Commissioner of Academic Institutes, 25 March 1848, No. 1024, AUJ, "Majątki uniwersyteckie, 1841–1849", ref. S I 204, no pagination.

86 Letter from the Treasury Office to the Government Commissioner for Academic Institutes of 25 October 1848, No. 926, AUJ, S I 204, no pagination. Notarial deed of 18 May 1848, drawn up by M. Strzelbicki in the chancellery at 101 Grodzka Street, ibidem. "The former heirs" had a right of first refusal should "the railway ever cease to exist"; the Society undertook to retain the right of propination in the acquired estates; it was to maintain the road crossings. The sale took place "together with the crossings, water drains, ditches and their banks"; under Article 19 of the Mortgage Act, the Jagiellonian University transferred to the Society a claim to separate the acquired land from the village of Łobzów and join it to the "mortgage whole" (*Corpus Tabulare*), which was to be created "for all the property of the Society". It was to be free of debts and burdens of mortgage; the Jagiellonian University allowed the deed to be entered in the mortgage books.

87 Letter from the head of the village of Krowodrza to the Administrative Council of 27 December 1852, ANK, 29/200/301 (WMK V-101 A), 77; Letter from the Administrative Council to the head of 10 December 1852 No. 18 618, ibidem; Letter from the Council to the General Directorate of Hospitals of 28 January 1853 No. 19 438, ibidem, 77–78, 83.

88 Letter of the Society's Directorate to the Ruling Senate, 26 April 1845, ANK, 29/200/301 (WMK V-101 A), 923–924.

89 Letter from the Office of Treasury Affairs to the Administrative Council of 23 July 1851 No. 1042, ANK, 29/200/301 (WMK V-101 A), 217–218.

("mortgage body"), and therefore the detachment or attachment of "adjuncts" and their subsequent entry in the mortgage list could only take place "with administrative and judicial approval".[90]

2.4 *The Delineation of the Route to the Podgórze Bridge*[91]

The second primary source for research into expropriations in the Free City of Cracow is the documentation from 1843–53, dedicated to the widening of the street leading from Wolnica Square and Wielicka Street towards the so-called Emperor Francis Joseph I Bridge (Podgórze bridge) linking Cracows's districts of Kazimierz and Podgórze. This investment, which was important not only for the inhabitants but also for the Imperial-Royal Army, was carried out between 1844 and 1850.[92]

The starting point for the work was the Senate's finding that the road building plan was in line with the conditions for the development of this part of Kazimierz that had been in force from 1843 ("the beautification plan").[93] In the first stage of the investment, the authorities were interested in the properties belonging to Ignacy Okoński, Leibel Judkiewicz, Dawid Birnbaum, Mrs Kempter and the monastery of the Brothers Hospitallers of Saint John of God.[94] Their exact location can be determined from the surviving situational plan.[95] In principle, the steps taken in this matter did not differ from the procedure followed in the construction of the railway line. Thus, landowners were summoned before the senator in charge of institute affairs to draw up an appropriate agreement, as long as the land was deemed necessary for the construction of a "public road leading towards the Podgórze bridge". The Government offered them remuneration, stipulating that if they refused, expropriation would take place through the courts. If the conditions offered proved unsatisfactory, the

90 Act of 17 June 1822, *O ustaleniu własności dóbr nieruchomych, o przywilejach i hipotekach* (*Prawo o hipotekach*), promulgated by the letter of the Ruling Senate of 6 September 1822, No. 2795 DGS, DRRz.WMK of 1822. On the Act, see Malec 2004, 79–95.

91 For a detailed discussion, see Mataniak 2020a, 85–90.

92 The work was carried out on the basis of a design by engineer Tomasz Kutschera, Imperial-Royal adjunct of the Galician Construction Directorate. The cost of construction was 200,000 Polish zlotys. For more, see Purchla 1981, 28–30.

93 On this subject, see Krasnowolski 2016, 59.

94 Letter from the Governorate Commission to the Administrative Council of 30 May 1850 No. 6774, ANK, 29/200/280 (WMK V-80), 1241–1242.

95 *Plan kierunku drogi do mostu stałego na Wiśle wybudować się mającego*, ANK, 29/200/280 (WMK V-80), 1269. The plan was approved by the Ruling Senate by resolution of 27 March 1843 No. 1554 DGS.

parties asked for them to be "withdrawn or relaxed".[96] Decisions of the Senate were based on the findings of a committee of real estate experts.[97]

From 1848 onwards, on the basis of a decision by the Imperial-Royal Military Headquarters, work was concentrated on the so-called "pre-bridge square", which enabled access to the crossing to be closed immediately in the event of military difficulties.[98] The first orders to this effect were received by the Imperial- Royal Circular Office; land measurements and redrawing of the modified route were to be done in consultation with engineer Kutschera, who supervised the bridge work.[99] The Imperial-Royal Military Headquarters left the final decision on the approval of the "general situational plan" to the Imperial-Royal Governorate Commission. The City Council was to ensure that no buildings were erected in the vicinity of the bridge.[100] In view of the above, the seizure was to include, in addition to the land of Okoński, Judkiewicz and the garden of the Brothers Hospitallers of Saint John of God, the real estate of Stanisław Szembek at No. 178, a house at No. 177, government land at No. 179 (on the site of the former turnpike) and a part of Józef Riedmüller's garden.[101]

In the discussed case, the biggest problem for the Government was the consistent opposition to the terms of the estimate it proposed, on the part of Judkiewicz and Okoński, owners of two key properties. The former was demanding an exchange of his land for another, but this had been already excluded from real estate trading, by decision of the military authorities. Okoński also

96 Letter from Okoński to the Ruling Senate of 4 February 1846, ANK, 29/200/280 (WMK V-80), 1463–1466; Letter from the Department of Internal Affairs to Okoński of 20 January 1846, No. 356, ibidem; *Plan Sytuacyi wykazujący plac Ignacego Okońskiego liniami czerwonymi oznaczony a-b-c-d, to jest z przybraniem placu publicznego w figurze a-b-e-f, i odstąpieniem od takowego na użytek publiczny figury f-g-h-i-e-d, a to z zastosowaniem się do form upiększnienia*, dated 12 February 1846, ibidem, 1459. The plan was prepared by Karol Kremer, the director of the Building Department.

97 Letter from the Department of Internal Affairs to the Administrative Council of 7 August 1846 No. 564, ANK, 29/200/280 (WMK V-80), 1463–1464.

98 Letter from the Director of Building to the Administrative Council of 2 July 1849 No. 22, ANK, 29/200/280 (WMK V-80), 1407–1408.

99 Letters from the Governorate Commission to the Administrative Council: of 14 May 1849, No. 5130, ANK, 29/200/280 (WMK V-80), 1423; of 22 June 1849, No. 8886, ibidem, 1417; Letter from the Governorate Commission to the Circular Office of 27 August 1848, No. 2555, ibidem.

100 Letter from the Administrative Council to the Governorate Commission of 2 July 1849, No. 8462, ANK, 29/200/280 (WMK V-80), 1413–1414; minutes of the military commission meeting of 22 July 1848.

101 Letter from the Director of Building to the Treasury Office of 17 February 1849, No. 121, ANK, 29/200/280 (WMK V-80), 1429–1430; Letter from the Administrative Council to the Governorate Commission of 1 March 1850, No. 1818, ibidem, 1259–1260.

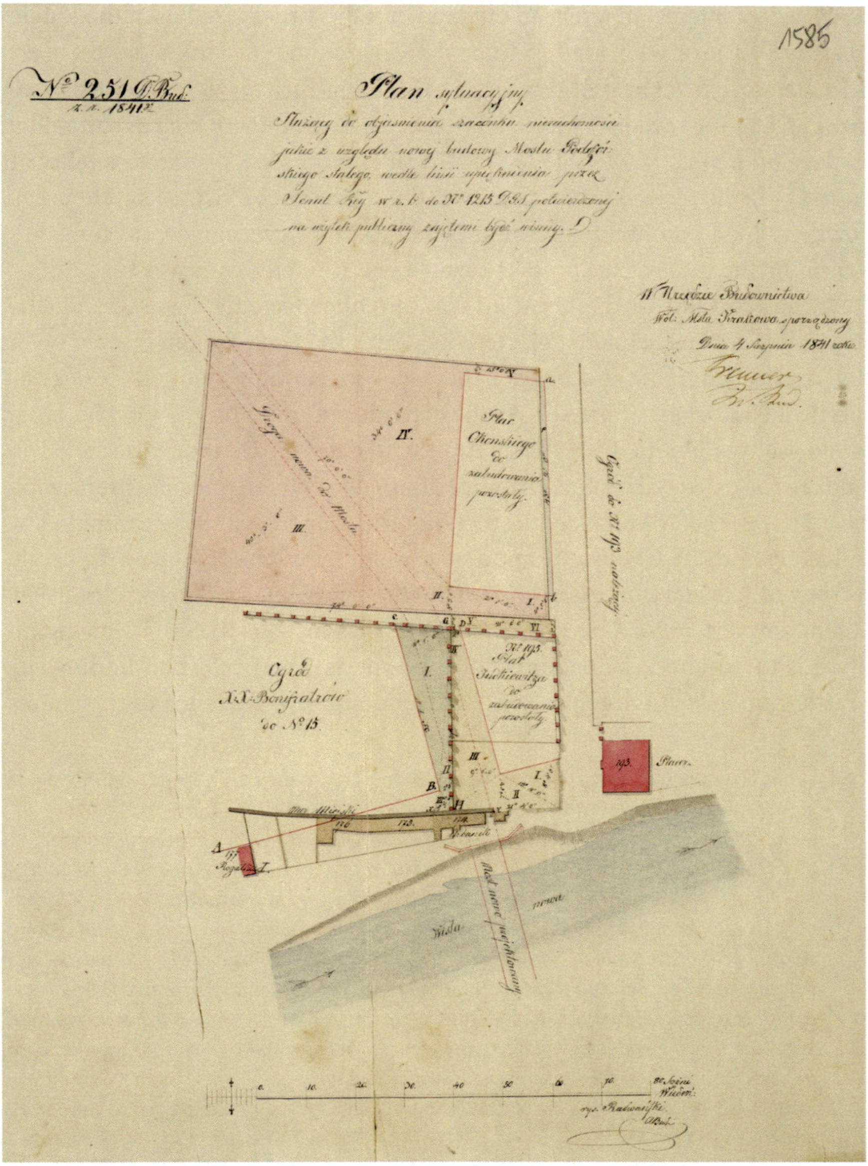

FIGURE 23 *Plan of real estate subject to expropriation for the construction of a road to the Podgórze bridge from 1841* (manuscript with drawing, paper, 1841)
SOURCE: NATIONAL ARCHIVES IN CRACOW, ANK, 29/200/280, 1585; PHOTO & PERMISSION BY NATIONAL ARCHIVES IN CRACOW

expressed an interest in replacement land, but this time seized from the Public Treasury.[102] Faced with urgings from the Governorate Commission, the next estimate, carried out by the Directorate of Building, turned out to be much more favourable to the owners.[103] It took into account parameters such as suitability for development, a favourable location near a main road, or the possibility of leasing the land for economic activities (the operation of Vistula warehouses). However, due to limited financial possibilities, the Government was forced to determine the value of the property using the arithmetic average.[104]

Since the results of the negotiations were unexpectedly unsuccessful (the majority of the participants rejected the offer), the Government carried out a kind of simulation of the scenarios that were conceivable before the Court, as part of the judicial estimate.[105] As the activities of the subsequent estimating commission, appointed in consultation with the City Council, also failed to produce the expected results, Okoński, disappointed in their calculations, took the matter to the Tribunal, requesting that the property value be estimated by judicial experts.[106] The Court appointed them by order ("judgment"), in the persons of masters (foremen) of construction (Kajetan Szydłowski, Stanisław Gołembiowski) and a surveyor (Karol Bełcikowski). The Tribunal, having no grounds to question the expertise of the experts, approved their findings by a further order.[107] In doing so, the Court did not give credence to the claims

102 Letter from the Governorate Commission to the City Council of 15 March 1851 No. 1659–3679, ANK, 29/200/280 (WMK V-80), 1193–1195.

103 *Oszacowanie gruntu P. Okońskiego przy Moście podgórskim na Kazimierzu położonego* of 28 June 1849, ANK, 29/200/280 (WMK V-80), 1273; *Oszacowanie Parkanu i Gruntu przy Moście podgórskim stałym na Kazimierzu położonego, do Lewka Judkiewicza należącego* of 3 December 1849, ibidem, 1283–1284; *Oszacowanie Parkanu od strony południowej i studni przy moście podgórskim stałym na Kazimierzu położonego, do Lewka Judkiewicza należącego* of 3 December 1849, ibidem, 1287; *Oszacowanie Parkanu i Ogrodu XX. Bonifratrom zająć się mającego* of 30 June 1849, ibidem, 1277–1279; *Oszacowanie Parkanu przy moście podgórskim stałym na Kazimierzu położonego, do OO. Bonifratrów należącego* of 3 December 1849, ibidem, 1291; *Oszacowanie Realności pod L. 175 w Gm. VI przy moście podgórskim pływającym położonej, do P. Stanisława Szembeka należącej* of 20 June 1849, ibidem, 1295–1304.

104 Letter from the Director of Building to the Administrative Council of 2 July 1849 No. 22, ANK, 29/200/280 (WMK V-80), 1409–1412.

105 Letter from the Administrative Council to the Governorate Commission of 1 March 1850 No. 1818, ANK, 29/200/280 (WMK V-80), 1257–1261.

106 Letter from the Governorate Commission to the City Council of 15 March 1851 No. 1659–3679, ANK, 29/200/280 (WMK V-80), 1191–1192; Proclamation of the Administrative Council of 4 April 1851 No. 3751, DRz.WMK No. 55 of 11 April 1851, 218.

107 Judgment of the Tribunal of the Grand Duchy of Cracow of 12 August 1852, ANK, 29/200/2088 (Tryb 285), no pagination; *Konkluzja ze strony Ignacego Okońskiego przeciwko c.k. Biurowi Spraw Skarbu*, ibidem; Extract from the delegation files of the Tribunal of

of the Government party, whose representative mainly pointed to the facts. Without waiting for Division II of the Court (which, under the 1842 Judicial Statute, was to hear appeals from judgments of Division I), to issue a judgment adjudicating the property to the Public Treasury, on terms unfavourable to it, the Office of Treasury Affairs brought an action against Okoński, thus challenging the above "judgment establishing the fee".[108] Division II upheld the ruling of Division I in its entirety.[109] The Administrative Council notified the Governorate Commission that the whole procedure had been finalised, requesting that the Imperial-Royal Branch National Fund issue an assignat necessary to deposit with the court the amount due for the land.[110]

2.5 *Other Cases and Conclusions*

Evidence of the Court's favourability towards expropriated persons is also provided by the case of properties in Cracow's Commune VIII on which buildings partially destroyed during the great fire of Cracow in 1850 were situated.[111] Particularly important in the proceedings in question was the amount of compensation for the residents, most of whom poor butchers were, along with their families. A commission of its own was appointed by the City Council, on which the residents of Cracow sat. The case ended with Division II confirming the judgment "establishing the fee" issued in Division I, by way of an adjudication of ownership for the benefit of the City of Cracow.[112]

It is worth reviewing the typical argumentation found in the pleadings of this case. During appeal proceedings, the Government assessor representing the interests of the Public Treasury argued that the fees were excessive. He described the land as low-lying, "damp and not favourable to plant vegetation";

---

the Grand Duchy of Cracow of 29 April 1852, ibidem. The court was composed of: Józef Pareński, Adam Karwacki and Tomasz Czech. The court also found justified the demand for an award of interest (5 per cent) from the date of seizure (pursuant to Article 1652 of the Civil Code) and reimbursement of costs of 15 Polish zlotys (Article 11 of the Expropriation Act).

108 Action by the Treasury Office against Okoński of 9 September 1852, ANK, 29/200/280 (WMK V-80), 1043–1047.

109 Letter from the Administrative Council to the Treasury Office of 21 March 1853 No. 4135, ANK, 29/200/280 (WMK V-80), 1087. The government defender was Herkulan Komar.

110 Letter from the Administrative Council to the Governorate Commission of 24 June 1853 No. 9498, ANK, 29/200/280 (WMK V-80), 1021–1022. Funds were allocated from the road fund.

111 For more, see Demel 1951, 66–74; Demel 1952. These were immovable properties: No. 281, 283 and 284.

112 Judgment of the Court of the Grand Duchy of Cracow of 27 October 1852, ANK, 29/200/2209 (Tryb 407), no pagination; Judgment of the Court of the GDC of 23 July 1852, ibidem.

the proximity of the road exposed the residents to "dust in the dry season and mud in the wet season"; besides, the neighbourhood was said to be depopulated and to fill up only on the occasion of cattle markets, which were disadvantageous factors "from the point of view of speculation"; moreover, the buildings were in any case situated at a considerable distance from the main road. He also had objections to the results of the Cadastral Office's measurements, which formed the basis of the experts' work; the assessor's objections also concerned the unauthorised invocation of the fact of the usucaption by persons who were not possessors (Article 2229 of the NC).[113]

The argumentation of the Treasury Office was rejected in its entirety by the advocates on behalf of their clients, expressing their conviction that the court "adhered strictly to the principles of law and aimed only at justice". They also alleged that the commission of the City Council had "generally taken the estimated price by mere approximation"; moreover, the city authorities had not appointed such a commission at the stage of the proceedings at first instance, and yet the court could only properly rule on the basis of official documents, including the reports of experts who, before acting, take an oath that they will "complete the work according to their conscience and knowledge of art". Further in the letter, the attorneys drew attention to the tragic situation of butchers deprived of places to earn a living, who had to "seek accommodation in areas far from the slaughterhouses". Not only did the clients "lose property in the fire", but also, unlike other victims, they did not participate "in the benefits of the contributions and loans to the fire victims". The Treasury Office's comments on the alleged unfavourable location of the land were also incorrect: after all, there was a "plant nursery" nearby, run by a Government gardener. The measurements of the Cadastral Office, however, were taken into account by experts whose level of expertise could hardly be questioned; the prices they established were "in accordance with cost estimates", and the estimate was not excessive; the attorneys also strongly protested against the appointment of new experts: Article 322 of the Code of Judicial Procedure provided for such a possibility only "if no sufficient explanation is found".[114]

A few words should also be devoted to indicating the sources of financing of the investments in question, an important element of which was the purchase

113 *Wywód uciążliwości ze strony C. k. Biura Spraw Skarbu i Instytutów Publicznych*, ANK, 29/200/2209 (Tryb 407), no pagination.

114 *Odpowiedź ze strony właścicieli realności nr 281/5, 283 i 284 na Wywód uciążliwości Biura Spraw Skarbu i Instytutów Publicznych*, ANK, 29/200/2209 (Tryb 407), no pagination. The last claim was thus "contrary to the law, seeking to delay and damage the appellees". The advocates in the case were Jan K. Kleszczyński and Adam Gołemberski.

of the necessary land. In particular, the acquisition of land for the needs of military administration, in connection with fortification works around Cracow, was the subject of serious disputes and controversy.[115] The cooperation of the Administrative Council with the Imperial-Royal Directorate of Fortifications, consisting mainly of the implementation of the orders of the Imperial-Royal Military Headquarters, was reported by its chairman, Piotr Michałowski.[116] In 1850, the Governorate Commission clarified that spending from the assigned funds should be strictly adhered to: the fortification fund (which was under the jurisdiction of the Directorate of Fortifications), the bridge fund ("construction of a permanent bridge"; it was administered by the Administrative Council), and the municipal fund ("for beautification").[117] The City Council tried to evade the cost-sharing, the reason being the disastrous financial situation of the municipality.[118]

Finally, it should be added that the seizure of land was not always carried out on the basis of the Expropriation Act. In the case of road and bridge works, the authorities of the Free City of Cracow followed the provisions of a regulation of 1817. It stipulated that when "straightening roads" in order to obtain the required width, the necessary part of the land should be compensated by a "part of the abandoned road"; monetary compensation was explicitly excluded.[119]

---

115 Rederowa 1957, 276; Bieniarzówna and Małecki 1979, 203–204. This was a result of the city being granted the status of a fortress. Between 1850 and 1854, individual forts were built around Kościuszko and Krakus Mounds, in Prądnik and Krzemionki, and at St Benedict's Church; work also covered the Wawel Hill.

116 *Sprawozdanie z czynności Rady Administracyjnej za rok 1850,* of 15 January 1851, No. 273, ANK, 29/645/171, 72. See the proclamation of the Administrative Council of 14 February 1851, No. 1949, DRz.WMK Nos. 29–30 of 1 March 1851, 113–115. The Council appointed officials of the Imperial-Royal National Building to sit in military-civil commissions.

117 Letters from the Governorate Commission to the Administrative Council: of 30 May 1850, No. 6774, ANK, 29/200/280 (WMK V-80), 1241–1242; of 15 March 1851, Nos. 1659–3679, ibidem, 1192–1193.

118 Letter from the Administrative Council to the Governorate Commission of 14 June 1851, No. 5494, ANK, 29/200/280 (WMK V-80), 1171; Letter from the Town Council to the Administrative Council of 14 April 1851, No. 4120, ibidem, 1173. According to the data of the Department of Administration and Treasury, the amount imposed on the municipality (84,440 zlotys 15 grosz) constituted almost half of the municipal revenue, and it was necessary to build a tollhouse in Podgórze and to pave the delineated roads.

119 Regulation of the Ruling Senate of 7 June 1817 No. 1525 DGS, *O funduszach rogatkowym i mostowym,* DRRz.WMK of 1817, Title II "On the Types of Roads and the Manner of their Maintenance" (Article 13). The width of the Lublin, Wrocław and Warsaw roads was to be 15 cubits, major roads 12, country roads 9 (Articles 2, 18).

The application of the above procedure is confirmed by the records in the case of the seizure of land necessary for the straightening of the Breslau (Wrocław) road, behind the Salt Warehouse, in which the owners received replacement land in the area occupied by the "old road".[120] In another case, in the seizure of a parcel of land between Mikołajska Street and Na Gródku Street, belonging to immovable property No. 653, the owners contented themselves with an estimate made by the Building Office, approved by the Senate.[121] In the case of the "resignation for public use" of a piece of land belonging to the manor of Retoryka, in order to "spread and straighten Wolska Street, to the tollhouses, towards the Kościuszko monument", the Senate allocated the necessary sums to the owners on the basis of an agreement reached before the Economic Committee.[122]

As can be seen from the above, the Act of 1821 introduced the French expropriation model in the Free City of Cracow, in which the necessity of expropriation was decided by the Government, which also issued an appropriate ruling. It was up to the courts – practically always, in view of the almost universal challenging of the Senate's decisions – to determine the amount of compensation and, as a mere formality, to issue judgments awarding ownership. This was a significant difference from the solutions in force in the Duchy of Warsaw; one of the reasons for this was undoubtedly the weaker structure of the State power apparatus.[123] In the Kingdom of Poland, the hearing of disputes in this regard belonged initially (formally from 1817) to the administration, i.e. the Voivodship Commissions, but in 1820 this competence was transferred to the ordinary (civil) courts.[124] The issue of expropriation attracted considerable

120 Letter from the Inspector of Roads and Bridges to the Department of Internal Affairs, 23 May 1840, No. 213, ANK, 29/200/859 (WMK VI-61), 467–468. Today this is the end of Długa Street.

121 Letter from the Ruling Senate to the Department of Internal Affairs of 6 July 1827, No. 3175, ANK, 29/200/858 (WMK VI-60), 515. Land of 3 square fathoms belonged to the Łopatkiewicz family, valued at 12 Polish zlotys.

122 Letters from the Department of Internal Affairs: to the delegated commissioner of 12 April 1826, No. 1433, ANK, 29/200/858 (WMK VI-60), 745–746; to the senator overseeing the affairs of public institutes of 15 April 1826 No. 1743, ibidem, 731; Letter from the Ruling Senate to the Department of Internal Affairs of 18 October 1826, No. 4401, ibidem, 725.

123 In the Duchy of Warsaw, "applications and disputes concerning compensation for the expropriation of private property for public needs" were dealt with by prefectural councils under the direction of the prefect, as "collegiate magistrates hearing and deciding administrative disputes", administrative bodies involved in the exercise of "administrative justice", Witkowski 1984, 55–56, 165–168, 182–183; Sójka-Zielińska 1998, 211.

124 Izdebski 1974, 134–135. This was confirmed by the Administrative Council on 18 June 1852 and then by the General Assembly of Warsaw Departments of the Ruling Senate on 24

interest there, as can be seen in the drafting activity of the lawyers in those courts.[125]

It seems that the solutions introduced in the Republic of Cracow can be regarded as beneficial for citizens. The examination of cases by judges made it possible to count on a more accurate interpretation of the provisions of the NC and the Code of Judicial Procedure, relatively speaking, compared to those made by officials of the Senate. It should be noted, however, that the number of code provisions referred to in judgments was negligible; apparently, judges concentrated more on the analysis of the facts, about which they were provided with information by court experts, who displayed a good level of expertise. A positive role, from the point of view of the protection of citizens' rights, may also have been played by the absence, at least formally, of personal relations between Senate officials and judges of the Tribunal and Court of Appeal, which allowed the parties to count on an impartial consideration of an appeal.[126] It seems that the preparation of deputies for their role as legislators can also be judged to be good. They were familiar with the solutions found in neighbouring countries and were aware of the possible consequences of the introduction of particular provisions of expropriation law.

3 Possessory Protection

3.1 *General Remarks*

A significant number of cases in Cracow's court records are taken by those of possessory protection. It concerned possession, one of the oldest legal institutions of Roman origin. From ancient times, it consisted of someone having actual control over a thing and exercising actual power over it, as opposed to the owner, who has the right to the thing, i.e. an entitlement recognised by the legal order. 'Possession' is therefore a factual circumstantial state of affairs protected by the legal system. It's essential elements are the *corpus*, i.e. the physical relationship of a person to a thing, in other words the ability to use

---

December 1859, "Dziennik Praw Królestwa Polskiego", Vol. XLV, 303–367. Sójka-Zielińska 1998, 212–219.

125 For more, see Filipiak 2020, 307–329.

126 No modification of the system was made in Cracow, unlike in France, where, in 1833, the issue of compensation was entrusted to commissions (landowners and a Tribunal's delegate). The reason for this was the lengthiness of court proceedings and overcompensation. The institution lasted for only two years. Zimmermann 1933, 199–200; Sójka-Zielińska 1998, 215.

the thing; and the *animus*, i.e. the will to control the thing like the owner (*animus rem sibi habendi*). Classical Roman law distinguished between "*possessio civilis*" and "*possessio naturalis*" (*detentio*, i.e. holding), as well as *possessio ad interdicta*: protected by possession measures in the form of praetorian interdicts. The protection covered *possessio* being the actual control over a thing, but not *possessio civilis*, which, in addition to the actual control over a thing, required a title to acquire it, i.e. a legal basis justifying the acquisition of ownership according to *ius civile*. What is particularly important in the context of the discussion here, in the interest of maintaining legal order, protection was granted not only to the owner, but also to the possessor in good faith (mistakenly believing himself to be the owner), and even to the possessor in bad faith, i.e. the one who knows that the thing is someone else's, but nevertheless wants to keep it for himself.[127] The issue of possession and its protection was present in all European codes of the 19th century, however the NC devoted very little attention to this issue. In addition to the provisions of Articles 2228–2235 (Book III, Title XX: "Of Prescription", Chapter II: "Of Possession"), Article 549 (on proceeds due to the possessor), Article 550 (on the good faith of the possessor), Article 1141 (on the surrender of movable property) and Articles 1605–1606 (on the surrender of the thing sold) can be mentioned in this regard. The definition provided in Article 2228 of the NC referred to Roman law.[128] The following Article 2229 of the NC sets out the method of acquiring possession by way of usucaption.[129]

Although the NC did not deal closely with the issue of possession, its protection was not forgotten, shaping it by means of lawsuits, described in the Code of Judicial Procedure. Interestingly, and which is often forgotten, these were taken over into the Code from Ordinance on Civil Procedure dating from 1667. This included the so-called *actio spolii* (*action reintegrande*), or action for the restoration of unlawfully lost possession of a thing, and a second post-possession complaint, called *action complainte*, or action for interference with possession. The former, in turn, was taken over in France from canon law, back in the 17th century.[130] The Roman-Canonical models underlying European systems of legal protection were primarily aimed at the elimination

127 Osuchowski 1988, 251–258; Litewski 1999, 200–204. See also: Wróblewski 1899; Ourliac, Malafosse 1971, 215–224.

128 "Possession is the retention or enjoyment of a thing or a right which we hold or which we exercise by ourselves, or by another who holds it or who exercises it in our name".

129 "In order to be able to prescribe, there is required possession continual and uninterrupted, peaceable, public, unequivocal, and under the title of proprietor".

130 Uruszczak 2017, 468–469.

of unauthorised self-help, and thus at the protection of social order and peace. Hence, the characteristic features of possessory proceedings included: a) the limited scope of the jurisdiction of a court, which examined only the fact of the infringement of possession; b) the provisional nature of the judgment, aimed only at the restoration of possession (the dispute over the title to possession was resolved in a petitory trial); and c) a shorter time limit for the assertion of a claim.[131]

It should also be noted that in the Free City of Cracow the legal basis for granting possessory protection was changing. Until 1825, Articles 23–27 of the Code of Civil Procedure (Title IV: "On Judgments Rendered on Actions Brought *in possesorio*") were decisive; later, with the introduction of the Act on Courts of the Peace, the provisions of this very regulation were decisive. It should be added that the two acts hardly differed from each other in this matter. A possessory complaint had to be filed within no more than one year from the moment of infringement of peaceful possession; this could be done by a person who had been in peaceful and "independent from another person's grace" possession for at least one year (Article 23 of the Code of Civil Procedure; Article 31 of the Act). The examination of a violation of possession, *inter alia* by means of a questioning of witnesses, could in no way concern the question of property rights. It was forbidden to bring a possessory complaint and a petitory complaint concerning the protection of property at the same time; it was only possible to apply for the latter after the possessory case had been concluded. At the same time, a person at whose request the court was examining his ownership right to the subject matter of the dispute (petitory issues) could not resort to the measures provided for possessory protection (Articles 24–27 of the Code of Civil Procedure; Articles 32–35 of the Act).[132]

The issue of the protection of possession, probably also because of its great practical importance, was of interest to Cracovian legal scholars. Lawyer Wiktor Kopff devoted a detailed study to it, drawing on the works of leading

131 Uruszczak 1974, 227–228. In connection with the blurring of the boundary between a special trial for the restoration of possession lost by violence and a petitory trial of a right, during the period of the Noble Republic, the drafters of the "Correction of the Laws" (1532) proposed new solutions to the traditional complaint "*pro violenta expulsione*", concerning the deprivation of possession of property (Articles 801–805). See, more extensively: Uruszczak 1990, 195–196.

132 Act of the Extraordinary Legislative Assembly of 1 June 1825, *Prawo oznaczające postępowanie przed Sądami Pokoju w kraju Rzeczypospolitej Krakowskiey,* promulgated by the letter of the Ruling Senate No. 3647 DGS, DPr.WMK of 1825. For more on possessory protection, see Jourdain 1995, 261–273.

jurists of the time.[133] Detailed questions in this area also appeared in the pages of a specialist periodical, *Themis*, published in the printing house of Stanisław Gieszkowski in Cracow; they were addressed to representatives of the legal community.[134]

3.2 *Examples of Cases Concerning Possessory Protection*

Using the court books, it can be seen that the issue of protection of possession can be understood in a variety of contexts. The most common possessory protection granted by the courts concerned the possession of real estate, both urban and rural.[135] A good example is the case of Bartłomiej Bałwański versus Zofia Wrońska. The focus of the dispute was whether a purchase and sale agreement had been concluded for land in Kazimierz, which was subsequently turned into treasury land, in connection with the construction of a road towards a bridge over the Vistula. The Court of Appeal saw in the judgment of the Court of the Peace "an improper examination and judgment" of the ownership issues. And although the essence of the case was about who was the current owner of the property (Wrońska had sold it to Bałwański, who had exchanged it for government land), the Court of Appeal accepted a request to question witnesses about the following circumstances: whether Wrońska had remained in peaceful possession of the land and the square at No. 184 for the previous year (i.e. until 20 July 1820) and "a little chamber not yet demolished", and whether she had only been "harassed in the possession" by Bałwański since July? The court instructed the Court of the Peace magistrate to examine the witnesses.[136] Interestingly, Bałwański's attorney not only pointed out that only the Tribunal of First Instance could deal with the examination of ownership issues, but also challenged the claim that his client's neighbour's possession of the land was "independent of anyone's grace" (as there was a dependence on

---

133 Kopff supported his considerations on the work of authors such as Robert Pothier, Raymond Troplong, Alexandre Duranton, Bénigne Poncet, Hyacinthe Blondeau, Charles Toullier and Christian F. Mühlenbruch. See also Burzyński 1871, 346–353. Piotr Burzyński (1819–79) was a deputy professor in the Department of French civil and commercial law (1851–54), and later professor of French civil law and Polish law and its history.

134 See *Themis* of 1834, vol. 2, 3–15. The author of the "Solutions to legal questions in civil law", which included a discussion of possessory protection, was Feliks Słotwiński, a Cracow advocate and professor at Jagiellonian University.

135 It should be added that this concerned not only private property, but also Government, Church and university property.

136 Judgment of the Court of Appeal of 25 October 1820, ANK, 29/200/1717 (WM 244), 627–630; *Nota Oppozycyjna z strony Zofii Wrońskiej*, ibidem, 631–634.

the Government), thus precluding her from being granted possessory protection under Article 25 of the Code of Civil Procedure.[137]

The case of the brothers Piotr, Józef and Kazimierz Feluś from Przeginia (a village in the district of the Free City of Cracow) is helpful for understanding another provision of the Code of Civil Procedure, concerning the protection of possession (Article 26).[138] They demanded that the Court of Appeal overturn a judgement of the Court of the Peace, whereby their neighbour, Jan Grzywa, was maintained in "peaceful possession" of benefits from agricultural land, which they had legally acquired through inheritance proceedings from their deceased father, Stanisław Feluś. The court correctly noted that the dispute had already been resolved by a judgment rendered following the partition of the estate, on the basis of which Grzywa was to withdraw from the property in question and hand over the accounts of its administration. The aforementioned Article 26 of the Code of Civil Procedure prohibited the initiation of a separate possessory lawsuit in such a situation. The court also ordered Grzywa to return to the owners the benefits taken from the property (Article 548 of the NC).[139] The prohibition on the combination of possessory and petitory actions (Article 25 of the Code of Civil Procedure) was addressed in the case of Ludwik Klemensiewicz from Zwierzyniec versus Erazm Antoni Fachinetty.[140]

Family disputes were also involved, for example in the case of two residents of Dąbie near Cracow: Katarzyna Twardowska, née Wójcik, and her mother-in-law Marianna Twardowska. In its judgement, the Court of Appeal declared the appeal against the judgment of the Court of the Peace to be unfounded and ordered that Katarzyna Twardowska be maintained in peaceful possession of a house with land. The facts of the case were as follows. In 1822, on the occasion of her marriage, Katarzyna Twardowska received, together with her husband Mikołaj, by donation between the living, land with buildings, previously granted to her in-laws by the Peasant Commission. In 1824, Mikołaj died, leaving a young widow with a young child. A contract ("voluntary settlement") between the groom's parents and the newlyweds provided life estate right for Marianna Twardowska. She was now demanding that

---

137 *Odpowiedź pko Oppozycji z strony Bartłomieja Bałwańskiego*, ANK, 29/200/1717 (WM 244), 635–637.

138 Article 26: "A plaintiff *in petitorio* will not be allowed to bring an action *in possesorio*".

139 Judgment of the Court of Appeal of 6 September 1820, ANK, 29/200/1717 (WM 244), 443–445; *Wywód uciążliwości z strony sukcesorów śp. Stanisława Felusia przeciwko wyrokowi sądu pokoju w dniu 3 sierpnia br. zapadłemu*, ibidem, 447–450.

140 Judgment of the Court of Appeal of 12 October 1838: ANK, 29/200/1761 (WM 288), 1599–1601. Art. 25: "*Possesorium* shall never be brought together with *petitorium*".

her daughter-in-law "step down from the house and land", which was probably the result of a family feud, with the obligation to pay 100 zloty for the use of the land. However, the justice of the peace found that the couple had remained in peaceful possession of the land with the buildings for two years, were independent of anyone's grace, and therefore, on the basis of Article 23 of the Code of Civil Procedure, Katarzyna Twardowska now deserved possessory protection, guaranteeing her continued possession. The judge also took into account the contents of the life agreement, allowing her mother-in-law to remain in the village cottage the rest of her life.[141] *Nota bene* a very similar course of action took place in the case of Agnieszka Kuleczkowa from Zagórze versus Wojciech Kulawik and Katarzyna Kulawik, née Kuleczek.[142]

A misapplication of Article 23 of the Code of Civil Procedure by the Court of the Peace concerned the case of Tomasz Grochowski from Zwierzyniec versus Bronisława Brożek, for maintaining peaceful possession of the house after Jacenty Grochowski, Tomasz's father. The Court of Appeal ruled that the above provision could not be applied to Brożkowa, who only administered the Grochowskis' house after Jacenty's death and in connection with Tomasz's departure outside the borders of the Free City of Cracow. Thus, the condition that the possession was "independent from the grace of another" was not fulfilled.[143]

Maintaining peaceful possession by a nephew in the house after his uncle, even against the deceased's stepchildren asserting their rights, was the situation in the case of Mateusz Wołek from Czernichów versus Wincenty Michna from Pasieka Czernichowska and Wojciech Sroka from Kępa Czernichowska. They began to disturb Wołek in the possession of land, "falsely proclaiming that they have the sacred right of inheritance" from Walenty Kowalski, as his closer relatives. On the ownership issues, a justice of the peace correctly referred the parties to the Tribunal. Wołek's attorney, Advocate Stanisław Boguński, drew attention to yet another circumstance, that the courts were appointed to settle

141 Judgment of the Court of Appeal of 24 May 1825, ANK, 29/200/1726 (WM 253), 369–370; *Wyciąg pierwszy wyroku sądu pokoju okręgu III w Mogile* of 1 September 1824, ibidem, 377–380.

142 Judgment of the Higher Court of 4 July 1850: ANK, 29/200/1849 (WM 336), 701–704; *Wywód rekursu z strony Agnieszki Kuleczkowej przeciwko Wojciechowi i Katarzynie Kulawikom właściwie Celarkom*, ibidem, 705–706. This might demonstrate to some extent the emergence of a line of rulings on this issue.

143 Judgment of the Court of Appeal of 5 January 1826, ANK, 29/200/1728 (WM 255), 41–43; *Wywód uciążliwości Tomasza Grochowskiego przeciwko Bronisławie Brożkowej*, ibidem, 45–46. What is more, Brożek was also to pay 200 Polish zlotys for using the farm and benefiting from it.

disputes "over ownership and inheritance", and not the Peasant's Commission, to which his client's opponents had applied to re-regulate the ownership of disputed land.[144] A similar idea was also used by Józef Lenda in the case versus Tomasz and Petronela Kossowski from Mogiła.[145]

Possessorial protection was also attempted in the case of an alleged infringement of the owner's rights to collect revenue from 'things' (Article 548 of the NC) and to use them (Article 578 of the NC), in the context of making vodka from planted potatoes. This led to a conflict between Father Józef Błoński, parish priest in Poręba, and Count Józef Szembek, who enjoyed the exclusive right to make and sell alcohol on his landed estates.[146] Nor were the courts much in doubt as to the admissibility of the Courts of the Peace in considering only possessory issues, including in cases concerning servitudes. This is demonstrated by the outcomes of the cases of Michał Okoński versus the successors of Stanisław Senderkowski,[147] and Peretz Pufeles versus Leibel Hartner.[148]

The overturning of an appeal and the upholding of the judgment of the Court of the Peace also occurred very often for formal reasons, most often due to the non-appearance of the appellant. This is evidenced by the case of Abraham Szauer versus Aszer Wappenstein before the Court of Appeal. Szauer claimed maintenance of peaceful possession of the property and the right to use the walkway across the common porch, as well as the disposal of rubbish in a box on the porch.[149] Similar was the fate of the appeal filed by Wawrzyniec and Stanisław Fic and other peasants from Nowa Wieś against

144 Judgment of the Court of Appeal of 4 October 1831, ANK, 29/200/1743 (WM 270), 235–238; *Wywód uciążliwości z strony Mateusza Wołka przeciwko Wincentemu Michno i Wojciechowi Sroce*, ibidem, 239–241. The Peasant Commission carried out an agrarian reform in the treasury and institute estates of the Free City of Cracow (as well as some private estates), involving the conversion of corvée into rent. The reform was combined with the transfer of used land into perpetual lease; buildings, livestock and crops became the property of the peasants: Rutkowski 1922, 62–63. For a detailed discussion of this issue, see Krzeczkowski 1916.

145 Judgment of the Court of Appeal of 19 January 1836, ANK, 29/200/1756 (WM 283), 285–287.

146 Judgment of the Tribunal of 19 December 1816, ANK, 29/200/1960 (Tryb 157), 1285–1288.

147 Judgment of the Court of Appeal of 13 August 1837, ANK, 29/200/1758 (WM 285), 121–124; *Appellacja incydentalna Okońskiego*, ibidem, 125–126; Judgment of the Court of the Peace of District II of 23 March 1836, ibidem.

148 Judgment of the Court of Appeal of 30 November 1830, ANK, 29/200/1739 (WM 266), 819–821; Judgment of the Court of the Peace of 1 September 1824, ibidem. For other examples of possessory protection in the context of land servitudes, see the chapter above on servitudes.

149 Judgment of the Court of Appeal of 18 June 1828, ANK, 29/200/1731 (WM 258), 315–317.

Tomasz and Zofia Fic, demanding that they maintain their peaceful possession of a meadow,[150] or Antoni Okoński's appeal against Jakub Łukaszkiewicz for peaceful possession of a garden in Kazimierz.[151] In terms of trivia, one can see that in one of the letters of Advocate Feliks Słotwiński, representing Antoni Kocik in a dispute with Count Artur Potocki over a mill in Krzeszowice, the previously discussed legal principle of "*remedium spolii – spoliatus ante omnia restituendus*" was explicitly mentioned.[152]

150 Judgments of the Court of Appeal: of 15 January 1836, ANK, 29/200/1756 (WM 283), 245–247; of 10 March 1836, ANK, 29/200/1757 (WM 284), 951–953.

151 Judgment of the Court of Appeal of 18 April 1837, ANK, 29/200/1768 (WM 295), 1425–1427. Similarly, the case of Jan Broczkowski versus Kazimierz Kratzer, Judgment of the Court of Appeal of 27 November 1834, ANK, 29/200/1753 (WM 280), 1545–1551.

152 Judgment of the Court of Appeal of 27 September 1831, ANK, 29/200/1743 (WM 270), 175–176; *Uciążliwości Antoniego Kocika przeciw JW. Arturowi hr. Potockiemu*, ibidem, 179–180.

CHAPTER 7

The Form of Contracts

Andrzej Dziadzio

1 *Pacta sunt servanda* and Freedom of Contract of the *Code Civil* in the Case Law of Cracow's Courts

The introduction of the Civil Code in the Free City of Cracow in place of the Austrian West Galician Code was not a legislative revolution, as both codes had an ideological foundation of the law of nature.[1] The law of obligations in both codes was based on the freedom of contract. It found direct expression in Article 1134 of the NC, which declared that "Agreements legally formed have the force of law over those who are the makers of them". Parties entering into a contract at their own discretion were obliged to perform it (*pacta sunt servanda*). The idea of the validity of voluntarily concluded contracts was even more clearly expressed in Austrian law. The creator of the Austrian ABGB Code admitted that in the case law of the Austrian courts, the view that "every intentional, more or less substantial breach of obligations should give rise to the right to annul the contract" did not find support.[2] For this reason, the principle was introduced into the Austrian Code that the non-performance or improper performance of a contract by one party entitled the other party only to claim performance of the contract and to claim compensation.[3] Cracow's courts also ruled in this vein, ignoring the concept of the validity of contracts in the *Code civil*. Nevertheless, the Legislative Assembly of the Free City of Cracow in 1818 – when enacting the principles which were to form the foundation of the future

1 On the law of nature in the NC, see Beignier 1986, 77–101; Kanayama 1989, 129–154; Sourioux 1989, 155–163; Wołodkiewicz 1993, 45–55.

2 F. Zeiller was of the opinion that a legislator which adopts a principle opposite to the content of § 919 of the ABGB – and this was, in his view, the case with the French Civil Code – allows de facto provisional contracts; he thus argued that the French Code was not aimed at protecting contracts by imposing an obligation to observe them, which the parties assume when they express their will to conclude a contract: see Zeiller 1814, 182.

3 § 919 of the ABGB thus includes the following provision: "If one of the parties to the contract has not fulfilled the contract at all, or not at the proper time, or not at the proper place, or not in the agreed manner; then, except in cases expressly stated in the law, or if it has been more particularly pronounced, the other party has no right to demand the termination of the contract, but only to insist on its strict fulfilment, and to claim compensation for damages".

 | DOI:10.1163/9789004688742_009

Civil Code – decided to adopt the general principles of French civil law in this respect. Indeed, it unanimously adopted the principle that in "the event of one party's failure to fulfil a contract, the other party was allowed to make either a demand for the fulfilment of the contract or for its termination".[4]

French and Austrian law similarly set limits on freedom of contract, the exceeding of which rendered the contract void.[5] These limits resulted from the obligation of the contracting parties to comply with acts, and to establish public order and good morals. The framework for freedom of contract was set out in Article 6 of the NC, which stated that "the laws relating to public order and good manners may not be violated by private contracts". The French provisions in the field of the law of obligations, thus did not pose a major challenge to Cracow's judges as to the meaning of contracts in a liberal, free-market legal system. Therefore, in the case law of the courts of the Free City of Cracow, we find few examples of erroneous rulings in which there was an unauthorised restriction of the will of the parties in arranging their contractual relations or sanctioning an abuse of the freedom of contract.

One such case in which the courts ignored the contractual arrangements of the parties, concerned the right of lien on real estate (mortgage), which provided security for possible claims under a concluded contract for the lease of landed property. The parties had entered into a temporary land lease contract in which the lessee encumbered his tenement with a certain sum, representing the amount of the deposit made in favour of the lessor, secured by a mortgage entry in his favour. However, the lessee stipulated in the contract that the lessor would only be able to enforce his claims against the mortgaged tenement house within six months of the termination of the lease. A few years after the termination of the lease, the lessee's successor, who had inherited the encumbered tenement house, brought an action to cancel the mortgage. The Courts of First Instance and the Court of Appeal unanimously dismissed the action for the deletion of the mortgage entry. It was only the Faculty of Law that found in appeal proceedings that the courts in their judgments had violated Articles 1134, 1162 and 1163 of the NC. In its opinion it assumed that the courts, in accordance with the provisions of the *Code civil*, should decide the case on the basis of the will of the parties arising from the content of the contract. The Faculty of Law held that the courts had violated substantive law because

4 *Gazeta Krakowska* No. 13 of 15 December 1818, 148.

5 Ibidem, 187. Zeiller wrote that if the most important point of the code is freedom of person and property, it must be guided by the principle that contracts containing express or tacit declarations of intent should be observed as long as they did not oppose the social order and the special relations of the State.

they should have granted the claim on the basis of the principle of freedom of contract and the autonomy of the will of the parties, which is fundamental to the Civil Code.[6]

An interesting example of the interpretation by Cracow's courts of Article 6 of the *Code civil* is a case of the termination of a lease agreement, in which they ruled on the admissibility of the judicial route. The courts of both instances declared invalid a provision of the contract in which the parties accepted only an administrative route for the settlement of any disputes arising from the contract. The dispute was between the Department of Public Revenue and Treasury in the Ruling Senate (as administrator of the national estate) and the lessee of an inn located on the public estate. The lessee brought an action before the Court of First Instance to terminate the lease. The Department of Revenue, as defendant, raised the objection of inadmissibility of court proceedings on the basis of the agreement, whereby the plaintiff abandoned court proceedings, agreeing to pursue the claims in administrative proceedings. The Court of First Instance and the Court of Appeal dismissed the plea that the court lacked jurisdiction to hear the dispute, finding the provision in the contract that the parties had waived the judicial route to be a breach of the limits of freedom of contract in Article 6 of the NC.[7] The courts cited Article XV of the constitution of the Free City of Cracow in the justification of their position, according to which: "these two courts shall adjudicate in all cases without any difference in their nature or in the condition of the persons". In the courts' view, the contractual waiver of the judicial route in the adjudication of a civil dispute was not within the limits of freedom of contract, as it contravened the existing legal order.

In its opinion, the Faculty of Law referred to the provisions of the Decree of 14 January 1812 from the time of the Duchy of Warsaw, still in force, according to which all receivables arising from contracts were subject to the jurisdiction of administrative authorities. On the basis of the cited provisions, the Faculty of Law argued that the parties, by excluding the judicial route in the lease agreement, acted in accordance with the applicable law, exercising their freedom of contract. It must be assumed that the courts deciding the case considered that the administrative route, provided for by the Royal Decree of 1812, concerned the administrative enforcement of the rent, but considered the claim for termination of the contract itself as a civil dispute, subject to the jurisdiction of the court on the basis of Article XV of the Constitution. The position of the

6 Dziadzio and Mataniak eds. 2022, 99–100. Meeting of 23 October 1822, AUJ, WP I 57, 118–122.

7 Dziadzio and Mataniak eds. 2022, 397–399. Meeting of 6 July 1829, AUJ, WP I 57, 569–572.

Cracovian courts in interpreting Article 6 of the Civil Code should be considered correct, in contrast to the legal view of the Faculty of Law.

2 The Form of a Contract for Evidentiary Purposes in French Law and in Cracow's Case Law

Cracow's judges applying Austrian law for almost a decade before the introduction of the *Code civil* had the greatest difficulty in implementing the provisions of the French Code, which were a legacy of the Roman legal tradition. In the field of contract law, the difference between Austrian and French law was mainly in the approach to the freedom to choose the form of a contract. Despite the fact that in the early modern period, European jurisprudence came under the strong influence of canon law, which thoroughly deformalised contracts, the history of contract law took somewhat different routes in Austria and France.

In contrast to the Bologna school of glossators and commentators (12th–14th century), the canonists propounded the thesis that from a mere agreement, a "bare contract" (*nudum pactum*), a complaint and obligation arise (*ex nudo pacto oritur actio et obligatio*). According to the canonists, the assertion before the court of claims arising from an informal oral contract was not prevented by the fact that the contract was neither written down nor supported by an oath. Canon law linked the thesis of the actionability of oral contracts to the proposal of new means of proof. Instead of oaths, duels and ordeals, it favoured rational means of proof, in particular witness evidence. Although canon law also took into account the evidentiary value of written documents, in view of cases of forgery it gave greater evidentiary weight to witness testimony. There was thus a shift in canon law away from the view that documentary evidence was superior to oral evidence. French common law at the end of the Middle Ages thus underwent a major transformation, taking over both the canonical idea of the actionability of mere informal contracts and the principle that witnesses were better than writs (*témoins passent lettres*).[8]

This changed in the 16th century when, in France, jurisdiction in civil matters passed to the royal judiciary (Ordinance of Villers-Cotterêts 1539). The royal courts, under their new jurisdiction, had to rely *nolens volens* in their case law on the substantive and procedural approach of canon law to the concept of contracts.[9] However, lacking the experience of the ecclesiastical courts

8 Landau 2013a, 778.

9 Ibidem, 778–779.

in adjudicating disputes over the performance of contracts, in practice they proved incapable of giving legal protection to any informal contract. Practical considerations therefore caused the French King to issue the Ordinance of Moulins in 1566. The royal act stipulated in Article 54 that all legal transactions concerning things worth more than 100 *livres* were to be performed either before notaries or drawn up in the form of a written document bearing signatures and a seal. In the event of a breach of the form prescribed by the Ordinance, witness evidence was inadmissible at trial.[10] The motives for the legal solution adopted emphasised the interests of the judiciary and the prompt adjudication of disputes.[11]

The Ordinance of 1566 thus aimed at eliminating lengthy proceedings with witnesses, and issuing without delay a court judgment whose evidentiary basis was based on the contents of a written document. Article 54 of the Ordinance of Moulins, however, limited the freedom of the parties to act at their own discretion, forcing them to write down a document. It was also, at the same time, a certain instrument of State control over legal transactions in the interests of French families.[12] They demanded that the King introduce safeguards against rash, imprudent and ill-considered property dispositions by their members. Implicit in the content of the Ordinance was also a certain disapproval by the State authorities of the effects of the theory of contracts adopted by canon law. The principle of *témoins passent lettres* was replaced in the Ordinance by its opposite, that documentary evidence has greater value than witness testimony (*lettres passent témoins*).

10 *Ordonnances du Roy pour la réformation et reiglement de la justice, tant ès cours souveraines que inférieures, faictes en l'assemblée des princes et seigneurs de son Conseil et des députez des cours de parlements et Grand Conseil, tenue à Moulins au mois de febvrier 1566*, https://gallica.bnf.fr/ark:/12148/bpt6k97398516/f50.item.texteImage (accessed on 13 February 2023).

11 The preamble to Article 54 of the Ordinance of Moulins included the following statement: "Pour obvier à la multiplication de faicts que l'on a vu cy-devant estre mis en avant en jugement, subjects à preuve de témoins, et reproches d'iceux, dont adviennent plusieurs inconveniens et involutions de proces".

12 The autonomy of the will of the parties was upheld by canon law with regard to marriage contracts, firmly promoting the principle of *consensus facit nuptias*. Although it was applied as a norm universally regulating personal marriage law in Western countries from the 13th century onwards, France was the first country in the 16th century to introduce an obstacle to the dissolution of marriage in the form of the absence of the family's consent to the marriage (Ordinance of Blois 1579). The royal courts ruled on the nullity of a marriage contracted in violation of this marital obstacle at the request of the family, which could oppose the marriage on the basis of financial considerations. French law in the 16th century thus found itself in opposition to canon law, which emphasised the freedom of an individual to shape his legal situation. See Landau 2013b, 111–129.

However, French legal scholarship later sought all the time to restore the importance of witness evidence in a civil trial. Hence, the legal construction of the so-called "commencement of written evidence" was born in the 17th century as a prerequisite for the admissibility of witness evidence in a trial, despite the fact that a contract had not been concluded for evidentiary purposes in the form prescribed by the Royal Ordinance. The construction of the "commencement of written evidence" was directly linked to the need to relax the provision of the Ordinance of 1566, which was regarded as a break in the general theory of contracts based on canon law. According to many French lawyers, witness evidence should always be admitted when it could serve to support written evidence.[13] In this modified form, the provision of the Ordinance of Moulins found its way into Articles II and III of Chapter XX of Louis XIV's Ordinance on Civil Procedure of 1667. In the same form, it was replicated by the NC in 1804, which only defined the content of the notion of the "commencement of written proof".[14]

A written form for evidentiary purposes was therefore a distinctive feature of the French legal system. Despite its liberal-egalitarian character, the *Code civil* adopted more restrictive solutions than Austrian law (the West Galician Code and ABGB) with regard to the forms of legal transactions. This resulted not only from the reference to the – mentioned above – pre-revolutionary legal culture, but also from the introduction of other solutions, formalising legal transactions (Article 1325 of the *Code civil*). The *Code civil* did not explicitly declare the principle of freedom to choose the form of a contract, as did the Austrian West

13 Such a view was presented by lawyer Philippe Bornier (1634–1711): "La rasion pour laquelle la preuve par témoins est reçûe en ce cas, est d'autant que cette preuve n'est ordonnée que pour fortifier l'écriture; que l'article 54 de l'Ordonnance de Moulins étant contre le Droit commun, doit être plutôt restraint qu'etendu, & que les moindres apparences qu'on voye la vérité de ce qu'on met en fait, on les doit recevoir & en faciliter la preuve", s. 149; see *Conférence des ordonnances de Louis XIV [d'avril 1667 et août 1669] … avec les anciennes ordonnances du Royaume, le droit écrit et les arrêts … par M. Philippe Bornier … Nouvelle édition corrigée et augmentée … des édits [de décembre 1716 et novembre 1717], déclarations et arrêts [du Conseil d'Etat, 1667–1670] donnez en interprétation des ordonnances*, https://gallica.bnf.fr/ark:/12148/bpt6k1166723/f176.item.texteImage# (accessed on 15 February 2023).

14 Article 1341 of the *Code civil* stipulated: "There shall be a deed before a notary public, or with a private signature, for any thing that exceeds a sum of the value of 150 francs … and no evidence shall be accepted by witnesses against or in excess of that which the deed covers, nor for that which would be cited to have been spoken before, at the time of, or after the deed was finished." The *Code civil* considered as the commencement of evidence "any act in writing coming from the person against whom the demand is made, or from his deputy, and which, when cited, gives the act a resemblance to the truth" (Article 1347 of the *Code civil*).

Galician Code of 1797, which explicitly stated that the parties were obliged to perform the contract regardless of whether it was concluded orally, in writing, before or out of court. Following canon law, the Austrian codes adopted the principle of *ex nudo pacto oritur actio et obligatio*, abandoning contractual nominalism altogether.[15] A form of contract for evidentiary purposes was alien to Austrian legal culture. Nevertheless, the obligation under French law to keep a specific form (a written form or a notarial deed) of a legal transaction on pain of inadmissibility at trial of evidence of witnesses' testimony, was supported by the members of the Legislative Assembly of the Free City of Cracow, who, in 1818, enacted the principles of the future Civil Code. This was because they recognised that not all contracts could be "verbally concluded", as was the case under Austrian law. The Cracovian codifiers noted in the enacted decisions that "in certain cases, which the law will designate, contracts should be written down".[16] The construction of the form of contract for evidentiary purposes from French law was corrected by the Legislative Assembly in such a way that the future Civil Code of the Free City of Cracow was to introduce the

15 F. Zeiller, in his commentary on § 883 of the ABGB (the provision, *inter alia*, stated that "except in the cases indicated in the law, the variety of forms makes no difference, as far as duty is concerned") wrote: "So hatte man bey uns keine dringende Ursache der alten Sitten: Ein Mann, ein Wort: ein Wort, ein Mann, ungetreu zu werden. Unser Gesetz läßt daher den Bürgern auch in der Form, ihre Verträge zu schließen, volle Freyheit": Zeiller 1812, 58. Full deformalisation had already been adopted by the drafters of the Theresian Code of 1766 on the assumption that the Roman division of *pactis nudis et contractibus* had not been adopted in Austrian domestic law. They therefore believed that even a simple oral agreement gave rise to an obligation. They derived the binding of a mere promise from the old Germanic principle of honesty (*nach dem alten Redlichkeitsgrundsatz*), which was expressed by the saying: *ein Mann, ein Wort, ein Wort, ein Mann* (Zeiller in 1812 only repeated this). According to this maxim, contracts were to be honoured because an honest man should not change his word. By referring to Germanic custom, the authors of the Theresian Code thus acknowledged that Austrian domestic law had absorbed the principle of canon law, according to which a binding obligation was created from a mere contract. It was not so much the Germanic principle of honesty that stood behind the modern idea of freedom of contract as canon law and the practice of the ecclesiastical courts. Indeed, canon law linked a legal obligation to a moral duty to keep promises made. See Codex Theresianus, Caput II, § XI Num.62 "Alle Verträge erhalten ihre Kraft und Bündigkeit von beiderseitiger Einwilligung, welche entweder durch deutliche den Willen genüglich erklärende Kennzeichen ausgedrucket, oder stillschweigend zu erkennen gegeben wird"; Caput II, § V Num. 33 "Die Verträge werden entweder durch ausdrückliche mündlich oder schriftlich, oder auch mit deutlichen Zeichen erklärte Vereinigung, oder stillschweigende Einwilligung geschlossen …", 26, Harras von Harrasowsky 1883–86, 30, https://repertorium.at/ns/codex_theresianus_inhalt.html (accessed on 16 June 2023).

16 *Gazeta Krakowska* No. 13 of 15 February 1818, 148.

written form of contracts for evidentiary purposes for a strictly defined group of contracts.

In other words, the form for evidentiary purposes was no longer to cover all legal transactions exceeding a fixed value in the Code, as the *Code civil* did. The Cracovian legislator did not – as mentioned above – implement the announced changes. The concept formulated in the era of the Free City of Cracow of defining the form of legal actions for evidentiary purposes in a different way than the French Code, was only implemented in the Polish Code of Obligations of 1933. The Code of Obligations no longer used the general clause according to which every legal action exceeding a certain amount of value should have a written form for evidentiary purposes. The Code referred to the form for evidentiary purposes only for strictly defined types of legal transactions, such as a lease agreement (Article 371 of the Code), a loan (Article 431 of the Code), a partnership (Article 550 of the Code) or a life contract (Article 600 of the Code).[17]

Thus, the judges of the Free City of Cracow, accustomed to the system of Austrian law, did not immediately recognise the peculiarities of the *Code civil* regulation regarding the form of a contract for evidentiary purposes. Namely, in the initial period of application of the provisions of the French Code, there was a case of misinterpretation of Article 1341 of the *Code civil*, providing for the form of a legal transaction for evidentiary purposes, which was demonstrated to the courts by the Faculty of Law in appeal proceedings. The subject

17 In the lands of the Kingdom of Poland, the NC retained the binding force of form for evidentiary purposes until 1876, when Russian civil procedure was introduced, which repealed its entire Section VI on the evidence of obligations. The form for evidentiary purposes provided for by the 1933 Code of Obligations was abolished in 1950 by the general provisions of civil law. It was retained only in arbitration practice. Behind the removal of the *ad probationem* form from the legal order in communist Poland, was the conviction that a court in a civil trial should seek to establish the material truth using all available means. The Civil Code of 1964, however, restored the written form for evidentiary purposes, and in a version closer to the regulations of the NC than to the Code of Obligations of 1933. It included in the Civil Code all legal transactions whose value of the subject matter exceeded the amount specified in the Code. The Civil Code only relaxed the rigour of failure to observe the written form, since – in addition to the cases provided for in the Code of Obligations – witnesses' evidence was also admissible due to special circumstances of the case (this regulation was repealed in the 2003 amendment to the Civil Code). Thus, the last interference of the Polish legislator in relation to the form for the purposes of evidence took place in 2003. At present, this form is reserved for the types of contracts specified in the Civil Code, just as it was in the Code of Obligations. However, there has been an exclusion of the application of the provisions on form for evidentiary purposes in business-to-business relations, as well as a restriction on its application in consumer trade.

matter of the courts' decision was an action for the annulment of a notarised contract for the sale of real estate concluded by the defendant with the purchaser. The plaintiff claimed as the basis of its claim that the content of the contract also included the building property, which was owned by the plaintiff under an oral land exchange agreement with the defendant. The plaintiff therefore demanded that the concluded sale agreement be annulled and that his title to the land on which his house stood be entered in the mortgage book. He claimed that he had become the owner of the land in question on the basis of an informal land exchange agreement with the defendant, which had been executed by the parties by mutual surrender of the property. The defendant did not generally deny the facts stated in the statement of claim, but presented their legal meaning differently. He claimed, however, that touched by "pity for the plight and crippledom" of the plaintiff, he agreed to the plaintiff's request to build a house on his land.[18] He obtained an assurance from the plaintiff, however, that he would leave the house on any demand. In other words, the defendant disputed the fact that there was a land exchange agreement between him and the plaintiff, offering, on his part, to take an oath.

In support of his claim, the plaintiff requested witness evidence. The Court of First Instance granted his request and took evidence from witnesses who confirmed the factual basis of the claim, i.e. the conclusion of the land exchange agreement. As a result of these findings, the Court ruled that the land sale agreement was invalid under Article 1108 of the *Code civil*.[19] At the same time, the Tribunal of First Instance ordered that the plaintiff be entered in the mortgage book as the owner of the disputed property. The judgment of the Court of First Instance was approved by the Court of Appeal as lawful! The content of the judgments was clearly a result of a misreading of the legal meaning of Article 1341 of the *Code civil*. For the courts persisted in the belief that it introduced a prohibition on contradicting the content of a written document by evidence of witnesses. By inferring *a contrario*, they assumed that if the parties had not concluded a contract in writing, witness evidence could be admitted by the court to establish the content of the oral contract.

The judges therefore completely overlooked the fact that the construction of a written form of contract for evidentiary purposes (*ad probationem*) was

---

18 Judgment of the Court of Appeal of 22 October 1828, ANK, 29/200/1732 (WM 259), 455–459.

19 Article 1108 of the *Code civil*: "Four conditions are essential to the validity of an agreement: The consent of the party who binds himself; his capacity to contract; a certain object forming the matter of the contract; a lawful cause in the bond". The contract was invalidated on the basis of the absence of the third condition set out in the cited provision.

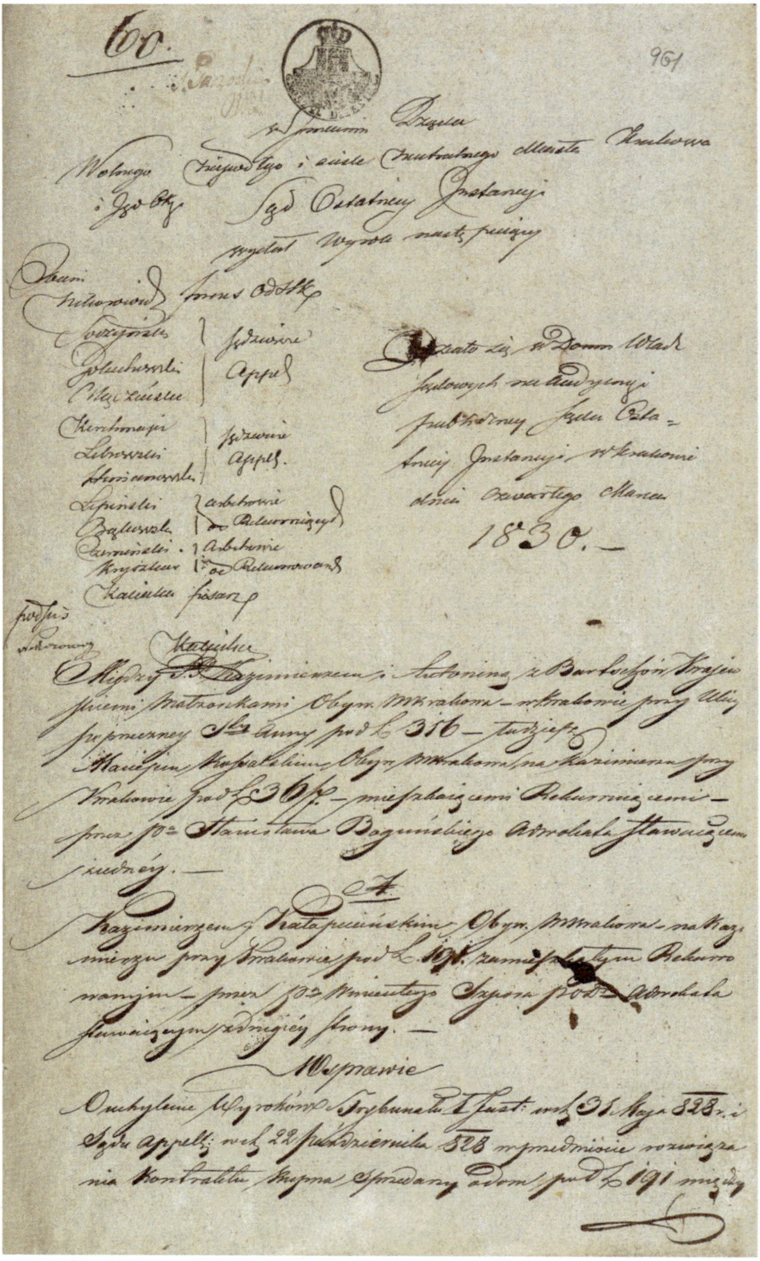

FIGURE 24 *Judgment of the Court of Last (Third) Instance of 4 March 1830 in case of Krajewscy*, (manuscript, paper, 1830)
SOURCE: NATIONAL ARCHIVES IN CRACOW, ANK, 29/200/1666, 961; PHOTO & PERMISSION BY NATIONAL ARCHIVES IN CRACOW

regulated in this provision. They gave judgment as if it was based on Austrian law and not French law! The Court of Last (Third) Instance, in its ruling – in accordance with the opinion of the Faculty of Law – found that the courts had violated the evidentiary prohibition of Article 1341 of the *Code civil*, but nevertheless supplemented the evidentiary proceedings with the taking of an oath by the defendant. After it was taken, the Court of Third Instance amended the judgments of the lower courts, declaring the disputed sale agreement valid. As a result, the purchaser of the disputed property was able to enter his title in the mortgage book. The claim for settlement between the parties arising from the construction of a house on someone else's land was referred back to the Tribunal of First Instance by the Court of Third Instance.[20]

The form for evidentiary purposes was made stricter in the *Code civil* by the introduction of a provision that formalised the requirements for the conclusion of bilateral (synallagmatic) agreements.[21] According to Article 1325 of the *Code civil*, the conclusion of a written bilateral contract was only valid if it was drawn up and signed in as many copies as there were parties to the contract. Each copy of the contract had to contain a clause stating that the contract was concluded in two (or more) copies. If the mention of the number of copies made was not included in the contract, it was on this basis that one could request the court to declare the contract invalid. This demand could not be brought by the party that had performed the contract. Thus, in the event of a lawsuit to enforce the contract, the other party could obtain judicial nullity of the contract when it showed one contract was drawn up in one copy or the copies of the contract did not mention the number of originals drawn up. The mere violation of the written form requirements for a bilateral contract, despite a declaration of intent properly made by the parties, could, according to the *Code civil*, lead to the invalidation of the contract, which was a manifestation of contractual nominalism. The obtaining by a party of a judgment declaring the invalidity of a concluded contract in the form of a deed with a

20 Judgment of the Court of Third Instance of 4 March 1830 and 1 April 1830, ANK, 29/200/1666 (WM 193), 961–964 and 1007–1010. The Court of Third Instance's ordering of an oath is questionable in the case, since it should not have been taken in this case under the *Code civil*. See comments below.

21 Article 1325 of the *Code civil* stated that "Acts under private signature which contain synallagmatical agreements are not valid except so far as there has been made a number of originals equal to that of the parties who have a distinct interest ... Every original must include mention of the number of originals which have been made thereof. Nevertheless, failure in mentioning that the originals have been made double ... cannot be objected by him who has executed on his part the agreement contained in the act".

private signature, closed the way for the other party to assert its claims through the possibility of witness evidence.

The strictness of the legal provisions of the NC with regard to the written form of bilateral contracts caused considerable difficulties of interpretation, which resulted in the case law of the Cracow, French and Baden courts being divergent.[22] Cracow's courts were confronted with the legal implications of Article 1325 of the *Code Civil* as early as the early 1820s in a case that concerned the performance of a bilateral contract concluded, albeit in duplicate, but in different forms. Namely, the parties first entered into a deed with a private signature and then drafted a notarial deed with identical contents for the greater security of their possible claims in the event of litigation. As one of the parties did not fully fulfil the terms of the contract, the other party filed a lawsuit in court to enforce it, which was accepted by the Tribunal of First Instance. The Court of Appeal upheld the judgment. For the Cracovian courts, the validity of the contract drawn up in the dual form of a written contract and a notarial deed was not in any doubt. Following the example of Austrian law, they took the view that it was up to the will of the parties to choose the form of the contract. In the spirit of Austrian law, they assumed the obligation of the parties to honour the terms of the contract, rejecting the defendant's request for termination.

The Court of First Instance and the Court of Appeal left Article 1325 of the *Code civil* completely aside in the decided case. The defendant did not even raise the objection of invalidity of the contract entered into by the parties during the trial, probably also based on the conviction that the contract was formally difficult to challenge. This was in fact the hitherto court practice based on Austrian law. Only after losing the case did the defendant's attorney (Adam Krzyżanowski, a professor at Jagiellonian University and an expert in French law) file an appeal with the Faculty of Law at Jagiellonian University, arguing that the courts had violated Article 1325 of the *Code civil* by failing to declare the contract between the parties invalid due to the lack of two identical copies. The Faculty of Law accepted this argument, stating that the courts had violated the provision, as they had considered contracts "only written in one hand" to be valid.[23] The problem in this case, however, was that the failure to mention the drafting of the contract in the two originals, which were consistent in content, could not be invoked by the party which had performed the contract.

22 The Civil Code was introduced in large areas of Germany at the same time as on Polish soil, including the Kingdom of Westphalia, the Grand Duchy of Berg and Baden. See Schubert 2011, 87–115. See also Müller 2004, 627–638 and Löhnig 2012, 255–269.

23 Dziadzio 2020b, 311.

Also in regard to this issue, the Faculty of Law reached for arguments that supported the appellant's view that the disputed contract was invalid. Namely, in its opinion, although Article 1325 of the *Code civil* did not allow the one who, on his part, performed the obligation to allege that the contract lacked a reference to the number of copies of the contract drawn up, it did not prohibit him from bringing an action for the invalidity of the contract on the ground that only one original with a private signature had been drawn up by the parties. In other words, in the Law Faculty's view, a claim for the invalidity of a contract raised by a party who had performed the contract would only be groundless if the parties had entered into a contract with a private signature in two copies, but in which there was no mention of the number of originals drawn up.

The judgment of the Court of Third Instance, consistent with the contents of the opinion of the Faculty of Law, set a case law precedent in the Cracow courts for the interpretation of Article 1325 of the NC, which was later reproduced in similar cases, despite the fact that the attorneys of the parties presented an interpretation of it that was developed over time by French case law.[24] The French courts adopted a more liberal interpretation of Article 1325 of the NC in an effort to better safeguard freedom of contract and the principle of *pacta sunt servanda*. However, in view of the inconsistent use of case law in the lower courts, the French Court of Cassation clearly took the position that the performance of a bilateral contract, concluded in a single copy, deprived a party of the right to request the annulment of the contract. The position of the Court of Cassation was supported by French legal scholarship.[25]

Some French and Baden courts, in view of the unclear legal nature of the sanction of nullity provided for by Article 1325 of the NC, explicitly sought to relax the rigour of the written form for bilateral contracts, which hindered legal transactions by limiting the autonomy of the will of the parties in establishing contractual relations.[26] Over time, case law developed according to which

---

24 See Dziadzio 2022b, 280.

25 Delsol 1874, 512. Delsol wrote that "the invalidity of an act due to the lack of duplicates can be covered by voluntary performance", justifying his position as follows: "But for what reason does voluntary performance cover these various nullities? This is because there would be a kind of bad will on the part of the person who, having performed the contract, would wish, by invoking a simple defect in the form, to undo the act performed, that is to say, a contract which he himself must have regarded as something very serious, since he had performed it at least in part. The legislator did not want – and rightly so – to authorise a similar overly delayed revocation of contracts".

26 It was a well-established view in French legal scholarship that the invalidity of a bilateral contract provided for in Article 1325 of the *Code civil* concerned the evidentiary force of the contract itself and not the statement of the parties expressed in its content. Legal academics pointed to the need to differentiate the concept of nullity found in this provision.

witness evidence became admissible to prove a bilateral agreement concluded in cases where the parties had concluded the agreement in writing in one copy only.[27] A bilateral agreement concluded in violation of Article 1325 of the *Code civil* treated it as the commencement of written proof, justifying the admissibility of witness evidence on the basis of Article 1347 of the *Code civil.* Eventually, the French Court of Cassation supported this position, thereby influencing the uniformity of case law on this debatable issue. In its judgment, it stated that an act with private signatures containing a bilateral contract, although invalid due to a violation of Article 1325 of the *Code civil* (not drawn up in as many originals as there are parties with different interests), could nevertheless be treated as the commencement of written evidence under Article 1347 of the *Code civil*, with the effect of admitting witness evidence of the conclusion of the contract.[28]

3 The Evidentiary Procedure of the Code Civil in the Practice of Cracow's Courts

It was not only issues of poor knowledge of French scholarship on civil law doctrine that posed a problem for Cracow's judges; they did not have any French commentaries on the provisions of the *Code civil* at that time. Unlike the Baden courts, which had easier access to French case law, Cracow's judges were forced to interpret the provisions of the French codes, both civil and civil procedure ones, on their own. It was also a challenge for the Cracovian judiciary to apply procedural rules that pertained to cases concerning the law of obligations. The largest percentage of court rulings that were appealed to the Faculty of Law of Jagiellonian University on the grounds of violation of procedural rules, were payment disputes (*c.*65 per cent).[29] It should therefore be assumed that the

Lawyers stressed that it was not nullity in the sense of a non-existent document, referred to by the term "*nulle*", but nullity in terms of lack of sufficient force, which was expressed by the word "*non valable*". Nullity in the latter sense meant that such an invalid document could not be given full evidentiary force in the sense that the act could not serve as evidence of the content contained therein (the declaration of intent of the parties), but was precisely applicable as the commencement of written proof under article 1347 of the *Code civil.* See Windscheid 1847, 30.

27 The case law of the Baden courts in the context of Articles 1325 and 1347 is discussed in more detail by Dziadzio 2022b, 281–283.

28 Judgment of the French Court of Cassation of 28 November 1864, Sirey ed. 1865, https://gallica.bnf.fr/ark:/12148/bpt6k57791653/f5.item (accessed on 16 February 2022).

29 Dziadzio 2020b, 189.

largest percentage of cases dealt with in Cracow's courts concerned disputes in the field of the law of obligations. This is because Cracow was a major centre of trade and commerce; landowners, burghers and the Jewish community occupied an important position in the socio-economic structure of the Free City.

The source of the claims brought before the courts was therefore, to a large extent, contracts, often concluded orally. In the appeals to the Faculty of Law in these type of cases, the most frequent allegations were most often concerning faulty conduct of the evidentiary proceedings, mainly through the violation of the conditions of admissibility of oath evidence set out in the Civil Code. Indeed, it was a feature of French legislation that in the *Code civil* the norms of substantive law occurred in conjunction with procedural provisions. An example of this integral treatment of civil law rules was precisely the law of obligations in the *Code civil*, where in Title III: "Of Contracts, or Contractual Obligations in General", all of Chapter VI was devoted to provisions on "Of the Proof of Obligations and of that of Payment". The *Code civil* contained, *inter alia*, provisions on the types of oaths and the legal conditions for the taking of

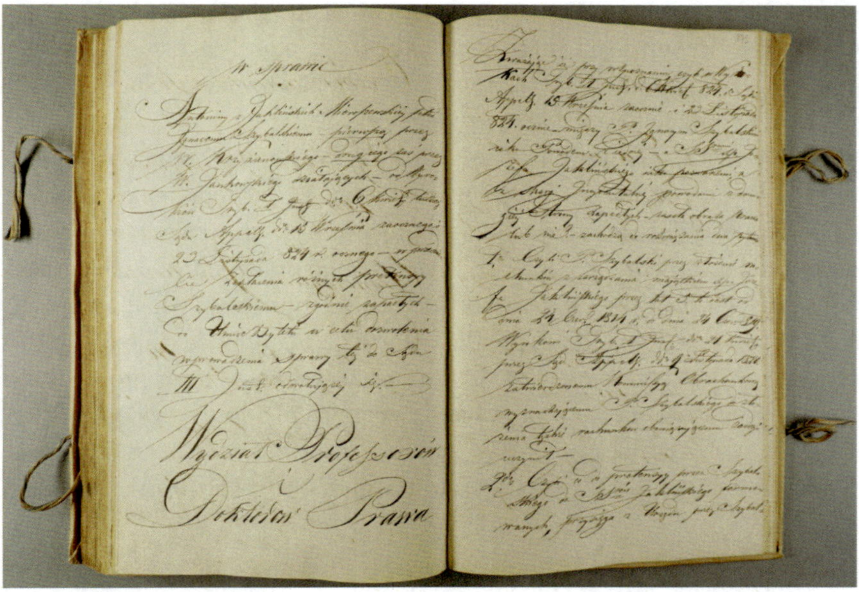

FIGURE 25 *Opinion of the Faculty of Law of 27 December 1824 in case of Mieroszewska*, (manuscript, paper, 1824)
SOURCE: JAGIELLONIAN UNIVERSITY ARCHIVES, AUJ, WP I 57, 274–275; PHOTO & PERMISSION BY JAGIELLONIAN UNIVERSITY ARCHIVES

this evidence, but the very definition of an oath was given in the Code of Civil Procedure.[30]

The provisions of French law with regard to oaths as a means of evidence in civil litigation confirm that not only was the very essence of a contract in the *Code civil* based on Roman law, but also the provisions on evidence in obligatory relations followed the Roman model. The *Code civil* followed Roman law in adopting, in articles 1357–1369, two types of oath: an oath deferred by one party to another, called a decisory oath, and an oath ordered to one or the other party by the court, called an officially administered oath. A decisory oath was only admissible to establish the personal acts of the party to whom it was deferred. It could be ordered in any state of the case, even before any other evidence was given. It could only be referred back to the opposing party if it concerned acts common to both parties. The decisory nature of a decisory oath and a referred oath consisted in the fact that their evasion entailed the acknowledgement of a proven fact contrary to that covered by its wording. The taking of an oath precluded the possibility of proving its falsity in civil proceedings; for when one of the parties requested an oath, the other was obliged either to refer it or take it, or to submit to the consequences of not taking it. It was not possible for the opposing party to refuse a proposed oath without the negative consequences of such a refusal. An officially administered oath could be ordered by a court to one of the parties in order to settle a dispute, but only if neither the action nor the allegations against it had been completely proved (justified) or completely devoid of evidence.[31]

Despite a clear tendency by the *Code civil* to eliminate religious aspects from the law, it is somewhat puzzling that an oath was retained as a means of evidence of a decisory nature in civil proceedings, which was a manifestation of the legal theory of evidence. Although the drafters of the code asked themselves whether the examples of societal corruption they had witnessed allowed the ancient institution of the oath to be maintained, this doubt did not result in the elimination of this means of evidence from proceedings. This was because French law prohibited the taking of witness evidence when a legal act with a value in excess of 150 francs was not concluded in written form or by notarial deed (Article 1341 of the *Code civil*). The form of the legal

30 Article 55 of the Code of Civil Procedure defined an oath as: "a solemn declaration of oneself, at which a party calls the Deity to witness that the truth is asserted". The Code of Civil Procedure defined the conditions for the conduct of an oath by a justice of the peace differently from the *Code Civil*, as a justice of the peace could not order an oath *ex officio*, as he was acting as a conciliator.

31 Rotwand 1918, 448.

transaction for the purposes of proof (*ad probationem*) appearing in the *Code civil*, which excluded in legal proceedings the evidence of witnesses, imposed, as it were, the necessity of maintaining an oath, since otherwise a party would be deprived of any possibility of asserting his claims if a written document had not been drawn up, or had been lost or destroyed. French law in such a case would be no different from the tenets of Roman law, which adhered to the principle that *ex nudo pacto non oritur actio et obligatio*.

For these reasons, it is understandable that in proceedings before Cracow's courts, the oath was a fairly frequently used means of evidence in payment disputes, as the majority of such claims arose from contracts mostly concluded orally, as already mentioned. The taking of evidence by oath was also the subject of numerous complaints to the Faculty of Law, alleging either a misclassification of the type of oath (decisory or officially administered) that was admissible in the factual and legal state of a particular case, or ordering by the court incompatibly with the Act. The wording of a decisory oath was determined by a party to the proceedings, but, as the Faculty of Law instructed the courts, it was the court's duty to amend it if it included circumstances that had been admitted by the opposing party. The Faculty in this case referred to the general rule of civil procedure that facts admitted by a party were to be considered by the court as proven.[32]

A common error reproduced in court rulings was the ordering of an officially administered oath according to wording set by the court when there was no "initial evidence" in the case, as the Law Faculty opinions put it. Cracow courts thus had some difficulty in applying the provisions of the *Code civil*, which distinguished between a decisory oath and an officially administered oath. The Law Faculty's opinions from the final period of its judiciary function, reflected a case in which the plaintiff, claiming payment of a certain amount, requested that the defendant take an oath, who, however, neither accepted it nor requested an oath in return. The court, however, in such a state of affairs, instead of awarding the amount to the plaintiff, imposed an oath *ex officio* on the plaintiff, although the court had no evidence in the case.[33]

---

32 Dziadzio and Mataniak eds. 2022, 27–30. Meeting of 4 June 1817, AUJ, WP I 57, 1–4. This principle was mentioned to the courts by the Faculty of Law in the first opinion issued under Article XV of the Constitution, see also the meetings of 19 November 1821 and of 23 October 1822, Dziadzio and Mataniak eds. 2022, 74–75 and 97–99; AUJ, WP I 57, 75–77 and 115–118.

33 Dziadzio and Mataniak eds. 2022, 640. Meeting of 12 September 1833, AUJ, WP I 57, 220–221. See also the meetings of 6 February 1828, 17 July 1829 and 15 June 1832, Dziadzio and Mataniak eds. 2022, 317–318, 399 and 576–577; AUJ, WP I 58, 411–413, 573–574 and WP I 59, 62.

In addition to instances of misapplication of officially administered oaths by the courts, where the action was completely devoid of evidence in the light of the facts established by the Law Faculty, a source of serious controversy between it and the courts was the issue of the very interpretation of the concept of "initial proof", conditioning, according to the Law Faculty, the statutory admissibility of an oath *ex officio.* Namely, in one case, the courts ordered the plaintiff to reimburse the successors of a deceased person for whom he had performed certain services under a power of attorney. This is because the courts held that the evidence of the power of attorney was precisely a prerequisite for the admissibility of the oath *ex officio* ("the demand was not completely devoid of evidence"), and, following its execution by the plaintiff, granted the claim. In contrast, the Faculty of Law, in its opinion in this case, assumed that such "initial evidence", justifying the admissibility of the plaintiff's oath *ex officio*, could only be the plaintiff's submission of receipts documenting the costs of actions arising from the power of attorney.[34] The Faculty of Law therefore concluded that there were grounds to allow the appeal. However, the Court of Last (Third) Instance confirmed the legality of the appealed judgments.[35] Which legal position should therefore be considered correct: that of the courts or that of the Faculty of Law?

The opinion of the Professors and Doctors of Law does not seem correct in that the conditions for the admissibility of witness evidence and evidence of oaths ordered *ex officio*, were treated equally. According to the *Code civil*, witness evidence could be admissible in respect of oral contracts exceeding 150 francs when a party had provided "the commencement of evidence in writing" (Article 1347 of the *Code civil*); similarly, evidence of oaths ordered *ex officio* could be taken if the demand was "not completely devoid of evidence" (Article

34 Dziadzio and Mataniak eds. 2022, 162–165. Meeting of 27 December 1824, AUJ, WP I 57, 273–288. In the opinion issued, the Faculty of Law stated, *inter alia*: "Given that such costs by Szybalski are not supported by detailed receipts, and so this claim cannot be sworn to at all, otherwise it would be up to the will of the swearing party to eliminate similar costs up to the amount preferred. However, the courts allowed Szybalski to take an oath in without any initial evidence as to each detail. And so they violated Articles 1315 and 1347 of the Civil Code".

35 Judgment of the Tribunal of First Instance of 6 April 1824, Judgments of the Court of Appeal of 15 September 1824 and 23 November 1824, ANK, 29/200/1724 (WM 251), 529–531 and 1067–1068. The Court of Third Instance, in a judgment of 14 April 1825, upheld the judgments of the lower courts, stating that the courts "gave place to the oath *ex officio*" on the "basis of the initial documents", which, according to the courts, were the "contracts of plenipotentiary power" given by the late Jakliński to Szybalski, and "in this respect they did not violate the provisions of the law and court proceedings", ANK, 29/200/1660 (WM 187).

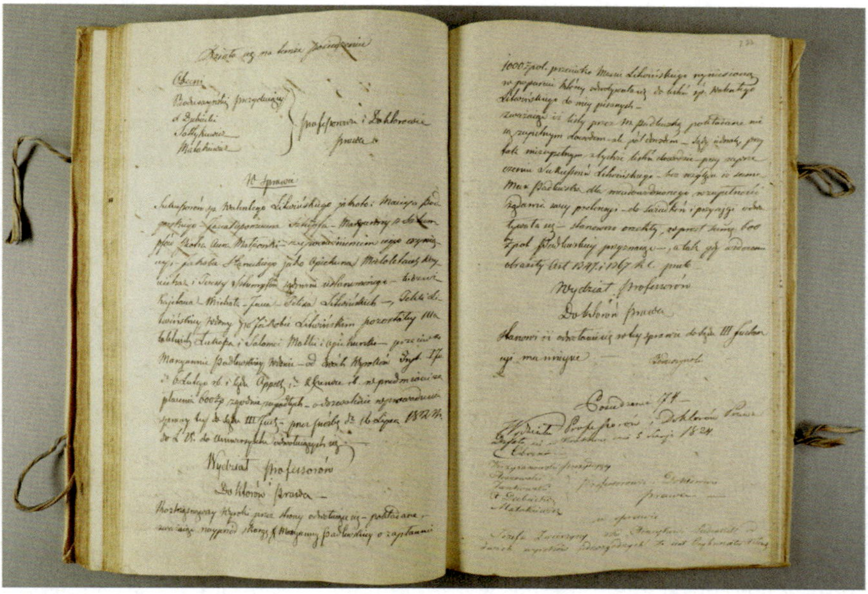

FIGURE 26 *Opinion of the Faculty of Law of 17 July 1824 in case of Litwiński's successors,* (manuscript, paper, 1824)
SOURCE: JAGIELLONIAN UNIVERSITY ARCHIVES, AUJ, WP I 57, 232–233; PHOTO & PERMISSION BY JAGIELLONIAN UNIVERSITY ARCHIVES

1367 of the *Code civil*). The Faculty of Law equated the legal meaning of the two terms, assuming that the court could admit an oath *ex officio* if a party presented "the commencement of evidence" (within the meaning of Article 1347 of the *Code civil*), rather than any evidence, however circumstantial, to justify the demand. The courts, on the other hand, rightly assumed that the two conditions of the evidentiary prohibition did not coincide, since the prohibition of proof of an oath *ex officio* was applicable when the claim or allegation was not supported by any (!) evidence. In the case analysed above, the courts considered the contents of the power of attorney on which the plaintiff based his claim, as evidence within the meaning of the *Code civil* provision on the oath *ex officio*.

Cracow's courts should also get credit for the fact that in adjudicating civil cases, they tried to follow the principle of free assessment of evidence, which was expressed in Article 1353 of the NC. The residue of the formal theory of evidence in French procedure was evident in, *inter alia*, the provisions on oaths cited above and the prohibition of refuting the content of a document by witness testimony. However, the legal theory of evidence, which had the acceptance of the Cracovian legal community, was nevertheless transferred to civil proceedings from the Austrian criminal procedure of 1803. Professors and Doctors of Law at Jagiellonian University were not free from this attachment to the legal theory of evidence. This is evidenced by one case, which concerned a claim for payment of a certain sum of money by the heirs of a professor and rector of Jagiellonian University, Walenty Litwiński, brought by a woman caring for the deceased professor's mentally ill wife.

As the basis of her claim, she presented a letter handwritten by Litwiński in which he promised to pay a certain amount for the service provided by the plaintiff. The courts of both instances awarded the amount of 600 Polish zlotys to the plaintiff, finding the evidence presented sufficient to rule in favour of the plaintiff.[36] However, following an appeal by the defendants, the Faculty of Law, in its opinion, found a violation of procedural law on the basis that the letter submitted, in its view, constituted only a "half of the evidence", with the result that the courts should order either an *ex officio* oath or the examination of witnesses.[37] As in the above-mentioned case, the Faculty of Law treated the letter submitted by the claimant merely as "the commencement of written evidence", which required supplementary proof.

The undoubtedly positive aspect of the Law Faculty's supervision of the case law of Cracow's courts, with regard to the use of a deferred (decisory) oath in court proceedings, was that it consistently instructed them that an oath was an extraordinary means of evidence with subsidiary application. In other words, the courts could not rely on a decisory oath as a means of evidence if they had other evidence in a given case, such as a letter presented by the defendant in which the plaintiff waived the benefit now claimed in the lawsuit. The court in such a case was to rule on the basis of the document presented and not a deferred oath.[38]

---

36 Judgment of the Court of Appeal of 2 June 1824, ANK, 29/200/1663 (WM 190), 285–289.

37 Dziadzio and Mataniak eds. 2022, 149–150. Meeting of 17 July 1824, AUJ, WP I 57, 232–233. The Faculty of Law in a short opinion concluded as follows: "Bearing in mind that the letters submitted by M. Padlewska do not constitute full proof, but half proof, the courts, however, in the face of such incomplete proof from these letters, in the face of denial from Litwiński's successors, regardless of the fact that Marianna Padlewska herself appealed to witnesses and oaths to substantiate her claim which was not fully proven, firmly decided to award the sum of 600 zlotys to Padlewska. Thus, as they violated Articles 1347 and 1367 of the Civil Code, the Faculty of Law Professors and Doctors stipulate that an appeal in this case to the Court of Third Instance shall take place".

38 Dziadzio and Mataniak eds. 2022, 236. Meeting of 3 June 1826, AUJ, WP I 57, 154–156. The Faculty in its opinion stated: "Considering further that proof by oath is extraordinary, and therefore only takes place where there are no ordinary ones, the courts of both instances, by giving place to the oath to be performed by Drobner, irrespective of the receipt given

4 Conclusion

The interpretation of the provisions of the *Code civil* in the form of a contract for evidentiary purposes (Articles 1325, 1341 of the *Code civil*), was not free from errors, as earlier judicial practice was different. Cracovian courts, guided by the fundamental assumptions of the freedom of contract of Austrian law, transferred its ideas to the application of French law, which sometimes led to rulings contrary to the letter of the *Code civil*. The implementation of the *Code civil* in the Free City of Cracow therefore did not proceed smoothly. The reason for this was not only the poor knowledge of French law and its traditions in Cracow. It was also due to the fact that, as its creators wrote, the *Code civil* had many advantages as well as gaps and deficiencies, the filling of which was left to case law and the judiciary. With greater or lesser success, the courts succeeded in meeting this imposed task. The difficulties that Cracow's courts had in applying the *Code civil* were also a challenge for French and Baden courts.

It is also reasonable to assume that Cracow's courts may have consciously ignored the provisions of French law in cases where a ruling made in accordance with the formalism of the *Code civil* may have been detrimental and unfair to a party to the proceedings. This can be evidenced by the previously described court case between a poor, crippled labourer and an entrepreneur – the owner of a brickyard – for evidence of an oral land exchange agreement. The circumstances of this case were of such a nature that the courts could become convinced that the action against the entrepreneur had factual justification. The circumstantial evidence for such a presumption can be found in the fact that the Court of Appeal in this case recognised the correctness of the decision of the Tribunal of First Instance, knowing the correct interpretation of Article 1341 of the *Code civil*. Moreover, in an earlier judgment in another similar case, the Court of Appeal conducted a legal reasoning in which it fully and correctly read the evidentiary prohibition provided for in this article of the Civil Code.[39]

---

by him, insofar as the plaintiff has not claimed payment of the claimed sum for eight years, have violated Article 1322 of the Civil Code". See also the meetings of 4 September 1826 and of 8 March 1828, Dziadzio and Mataniak eds. 2022, 252–254 and 324; AUJ, WP I 58, 202–212 and 426–427.

39 Judgment of the Court of Appeal of 21 March 1820, ANK, 29/200/1716 (WM 243), 565–567. The Court of Appeal in a dispute over an oral contract for the lease of a house stated: "The Court of First Instance, in spite of the evidence offered by Zofia Trynczyńska (the defendant) by witnesses on a circumstance conclusive of the dispute, did not give place to such evidence, and yet such evidence on a subject not exceeding 150 francs may by law be admitted".

FIGURE 27 *Seal of the Faculty of Law of Jagiellonian University introduced in 1817,* (seal matrix, brass, 1817)
SOURCE: JAGIELLONIAN UNIVERSITY ARCHIVES, AUJ, COLLECTION OF THE SEAL MATRIXES, 21; PHOTO & PERMISSION BY JAGIELLONIAN UNIVERSITY ARCHIVES

CHAPTER 8

Inheritance

Piotr Michalik[1] *and Mateusz Mataniak*[2]

1 Introduction

In the impressive body of rulings of the courts of the Free City of Cracow, inheritance cases form a small group,[3] but are particularly rich in legal scholarly content. Some court battles between the wealthier inhabitants of the Republic of Cracow fought over substantial inheritance estates lasted for years, and lavishly rewarded legal argumentation was used as a weapon. This was guaranteed by the best Cracowian lawyers and professors of the Faculty of Law at Jagiellonian University, with Adam Krzyżanowski, a lecturer in French civil law, at the forefront, whose interpretation of the provisions of the NC enjoyed the highest level of authority among Cracow's judges. The most prominent example of this was the struggle between several powerful families (the Sołtyk, Parys, the Potocki and Wielogłowski families) over the inheritance of Father Michał Sołtyk, dean of the Cracow Cathedral Chapter, who died in 1815.[4] It encompassed seven lawsuits directly related to the acquisition and partition of the estate, fought almost continuously between 1818 and 1832. Over the course of them, Cracow's courts issued 19 judgments (three in default), including two by the Court of Last Instance. The case was also the subject of five legal opinions of the Faculty of Law of Jagiellonian University, and it was once litigated as *restitutio in integrum.*[5]

As far as the source material is concerned, the starting point for the presented research on the application of the law of succession of the NC by Cracow's courts, are the opinions issued on this matter between 1818 and 1833 by the Faculty of Law of Jagiellonian University. According to the findings of Andrzej Dziadzio, Mateusz Mataniak and Piotr Michalik, there were 49 such

1 Author of Chapters 8, Sections 1–6, 9 and Table 4.

2 Author of Chapters 8, Sections 7, 8 and 9.

3 See above, Chapter 2.

4 The part of the inheritance not covered by the dispute in question was the rich mineralogical collection, which Michał Sołtyk bequeathed as a legacy to Jagiellonian University, which has kept it to the present day. For more, see Śmiałowski 2000.

5 See below, pp. 232 and 239–241.

 | DOI:10.1163/9789004688742_010

opinions, 17 of which were issued by professors and doctors of law stating a violation of law, constituting grounds for a party to file an appeal to the Court of Last Instance.[6] In addition to the 49 cases in question, a further 40 cases were found in the Court of Appeal's court books from the years 1816–33, 12 of which were finally resolved by the Court of Last Instance because, due to the incompatibility of the judgments of the First and Second Instances, an appeal could be brought to the Third Instance without the opinion of the Faculty of Law of the university. This amounts to a total of 89 cases in which judgments were issued by the Tribunal of First Instance and the Court of Appeals, including 49 cases with the opinion of the Faculty of Law of Jagiellonian University, and 25 cases finally settled only by the judgment of the Court of Last Instance. In these cases – which procedurally were mainly actions for the partition of an estate, a declaration of the invalidity of a will, a surrender of the bequest and the payment of inherited debts – Cracow's courts decided on a broad range of issues, applying provisions from all sections of Title I: "Of Successions" and II: "Of Donations during Life and of Wills" of Book III of the NC.

2 Order of *ab intestato* Succession

Undoubtedly, the least problematic challenge for the courts of the Free City of Cracow was the application of the provisions of the NC regarding the order of *ab intestato* succession. Both the Tribunal of First Instance as well as the Court of Appeals and the Court of Last Instance, correctly determined the heirs entitled to inheritance and the number of portions due to them. It is noteworthy that this was also the case in cases of statutory succession of legally recognised natural children, to whom Articles 756 and 757 of the NC granted the right to inherit from their parents concurrently with the lawful heirs, as Cracow's courts pointed out in the cases of the Molak (1828–29)[7] and Nowicki (1831–32) families.[8] In contrast, doubts arose in the case of the succession rights of the spouse, where French law diverged from Austrian and old-Polish regulations, but the issue only became relevant in the event of a dispute as to the existence or validity of a will or a donation. In the case of statutory succession, the unambiguous wording of Article 767 of the NC left no chance for the spouse

6 See above, Chapter 1 and Dziadzio 2020d, 198, and below, Table 4.

7 Judgment of Tribunal of First Instance of 26 April 1828, ANK, 29/200/2126 (Tryb 324), 1335–1337, 1351–1362; judgment of the Court of Appeal of 17 February 1829, ANK, 29/200/1733 (WM 260), 669–672.

8 See below, pp. 233–234.

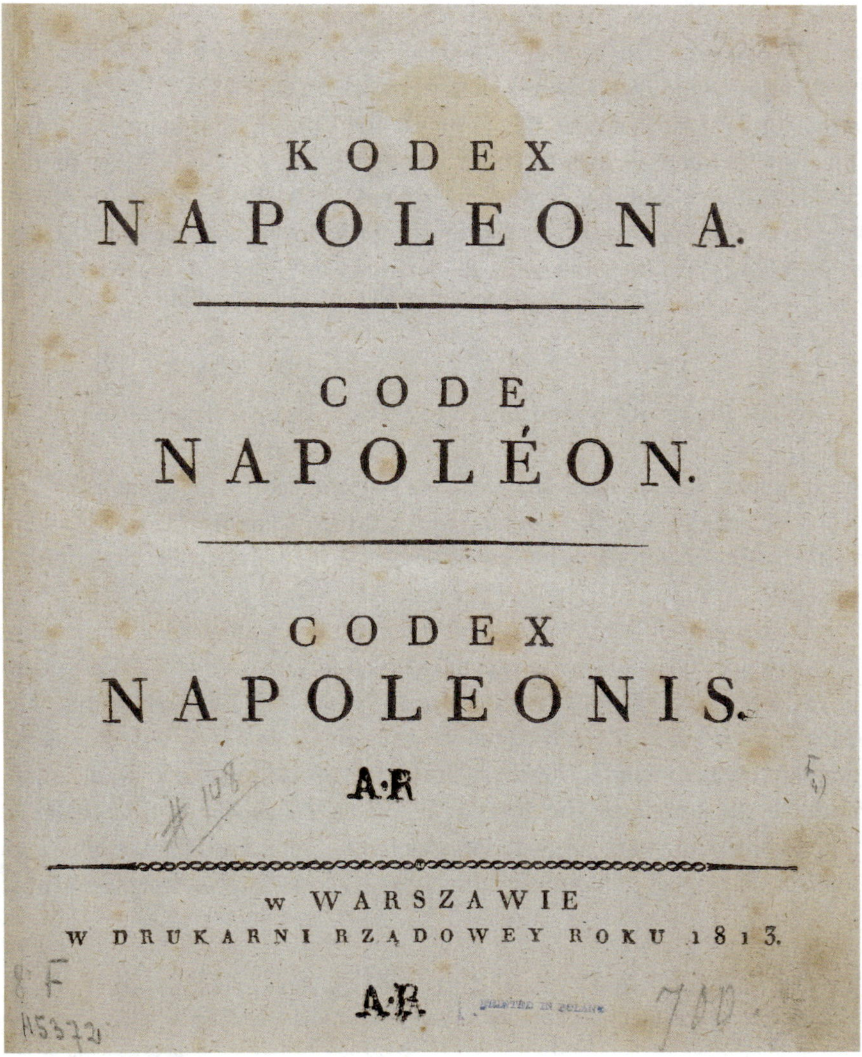

KODEX
NAPOLEONA.

CODE
NAPOLÉON.

CODEX
NAPOLEONIS.

A·R

W WARSZAWIE
W DRUKARNI RZĄDOWEY ROKU 1813.

A·R

FIGURE 28 *Kodeks Napoleona* (*polish translation of 1808*), (print, paper, 1813)
SOURCE: NATIONAL LIBRARY OF FRANCE, 8-F-45372; SCAN BY GALLICA DIGITAL LIBRARY IN PUBLIC DOMAIN (WIKIMEDIA COMMONS)

to be included in the circle of lawful heirs, a place provided for him by the draft civil code of the Free City of Cracow, which was being prepared between 1816 and 1818.[9] For these reasons, the order of *ab intestato* inheritance itself did

9 See Michalik 2022, 13–36.

not as a rule constitute the essence of the dispute, but was established on the occasion of a ruling on another issue forming the basis of the action. This was the situation in the Wypiór family case (1818–20), in which two lawsuits ended with Court of Last Instance judgments on the validity of a judgment of the Chrzanów *dominium* court (in Polish: *sąd dominialny*) of 18 May 1803, on the division of the inheritance of Kazimierz Wypiór.[10] In the Sołtyk family's case, the question of the order of succession according to stocks and heads (Article 743 of the NC) arose only after the fideicommissary substitutions were found to be invalid as to part of the inheritance.[11]

3 The Rights of Compulsory Heirs – The System of Reserve

The system of reserve (*réserve héréditaire*) introduced by the creators of the *Code civil*[12] was alien to Cracow's lawyers, but the mechanism itself for securing the rights of compulsory heirs was familiar to them from the system of legitime under Austrian law. The courts of the Free City of Cracow therefore had no problems in applying the new institution in simple cases, where knowledge of the statutory order of succession and a literal interpretation of Article 913 *et seq.* of the NC was sufficient. This was the situation in the Lebowski family case (1820), in which the Tribunal of First Instance and the Court of Appeal unanimously limited Franciszek Wolff's testamentary disposition to half of the inheritance, i.e. the amount of the disposable portion.[13] This was also the scenario in the Rohlik family case (1825–26), in which the Tribunal of First Instance and the Court of Appeal unanimously dismissed a claim "for the designation of a

10 Judgment of the Tribunal of First Instance of 15 June 1818, ANK, 29/200/1966 (Tryb 163), 683–685; judgment of the Court of Appeal of 2 December 1818, ANK, 29/200/1713 (WM 240), 1069–1071; judgment of the Court of Last Instance of 4 May 1819, ANK, 29/200/1694 (WM 221), No. 11; judgment of the Court of Appeal of 24 November 1819, ANK, 29/200/1715 (WM 242), 1073–1076; judgment of the Court of Last Instance of 16 March 1820, ANK, 29/200/1695 (WM 222), No. 8.

11 Judgment of the Tribunal of First Instance of 30 November 1819, ANK, 29/200/1970 (Tryb 167), 1089–1093; judgment of the Court of Appeal of 1 March 1820, ANK, (WM 243), 367–369; judgment of the Tribunal of First Instance of 27 March 1821, ANK, 29/200/2112 (Tryb 310), 823–829; judgment of the Court of Appeal of 25 June 1822, ANK, 29/200/1718 (WM 245), 1245–1248; judgment of the Court of Last Instance of 22 May 1823, ANK, 29/200/1659 (WM 186), 329–330.

12 On the origins of the system of reserve, see Peguera Poch 2009.

13 Judgment of the Tribunal of First Instance of 21 July 1820, ANK, 29/200/1972 (Tryb 169), 993–995; judgment of the Court of Appeal of 6 September 1820, ANK, 29/200/1717 (WM 244), 431–433.

legitime" for a son from the estate of Wacław Rohlik, who had allocated in his will the share of the inheritance due to his son under the reserve.[14] More complex was the aforementioned Nowicki family case, in which a Cracow clerk, Szymon Nowicki, as the natural son of Jan Nowicki, claimed his compulsory portion from the inheritance of his father, who, having no legitimate descendants, had bequeathed his entire estate to his wife Marianna Nowicka. Both the Tribunal of First Instance and the Court of Appeal had no doubt that Szymon was Jan's son, which was confirmed, *inter alia*, by the parish baptismal certificate of 1797, but it was disputed whether the plaintiff was entitled to the status of a natural child legally recognised under Article 756 of the NC.[15]

Referring to the wording of Article 334 of the NC, which required an official act of acknowledgement for the recognition of a natural child, and which could be expressed in a birth certificate, the Tribunal of First Instance correctly dismissed the claim, as the plaintiff had not submitted such a document and the baptismal certificate did not contain a relevant statement by Jan Nowicki. However, based on the argument of nuisance (appeal) of the plaintiff's attorney Wincenty Szpor, the appellate court changed the first instance judgment granting Jan Nowicki the status under Article 756 of the NC. This was because the Court of Appeal assumed that the baptismal certificate had been drawn up before the NC came into force, so the formal requirements of Article 334 of the NC did not apply to it. However, the baptismal certificate itself, which states that Szymon is John's son out of wedlock, and that he was nevertheless given his father's surname, shows that the latter had the will to acknowledge him legally. What is more, he did not change this will until his death, and in his handwritten will of 1829 he gave him his blessing as a "recognised son", which, after the will had been officially presented in accordance with Article 1007 of the NC, gave this declaration the value of an official act.[16]

The argumentation of the Court of Appeal (composed of Nikorowicz, Piekarski, Januszewicz, Gołuchowski and Mączeński), although erroneous in the light of the letter and spirit of French law, as demonstrated by the defendant's attorney Adam Krzyżanowski in his response to the appeal,[17] is

14 Judgment of the Tribunal of First Instance of 8 October 1825, ANK, 29/200/1988 (Tryb 185), 415–422; judgment of the Court of Appeal of 28 June 1826, ANK, 29/200/1729 (WM 256), 355–358.

15 Judgment of the Tribunal of First Instance of 20 May 1831, ANK, 29/200/2132 (Tryb 330), 1727–1733; judgment of the Court of Appeal of 11 November 1831, ANK, 29/200/1743 (WM 270), 535–541.

16 ANK, 29/200/1743 (WM 270), 535–546.

17 Ibidem, 547–550.

an excellent illustration of the adaptation of the provisions of family law in the NC to the social realities of the Free City of Cracow, something well known from other rulings in Cracow's courts.[18] Undoubtedly, the overriding objective of the Court of Appeal was to award Szymon Nowicki a portion of his father's inheritance, even if it was not due to him under the letter of the applicable law of succession. This is confirmed by the second part of the judgment, in which the Court of Appeal laconically rejected Krzyżanowski's very serious argument against the natural child's right to a reserve. For, in accordance with the position of part of French legal scholarship in the first half of the 19th century, Marianna Nowicka's attorney argued that Article 913 of the NC establishes a compulsory portion only when the testator had legitimate children (by virtue of Article 333 of the NC also legitimated); *a contrario* natural children, also legally recognised, have no right to a reserve. Meanwhile, the Court of Appeal, referring to Article 757 of the NC, which in no way makes a natural child legitimate, but only grants him or her an entitlement to a part of the inheritance of his or her parents, ruled that the plaintiff, by virtue of the compulsory portion, was entitled to half of that part of the inheritance which he or she would have received under Article 913 of the NC had he or she been a legitimate child, i.e. ultimately one-quarter of the inheritance.[19] It is significant that this interpretation was also adopted by French jurisprudence at the time, but there is no evidence that Cracow's judges were aware of it. A similar ruling was also made in 1842 by the Ninth Department of the Senate in Warsaw, in the case of Frankiewicz's successors versus the Jaroszyński family.[20]

A real challenge for the legal elite of the Free City of Cracow, however, was the court battle that lasted from 1827 to 1830 over the estate of Józef Sawiczewski, a well-known Cracow pharmacist and professor at Jagiellonian University, who died in 1825. It encompassed two lawsuits over the partition of the estate, the first of which in the years 1827–28 was, in terms of legal scholarship, one of the most interesting cases settled by the courts of the Republic of Cracow.[21] The parties to the dispute were testamentary heirs, each of whom received one-sixth of the estate from the testator: the deceased's adult sons from his first marriage (Julian, Florian and Ignacy Sawiczewski), the widow from his third marriage, Aniela Sawiczewska (*secundo voto* Eminowiczowa), together with her minor children Konstanty and Bolesława from that marriage. Since the testator not only disposed of his property through his will but also

18 See above, Chapter 1.

19 ANK, 29/200/1743 (WM 270), 535–541.

20 Kapuściński ed. 1869, 9–10. See also Bieda, Wiśniewska-Jóźwiak 2014, 113–115.

21 See Michalik 2021, 307–330.

through donations to his sons and wife, it was necessary to apply not only the provisions on testamentary legacies and donations, including those between spouses, but also the provisions on the disposable portion, restitutions and reductions to resolve the case.[22]

In the case of the Sawiczewski family, the Tribunal of First Instance erroneously adopted Article 913 of the NC as the basis for determining the amount of the disposable portion, which, according to this court, in view of the testator leaving five children, amounted to one-quarter of the inheritance. Based on Krzyżanowski's appeal, the Court of Appeal (composed of Piekarski, Januszewicz, Soczyński, Gołuchowski and Mączeński) correctly pointed out that Article 1098 of the NC, which reduced the amount of the disposable portion in the case of generosity in favour of the testator's subsequent spouse to the amount of the portion of the child receiving the least, which in this case amounted to one-sixth of the inheritance (which the courts did not specify). This position was supported by the Faculty of Law of Jagiellonian University (composed of Słotwiński, Jaworski, Szpor, Soświński and Kojsiewicz) and was finally approved by the Court of Last Instance (composed of: Nikorowicz, Januszewicz, Soczyński, Gołuchowski, Mączeński, Dzianotty and Himonowski), thanks to which Cracow's courts also correctly determined the amount of the reserve in this case. This, however, was the end of adjudication in accordance with the NC, as Cracow's lawyers, educated on Roman and Austrian law, did not accept the French system of the law of succession based on the precedence of statutory inheritance over testamentary inheritance.

4 Testamentary Legacies

Under both Roman law, which Cracow's lawyers continued to regard as the model *ius commune*,[23] and the Austrian West Galician Code of 1797, which was in force in Cracow before the NC was introduced there, the establishment of an

22 Judgment of the Tribunal of First Instance of 28 August 1827, ANK, 29/200/1993 (Tryb 190), 1975–1986; judgment of the Court of Appeal of 17 January 1828, ANK, 29/200/1730 (WM 257), 141–148; opinion of the Faculty of Law of Jagiellonian University of 22 February 1828, AUJ, WP I 58, 413–417; Dziadzio and Mataniak eds. 2022, 318–320; judgment of the Court of Last Instance of 13 March 1828, ANK, 29/200/1665 (WM 192), 751–760.

23 See e.g. ANK, 29/200/1715 (WM 242), 241 and ANK, 29/200/1717 (WM 244), 439. This is evidenced above all by letters from lawyers in which they not infrequently refer to Roman law. By virtue of his academic specialisation, the protagonist of this practice was Professor of Roman law Feliks Słotwiński who, when arguing in favour of his client, would casually remind the court of the Roman law principles of the institution in question.

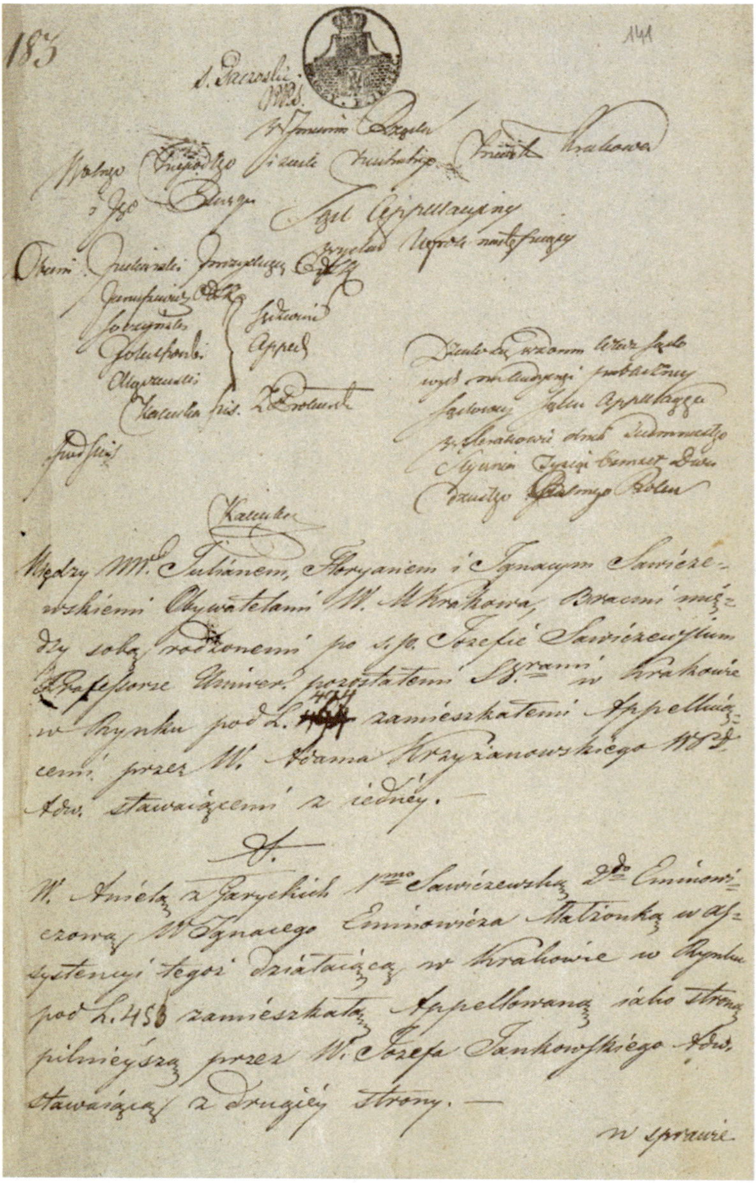

Między WW. Julianem, Floryanem i Ignacym Sawiczewskiemi Obywatelami W. M. Krakowa, Braćmi między sobą rodzonemi po s.p. Józefie Sawiczewskim Professorze Univer. pozostałemi ... w Krakowie w Rynku pod L. 404 zamieszkałemi Appellującemi przez W. Adama Krzyżanowskiego ... Adw. stawaiącemi z iedney. —

A.

W. Amelią z Garyckich 1mo Sawiczewską 2do Emmanowiczową W. Ignacego Emmanowicza Matronką w assystencyi tegoż działaiącą w Krakowie w Rynku pod L. 456 zamieszkałą Appellowaną iako stroną pilnieyszą przez W. Józefa Jankowskiego Adw. stawaiącą z drugiey strony. —

w sprawie

FIGURE 29 *Judgment of the Court of Appeal of 17 January 1828 in case of Sawiczewscy*, (manuscript, paper, 1828)
SOURCE: NATIONAL ARCHIVES IN CRACOW, ANK, 29/200/1730, 141; PHOTO & PERMISSION BY NATIONAL ARCHIVES IN CRACOW

heir took place through a will.[24] Only in the case of the absence of a will did the statutory succession apply. Also in French law, the testator could draw up a will and also establish an heir within it (Article 967 of the NC). However, according to the compromise conception in the NC, combining the institutions of written law (*droit écrit*) with the institutions of customary law (*droit coutumière*) of pre-revolutionary France, the testamentary heir thus appointed was not an heir (*héritier*), but only a legatee (*légataire*). The most important consequence of this was that the legatee did not come into possession of the estate (*saisine*) as soon as it was opened (Article 724 of the NC), unless he or she was at the same time a compulsory heir (*héritier réservataire*) or none of the compulsory heirs lived to see the opening of the estate (article 1006 of the NC). In addition, the NC introduced a system – backbreaking for practice – of testamentary legacies which, in France itself, has been flattened over time by legal scholarship and case law. Article 1002 of the NC divided testamentary dispositions into three types: general legacies (*legs universel*), which introduced legatees in place of heirs to the entire estate (*heredis loco*); legacies under a general title (*legs à titre universel*), which introduced legatees in place of heirs to part of the estate, but with limitations; and legacies under a specific title (*legs à titre particulier*), which gave legatees a right to specific items of the estate.

In the majority of the inheritance cases heard by the courts of the Free City of Cracow, the testators disposed of their property by will,[25] and also appointing "universal heirs" in it.[26] It is clear from the court records of these cases, that both judges and attorneys-at-law, including professors of law at Jagiellonian University, treated the heirs so appointed as true heirs, trying to match specific provisions of the NC to this assumption. The consequences, judged in terms of the correctness of the interpretation of French law, varied. In the Styrio family case, which took place between 1821 and 1822, the dispute was over the inheritance of Tomasz Styrio, who bequeathed his entire estate to his wife Agnieszka Styrio in his will with the exclusion of the children of his sister Maria Roża née Styrio, entitled to inherit under Article 750 of the NC. In this case, both the Tribunal of First Instance and the Court of Appeal (composed

24 See § 331 and 346, part II of the West Galician Code.

25 The subject of the presented research did not include the establishment of a statistical study of inheritance as a socio-legal phenomenon, so at present it is impossible to say to what extent the conclusions derived from the courts' case law alone reflect the actual socio-legal processes related to inheritance. For example, it is still not known what percentage of Cracow's testators made a will and what percentage of these wills were subsequently the subject of litigation between heirs.

26 See e.g. ANK, 29/200/1993 (Tryb 190), 1977 and ANK, 29/200/1730 (WM 257), 143.

of: Nikorowicz, Piekarski, Litwiński, Januszewicz, Gołuchowski and Soczyński) correctly recognised the defendant Agnieszka Styrio as the sole successor of the testator, which was also tacitly acknowledged by the Faculty of Law.[27] Due to this and the laconic content of the Court of Appeal 's judgment, it is impossible to ascertain whether the argumentation presented in the plaintiffs' appeal by attorney Michał Stróżecki was considered by the Court of Appeal judges and professors of the Faculty of Law of Jagiellonian University. He pointed out that pursuant to Article 724 of the NC, it was the statutory heirs who took possession of the inheritance upon its opening and, consequently, the defendant illegally took possession of the inheritance. This objection indicates that Stróżecki was referring to the defendant's status as a legatee, but erroneously ignoring the wording of Article 1006 of the NC, as the plaintiffs were not compulsory heirs.[28]

The situation was different in the above-mentioned case of the Sawiczewski family, in which Cracow's lawyers demonstrated *en masse* a lack of understanding of the NC. Of Józef Sawiczewski's testamentary heirs, all of his children were compulsory heirs, and as such they took joint possession of the entire estate as soon as their father died. Aniela Sawiczewska, on the other hand, as his wife, not being a legitimate heir, was only a legatee under a general title, who, pursuant to Article 1011 of the NC, should apply to the heirs for the legacy due to her. However, based on the intention of the testator as expressed in his will, the courts of all instances recognised Florian Sawiczewski as a "universal heir", who took possession of the entire estate *in natura* and was obliged to pay the other testamentary heirs in equal shares. Contrary to the appearance created by the actual consent of the other heirs to Florian's taking possession of the inheritance, the consequence of this state of affairs was not merely a formal breach of the Code, but a defective partition of the estate. The recognition of Aniela Sawiczewska as an heir resulted in her taking part in the settlements prescribed by Article 843 of the NC for the return to the inheritance estate of donations received from Józef Sawiczewski by his sons. This in turn led to a defective reduction of the testator's generosity under Article 922 of the NC.

27 Although it also correctly stated that both courts had violated Articles 1007 and 1008 of the *Code civil*, that could not, however, have the effect of depriving Agnieszka Styrio of her inheritance when the courts had found the will to be valid. Perhaps for this reason, the plaintiffs did not ultimately file an appeal with the Court of Last Instance.

28 Judgment of the Tribunal of First Instance of 7 July 1821, ANK, 29/200/1975 (Tryb 172), 789–791; judgment of the Court of Appeal of 7 May 1822, ANK, 29/200/1720, (WM 247), 717–718; opinion of the Faculty of Law of the Jagiellonian University of 4 July 1822, AUJ, WP I 57, 104–106; Dziadzio and Mataniak eds. 2022, 91–92.

Ultimately, it was the widow who was harmed by the judges who charged her with the status of heir and spouse, dual and mutually exclusive under the NC.[29]

5 Inherited Debts

Among the issues determined by the interpretation of testamentary legacies, one of the most important was liability for inherited debts. Disputes about them usually took the form of actions for payment. In the course of these, the courts decided on the extent of the liability of individual heirs, both towards the creditors of the estate and towards each other. In the majority of cases, the question of the extent of liability for the debts of individual heirs, as regulated by the provisions of the law of succession (Articles 870–882 of the NC), was not in dispute, and the subject of the decision was the proper application of the provisions of contract law. This was the situation in the case of the Dyktarski family (1824–25), where the dispute concerned the set-off of debts,[30] and in the Kubecki family case (1826–29), where the application to co-heirs of the provisions on solidarity of debtors and divisibility of obligations, was disputed.[31] However, in more complex cases, the issue of liability for inherited debts was only one element of the dispute, which concerned the determination of the acquisition and partition of the estate itself on the basis of the interpretation of the testamentary legacies. This was the case, *inter alia*, in the aforementioned multi-year court battle of the Sołtyk family, in which Michał Sołtyk's nephews and testamentary heirs, Władysław and Karol Sołtyk, represented by Feliks Słotwiński, clashed with the testator's other heirs, represented by Adam Krzyżanowski.[32]

---

29 For more, see Michalik 2021, 325–327.

30 Judgment of Tribunal of First Instance of 15 October 1824, ANK, 29/200/1985 (Tryb 182), 614–632; judgment of the Court of Appeal of 15 March 1825, ANK, 29/200/1715 (WM 242), 563–565; opinion of the Faculty of Law of Jagiellonian University of 11 May 1825, AUJ, WP I 58, 37–39; Dziadzio and Mataniak eds. 2022, 180–181; judgment of the Court of Last Instance of 20 July 1825, ANK, 29/200/1700 (WM 227), No. 12.

31 Judgment of the Tribunal of First Instance of 19 June 1827, ANK, 29/200/1993 (Tryb 190), 505–513; judgment of the Court of Appeal of 4 February 1828, ANK, 29/200/1730 (WM 257), 257–261; opinion of the Faculty of Law of the Jagiellonian University of 8 March 1828, AUJ, WP I 58, 422–426; Dziadzio and Mataniak eds. 2022, 322–323; judgment of the Court of Last Instance of 19 February 1829, ANK, 29/200/1665 (WM 192), 725–730.

32 This battle ended in 1832 with the final defeat of Władysław and Karol Sołtyk, who incidentally both died the year before, at the relatively young ages of 44 and 40.

The Sołtyk family case is particularly valuable for the study of the application of the NC provisions by the courts of the Free City of Cracow, not least because it provides an insight into the way in which Cracow's lawyers understood the principle of *favor testamenti*. Michał Sołtyk drew up his will in 1808, i.e. under the West Galician Code. In this will, in accordance with § 400, Part II of this Act, he established two fideicommissary substitutions. The first comprised a portion of the testator's landed estates (the Niegoszowice estate and immovable properties in Cracow) bequeathed to Władysław Sołtyk and his "successors in the name and our Family". The second comprised a collection of valuables ("family jewels") bequeathed to each of the "eldest Sołtyk of my line", who was also Władysław Sołtyk at the time.[33] The opening of this will, however, took place in 1815, i.e. under the NC, which meant that the provisions of the French Code had to be applied to the validity of the will under the transitive regulations of the Duchy of Warsaw.[34] These provisions, in Article 896 of the NC, following the revolutionary legislation, declared the *substitution fidéicommissaire* to be absolutely invalid, i.e. both as regards the proximate (*le grevé*) and the distant legatee (*l'appelé*). The Tribunal of First Instance, the Court of Appeal and the Faculty of Law of Jagiellonian University therefore declared the will invalid in this respect, and ruled that the succession items covered by both substitutions were subject to statutory succession with the exclusion of Władysław Sołtyk and his descendants.[35] Finally, by a judgment of 22 May 1823 in the third successive lawsuit of the Sołtyk family, the Court of Last Instance awarded one-third of the would-be substitutions to Karol Sołtyk and two-thirds to the plaintiffs.[36]

This ruling was incorrect. It was Krzyżanowski who, using his legitimate arguments concerning the invalidity of the substitution, pushed through a ruling favourable to his clients, recognising them as statutory co-heirs of the property that the testator undoubtedly wished to preserve in the male line of the Sołtyk family. However, the sanction of Article 896 of the NC did not apply to Karol Sołtyk, who continued to be a legitimate "universal heir", i.e. in effect a general legatee. In accordance with the principle of *favor testamenti*, the courts

33 Kielce, State Archives, *Testament Michała Sołtyka*, Akta notariusza Andrzeja Kossowicza, 1815, file No. 3, 205–211v.

34 See *Dekret z 10 października 1810 r.*, DPKW, vol. 2, 84–96.

35 Judgement of the Tribunal of First Instance of 24 May 1819, ANK, 29/200/1969 (Tryb 166), 35–40; judgment of the Court of Appeal of 3 August 1819, ANK, 29/200/1715 (WM 242), 233–236; opinion of the Faculty of Law of Jagiellonian University of 11 October 1819, AUJ, WP I 57, 26–27; Dziadzio and Mataniak eds. 2022, 45–46.

36 See above, footnote 11.

should have held that if Michał Sołtyk had known that he was not allowed to establish substitutions, he would have bequeathed the part of the estate covered by them together with the rest of his hereditary estate to his two nephews. However, as Władysław's succession was ruled out in this respect, the object of the substitution should have been assigned to Karol Sołtyk on the basis of accrual, and should not have been divided among the legal heirs. Belatedly, i.e. in the fourth successive case of the Sołtyk family (1824–25), this error came to light in connection with a dispute over liability for inherited debts. The Tribunal of First Instance and the Court of Appeal, on the basis of the latter's final judgment of 1819, held that Władysław and Karol Sołtyk were in the will only legatees under a special title, and were not liable for inherited debts under Article 871 of the NC. The inconsistency of this reasoning with Michał Sołtyk's intention expressed in his will, was noted by the Faculty of Law of Jagiellonian University, and on this basis the Court of Last Instance recognised the testator's nephews as legatees under a general title (general legatees).[37] This by no means meant an improvement in the situation for the Sołtyk family. On the contrary, it represented another brilliant victory for Krzyżanowski, who this time burdened Słotwiński's clients with the obligation to participate in the inherited debts also on the basis of a testamentary bequest (Articles 871 and 1012 of the NC).

6 Law and Justice

The already repeated claim that Cracow's lawyers had problems with understanding the classification of the law of succession in the NC and, as a result, in intricate cases made a wrong subsumption of its provisions, is, in the light of the sources, justified insofar as we analyse them solely at the level of legal scholarship, disregarding other factors which influenced specific decisions of the judges. Even then, however, there are cases in which the courts of the Free City of Cracow, like other tribunals in the past and today, ruled *de iure* on the basis of the law and *de facto* on the basis of equity understood as the fulfilment of social justice. This was the situation in the Czałczyński family case (1820–21), in which the Tribunal of First Instance and the Court of Appeal settled

37 Judgment of the Tribunal of First Instance of 31 July 1824, ANK, 29/200/1984 (Tryb 181), 980–988; judgment of the Court of Appeal of 1 February and 2 March 1825, ANK, 29/200/1725 (WM 252), 231–236; opinion of the Faculty of Law of Jagiellonian University of 7 November 1825, AUJ, WP I 58, 97–101; Dziadzio and Mataniak eds. 2022, 208–210; judgment of the Court of Last Instance of 15 June 1826, ANK, 29/200/1663 (WM 190), 25–29.

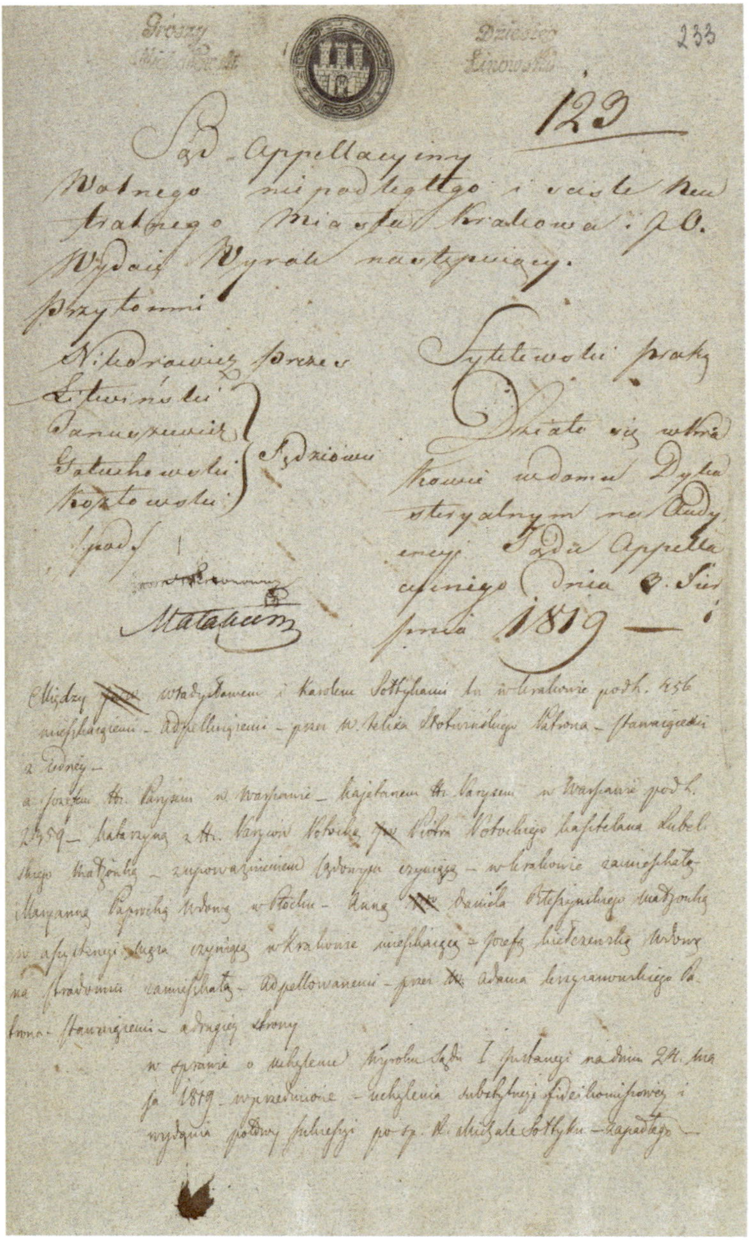

FIGURE 30 *Judgment of the Court of Appeal of 3 August 1819 in case of Sołtykowie*, (manuscript, paper, 1819)

SOURCE: NATIONAL ARCHIVES IN CRACOW, ANK, 29/200/1715, 233; PHOTO & PERMISSION BY NATIONAL ARCHIVES IN CRACOW

a dispute over the estate of a Carmelite monk, Franciszek Czałczyński, who had died without a will. The plaintiffs in the case were his parents Franciszek Czałczyński and Marianna Czałczyńska, poor people who were dependent on their son before his death; the defendant was Alojzy Bartosiewicz, provincial of the Congregation of Carmelite Fathers. The Tribunal of First Instance, referring to the fact that the NC does not regulate the inheritance of a monk's estate, held, on the basis of transitive provisions, that the case should be adjudicated on the basis of old law, i.e. Austrian law.[38] Thus, in accordance with the canonical maxim adopted therein, *monachus quidquid adquirit, monasterio adquirit*, the Tribunal of First Instance dismissed the action, ruling that Czałczyński did not leave any inheritance at all, as all the funds accumulated by him after his perpetual monastic vows are the property of the Congregation.[39]

The judgment of the Tribunal of First Instance was clearly contrary to the law, as the transitive decree in no way gave grounds to apply old law to the succession of an estate opened in 1819, i.e. nine years after the entry into force of the NC. This Code, enacted in post-revolutionary France, no longer recognised the category of civil death following perpetual monastic vows, and the rules of statutory succession should apply to the case. The fact was, however, that as a result of legislative negligence, no specific order of succession to the clergy had been established in the Free City of Cracow until that time, although in the socio-economic realities of the Republic this was an important issue.[40] This did not occur until the Act of the Assembly of Representatives of 2 January 1821,[41] incidentally enacted before the Court of Appeal issued its judgment in this case. The latter acknowledged the plaintiffs' appeal written by Słotwiński, in which he presented a way out of the situation that would simultaneously preserve the appearance of legalism and elementary social justice.[42] The Court of Appeal (composed of Nikorowicz, Piekarski, Januszewicz, Gołuchowski and Soczyński) thus ruled that, due to the fact that Czałczyński had been secularised by papal dispensation in 1815, the property accumulated from then until his death constituted his legacy and, pursuant to Article 748 of the NC, passed it in equal portions to his parents as legal heirs.[43]

38 See *Dekret z 10 października 1810 r.*, DPKW, vol. 2, 84–96.

39 Judgment of the Tribunal of First Instance of 28 October 1820, ANK, 29/200/1973 (Tryb 170), 707–710.

40 It was regulated in the draft civil code of 1816–18. See above, Chapter 3.

41 See below, Chapter 8, Section 8.

42 ANK, 29/200/1718 (WM 245), 535–541.

43 Judgment of the Court of Appeal of 14 March 1821, ANK, 29/200/1718 (WM 245), 531–533.

7 Heirless Estates

A significant role in the legal practice of the Free City of Cracow was also played by so-called heirless estates. They are among the institutions present in all the codes that were in force in the Polish lands in the 19th century.[44] As a general rule, in the absence of statutory heirs from among the family of the deceased or the renunciation by all those entitled to inherit from accepting the inheritance, the entity entitled to the inheritance in last place was the Public Treasury. Heirless estates belonged to the State *iure imperii*, i.e. by virtue of its sovereignty over a territory. This principle appeared in the NC in Article 768, which proclaimed that "if there is no surviving spouse, the inheritance belongs to the people". This provision also reaffirmed the general rule expressed in Articles 539 and 713 of the NC, which placed all vacant and ownerless estates in the category of public property. Acquisition of escheats took place on a statutory basis, following entry into possession by the decision of the competent court (Article 770 of the NC).[45] The aforementioned Article 713 of the NC was a historical remnant of the medieval land regalia, under which all land with no other owner belonged to the ruler.[46] The provision proclaimed that "Property which has no owner belongs to the nation".[47]

The provisions of Articles 811 to 814 of the NC were specifically devoted to heirless estates. The former pointed to the circumstances in which an estate could be considered as heirless. These concerned the expiry of the time limit set for the notification to take possession of the inheritance, if it turned out that the heirs were not known or had renounced the inheritance. An additional condition was also the expiry of the time limit for making of the inventory (Article 811 of the NC). Article 812 of the NC required the Court of First Instance, in whose district the inheritance had been opened, to appoint a curator of the inheritance at the request of persons with a legal interest in it or the Government prosecutor. A further provision required the curator of the estate to make an inventory of the estate and to take all measures that would enable the estate's rights to be effectively sought and protected, including litigation with those claiming against the estate. The curator also managed the estate's assets, including transferring to the government coffers all funds belonging to the estate, in particular those obtained through the sale of movable and

44 The belief that the State is the last and necessary successor of a natural person was already present in Roman law. See Blicharz 2016, 263–264.

45 Stus 2005, 72. The Public Treasury was therefore not among the statutory heirs.

46 Dąbkowski 1922, 220.

47 For more about Article 713 of the NC, see Sokołowski 2016, 64–67.

immovable property. He was to submit accounts of his management activities (Article 813 of the NC). The provisions concerning heirs taking possession of an inheritance up to the level of net assets (814 of the NC), and the provisions of Articles 998–1002 of the NC were to be applied by the curator.

Under the conditions of the Free City of Cracow, the implementation of Article 768 of the NC belonged to the senator overseeing institute affairs and the care of minors (in the original: on the administration of the treasury estate). It was incumbent on him to apply for affixing of a seal by the justice of the peace with jurisdiction over the location of the estate. It was also required to draw up an inventory of the estate, in accordance with the rules laid down for the acceptance of inheritances up to the level of net assets (Article 769). The senator also had to apply to the competent Court of First Instance for the introduction of possession of the estate. The adjudication of possession could only take place after the potential heirs had been summoned three times, following the legal opinion of the Government prosecutor.[48] Procedural issues concerning the sealing of inheritances by justices of the peace were also regulated in the Code of Civil Procedure. This was primarily dealt with by the provisions of Articles 907–925 of said procedure. The above-mentioned provisions gave rise to numerous doubts, and perhaps they were not applied in accordance with the letter of the law, in any case, in 1820, the Court of Appeal, through the Senate, ordered their contents to be recalled to commune heads and their deputies.[49]

The number of proceedings for the declaration of inheritance by the Public Treasury was quite considerable in the Free City of Cracow. By way of example, in the period between 1 June 1822 and 30 May 1823 alone, 32 heirless estates were awarded to the Public Treasury. In the reporting period 1824/25, this number rose to 53, consisting of "various things and cash". The correspondence of the Ruling Senate with the Accounts Office shows that the awarding of inheritances was done in compliance with the applicable procedural provisions.[50]

48 In the original: Imperial prosecutor (Article 770).

49 Proclamation of the Ruling Senate of 14 June 1820 No. 1647 DGS, DRz. WMK, No. 40 of 21 October 1820, 161–168; ibidem, No. 41 of 28 October 1820, 169–172. They concerned the provisions of Articles 907–944 of the Code of Civil Procedure.

50 Adjudication of ownership was made by the Tribunal of the First Instance, by way of judgments, at the request of the public prosecutor at this court, after the successors' summonses had been declared ineffective ("they did not appear despite the required announcements"), with reference to the provisions of Articles 768 and 770 of the NC, etc. Cash and other movable property previously deposited at the Deposit Office were collected by the Government assessor or cashier and brought to the Government's General Cash Office.

In 1825, the Senate proposed to the Court of First Instance the creation of a separate "cadastre of heirless estates", the maintenance of which was to rest with the General Cash Office. The most important purpose of keeping the list was to safeguard the ability of successors to claim inheritances previously granted to the Public Treasury. This was a consequence of the fact that they were entitled to claim the inheritance until the expiry of the limitation period, set at 30 years. This period, according to the interpretation made by Government lawyers of Article 2229 of the NC, was to be counted from the moment the inheritance was adjudicated by the Tribunal of First Instance. However, there were doubts as to whether, in the event of recovery of the estate, the heirs had a claim against the Public Treasury for the return of the benefits.[51]

In view of the conceivable liability of the Public Treasury for the inheritance assets of private individuals, the Government had the intention of appointing a separate official to supervise the assets acquired in this way, and to deal with the acts of negotiation, based on the files of the Tribunal of First Instance. In doing so, he was to be authorised to collect from the court depository movable properties, cash and debentures that had not been submitted to the Mortgage Commission as not having been brought to the mortgage file (not entered). It may be added that the value of an heirless estate was often negligible. This is because the most frequent cases involved non-entered debentures. In order to limit the court costs charged to the estate, the appointed officials were therefore to summon the debtors to accept the debt, to secure it and to settle voluntarily and, in addition, to pay the outstanding commissions, within a five-year period, with the possibility of instalments.[52] According to a list kept in the Senate's Main Archives, some 365 heirless estates were adjudicated for the benefit of the Public Treasury between 1839 and 1853, of which, however, a large proportion was later returned to the heirs.[53] It is not possible today to

51 Since, in the Senate's view, this was certainly not the case with regard to the benefits collected by the Government before a court judgment awarding the inheritance to the Public Treasury was made, it was necessary to classify them as special treasury capital for remedies, with the obligation to record them in a separate register.

52 Letter from the Ruling Senate to the Senator overseeing institute affairs and the care of minors, the Accounts Office, the Public Revenue Department, the General Treasury and the Tribunal of the First Instance, 7 June 1826, ANK, 29/200/1289 (WM 355), 5–10, 51.

53 Letter from the Administrative Council to the Tribunal of First Instance and the Governorate Commission of 25 May 1853, ANK, 29/200/253 (WMK V-54A), 35–36; *Konsygnacja Akt byłego Senatu Rządzącego odnoszących się do mass bezdziedzicznych Skarbowi Publicznemu przez były Trybunał Krakowski przyznanych* of 5 January 1853, ibidem, 7–32.

determine their exact number, although the Government informed the judicial authorities of the estates seized by the Public Treasury in separate reports.[54]

Referring to archival sources, it can be stated that the adjudication of assets in favour of the Public Treasury did indeed take place as a result of a resolution of the Tribunal of the First Instance.[55] This took place only after the expiry of the time limit set for the heirs in press notices.[56] The collection of sums from the deposit and their payment to the General Cash Office was carried out by authorised officials from the office of the senator overseeing institute affairs and the care of minors, or from the Office of Treasury Affairs.[57] The return of assets already granted to the Public Treasury was only possible after the applicants had demonstrated that they were "indeed successors".[58] Various documentation was used to establish the legal and factual status of the estates to be taken over by the Public Treasury, including "Tables of the deed of sealing", which contain detailed data on the family status of the deceased, the assets left by them – movable and immovable – as well as the activities already carried out in relation to the estate (e.g. auctions held).[59]

It may be added that the adjudication in favour of the Public Treasury could concern only a small part of the succession estate, in view of the fact that the remainder was taken over by heirs: statutory or testamentary. This is demonstrated by the example of the estate of Marcin Krzyżanowski, who died in 1802, and whose entire estate, consisting of movable property and a town house at Grodzka Street No. 37, was acquired by his adult children, Tomasz Krzyżanowski and Elżbieta Chryścińska, née Krzyżanowska. The case involved the sealing of the inheritance and negotiations at the magistrate's office of the City of Cracow, followed by a judicial division of the inheritance. Each successor took the share falling to him, with only 98 zlotys 10 grosz left in the

54 Letter from the Ruling Senate to the Tribunal of 3 July 1843, ANK, 29/200/2300 (Tryb 103), 2907–2908. The reports have not survived to the present day.

55 The case of Mikołaj Jurkowski's estate: the Tribunal's resolution of 28 December 1843, ANK, 29/200/2333 (Tryb 136), 13–14.

56 The case of the estate of Jacek and Jadwiga Czech: Letter from the Tribunal to the Ruling Senate of 25 January 1841, ANK, 29/200/2334 (Tryb 137), 437.

57 The case of the estate of Kazimierz Pałka and Antoni Strzelbicki: Letter from the Ruling Senate to the senator overseeing institute affairs and the care of minors and the Tribunal, 20 October 1840, ANK, 29/200/2333 (Tryb 136), 45.

58 A certificate could be issued, for example, by a family council, in the case of minors. The case of the successors of Salomea Majewska née Haller: Letter from the Ruling Senate to Wincenty Wolff, attorney for the Majewski family of 3 December 1840, ANK, 29/200/2333 (Tryb 136), 871.

59 Letter from the Ruling Senate to the Tribunal of 13 September 1844, ANK, 29/200/2301 (Tryb 104), no pagination.

deposit, as well as a bond from Michał Wołowski for 1,500 Rhine zlotys (i.e. 6,000 Polish zlotys), attached to the file and secured on a house in Mikołajska Street No. 672. The situation of the estate was announced in 1819, and since no one appeared for the deposited money and debenture for 20 years, it was awarded to the Public Treasury.[60]

8 The Protection of the Succession Rights of the Catholic Church

A special place in the application of succession law in the Free City of Cracow was occupied by cases concerning the clergy and institutes of the Catholic Church. Its privileged constitutional and material position and the still living traditions of Josephinism, were the basis for the modification of French succession law, guaranteeing both the protection of the public interest and the property interests of the Catholic Church itself. This found a legal basis in the constitutions of the Republic of Cracow, which recognised Roman Catholicism as the religion of the state.[61] Also, the *de facto* position of the Catholic Church in the Free City fully justified granting it the position of *primus inter pares* among the Christian denominations.[62] In Cracow, together with the District, 46 parishes were involved in pastoral activities, 13 of them in Cracow. The District had three deaneries (Czernichów, Bolechowice and Nowa góra) comprising 33 parishes. In total, the Catholic Church in the Republic of Cracow had about 70 churches. There were also very numerous monasteries, both male and female.[63] As was the case in the period of the Duchy of Warsaw, contacts between the Government and the clergy were maintained through the General Consistory of the Diocese of Cracow, i.e. the so-called diocesan curia, and the Cracow Cathedral Chapter, i.e. an auxiliary organ of the Bishop of Cracow.[64]

The starting point for the modification of the succession provisions of the *Code civil*, which based the question of succession to and by clergy and

60 Letter from the Tribunal to the Ruling Senate of 20 July 1840, ANK, 29/200/2333 (Tryb 136), 215; *Stan masy śp. Marcina Krzyżanowskiego*, ibidem, 217; copy of the rescript of the Ruling Senate of 7 August 1840, ibidem, 219–220.

61 "The Catholic, Apostolic and Roman religion is maintained as the national religion": Article 1 of the 1815 Constitution.

62 Whose followers were equal in political and civil rights: Articles 2 and 3 of the 1815 Constitution.

63 Urban 2016, 123–141.

64 Numerous tasks were also performed by ecclesiastical janitors, appointed at parishes as management and consultative bodies. For more, see Mataniak 2017a, 123–149; Mataniak 2019a, 321–323.

ecclesiastical institutes on general principles, was the enactment at the Legislative Assembly in 1818 of five principles of law governing these issues.[65] However, unlike most of the principles enacted at the time, the principles mentioned above were reflected in the laws passed by the Assemblies of Representatives. This occurred firstly in the 1821 Act relating to the treatment of property left by priests who died without having made a will.[66] According to the preamble to the Act, its main purpose was to provide relief to certain parishes, as well as to subsidise the Charitable Society's meagre financial resources.[67] According to Article 1 of the Act, non-testamentary inheritances from clergy, both lay and religious, including members of abolished monasteries, were to be divided into three parts. In the case of clergymen holding an ecclesiastical benefice ("installed" on *benefitio curiata or benefitio simplicia*) or other paid ecclesiastical posts, one part went to the church, the second to the poor and the third to the successors. The inheritances of clergymen who were not attached to the parish church for life, but only "temporarily, substitutively or auxiliary", performed paid clerical duties or remained in an office paid from the Public Treasury, were to be received in two-thirds by the successors and one-third by the poor.[68]

In doing so, a stipulation was introduced that relatives remaining "in a truly poor condition", once confirmed by the Senate, could also request the share due to the poor (Article 2).[69] This provision was applied in the case of the Uszewski siblings Bernard, Józef, Napoleon, Helena and Teodozja, the survivors of Wincenty and Barbara née Janowska. They applied to the Senate to be granted one-third of the "remainder of the pure estate" of their uncle, Father Jacek Janowski, a share which, under ordinary circumstances, would have gone to the poor people's fund. As the documents they submitted did indeed confirm the state of poverty, the Senate agreed to the passing of one-third of the estate to the nephews and nieces of the late priest.[70] It should be pointed

65 See above, Chapter 3.

66 The Act of 2 January 1821, *Postępowanie z majątkiem po zmarłych xx. bez testamentu pozostałym*, promulgated by the letter of the Ruling Senate of 12 January 1821, No. 110 DGS, DRRz.WMK of 1821 (hereinafter: Act of 1821).

67 The Charitable Society financed, *inter alia*, the stay of people in the Shelter Home for the Poor. The preamble also referred to the financial difficulties of the parish hospitals in the district, where "peasants commonly sought shelter because of their age or infirmity".

68 Act of 1821.

69 Ibidem. The remainder of the Act set out the rules for calculating the shares for individual heirs (Articles 3–5).

70 Letter from the Governing Senate to the Accounts Office of 10 October 1835, ANK, 29/200/1291 (WM 357), 529–530. The Senate also exempted the Uszewski family from the stamp duty on inheritances.

out, however, that in court records from the period of the Republic of Cracow, examples can be found to show that succession after clergymen took place not on the basis of the 1821 Act, but on the basis of general principles.[71]

Closely related to the above regulation was the 1819 Act for the protection of estates left by priests who had been benefice holders.[72] Its purpose was to safeguard "the entire funds of religious institutes". This exposure to loss occurred when the estate of a deceased benefice-holder was taken over by heirs who refused to compensate for the damage caused by the testator to the fund property. The remedies consisted of several solutions. First, it was to be mandatory to seal the succession property, which, according to Article 907 of the Civil Procedure Code, belonged to a justice of the peace or his deputy. This act was to be attended by the commune head, as a representative of the local administration, the local dean (i.e. the clergyman in charge of the deanery, i.e. a unit of the ecclesiastical administrative division) and a *collator* (i.e. the person exercising the "right of collation" with respect to the parish). Not infrequently the latter was the founder of the local church.

All of them were to ensure that the assets constituting the institute's property were nevertheless excluded from the sealing (the data from the church's *fundi instructi* inventories were a source of information in this regard). A further act was the drawing up of the inventory by a notary (designated by the Tribunal of First Instance). He summoned the commune head, the dean and the *collator* to participate, who were to compare the current state of the estate with the inventory drawn up when the deceased benefice-holder became the parish priest, and then determine the extent of any damage, which was to be assessed by experts; any claims to the estate were to be reported in the inventory. Civil status records and church records were to be handed over to an administrator appointed "*in spiritualibus*" by the ecclesiastical authorities. There was also a rule that the inheritance of a deceased benefice-holder could only be taken over by the heirs after obtaining a court award. This could take place no sooner than after the heirs had produced a certificate issued by the

---

71 See the cases of the successors of: Father Kasper Małecki, Judgment of the Court of Appeal of 4 November 1832, ANK, 29/200/1748 (WM 275), 29–33; Father Mateusz Dubiecki, Judgment of the Court of Appeal of 1 March 1836, ANK, 29/200/1756 (WM 283), 829–832; Father Florian Kudrewicz, Judgment of the Court of Appeal of 29 April 1836, ibidem, 1415–1418, 1421–1426.

72 The Act of 27 December 1819, *O zabezpieczeniu funduszów po zmarłych Beneficjantach,* promulgated by the letter of the Ruling Senate of 31 December 1819, No. 4557 DGS, DRRz. WMK of 1820.

Senate to the effect that the "institute fund" did not make any claim to the inheritance or that it had already been satisfied in full.[73]

A good illustration of the implementation of the above regulations is the case of the estate of Father Sebastian Czochron, a parish priest in Luborzyca, who died in 1819.[74] The fund of the institute, i.e. the Luborzyca parish, was represented by legal assessor Adam Ekielski, suing Jadwiga Nowakiewiczowa as Father Czochron's heir. After his death, the General Consistory of the Diocese of Cracow appointed a civil-ecclesiastical commission, which found a loss in the *fundi instructi* inventory, in the amount of 2,627 Polish zlotys, six grosz, as well as the parish priest's tax arrears. After reviewing the opinion of the Government prosecutor, the Court of Appeal held that the minutes of the commission could not be evidence in the case, as it had been administratively appointed. In addition, Father Czochron's heirs were not called to participate in its work. Thus, it approved the Tribunal's decision, which gave space to an experts' report, and ordered an assessment of the parish property. As Luborzyca was located in the Kingdom of Poland, it also summoned the Civil Tribunal of the Cracow Voivodship there for legal assistance. The key issue in the case was to establish whether the damage found had been caused by the parish priest's negligence or was the natural result of the passage of time.[75]

The case of Father Franciszek Flaszkiewicz, a parish priest in Chrzanów, involved doubts about the inventories, according to which the current state of the parish estate should be compared with that which had been taken over by the deceased parish priest. An estimate of the claims of the parish fund to the estate of the deceased priest was also made by a civil-ecclesiastical commission.[76] According to the Tribunal, the inventories from 1800–01, when Father

73 Ibidem, Articles 1–6. As verification of the estate and liquidation of damages tended to take a long time, a prohibition on claiming an inheritance before three months from the date of death of a benefice-holder was introduced.

74 Sebastian Czochron (1750–1819). He was in 1787 a professor of the Moral College of the Crown Main School, then in 1790–1803/04 a professor at the Department of Canonical Procedure of the Crown Main School. He was a supporter of the school of natural law, a representative of the humanitarian trend in criminal law, and a parish priest in Luborzyca from 1803. Żukowski 2014, 71–72.

75 Judgment of the Court of Appeal of 26 February 1828, ANK, 29/200/1730 (WM 257), 589–593; *Uciążliwości ze strony funduszu Kościoła Farnego w Luborzycy założonego*, ibidem, 597–603. The assessor argued that Father Czochron was obliged to do the main work resulting from being a parish priest, which entailed a corresponding salary, and ancillary work, which he was alleged to have neglected.

76 The estimate covered not only the church, presbytery and belfry, but also the cemetery wall and, of the movable property, also the organ and chasubles, a clock and even an oil painting and an iron for baking wafers. *Odpowiedź ze strony funduszu Kościoła*

Flaszkiewicz obtained a benefice and took over the parish, should have been taken as the basis for the estimate. According to the Government Assessor, this was an inaccurate assumption, since, as a result of the civilisational development and population increase, the existing value of the parish property was undoubtedly higher. Finally, the Court of Appeal, in modifying the amount of compensation awarded by the Tribunal, confirmed that parish priests should "out of their duty take care of the whole" and prevent any damage to the parish property.[77] The provisions of the Act of 1819 were also applied in a very large number of similar cases, including that of the prebendary of the church in Czernichów, Father Izydor Teresiński,[78] as well as the parish priests: Father Bartłomiej Opłatkiewicz in Nowa Góra;[79] Father Tomasz Hurko vel Heczko in Zalas;[80] and Father Jan Drobich in Regulice.[81]

Of the provisions of the NC that were frequently applied in the practice of the authorities of the Republic of Cracow, Articles 910 and 937 of the NC, concerning the approval of donations and bequests to ecclesiastical institutes, should certainly also be mentioned. An example of the application of the former[82] was the Senate's approval of the bequests of Father Jan Dzianotty, a Cracow canon and parish priest of St Anne's Church, who included in his will bequests of 100–200 zlotys to several Cracow monasteries. Their announcement "through

---

Jaworznickiego i plebanii przeciwko sukcesorom x. Flaszkiewicza, ANK, 29/200/1738 (WM 265), 479–482.

77 Judgment of the Court of Appeal of 7 July 1830, ANK, 29/200/1738 (WM 265), 471–477; *Odpowiedź sukcesorów x. Flaszkiewicza*, ibidem, 483. It is worth mentioning here that the rules for the contribution of parish priests to the renovation of churches and presbytery buildings, which, incidentally, were referred to by the Court of Appeal, were defined in detail first by a decree of the Court Commission of 1800, and then by legal acts of 13 September 1833 and 1 March 1843 on the functioning of church caretakers. For more, see Mataniak 2017a, 123–124, 127–134. The 1833 Act took into account the provisions of the Act on heirless estates from deceased benefice-holders. These were to finance (to the extent of one-third) the permanent parish funds. Where a parish priest had disposed of property by will prior to his death, a quarter part of it – movable and immovable property – was due to the parish church as a so-called 'mandatory part'; this did not apply only to property acquired by inheritance.

78 Judgment of the Court of Appeal of 8 March 1833, ANK, 29/200/1749 (WM 276), 93–96; *Uciążliwości ze strony funduszu kościoła Czernichowskiego przeciwko Wierzycielom śp. x. Izydora Teresińskiego*, ibidem, 97–100.

79 Judgment of the Court of Appeal of 7 July 1835, ANK, 29/200/1742 (WM 269), 105–109.

80 Judgment of the Court of Appeal of 14 May 1833, ANK, 29/200/1749 (WM 276), 661–663.

81 Judgment of the Court of Appeal of 29 May 1833, ANK, 29/200/1749 (WM 276), 905–908.

82 Article 910: "Dispositions during life or by will, for the benefit of hospitals, of the poor of a commune, or of establishments of public utility, shall not take effect, except so far as they shall be authorised by an ordinance of the government".

public writs" was to be made by the Department of Internal Affairs.[83] Such bequests were usually aimed at "the welfare of suffering humanity, by multiplying the funds for this purpose". This formula appeared, for example, in the charitable deed of Maciej Dziedzicki.[84]

What was exceptional, however, was the case of Father Jacek Janowski, vice-chancellor and secretary of the Cracow Cathedral Chapter, who deposited 10,000 Polish zlotys in the coffers of the Brotherhood of Mercy for a "perpetual fund", with the reservation of drawing a percentage from it for the rest of his life. The capital was to be temporarily invested on landed estates, at 5 per cent. After the priest's death, the percentage was to be paid to various institutes. In an open letter to Father Janowski, published in the Cracovian press, the Senate thanked him on behalf of "suffering humanity" for this "proof of indefatigable diligence in the fulfilment of pious deeds". As this "perpetual foundation" was made in the form of a donation between the living, it nevertheless required official form in accordance with Article 931 of the NC for its validity.[85] The act of donation was approved by the Senate under Article 910 of the NC. Subsequently, the provisions of Article 937 of the NC became the basis for the Government to authorise the Brotherhood of Mercy and the General Consistory to delegate commissioners from among themselves to accept donations on behalf of the recipients, in the presence of a legal assessor.[86]

A serious problem faced by the authorities of the Free City of Cracow was the failure of those making bequests, either by wills or *inter vivos*, to indicate the names of institutes for the benefit of "poor people's funds", which gave rise

83 Letter from the Ruling Senate to the Accounts Office of 24 September 1835, ANK, 29/200/1291 (WM 357), 357–358. The beneficiaries were the Capuchin, Dominican, Augustinian and Bernardine monasteries, the congregation of vicars at St Anne's and Cathedral (Castle) churches, as well as the Brotherhood of Mercy; the information was also sent to the Court of Third Instance and the General Consistory, who was to inform the Cracovian clergy, as well as to the Brotherhood of Mercy and the St Catherine's Church restoration committee.

84 Letter from the Ruling Senate to the Accounts Office of 24 September 1835, ANK, 29/200/1291 (WM 357), 361. As the bequest of 500 zlotys to the Brotherhood of Mercy was made on 14 June 1823 in Radom, information about this fact was provided by the General Counsel of the Kingdom of Poland in the letter to the Senate of 20 May 1833.

85 Article 931 of the NC: "All acts importing donation during life shall be passed before notaries, in the ordinary form of contracts; and a minute thereof shall be left, on pain of nullity".

86 Letter of Ruling Senate to Accounting Office of 24 February 1835, ANK, 29/200/1291 (WM 357), 411–412. Article 937 of the NC: "Donations made for the benefit of hospitals, for the poor of a commune, or for establishments of public utility, shall be accepted by the managers of such communes or establishments, having been thereto duly authorised".

to disputes between charitable institutions whose "principles and aims were in contact". In 1821, therefore, a list was enacted of the institutions which were to be presumed to have become bestowed in the manner indicated above.[87] Charity bequests were also the basis for litigation, which were sometimes resolved by settlement. This was the situation in the case of the estate of Father Bernard Bittner, where a settlement was reached between the Government and the heirs.[88] The judicial division of the amounts due to the testator's relatives and the bestowed institutes took place on the basis of a settlement concluded between them in connection with the death of the Cracow canon Father Andrzej Trzciński.[89]

9 Conclusion

The presented analysis clearly shows that the courts of the Free City of Cracow applied the provisions of the *Code civil* in the vast majority of succession law cases. It was indeed treated by Cracow's lawyers as the binding civil code. Only exceptionally, and evidently for reasons of justice, did the judges decide to depart from the letter of French law, directly applying the provisions of Austrian law previously in force in Cracow. On the other hand, however, it was not uncommon for them to interpret the norms of the NC inconsistently

87 Act of 2 January 1821, *O zapisach dla ubogich,* promulgated by the letter of the Ruling Senate of 8 January 821, No. 79 DGS, DRRz.WMK of 1821. In general, bequests could be made to the following institutes: Archconfraternity of Charity and Pious Bank, St Lazarus Hospital, the Congregation of the Brothers Hospitallers of Saint John of God ("Brothers of Charity") and the Charitable Society. It was obligatory to indicate the institute or "species of the poor" cared for by one of the indicated institutions, otherwise it was assumed to be the Shelter Home for the Poor, administered by the Charitable Society; similarly, when the term "beggars" was used (Articles 2–3).

88 Act of 22 December 1817, *Odkazanie sumy pozostałej po x. Bernardzie Bittnerze przypadłej Skarbowi Publicznemu na rzecz zakładu dla sposobienia do życia moralnego dzieci osób pozostających w Domu Ogólnego Schronienia,* promulgated by the letter of the Ruling Senate of 5 January 1818 No. 53 DGS, DRRz.WMK of 1818. The funds due to the Public Treasury were given by the Government for the benefit of the infants in the care of the Shelter Home for the Poor. They were to be secured by mortgage on landed estates in the Free City of Cracow, charging 5 per cent per annum.

89 Resolution of the Ruling Senate of 4 April 1826 No. 1235 DGS, ANK, 29/200/1292 (WM 358), 883–885. The parties were called upon by the First Instance Tribunal to divide the property according to the partition of the estate, as determined by the settlement reached before the Senate. The beneficiaries were: the St Lazarus Hospital, the stipend fund of the poor students of Jagiellonian University, the Brotherhood of Mercy, the Hospital of the Brothers of St John of God, Józef Marxen and the relatives of Father Trzciński.

with its principles, especially if they were based on pre-revolutionary customary law, unknown to lawyers of the Republic of Cracow educated on Roman and Austrian law. This was the case in particular with the commonly accepted priority of testamentary inheritance over statutory inheritance by Cracow's courts. This resulted in the automatic recognition of a testamentary heir as an heir to the estate. However, in the light of the classification and principles of the NC, such a situation occurred only in event of a lack of statutory compulsory heirs. Indeed, their status was guaranteed by the reserve system derived from the principle of protection of the family/lineage in the customary law. This system was, however, unacceptable to the lawyers of the Free City of Cracow, whose conception of succession was based on the Roman precedence of an individualistic will of the testator over the law expressing the solidarity of the community (*uti legassit, ita ius esto*).

Particularly noteworthy is also the fact that the strong position of the Catholic Church in Cracow – sanctified by centuries of tradition, as well as the considerable influence and authority of the local clergy – led the authorities of the Free City to introduce regulations, unknown in the post-revolutionary *Code civil*, that protected the inheritance rights of the Church in a special way. This consisted not only in the privileging of ecclesiastical institutes at the time of the partition of estates of clergy, but also in the creation of the possibility of claiming damages caused to parish property, also by profligate parish priests. The number of cases of this kind, settled using the procedural provisions of the NC, was very high in relation to the total number of succession cases settled in court. The same was true of the application of the provisions of the *Code civil* concerning the approval by public authorities of donations to religious institutes.

TABLE 4 Inheritance cases adjudicated by the Faculty of Law of Jagiellonian University (1818–33)

No.	Year	Parties	Subject matter of the case	Judgment of the Tribunal of First Instance	Judgment of the Court of Appeal	Opinion of the Faculty of Law	Judgment of the Court of Last Instance
1	1818	Bernard and Franciszka Michalczewscy v Marianna Stawowa	Handing over the estate	29.11.1817	14.05.1818	10.06.1818 no appeal	There was not
2	1819	Władysław and Karol Sołtyk v Józef Parys and Katarzyna Potocka	Invalidity of the will	24.05.1819	3.08.1819	11.10.1819 no appeal	There was not
3	1821	Heirs of Tekla Różycka v Legatess	Invalidity of the will	13.07.1818	9.11.1819	18.07.1821 no appeal	There was not
4	1822	Tekla Girtlerowa v Institutes	Entry of inheritance claims in the mortgage	28.01.1819	18.05.1819	13.04.1822 no appeal	18.07.1822
5	1822	Antonina Schmidowa v Jan Raubach	Validity of the contract in the event of death	12.01.1822	8.05.1822	20.06.1822 there is an appeal	30.11.1822
6	1822	Anastazy Roża v Agnieszka Styrio	Partition of the estate	7.07.1821	12.03.1822	4.07.1822 there is an appeal	Not found

TABLE 4 Inheritance cases adjudicated by the Faculty of Law of Jagiellonian University (1818–33) (*cont.*)

No.	Year	Parties	Subject matter of the case	Judgment of the Tribunal of First Instance	Judgment of the Court of Appeal	Opinion of the Faculty of Law	Judgment of the Court of Last Instance
7	1822	Father Adam Domaradzki v Heirs of Father Kajetan Kulpiński	Account of the execution of the will	3.05.1822	23.07.1822	23.10.1822 there is an appeal	3.07.1823
8	1822	Eufrozyna Sawicka v Heirs of Antoni Stadnicki	Handing over the legacy	8.06.1821 (in default) 9.11.1821 (standard procedure)	26.03.1822 (in default) 15.05.1822 (standard procedure)	28.10.1822 there is an appeal	Not found
9	1823	Katarzyna Banasińska v Kacper Banasiński	Partition of the estate	17.08.1822 (in default) 21.09.1822 (standard procedure)	19.11.1822	22.02.1823 no appeal	There was not
10	1823	Institute of Franciscan Fathers v Mateusz Witkowski	Payment of the legacy	6.07.1822	5.03.1823	29.04.1823 no appeal	There was not

TABLE 4 Inheritance cases adjudicated by the Faculty of Law of Jagiellonian University (1818–33) (*cont.*)

No.	Year	Parties	Subject matter of the case	Judgment of the Tribunal of First Instance	Judgment of the Court of Appeal	Opinion of the Faculty of Law	Judgment of the Court of Last Instance
11	1824	Jan Brożek v Heirs of Antoni Brożek	Invalidity of the will	22.11.1822 (in default z) 21.03.1823 (standard procedure)	14.01.1824	6.02.1824 no appeal	There was not
12	1824	Mateusz Konieczny v Heirs of Tomasz Czałczyński	Interest on legacies	19.07.1823	10.02.1824	22.04.1824 there is an appeal	21.10.1824
13	1824	Leon Pszczółkowski, curator of the absent heirs of Father Andrzej Trzciński v Institutes	Partition of the estate and invalidity of the will	17.01.1824	2.04.1824	22.04.1824 no appeal	There was not
14	1824	Regina Czuprynowa v Jadwiga Krawczykowa	Handing over the estate	19.07.1822	27.04.1824	10.07.1824 no appeal	There was not
15	1824	Heirs of Walenty Litwiński v Marianna Padlewska	Payment of inheritance debts	6.02.1824	2.06.1824	17.07.1824 there is an appeal	26.10.1826

TABLE 4 Inheritance cases adjudicated by the Faculty of Law of Jagiellonian University (1818–33) (*cont.*)

No.	Year	Parties	Subject matter of the case	Judgment of the Tribunal of First Instance	Judgment of the Court of Appeal	Opinion of the Faculty of Law	Judgment of the Court of Last Instance
16	1824	Curator of the estate of Piotr Cerpondt v Creditors of the estate of Józef Petra	Classification of the estate	4.06.1824	1.09.1824	28.09.1824 no appeal	There was not
17	1824	Rafał Spira v Adam Kezewski	Heirless inheritance	2.07.1824	27.10.1824	27.11.1824 incompatible judgements	Not found
18	1825	Adam and Karolina Rogawscy v Heirs of Feliks Rogawski	Invalidity of the will	21.05.1824	2.12.1824	3.02.1825 no appeal	There was not
19	1825	Heirs of Aleksander Kronegold v Trade of Piotr Steinkeller	Establishing mortgage on the estate	30.07.1824	18.01.1825	7.02.1825 there is an appeal	23.10.1828
20	1825	Heirs of Antoni Rechowicz v Count Józef Szembek	Payment of inheritance debts	3.02.1824 (in default) 15.05.1824 (standard procedure)	22.12.1824	5.03.1825 no appeal	There was not

TABLE 4 Inheritance cases adjudicated by the Faculty of Law of Jagiellonian University (1818–33) (*cont.*)

No.	Year	Parties	Subject matter of the case	Judgment of the Tribunal of First Instance	Judgment of the Court of Appeal	Opinion of the Faculty of Law	Judgment of the Court of Last Instance
21	1825	Jacek and Franciszka Gołemberscy v Heirs of Sebastian Dyktarski	Payment of inheritance debts	6.12.1823 (in default) 15.10.1824 (standard procedure)	15.03.1825	11.05.1825 there is an appeal	20.07.1825
22	1825	Jan and Marianna Wilk v Antoni and Katarzyna Sadowscy	Invalidity of the will	25.01.1825	26.05.1825	2.07.1825 Incompatible judgments	27.10.1825
23	1825	Katarzyna Potocka v Władysław and Karol Sołtyk	Payment of inheritance debts	31.07.1824	1.02.1825 and 2.03.1825	7.11.1825 there is an appeal	15.06.1826
24	1826	Tomasz Wąsik v Heirs of Wojciech Wąsik	Partition of the estate	8.04.1826	4.07.1826	22.07.1826 there is an appeal	5.04.1827
25	1827	Paweł Jarok and Jadwiga Nowakowa v Mateusz Jarok	Partition of the estate	23.06.1827	16.10.1827	17.11.1827 no appeal	There was not

TABLE 4 Inheritance cases adjudicated by the Faculty of Law of Jagiellonian University (1818–33) (*cont.*)

No.	Year	Parties	Subject matter of the case	Judgment of the Tribunal of First Instance	Judgment of the Court of Appeal	Opinion of the Faculty of Law	Judgment of the Court of Last Instance
26	1827	Stanisław Sobierajski v Regina Matuszewska	Handing over the legacy	21.08.1826 (Court of the Peace)	19.05.1826 (in default) 27.10.1827 (standard procedure)	17.11.1827 there is an appeal	13.03.1828
27	1828	Heirs of Józef Sawiczewski v Aniela Eminowiczowa	Partition of the estate	28.08.1827	17.01.1828	22.02.1828 there is an appeal	13.03.1828
28	1828	Heirs of Józef Kubecki v Counts Hieronim and Stanisław Ankwicz	Payment of inheritance debts	16.12.1826 (in default) 19.06.1827 (standard procedure)	4.02.1828	8.03.1828 there is an appeal	19.02.1829
29	1828	Wincenty Piegłowski v Barbara Marianna Piegłowska	Partition of the estate	23.02.1828	24.06.1828	15.07.1828 no appeal	There was not
30	1828	Władysław and Karol Sołtyk v Katarzyna Potocka	*Restitutio in integrum*	5.02.1828	6.05.1828 (in default) 17.06.1828 (standard procedure)	15.07.1828 no appeal	There was not

TABLE 4 Inheritance cases adjudicated by the Faculty of Law of Jagiellonian University (1818–33) (*cont.*)

No.	Year	Parties	Subject matter of the case	Judgment of the Tribunal of First Instance	Judgment of the Court of Appeal	Opinion of the Faculty of Law	Judgment of the Court of Last Instance
31	1828	Treasury of the Kingdom of Poland v Leon Pszczółkowski curator of the heirless estate of Father Sebastian Sierakowski	Payment of legacies and inheritance debts	11.05.1827	26.03.1828	25.07.1828 there is an appeal	Not found
32	1828	Teresa Knotz v Maciej Knotz	Abolishment of the legacy	22.04.1828	22.07.1828	19.08.1828 no appeal	There was not
33	1828	Walenty Rosenthal v Father Wojciech Danielkiewicz	Agreement over the estate	1.03.1828	7.10.1828	10.11.1828 there is an appeal	Not found
34	1829	Heirs of Teresa Gaszyńska v Karol Gaszyński	Invalidity of the will	18.10.1828	18.02.1829	5.06.1829 no appeal	There was not
35	1829	Władysław and Karol Sołtyk v Katarzyna Potocka	Disclosure of the succession property	13.01.1829	10.06.1829	6.07.1829 no appeal	There was not

TABLE 4 Inheritance cases adjudicated by the Faculty of Law of Jagiellonian University (1818–33) (*cont.*)

No.	Year	Parties	Subject matter of the case	Judgment of the Tribunal of First Instance	Judgment of the Court of Appeal	Opinion of the Faculty of Law	Judgment of the Court of Last Instance
36	1829	Szymon Zbroja v Ignacy and Mateusz Uznańscy	Partition of the estate	31.07.1828	3.12.1828	6.07.1829 no appeal	There was not
37	1829	Creditors of the Wacław Rohlik estate v Szczepan and Rozalia Zawadzcy	Partition of the estate by auction of immovable property	1.06.1829	5.08.1829	16.09.1829 there is an appeal	22.10.1829
38	1829	Franciszek Starowieyski v Cracow Chapter	Payment of the legacy	20.01.1829	9.09.1829	30.09.1829 no appeal	There was not
39	1830	Heirs of Filip Bonde v Heirs of Freyndla Bonde	Partition of the estate	25.11.1820	5.02.1830	6.04.1830 no appeal	There was not
40	1830	Aniela Eminowiczowa v Heirs of Józef Sawiczewski	Partition of the estate	26.06.1829	3.03.1830	10.05.1830 no appeal	1.07.1830
41	1830	Ignacy Ulrych v Wincent Szpor, executor of the will of Ewa Ulrych	Invalidity of the will	27.10.1829	11.05.1830	11.06.1830 no appeal	There was not

TABLE 4 Inheritance cases adjudicated by the Faculty of Law of Jagiellonian University (1818–33) (*cont.*)

No.	Year	Parties	Subject matter of the case	Judgment of the Tribunal of First Instance	Judgment of the Court of Appeal	Opinion of the Faculty of Law	Judgment of the Court of Last Instance
42	1830	Tekla Frytzowa v Konstancja Kosicka and Marianna Bulińska	Partition of the estate	5.02.1830	22.06.1830	19.07.1830 no appeal	There was not
43	1830	Tekla Girtlerowa v Heirs of Franciszek and Barbara Dziannotty	Partition of the estate	13.05.1830	28.09.1830	8.11.1830 no appeal	There was not
44	1830	Tekla Frytzowa v Konstancja Kosicka and Marianna Bulińska	Partition of the estate by the auction of immovable property	5.08.1830	19.10.1830	8.11.1830 no appeal	There was not
45	1832	Emilia Sołtykowa v Katarzyna Potocka	Partition of the estate	8.01.1831	22.02.1832	28.04.1832 no appeal	7.05.1832
46	1832	Adam Ekielski, legal assessor of institutes v Józef Kwaśniewski, executor of the will of Józef Miłkowski	Recovery of legacies	7.05.1831	14.01.1832	19.05.1832 no appeal	There was not

TABLE 4 Inheritance cases adjudicated by the Faculty of Law of Jagiellonian University (1818–33) (*cont.*)

No.	Year	Parties	Subject matter of the case	Judgment of the Tribunal of First Instance	Judgment of the Court of Appeal	Opinion of the Faculty of Law	Judgment of the Court of Last Instance
47	1832	Wiktoria Worytkiewiczowa v Regina and Franciszek Sikora	Partition of the estate	18.05.1830	11.07.1832	2.10.1832 no appeal	There was not
48	1833	Fund of Czernichów church v Creditors of the estate of Izydor Teresiński	Payment of inheritance debts	21.11.1832	8.03.1833	21.05.1833 no appeal	There was not
49	1833	Antoni Wideński v Katarzyna Wideńska	Partition of the estate	21.10.1830 (in default) 8.10.1831 (standard procedure)	10.07.1832 (in default) 23.07.1833 (standard procedure)	12.09.1833 no appeal	There was not

SOURCE: AUTHORS' OWN COMPILATION ON THE BASIS OF ANK: 29/200/1658 (WM 185) – 29/200/1668 (WM 195); 29/200/1712 (WM 239) – 29/200/1750 (WM 277); 29/200/1964 (TRYB 161) – 29/200/2009 (TRYB 206); 29/200/2105 (TRYB 303) – 29/200/2135 (TRYB 333); AND AUJ, WP I 57 – WP I 59

Conclusion

Andrzej Dziadzio, Mateusz Mataniak, and Piotr Michalik

When, at the Congress of Vienna, the representatives of the powers victorious in the Napoleonic wars (Austria, Russia and Prussia) imposed a constitution for the Free City of Cracow, they left the regulation of its legal order to the decision of the Assembly of Representatives of the new city-state. Formally, they did so in accordance with the Montesquieu's "spirit of the law", ordering the Cracow legislature to take into account "the localisation of the country and the spirit of its inhabitants" (*aux localités du pays et à l'esprit des habitants*). This was intended to lead, *inter alia*, to the enactment of a new civil code and code of civil procedure. These were to replace the *Code civil* and *Code de procédure civile* that had been in force in the Napoleonic Duchy of Warsaw from 1808, as explicitly stated by the Prussian resident in Cracow, Ernest Reibnitz, who described the French codes as "a shocking memory of Bonaparte's usurpation".

Certainly these residents' expectations were not unfounded. Twenty years had passed from 1795, when Cracow and its surroundings were incorporated into Austria as part of the Third Partition of Poland, an exceptional period in terms of the dynamics of political and legal changes. During the so-called "one generation", Poles first experienced the bitterness of the final collapse of the old order of the Polish-Lithuanian Commonwealth, then the rebirth of statehood under the Duchy of Warsaw, which was part of the Napoleonic system, and finally experienced another defeat brought about by the fall of the French Emperor in 1815. This sequence seemed a sufficient lesson to recognise the necessity of subordination to the victors, including acceptance of the legal order imposed by them. All the more so since this order, i.e. Austrian civil law in the form of the West Galician Code, had already been in force in Cracow from 1798 to 1810, much longer than the Napoleonic Code. Likewise, the generation of Cracow lawyers at the turn of the 19th century had been educated primarily in Austrian law, and it was not until 1809 that Professor Adam Krzyżanowski began lecturing on French law at Jagiellonian University.

The position of the Austrian Code, as a rival to the *Code civil*, was also strengthened by the fact that Francis I promulgated a universal civil act for the Austrian monarchy (ABGB) in 1811. Although the new code was based on solutions already adopted in the West Galician Code, which was the first modern and complete codification of civil law in Europe, it was only the universal character of the ABGB and the high level of legislative technique that made it

 | DOI:10.1163/9789004688742_011

an Austrian response to the Napoleonic Code.[1] Both codes were based on the assumptions of the natural law school, but the legal solutions adopted in them differed significantly. This is because both were affected by their domestic legal tradition and their attitude to the revolutionary legal legacy. Consequently, the systems of marriage law, both personal (lay and mixed) and property marriage (joint and divided property), were different in the *Code civil* and ABGB, resulting in a different legal position for a wife and illegitimate children in a family and society. Differences also existed in property rights, where the Austrian Code allowed feudal divided property, and in the law of obligations, e.g. with regard to the provisions on the forms of contracts. Inheritance law differed considerably, above all with regard to the meaning and form of the will or the safeguarding of the inheritance rights of necessary heirs (legitime in Austrian law and reserve in the French Code).

With the awareness of the differences in the systems of Austrian and French civil law, there was a clear conviction among both the residents of the powers and the inhabitants of the Free City of Cracow themselves, that it was impossible to return to the uncodified and estate-based Polish law of the period of the Polish-Lithuanian Commonwealth. This did not mean a complete abandonment of its application; it was marginally present in Cracovian judicial practice throughout the existence of the Free City. This is, however, a significant fact, showing how the philosophy of the Enlightenment and dynamic political and social changes at the turn of the 19th century interrupted the continuity of the development of the Polish legal tradition. The role of the *Code civil* in this process was significant, although not exceptional and rather instrumental. Just as Cracovian society adapted to the Austrian law introduced after the Partitions, it adopted the French solutions imposed by Napoleon in the Constitution of the Duchy of Warsaw. Furthermore, Austrian law acted as a catalyst in adapting those norms of French law which, if introduced directly, would have been too revolutionary for Cracow's society. An excellent example of this was the gradual introduction in Cracow of civil registration, which did not exist in the pre-partition Republic. The first stage of this was the introduction of Austrian record books in 1797, and the second the introduction of French civil status registers in 1810, in both cases kept mainly by the clergy on the orders of the State authorities, i.e. in the spirit of Habsburg jurisdictionalism rather than the revolutionary separation of Church and State.

1 In contrast to the Prussian *Landrecht* of 1794, which could not match either the French Code or the Austrian Code in the latter aspect: see Halpérin 2018, 915–916.

However, it was not these or other principles and solutions adopted in the Napoleonic Code and the ABGB that determined the final decision to replace the French Code with a domestic or foreign act. The Civil Code of the Free City of Cracow, as adopted at the Legislative Sejm of 1818, would have been an eclectic act, based overwhelmingly on the solutions adopted in both great codifications. Cracow's legislators, however, opted for a more pragmatic solution of keeping the *Code civil* in force, followed by the *Code de procédure civile*. First, this was politically significant, emphasising the autonomy of the city-state and its connection to the Kingdom of Poland, where the French Codes were also still in force. Second, the Napoleonic Code generally worked well in Polish realities, and in the vast majority of cases was directly applied by Cracow's judges and officials. It was therefore better to remove or correct its shortcomings than to experiment with a new codification. Necessary amendments to the provisions of the *Code civil* were made by the passing of the Mortgage (1822) and Guardianship (1825) Acts by the Assembly of Representatives. Similarly, the rules of civil procedure were also modified by the enactment of the Enforcement Act (1823) and the Act on Courts of the Peace (1825). The rest was limited to adapting the regulations of the *Code civil* to local realities in the course of its application by the courts and offices of the Free City of Cracow.

From an analysis of the court records of the Free City of Cracow (the Court of First Instance and the Court of Appeal), it is clear that in the first decades of the application of the provisions of the Napoleonic Code, Cracow's judges had difficulties in interpreting them correctly. This is also evidenced by legal opinions issued by Professors and Doctors of Law at Jagiellonian University. Between 1815 and1833, under the Constitution of the Free City of Cracow, they exercised judicial supervision over the case law of these courts, under a unique procedure combining elements of the French cassation and the German procedure of sending files to law faculties (*Aktenversendung*). Of the 49 inheritance cases referred to the Faculty of Law at the time, in as many as 17, or one-third, it found serious breaches of substantive or procedural law, opening the way for an appeal to the Court of Last (Third) Instance. However, a detailed analysis of the cases in question shows that Cracovian judges did not so much fail to understand the principles of the *Code civil* inheritance law, but rather did not fully accept the solutions adopted in them. For example, on the one hand, they correctly resolved most of the cases of violation of the mandatory part (reserve). On the other hand, however, they attempted to limit this key institution of French inheritance law where it led to a restriction of the freedom to testate in favour of those closest to the testator, such as the wife and natural children, who were not heirs (*héritiers*) entitled to the reserve under the Napoleonic Code. This tendency resulted from the conviction of Cracovian lawyers, based on Roman and Austrian law, of the primacy of testamentary inheritance over statutory inheritance, and of the guarantee in Polish legal tradition of securing the wife's (widow's) property through both *inter vivos* and *mortis causa* actions.

A similar attitude to the regulations of the *Code civil* occurred in the course of the implementation in the Free City of Cracow of the institution of French secular marriage law. Representing a departure from Polish legal culture, the acceptance of civil marriage and the admissibility of divorce for Catholics, were not, however, of a revolutionary nature. Although the Catholic Church, which had the status of the State Church according to the Constitution of the Free City of Cracow, opposed both institutions, this opposition was mainly formal. In practice, it only led to the maintenance of the exclusion of clergy from pronouncing divorce judgments and granting civil weddings to divorcees, which had already been introduced in the era of the Duchy of Warsaw. At the same time, Catholic clergy exemplarily performed their duties as civil registrars under the provisions of the Napoleonic Code. Consequently, for the Catholic majority of the inhabitants of the Free City of Cracow, a civil wedding was a *de facto* official form of marriage registration performed in front of a clergyman in a parish church, and divorce an acceptable, but still rare, form of the cessation of marriage. In contrast, the situation was different for the large Jewish minority. They generally rejected the secular model of marriage, regarded as an element of forced assimilation into the Christian community. In practice, therefore, Jews either did not enter into civil marriages at all or, when necessary, tried by various means to circumvent the formal requirements associated with them, in particular the obligation, unknown to the *Code civil*, to obtain the *wójt*'s consensus for marriage.

The application of the Napoleonic Code by Cracovian judges was not only its adaptation to Polish realities, but it also had the character of a mitigation of rigour or even a rectification of the errors of the French codification. This was the case in the adjudication of payment cases, which constituted the majority of those heard by the Court of First Instance and the Court of Appeal, where the decisive issue was to prove the basis of the liability and its amount. In this respect, the judges had to face the discrepancy between the principle of freedom of contract declared in the *Code civil* and the strict regulation of the written form for evidentiary purposes, as well as the inconsistency between the introduction in French procedure of the principle of free assessment of evidence while preserving the special role of the oath as the *ultima ratio* means of proof. In this case, the practice derived from the application of Austrian law, which in the West Galician Code fully implemented the canonical principle *ex nudo pacto oritur actio et obligatio*, proved helpful. On this principle, and on the principle of equity, were based those decisions of the Cracow courts, which recognised the validity of contracts concluded in violation of the formalism of the Napoleonic Code by admitting evidence from witnesses and oaths. Incidentally, the latter means of proof, well-established in Polish legal culture, was used by Cracovian judges very often, also in violation of the inconsistent provisions of the *Code civil* in this matter, as indicated in the opinions of the Doctors and Professors of Law of Jagiellonian University.

From the wealth of case law and clerical practice of the Free City of Cracow, there emerges a picture in which its inhabitants were consciously and consistently building the structure of a modern State. As far as was possible in the realities of post-feudal society, this State was already based on the rule of law. One of the basic elements of this structure was precisely the Napoleonic Code, which set the framework for the private law of the Cracovian Republic. There is no doubt that over the course of almost half a century of its application in Cracow (1810–55), the French Code was received into Polish legal culture. The *Code civil* took the place prepared for it after the Partitions by the legislation of the partitioning states; in the case of the Free City of Cracow by the Austrian West Galician Code. Although the *Code civil* was initially imposed by Napoleon, due to the political situation it was quickly accepted. The consolidation of its position as the domestic "civil code", as it appears under that name in the records of Cracovian courts, took place gradually. This was thanks, first, to its practical qualities, far surpassing the Old Polish legacy; second, it was due to the fact that its regulations were based on the European, post-Enlightenment legal tradition, understood and expected by Cracovian society. Thirdly, it was thanks to the necessary modifications that were made, both through legislative changes and in the course of the application of the code by Cracow's judges and clerks, in accordance with the Praetorian maxim *adiuvandi vel supplendi vel corrigendi iuris civilis gratia.*

Bibliography

Archival Sources (Manuscripts)

Archiwum Narodowe w Krakowie (National Archives in Cracow).

Archiwum Wolnego Miasta Krakowa [fond: 29/200/0] [former fond: WMK]:

- 29/200/3 (WMK I-3), 29/200/7 (WMK I-7), 29/200/8 (WMK I-8) – akta Komisji Organizacyjnej;
- 29/200/200 (WMK V-1), 29/200/201 (WMK V-2), 29/200/202 (WMK V-3 B), 29/200/204 (WMK V-5), 29/200/206 (WMK V-7), 29/200/219 (WMK V-20 B), 29/200/220 (WMK V-21), 29/200/221 (WMK V-22 A), 29/200/221 (WMK V-22 B), 29/200/253 (WMK V-54A), 29/200/280 (WMK V-80), 29/200/301 (WMK V-101 A), 29/200/301 (WMK V-101 B), 29/200/302 (WMK V-102 B), 29/200/407 (WMK V-196) – *akta główne Senatu Rządzącego*;
- 29/200/1289 (WM 355), 29/200/1291 (WM 357) – *akta hipoteczne Senatu*;
- 29/200/27 (WMK II-7), 29/200/38 (WMK II-18), 29/200/39 (WMK II-19), 29/200/41 (WMK II-21), 29/200/43 (WMK II-23), 29/200/46 (WMK II-26), 29/200/50 (WMK II-30), 29/200/56 (WMK II-36), 29/200/62 (WMK II-42) – *akta Zgromadzenia Reprezentantów*;
- 29/200/117 (WMK III-3), 29/200/188 (WMK III-7 B), 29/200/139 (WMK III-28 A), 29/200/142 (WMK III-31 B) – *akta prezydialne Senatu Rządzącego*;
- 29/200/858 (WMK VI-60) – 29/200/859 (WMK VI-61) – *akta Wydziału Spraw Wewnętrznych w Senacie Rządzącym*;
- 29/200/1960 (Tryb 157), 29/200/1964 (Tryb 161) – 29/200/2009 (Tryb 206); 29/200/2105 (Tryb 303) – 29/200/2135 (Tryb 333); 29/200/2209 (Tryb 407) – *akta Trybunału I Instancji;*
- 29/200/1712 (WM 239) – 29/200/1750 (WM 277), 29/200/1756 (WM 283), 29/200/1758 (WM 285), 29/200/1761 (WM 288), 29/200/1763 (WM 290), 29/200/1768 (WM 295) – *akta Sądu Apelacyjnego*;
- 29/200/1656 (WM 183), 29/200/1658 (WM 185) – 29/200/1668 (WM 195); 29/200/1670 (WM 197), 29/200/1677 (WM 204), 29/200/1683 (WM 210), 29/200/1687 (WM 214), 29/200/1694 (WM 221), 29/200/1695 (WM 222) – *akta Sądu III (Ostatniej) Instancji*;
- 29/200/1769 (WM 296), 29/200/1770 (WM 297), 29/200/1772 (WM 299) – *wyroki hipoteczne Sądu Apelacyjnego*;
- 29/200/1690 (WM 217) – *wyroki hipoteczne Sądu Najwyższej Instancji*;
- 29/200/1849 (WM 336) – *wyroki Sądu Wyższego*;
- 29/200/1627 (WM 114), 29/200/1814 (WM 150), 29/200/1818 (WM 154), *"Ksiega normalίów Sądu Wyższego od 1842 r."*, 29/200/4658 (WM 586) – *akta sądowe różne*;

– 29/200/2300 (Tryb 103), 29/200/2301 (Tryb 104), 29/200/2333 (Tryb 136), 29/200/2334 (Tryb 137) – *akta spadkowe Wolnego Miasta Krakowa*;
– 29/200/66 (WM 15), 29/200/67 (WM 16), 29/200/71 (WM 20) – *akta budżetowe.*
Akta stanu cywilnego Izraelickiego Okręgu Metrykalnego w Krakowie [fond: 29/1472/0].
Akta stanu cywilnego Parafii Rzymskokatolickiej Najświętszej Marii Panny w Krakowie [fond: 29/328/0].
Akta rozwodowe z terenu gmin, powiatu i miasta Krakowa [fond: 29/336/0].
Archiwum Uniwersytetu Jagiellońskiego (Jagiellonian University Archives).
S I 204 – *Akta Senatu Akademickiego.*
WP I 57, WP I 58, WP I 59 – *Akta Wydziału Prawa.*

Printed Sources

Allgemeines Landrecht für die Königlich Preussischen Staaten, Berlin 1794.
Code Napoléon. Édition originale et seule officielle. De l'imprimerie impériale, Paris 1807.
Conférence des ordonnances de Louis XIV [d'avril 1667 et août 1669] … avec les anciennes ordonnances du Royaume, le droit écrit et les arrêts … par M. Philippe Bornier … Nouvelle édition corrigée et augmentée … des édits [de décembre 1716 et novembre 1717], déclarations et arrêts [du Conseil d'Etat, 1667–1670] donnez en interprétation des ordonnances, https://gallica.bnf.fr/ark:/12148/bpt6k1166723/f176.item.texteImage# (accessed on 15 February 2023).
Dziennik Praw Królestwa Polskiego. Tom XLV, Nr 138–139. Drukarnia Rządowa, Warszawa 1852.
Dziennik Praw Księstwa Warszawskiego. W Drukarni Xięży Piarów, Warszawa 1810.
Dziennik Rozporządzeń Rządowych Wolnego, Niepodległego i Ściśle Neutralnego Miasta Krakowa i Jego Okręgu. Drukarnia J.A. Maya, Kraków 1816–1822.
Dziennik Rządowy Wolnego Miasta Krakowa i Jego Okręgu. Drukarnia J.A. Maya, Kraków 1816–1846.
Dziennik Praw Rzeczypospolitey Krakowskiey. Kraków 1823–1829.
Dziennik Praw Wolnego Miasta Krakowa. Drukarnia S. Gieszkowskiego, Kraków 1833–1846.
Gazeta Krakowska. Kraków 1794–1849.
Jahrbücher der Großherzogliche Badischen Oberhofgerichts. Schwan & Götz, Mannheim 1825, https://dlc.mpdl.mpg.de/dlc/viewMulti/escidoc:14679 (accessed on 3 April 2023).
Kalendarzyk polityczny krakowski na rok 1844. Nakładem J. Cypcera, Kraków 1844.
Kalendarzyk polityczny krakowski na rok 1846. Drukarnia Stanisława Gieszkowskiego, Kraków 1846.
Kodex Napoleona z przypisami. Tom I–II. W Drukarni Xięży Piarów, Warszawa 1808.

Kodex postępowania cywilnego. ... podług drugiéy edycyi przez J.A. Rogrona; przeł. na polski język z zastosowaniem prawodawstwa polskiego i własnem staraniem i nakładem wyd. przez Damazego Dzierożyńskiego, Warszawa 1829.

*Kodex postępowania sądowego cywilnego, przez Antoniego Łabęckiego mecenasa S.K.X.W. Członka Kommisyi przez N. Pana do układania Proiektów do Praw ustanowioney wytłumaczony i poprawiony.*Drukarnia Xięży Piarów, Warszawa 1810.

Księga ustaw na zbrodnie i ciężkie policyjne przestępstwa, cz. 1: O zbrodniach, cz. 2: Księga ustaw o ciężkich przestępstwach policyjnych i o sposobie z tymiż postępowania. W drukarni Józefa Jerzego Trasslera, Kraków 1804.

Obraz Kraju 1822 roku, ogłoszony pismem Senatu Rządzącego nr 4276, "Dziennik Rozporzadzeń Rządowych WMK" z 1822 roku.

Ordonnances du Roy pour la réformation et reiglement de la justice, tant ès cours souveraines que inférieures, faictes en l'assemblée des princes et seigneurs de son Conseil et des députez des cours de parlements et Grand Conseil, tenue à Moulins au mois de febvrier 1566, https://gallica.bnf.fr/ark:/12148/bpt6k97398516/f50.item.texteImage (accessed on 13 February 2023).

Polski Słownik Bibliograficzny, Wrocław–Warszawa–Kraków.

Powszechna księga ustaw cywilnych dla wszystkich krajów dziedzicznych niemieckich Monarchii Austryackiej. Część I–III. Z c. k. drukarni nadwornej i rządowej, Wiedeń 1811.

Stan kraju Rzeczypospolitej, ogłoszony pismem Senatu Rządzącego z 16 grudnia 1820 r. nr 4542 DGS, "Dziennik Rozporzadzeń Rządowych WMK" z 1821 roku.

Themis. Drukarnia Stanisława Gieszkowskiego, Kraków 1834.

Ustawy cywilne dla Galicyi Wschodniey. Część I–III. Drukiem Józefa Hraszańskiego, Wiedeń 1797.

Zdanie sprawy Zgromadzeniu Reprezentantów o położeniu Interessów krajowych, przez delegowanego do teyże Reprezentacyi Senatora na posiedzeniu seymowym w dniu 3 grudnia 1817 roku, ogłoszone pismem Senatu Rządzącego z 5 stycznia 1818 r. nr 80 DGS, "Dziennik Rozporzadzeń Rządowych WMK" z 1818 roku.

Zdanie sprawy Zgromadzeniu Reprezentantów o położeniu interessów krajowych, przez delegowanego do tejże Reprezentacyi senatora, na posiedzeniu seymowym w dniu 10 grudnia 1818 roku, ogłoszone pismem Senatu Rządzącego z 11 marca 1819 r. nr 88 DGS, "Dziennik Rozporzadzeń Rządowych WMK" z 1819 roku.

Zdanie sprawy Zgromadzeniu Reprezentantów o położeniu interessów krajowych, przez Delegowanego do teyże Reprezentacyi Senatora na Posiedzeniu Seymowym 9 Grudnia 1819 roku, ogłoszone pismem Senatu Rządzącego z 25 stycznia 1820 r. nr 122 DGS, "Dziennik Rozporzadzeń Rządowych WMK" z 1820 roku.

Zdanie sprawy o Stanie i Położeniu Kraju Wolnego Miasta Krakowa, dla Zgromadzenia Reprezentantów 1823, ogłoszone pismem Senatu Rządzącego nr 3854, "Dziennik Rozporzadzeń Rządowych WMK" z 1823 roku.

Zdanie sprawy o Stanie i Położeniu Kraju Wolnego, Niepodległego i ściśle Neutralnego Miasta Krakowa i Jego Okręgu dla Zgromadzenia Reprezentantów 1824 roku, ogłoszone pismem Senatu Rządzącego nr 4367 DGS, Dziennik Praw Rzeczypospolitey Krakowskiey z 1824 roku.

Zdanie sprawy o Stanie i Położeniu Kraju Wolnego, Niepodległego i ściśle Neutralnego Miasta Krakowa i Jego Okręgu dla Zgromadzenia Reprezentantów 1825 roku, ogłoszone pismem Senatu Rządzącego nr 4793 DGS, Dziennik Praw Rzeczypospolitey Krakowskiey z 1825 roku.

Zdanie sprawy o Stanie i Położeniu Kraju Wolnego, Niepodległego i ściśle Neutralnego Miasta Krakowa i Jego Okręgu dla Zgromadzenia Reprezentantów 1826 roku, ogłoszone pismem Senatu Rządzącego nr 4925 DGS, ANK, 29/200/407 (WMK V-196).

Zdanie sprawy o Stanie i Położeniu Kraju Wolnego, Niepodległego i ściśle Neutralnego Miasta Krakowa i Jego Okręgu dla Zgromadzenia Reprezentantów 1827 r., ogłoszone pismem Senatu Rządzącego nr 5415 DGS, Dziennik Praw Rzeczypospolitey Krakowskiey z 1827 roku.

Zdanie sprawy o Stanie i Położeniu Kraju Wolnego, Niepodległego i ściśle Neutralnego Miasta Krakowa i Jego Okręgu Zgromadzeniu Reprezentantów na dzień 21 Sierpnia 1833 roku zwołanym, ogłoszone pismem Senatu Rządzącego nr 6174 DGS, ANK, 29/200/407 (WMK V-196), 1265–1266; Dziennik Praw WMK z 1833 roku.

Zdanie sprawy o Stanie i Położeniu Kraju Wolnego, Niepodległego i ściśle Neutralnego Miasta Krakowa i Jego Okręgu dla Zgromadzenia Reprezentantów r. 1837, ANK, 29/200/863 (WMK VI-65).

Zdanie sprawy o stanie i położeniu Kraju W.M. Krakowa i Jego Okręgu w Zgromadzeniu Reprezentantów w r. 1844 przedłożone przez Senatora do tegoż Zgromadzenia delegowanego, DPr.WMK z 1844 roku; ANK, 29/200/407 (WMK V-196).

Bartel, Wojciech, Jan Kosim, and Władysław Rostocki, ed. 1964–1969. *Ustawodawstwo Księstwa Warszawskiego. Akty normatywne władzy najwyższej*. Warszawa: Państwowe Wydawnictwo Naukowe.

Burzyński, Piotr. 1852. *Wykład prawa cywilnego francuzkiego. Tom I.* Kraków: nakładem autora, czcionkami Drukarni „Czasu".

Burzyński, Piotr. 1871. *Prawo polskie prywatne: napisane i poświęcone pamięci ubiegłych w roku 1864 pięciuset lat istnienia Uniwersytetu Krakowskiego. Tom 2 obejmujący Część II Prawo rodzinne i Część III Prawo majątkowe*. Kraków: nakładem autora, Drukarnia c.k. Uniwersytetu Jagiellońskiego.

Delsol, Jean Jacques. 1873. *Zasady Kodeksu Napoleona w związku z nauką i jurysprudencyą przedstawione, t. 1.* Warszawa: Redakcja Biblioteki Umiejętności Prawnych.

Delsol, Jean Jacques. 1874. *Zasady Kodeksu Napoleona w związku z nauką i jurysprudencyą przedstawione*, t. 2. Warszawa: Redakcja Biblioteki Umiejętności Prawnych.

Dippel, Horst, ed. 2008. *Constitutions of the World from the late 18th Century to the Middle of the 19th Century. Sources on the Rise of Modern Constitutionalism. Europe: Volume 5*. München: K.G.Saur Verlag.

Dziadzio, Andrzej, and Mateusz Mataniak, eds. 2022. *Protokoły posiedzeń Wydziału Profesorów i Doktorów Prawa Uniwersytetu Jagiellońskiego (1817–1833). Opinie o stosowaniu Kodeksu Napoleona przez sądy Wolnego Miasta Krakowa*. Kraków: Księgarnia Akademicka.

Estreicher, Stanisław, ed. 1909. *Wspomnienia Ambrożego Grabowskiego*. „Biblioteka Krakowska", no 40. Kraków: Towarzystwo Miłośników Historii i Zabytków Krakowa.

Fierich, Maurycy. 1888. *Historya ksiąg hipotecznych byłego Wolnego Miasta Krakowa*, „Gazeta Sądowa Warszawska", no 29, vol. 8 (20): 489–500.

Harras von Harrasowsky, Philip. 1883–1886. *Der Codex Theresianus und seine Umarbeitungen, teil I–IV*. Wien, https://repertorium.at/ns/codex_theresianus_inhalt.html (accessed on 16 June 2023).

Hoszowski, Konstanty. 1869. *Biografie ośmiu zgasłych członków Towarzystwa Naukowego Krakowskiego*. Kraków: nakładem autora, Drukarnia Uniwersytetu Jagiellońskiego.

Hube, Romuald. 1828. "O prokuratorach we Francji", *Themis Polska* 2: 1–32.

Hube, Romuald. 1829. "Uwagi nad systematem kodeksu cywilnego francuzkiego", *Themis Polska* 5: 297–339.

Hube, Karol. 1877. *Prawo cywilne obowiązujące w Guberniach Królestwa Polskiego*. Warszawa: Gebethner & Wolff; Gustaw Sennewald.

Kapuściński, Piotr. 1869. *Jurysprudencja Senatu z lat dwudziestu sześciu (1842–1867) opatrzona skorowidzem wyrazowym zebrał i wydał z up. Kommissji Rządowej Sprawiedliwości Piotr Kapuściński*. Warszawa: Kommisja Rządowa Sprawiedliwości.

Kallas, Marian, and Marek Krzymkowski, ed. 2006. *Historia ustroju i prawa w Polsce 1772/1775–1918. Wybór źródeł*. Warszawa: Wydawnictwo Naukowe PWN.

Kopff, Wiktor. 1836a. "O posiadaniu i skargach posesoryjnych. Część I". *Kwartalnik Naukowy* t. 3, z. 1: 50–85. Kraków: Drukarnia Kwartalnika Naukowego.

Kopff, Wiktor. 1836b. "O posiadaniu i skargach posesoryjnych. Część II". *Kwartalnik Naukowy* t. 3, z. 2: 277–314. Kraków: Drukarnia Kwartalnika Naukowego.

Kopff, Wiktor. 1906. *Wspomnienia z ostatnich lat Rzeczypospolitej Krakowskiej*. „Biblioteka Krakowska", no 31. Kraków: Towarzystwo Miłośników Historii i Zabytków Krakowa.

Królasik, Tomasz. 2018. „Francuski model postępowania egzekucyjnego w Księstwie Warszawskim i w Królestwie Polskim w latach 1808–1823" (unpublished doctoral thesis).

Krzeczkowski, Konstanty. 1916. *Komisja Włościańska w Rzeczypospolitej Krakowskiej*, „Sprawozdania Akademii Umiejętności w Krakowie", Kraków.

Malinowski, Antoni. 1811. *Opieka podług Kodexu Napoleona dla Xięstwa Warszawskiego*. Poznań: Drukiem Dekkera i Komp.

Meciszewski, Hilary. 1840. *Memoriał historyczny i polityczny o stanie obecnym Wolnego Miasta Krakowa i Jego Okręgu. Na poparcie adresu obywateli krakowskich podanego rządowi francuskiemu i angielskiemu w październiku 1839 roku. Z dołączeniem zbioru dokumentów*. Paryż: Dufart.

Meciszewski, Hilary. 1849. *Do historyi ustawodawstwa karnego tudzież Sejmów Prawodawczych byłej Rzeczypospolitej Krakowskiej. Odpowiedź na objaśnienie artykułu wstępnego w N. 200 Czasu z strony Redakcyi dane*. Kraków: Drukarnia „Czasu".

Meciszewski, Hilary. 1851. *Historya Rzeczypospolitej Krakowskiej (Epoka czasu od miesiąca maja 1815 do listopada 1846 roku)*. Kraków: Drukarnia „Czasu".

Mieroszewski, Jacek. 1886. *Dzieje Rzeczypospolitej Krakowskiej. Przewodnik Naukowy i Literacki* 14. Lwów: Wydawnictwo Gazety Lwowskiej.

Piller, Thomas et al., eds. 1789–1794. *Continuatio Edictorum et Mandatorum Universalium in Regnis Galiciae et Lodomeriae*. Lwów: Typis Piller.

Sirey, Jean Baptiste, ed. 1865. *Recueil général des lois et des arrêts: En matière civile, criminelle, commerciale et de droit public*. Paris, https://gallica.bnf.fr/ark:/12148/bpt6k57791653/f5.item (accessed on 16 February 2022).

Thomine-Desmazures, Pierre Jacques Henry. 1833. *Commentaire sur le Code de procédure civile, t. 3*. Bruxelles: Société Typographique Belge. Adolphe Wahlen.

Tokarz, Wacław ed. 1932. *Pomniki prawa Rzeczypospolitej Krakowskiej 1815–1818. Tom 1*. Kraków: Polska Akademia Umiejętności.

Wawel-Louis, Józef. 1977. *Sądownictwo Rzeczypospolitej Krakowskiej*. In Józef Wawel-Louis, *Urywki z dziejów i życia mieszkańców Krakowa*, edited by Janina Bieniarzówna and Wiesław Bieńkowski, „Biblioteka Krakowska", no 117. Kraków: Wydawnictwo Literackie; Towarzystwo Miłośników Historii i Zabytków Krakowa.

Windscheid, Bernard. 1847. *Zur Lehre des Code Napoleon von der Ungültikeit der Rechtsgeschäfte,* Düsseldorf: Verlag von Julius Buddeus.

Wróblewski, Stanisław. 1899. *Posiadanie na tle prawa rzymskiego*, „Rozprawy Wydziału Historyczno-Filozoficznego Akademii Umiejętności w Krakowie", vol. 37. Kraków: Nakładem Akademii Umiejętności.

Zeiller, Franz 1812. Kommentar über das allgemeine bürgerliche Gesetzbuch für die gesammten Deutschen Erbländer der Österreichischen Monarchie. Dritter Band. Erste Abtheilung, Wien: Im Geistingers Verlagshandlung.

Zeiller, Franz. 1814. *Anzeigen und Recensionen des Őesterreichischen bürgerlichen Gesetzbuches in auswärtigen Schriften, nebst Bemerkungen.* In *Materialien für Gesetzkunde und Rechtspflege in den österreichischen Staaten,* edited by C.J. Pratobevera, Erster Band, 169–191. Wien: Im Verlag der Geistingerschen Buchhandlung.

Literature

Ajnenkiel, Andrzej. 2001. *Konstytucje Polski w rozwoju dziejowym 1791–1997*. Warszawa: Oficyna Wydawnicza Rytm.

Arnaud, André-Jean. 1969. *Les origines doctrinales du Code civil Français*. Paris: Libraire generale de droit et de jurisprudence.

Atias, Christian 1985. "La controverse et l'enseignement du droit". *Annales d'historie des Facultés des Droits et de la science juridique* 2: 107–123.

Bartel, Wojciech. 1976. *Ustrój i prawo Wolnego Miasta Krakowa 1815–1846*. Kraków: Wydawnictwo Literackie.

Bartel, Wojciech. 1981. "Ustrój i prawo Wolnego Miasta Krakowa (1815–1846)". In *Historia państwa i prawa Polski,* edited by Juliusz Bardach. Vol. 3: *Od rozbiorów do uwłaszczenia,* edited by Juliusz Bardach and Monika Senkowska-Gluck, 792–823. Warszawa: Wydawnictwo Naukowe PWN.

Bartel, Wojciech. 1984. "Zgromadzenie Reprezentantów Wolnego Miasta Krakowa". *Czasopismo Prawno-Historyczne* 36, no.1: 143–154.

Basdevant-Gaudemet, Brigitte, and Jean Gaudemet. 2000. *Introduction historique au droit XIIIe–XXe siècles*. Paris: LGDJ (Libraire générale de droit et de jurisprudence).

Beignier, Bernard 1986. "Portalis et le droit naturel dans le Code civil", *Revue d'historie des Facultés des Droits et de la science juridique* 6: 77–101.

Bieda, Justyna, and Dorota Wiśniewska-Jóźwiak. 2014. "Zasady dziedziczenia ustawowego na ziemiach Królestwa Polskiego po 1826 roku". *Czasopismo Prawno-Historyczne* 66, no 1: 105–120.

Bieniarzówna, Janina, and Jan M. Małecki. 1979. *Dzieje Krakowa. T.3: Kraków w latach 1796–1918*. Kraków: Wydawnictwo Literackie.

Blanc-Jouvan, Xavier. 2004. "L'influence du Code Civil sur les codifications étrangères récentes". In *Le Code civil 1804–1904: livre du Centenaire*, edited by Jean-Louis Halpérin, 477–512. Paris: Dalloz.

Blicharz, Grzegorz. 2016. *Udział państwa w spadku. Rzymska myśl prawna w perspektywie prawnoporównawczej*. Kraków: Wydawnictwo Od. Nowa.

Bouineau, Jacques, and Jérôme Roux. 2004. *200 ans de Code civil*. Paris: ADPF.

Broniewicz, Witold. 1993. "La réception du Code de français de procédure civile de 1806 en Pologne". In *Code Napoléon et son héritage. Colloque international, Łódź, 12–14 septembre 1989*, edited by Biruta Lewaszkiewicz-Petrykowska, 217–221. Łódź: Wydawnictwo Uniwersytetu Łódzkiego.

Carbonnier, Jean 2004. "Le Code civil". In *Le Code civil 1804–2004: Livre du Bicentenaire,* 17–37. Paris: Dalloz/Litec LexisNexis.

Catala, Pierre 2005. "Le modèle de la codification napoléonienne et les temps modernes", *Czasopismo Prawno-Historyczne,* 57, no. 2: 19–26.

Cavanna, Adriano 1994. "L'influence juridique française en Italie au XIXe siècle", *Revue d'historie des Facultés des Droits et de la science juridique* 15: 87–112.

Cichoń, Paweł. 2012. "Droga do zawodu sędziego w Księstwie Warszawskim", *Studia z Dziejów Państwa i Prawa Polskiego* 15: 43–58.

Cichoń, Paweł. 2016. "Z orzecznictwa Dyrekcji Policji Wolnego Miasta Krakowa – casus Oszyków". *Studia Iuridica Lublinensia* 25, no. 3: 179–190.

Cichoń, Paweł. 2021. "Zmiany prawnoustrojowe w «napoleońskim» Krakowie w latach 1809–1815". *Studia z Dziejów Państwa i Prawa Polskiego* 24: 31–48.

David, René, and John E.C. Brierley. 1985. *Major legal systems in the world today: an introduction to the comparative study of law*. London: Stevens&Sons.

Dąbkowski, Przemysław. 1922. *Zarys prawa polskiego prywatnego: podręcznik do nauki uniwersyteckiej*, Lwów: K.S. Jakubowski.

Decourt-Hollender, Bénédicte. 2012. "La notion de faits injurieux dans le divorce et la séparation de corps au XIX-e siècle". *Revue historique de droit français et étranger* 90, no. 3: 329–378.

Demel Juliusz. 1951. *Stosunki gospodarcze i społeczne Krakowa w latach 1846–1853*, "Biblioteka Krakowska" no. 107, Kraków: Towarzystwo Miłośników Historii i Zabytków Krakowa.

Demel, Juliusz. 1952. "Pożar Krakowa 1850 r.". *Rocznik Krakowski* 33, no 3. Kraków: Towarzystwo Miłośników Historii i Zabytków Krakowa.

Dziadzio, Andrzej. 2018. "Vertragsfreiheit in der Donaumonarchie. Das Gesetz für Galizien über das Wucherverbot". *Journal on European History of Law* 9, no 2: 216–222.

Dziadzio, Andrzej. 2020a. "Der Code civil in der Rechtsprechung der Freien Stadt Krakau (1815–1846). Zwischen französischer und österreichischer Rechtskultur". *Beiträge zur Rechtsgeschichte Ősterreichs* 10, no 2: 269–277.

Dziadzio, Andrzej. 2020b. „Opinie profesorów i doktorów Wydziału Prawa Uniwersytetu Jagiellońskiego jako źródło badań nad stosowaniem Kodeksu Napoleona w Wolnym Mieście Krakowie". *Krakowskie Studia z Historii Państwa i Prawa* 13, no 3: 309–319.

Dziadzio, Andrzej. 2020c. *Powszechna Historia Prawa*. Warszawa: Wydawnictwo Naukowe PWN.

Dziadzio, Andrzej. 2020d. „Udział Wydziału Prawa Uniwersytetu Jagiellońskiego w stosowaniu *Code Civil* w Wolnym Mieście Krakowie (1815–1833)". In *Miasto i państwo na przestrzeni dziejów. Studium historyczno-prawne. Księga Jubileuszowa z okazji czterdziestopięciolecia pracy naukowej oraz 70. urodzin profesora Tadeusza Maciejewskiego*, edited by Michał Gałędek, 185–199. Warszawa: C.H. Beck.

Dziadzio, Andrzej. 2022a. „Powstanie austriackiego kodeksu cywilnego ABGB i jego twórca". *Prawo i Więź* 42: 449–474.

Dziadzio, Andrzej. 2022b. "Vertragstypenzwang im Code civil? Die Gültigkeit gegenseitiger Verträge in der Judikatur der Freien Stadt Krakau (1815–1846)" *Zeitschrift der Savigny –Stiftung für Rechtsgeschichte* 139: 270–283.

Eisenbach, Artur. 1983. „Emancypacja Żydów na ziemiach polskich w XIX w. na europejskim tle porównawczym". *Przegląd Historyczny* 74, no 4: 615–629.

Erp van, Sjef. 2019. "Comparative Property Law". In: *The Oxford Handbook of Comparative Law* (2nd edition), edited by Mathias Reimann and Reinhard Zimmermann, 1031–1057. Oxford: Oxford University Press.

Fehrenbach, Elisabeth. 1983. *Traditionale Gesellschaft und revolutionäres Recht. Die Einführung des Code Napoleon in den Rheinbundstaaten*, ed.3: Göttingen: Vandenhoeck Ruprecht.

Fierich, Franciszek Xawery. 1917. *Sąd trzeciej instancji i najwyższy sąd sejmowy na tle całokształtu organizacji sądownictwa Rzeczypospolitej Krakowskiej (1815–1833)*. Kraków: Nakładem Akademii Umiejętności.

Filipiak, Zbigniew. 2016. „Projekt urządzenia ogólnego ludności żydowskiej w Księstwie Warszawskim z 1809 r.". *Czasopismo Prawno-Historyczne* 68, no 2: 147–166.

Filipiak, Zbigniew. 2020. *Prawo własności nieruchomości w działalności legislacyjnej Księstwa Warszawskiego i Królestwa Kongresowego (1807–1830)*. Toruń: Wydawnictwo Naukowe Uniwersytetu Mikołaja Kopernika.

Gaudemet, Jean. 1999. *La naissance du droit. Les temps, le pouvoir et la science au service du droit*. Paris: Montchrestien.

Gergen, Thomas. 2014. "The Reception of the Code civil (Napoléonic Code) of 1804: An Example of «Juridical Migration»?" *Journal on European History of Law* 5, no 1: 26–30.

Geyer, Stefan. 2009. *Den Code civil »richtiger« auslegen. Der zweite Zivilsenat des Reichsgerichts uns das französische Zivilrecht*. Frankfurt am Main: Klostermann.

Gilissen, John. 1979. *Introduction historique au droit. Esquisse d'une histoire universelle du droit. Les sources du droit depuis XIIIe siécle. Éléments d'historie du droit privé*. Bruxelles: Bruylant.

Goclon, Jacek. 1990. "Konstytucje Wolnego Miasta Krakowa z 1815, 1818 i 1833 roku". In *Konstytucje Polski. Studia monograficzne z dziejów polskiego konstytucjonalizmu*, edited by Marian Kallas, 233–292. Vol. 1. Warszawa: Wydawnictwo Naukowe PWN.

Gordley, James. 2014. *The Jurists: A Critical History*. Oxford: Oxford University Press.

Górnicki, Leonard. 2002. "Problem prawnej ochrony własności nieruchomości, nie wpisanej do ksiąg gruntowych w okresie zaborów i w Polsce niepodległej". *Acta Universitatis Wratislaviensis* 2367. Prawo CCLXXVI: 169–203.

Grimaldi, Michel. 2003. "L'exportation du Code civil". *Pouvoirs* 107, no 4: 80–96.

Grodziski, Stanisław. 2007. "Stanowisko prawne Żydów w Galicji: reformy Marii Teresy i Józefa II (1772–1790)". In *Studia Galicyjskie. Rozprawy i przyczynki do historii ustroju Galicji*, edited by Stanisław Grodziski and Grzegorz Nieć: 73–85. Kraków: Księgarnia Akademicka.

Gross, Norbert J. 1993. *Der Code Civil in Baden. Eine deutsche-französische Rechtsbegegnung und ihr Erbe*. Baden-Baden: Nomos Verlagsgesellschaft.

Grynwaser, Hipolit. 1951. "Kodeks Napoleona w Polsce". In Grynwaser, Hipolit. *Pisma*. Vol. I, 15–174. Wrocław: Wydawnictwo Zakładu Narodowego im. Ossolińskich.

Halpérin, Jean-Louis, ed. 1996. *Avocats et notaires en Europe. Les professions judiciaires et juridiques dans l'histoire contemporaine*. "Droit et Société" 19. Paris: LGDJ. (Libraire générale de droit et de jurisprudence).

Halpérin, Jean-Louis. 2003. *Le code civil*. Paris: Dalloz.

Halpérin, Jean-Louis, ed. 2004a. *Le Code civil 1804–1904: Livre du Centenaire*. Paris: Dalloz.

Halpérin, Jean-Louis. 2004b. "Le regard de l'historien". In *Le Code civil 1804–2004. Livre du Bicentenaire: 2004*, 43–58. Paris: Dalloz/Litec LexisNexis.

Halpérin, Jean-Louis. 2018. "The Age of Codification and Legal Modernization in Private Law". In *The Oxford Handbook of European Legal History*, edited by Heiki Pihlajamäki, Markus D. Dubber and Mark Godfrey: 907–928. Oxford: Oxford University Press.

Haferkamp, Hans-Peter. 2019. "Die Rheinische Apellationsgerichtshof zwischen dem Rheinland, Frankreich und Preußen – Überlegungen anhand der rheinischen Judikatur zu Art. 1133 CC". In *Das Oberlandesgericht Köln zwischen Rheinland, Frankreich und Preußen*, edited by Hans-Peter Haferkamp and Margarete Gräfin von Schwerin, 15–34. Köln: Böhlau Verlag.

Hattenhauer, Christian and Klaus-Peter Schroeder, ed. 2011. *200 Jahre Badisches Landrecht von 1809/1810*. Frankfurt am Main: Peter Lang GmbH.

Izdebski, Hubert. 1974. "Sądownictwo administracyjne w Księstwie Warszawskim i w Królestwie Polskim do 1867 roku". *Czasopismo Prawno-Historyczne* 26, no 2: 119–149.

Jakimyszyn, Anna. 2005. "The Jewish Community in Cracow – analysis based on the Cracow Community Charter of 5355 and supplements". *Scripta Judaica Cracoviensia* 3: 41–49.

Jakimyszyn, Anna. 2008. *Żydzi krakowscy w dobie Rzeczypospolitej Krakowskiej. Status prawny. Przeobrażenia gminy. System edukacyjny*. Kraków-Budapeszt: Wydawnictwo Austeria.

Janicka Danuta 2005. "Niektóre problemy stosowania francuskiego prawa zobowiązań w praktyce orzeczniczej Sądu Najwyższego (1918–1939)", *Czasopismo Prawno-Historyczne* 57, no. 2: 89–108.

Jean, Jean-Paul, and Jean-Pierre Royer. 2003–04. "Le droit civil, de la volonté politique à la demande sociale. Essai d'évaluation sur deux siècles". *Pouvoirs* 107: 127–142.

Jemielity, Witold. 1995. „Akta stanu cywilnego w Księstwie Warszawskim i Królestwie Polskim". *Prawo Kanoniczne: kwartalnik prawno-historyczny* 38, no 1–2: 163–188.

Jourdain, Patrice. 1995. *Les biens*. Paris: Dalloz.

Kanayama, Naoki. 1989. "Les civilistes français et le droit naturel au XIXe siècle. À propos de la prescription". *Revue d'historie des Facultés des Droits et de la science juridique* 8: 129–154.

Kannowski, Bernd. 2011. "Das Badische Landrecht in der Rechtsprechung des Reichsgerichtes". In *200 Jahre Badisches Landrecht von 1809/1810*, edited by Christian Hattenhauer and Klaus-Peter Schroeder, 217–244. Frankfurt am Main: Peter Lang GmbH.

Karabowicz, Anna. 2004. "Rewolucja w prawie osobowym małżeńskim na ziemiach polskich (1808–1825)". *Zeszyty Naukowe Uniwersytetu Jagiellońskiego. Towarzystwo Biblioteki Słuchaczów Prawa. Zeszyty Prawnicze* 11–12: 171–194.

Kasprzyk, Bogdan, ed. 2010. *Poczet sołtysów, wójtów, burmistrzów i prezydentów miasta Krakowa: (1228–2010)*. Kraków: Urząd Miasta Krakowa.

Klimaszewska, Anna. 2020. "The Reception of the French Commercial Code in Nineteenth-Century Polish Territories: A Hollow Legal Shell" In *Modernisation, National Identity and Legal Instrumentalism (Vol. I: Private Law)*, edited by Michał Gałędek and Anna Klimaszewska, 143–163. Leiden/Boston: Brill/Nijhoff.

Kodrębski, Jan. 1993. "Le Code Napoléon en Pologne sous la domination russe" In *Code Napoléon et son héritage. Colloque international, Łódź, 12–14 septembre 1989*, edited by Biruta Lewaszkiewicz-Petrykowska, 135–142. Łódź: Wydawnictwo Uniwersytetu Łódzkiego.

Korobowicz, Artur. 1993. "La jurisdiction du Royaume de Pologne et la codification napoléonienne" In *Code Napoléon et son héritage. Colloque international, Łódź, 12–14 septembre 1989*, edited by Biruta Lewaszkiewicz-Petrykowska, 143–153. Łódź: Wydawnictwo Uniwersytetu Łódzkiego.

Korobowicz, Artur. 1998. "Rys dziejów kasacji w polskim systemie sądowoodwoławczym" In *Polska lat dziewięćdziesiątych: przemiany państwa i prawa: materiały z konferencji, Lublin-Kazimierz, 27–29 kwietnia 1998 r.*, edited by Lech Antonowicz et al., 397–413. Vol. 2. Lublin: Wydawnictwo Uniwersytetu Marii Curie-Skłodowskiej.

Krasnowolski, Bogusław. 2016. "Urbanistyka i sztuka Wolnego Miasta Krakowa" In *Rzeczpospolita Krakowska 1815–1846. Materiały z sesji naukowej, 23 maja 2015 roku*, edited by Jerzy Wyrozumski, *Kraków w Dziejach Narodu* 35: 55–91. Kraków: Towarzystwo Miłośników Historii i Zabytków Krakowa.

Królasik, Tomasz. 2019. "Potioritas czy subhastacja? Pomiędzy dawnym prawem polskim a prawem francuskim w egzekucji sądowej w Księstwie Warszawskim i Królestwie Polskim". *Krakowskie Studia z Historii Państwa i Prawa* 12, no. 1: 39–54.

Landau, Peter. 2013a. "Pacta sunt servanda. Zu den kanonistischen Grundlagen der Privatautonomie". In *Europäische Rechtsgeschichte und kanonisches Recht im Mittelalter. 40 ausgewählte Aufsätze aus den Jahren 1967 bis 2006*: 763–781. Badenweiler: Wissenschaftlicher Verlag Bachmann.

Landau, Peter. 2013b. "Reflexionen über Grundrechte der Person in der Geschichte des kanonischen Rechts". In *Europäische Rechtsgeschichte und kanonisches Recht im Mittelalter. 40 ausgewählte Aufsätze aus den Jahren 1967 bis 2006*: 111–129. Badenweiler: Wissenschaftlicher Verlag Bachmann.

Laufs, Adolf. 2011. "Das Großherzogtum Baden und sein Bürgerliches Gesetzbuch". In *200 Jahre Badisches Landrecht von 1809/1810*, edited by Christian Hattenhauer and Klaus-Peter Schroeder, 1–16. Frankfurt am Main: Peter Lang GmbH.

Le Code civil 1804–2004: Livre du Bicentenaire, 2004. Paris: Dalloz/Litec LexisNexis.

Lequette, Yves, and Laurent Leveneur, ed. 2004. *1804–2004. Le code civil. Un passé, un présent, un avenir*. Paris: Dalloz/Université Paris II Pantheon-Assas.

Lewaszkiewicz-Petrykowska, Biruta, ed. 1993. *Code Napoléon et son héritage. Colloque international, Łódź, 12–14 septembre 1989*. Łódź: Wydawnictwo Uniwersytetu Łódzkiego.

Litewski, Wiesław. 1999. *Rzymskie prawo prywatne*. Warszawa: Wydawnictwa Prawnicze PWN.

Lityński, Adam. 1994. "Die geschichte des Code Napoléon in Polen" In *Französisches Zivilrecht in Europa während des 19. Jahrhunderts*, edited by Reiner Schulze, 253–269. Berlin: Dunker&Humboldt.

Löhnig Martin 2012. "La réforme de la justice dans le Grand-Duché de Berg: de la réception de l'organisation judiciaire française en Allemagne", *Revue historique de droit français et étranger* 90, no 2: 255–269.

Machut-Kowalczyk, Joanna. 2010. "Dzieje opieki na ziemiach polskich". *Studia z Dziejów Państwa i Prawa Polskiego* 13: 57–73.

Machut-Kowalczyk, Joanna. 2014. *Rada familijna pod powagą sądu pokoju w świetle akt łęczyckich, zgierskich i łódzkich z lat 1809–1876*. Łódź-Gdańsk: Wydawnictwo Head Republic.

Maciejewski, Tadeusz. 2003. *Historia ustroju i prawa sądowego Polski*. Warszawa: Wydawnictwo C.H. Beck.

Maciejewski, Tadeusz. 2016. *The history of Polish legal system: from the 10th to the 20th century*. Warszawa: C.H. Beck.

Malec, Dorota. 2001. "Notariat w Departamencie Krakowskim Księstwa Warszawskiego oraz w Rzeczypospolitej Krakowskiej". *Czasopismo Prawno-Historyczne* 53, no. 2: 185–202.

Malec, Dorota. 2004. "Z dziejów prawa hipotecznego Wolnego Miasta Krakowa". *Czasopismo Prawno-Historyczne* 56, no 1: 75–96.

Malec, Dorota. 2007. *Dzieje notariatu polskiego*. Kraków: Wydawnictwo Uniwersytetu Jagiellońskiego.

Malec, Dorota, and Jerzy Malec. 2010. "Wincenty Szpor (1796–1856) i jego program wykładu umiejętności politycznych. Z Dziejów Katedry Umiejętności Politycznych Uniwersytetu Jagiellońskiego". *Krakowskie Studia z Historii Państwa i Prawa* 3: 99–109.

Martin, Gilles J. 1993. "L'evolution du droit de propriété de puis le Code civil" In *Code Napoléon et son héritage. Colloque international, Łódź, 12–14 septembre 1989*, edited by Biruta Lewaszkiewicz-Petrykowska, 233–244. Łódź: Wydawnictwo Uniwersytetu Łódzkiego.

Mataniak, Mateusz. 2017a. "Dozory kościelne w Krakowie w latach 1800–1853. Organizacja i zakres kompetencji". *Rocznik Biblioteki Naukowej PAU i PAN w Krakowie* 62: 123–149.

Mataniak, Mateusz. 2017b. "Funkcjonowanie więzienia w Wolnym Mieście Krakowie w I połowie XIX w.". *Przegląd Więziennictwa Polskiego* 96: 213–249.

Mataniak, Mateusz. 2017c. "System emerytalny dla urzędników Wolnego Miasta Krakowa. Część I: lata 1815–1837". *Krakowskie Studia z Historii Państwa i Prawa* 10, no. 2: 77–106.

Mataniak, Mateusz. 2017d. "System emerytalny dla urzędników Wolnego Miasta Krakowa. Część II: lata 1838–1854". *Krakowskie Studia z Historii Państwa i Prawa* 10, no. 3: 493–519.

Mataniak, Mateusz. 2017e. "Wprowadzenie «Monety Krajowej» w Wolnym Mieście Krakowie w 1833 r. Z dziejów skarbowości na ziemiach polskich w XIX w". *Studia z Dziejów Państwa i Prawa Polskiego* 20: 93–116.

Mataniak, Mateusz. 2018. "Bank Krajowy Wolnego Miasta Krakowa. O nieudanych próbach jego utworzenia w latach 1833–1835". *Czasopismo Prawno-Historyczne* 70, no. 2: 267–298.

Mataniak, Mateusz. 2019a. *Rada Administracyjna Miasta Krakowa i Jego Okręgu (1846–1853)*, „Biblioteka Krakowska", no 165. Kraków: Księgarnia Akademicka, Towarzystwo Miłośników Historii i Zabytków Krakowa.

Mataniak, Mateusz. 2019b. "Urzędnicy sądowi Wolnego Miasta Krakowa (1815–1846) na tle zasad organizacji jego sądownictwa. Zarys problematyki". In *Dzieje biurokracji* 9, edited by Artur Górak, Julia Kukarina and Jacek Legieć, 63–103. Lublin: Towarzystwo Nauki i Kultury „Libra".

Mataniak, Mateusz. 2020a. "The Judicial Circle in the Free City of Cracow (1815–1846)". *Beiträge zur Rechtsgeschichte Österreichs* 10, no 2: 325–332.

Mataniak, Mateusz. 2020b. "Wywłaszczenia na użytek publiczny w Wolnym Mieście Krakowie (1815–1846) a ochrona prawa własności". *Studia z Dziejów Państwa i Prawa Polskiego* 22: 71–98.

Mataniak, Mateusz. 2021. "Spory wśród mieszkańców Krakowa o służebności gruntowe miejskie (mur środkowy i prawo widoku). W świetle orzecznictwa sądów cywilnych Wolnego Miasta Krakowa (1815–1846)". *Krakowski Rocznik Archiwalny* 27: 11–65.

Mataniak, Mateusz. 2022a. "Egzekucja z nieruchomości w Wolnym Mieście Krakowie (1815–1846) – w świetle ustawy «Prawo o egzekucji sądowej» z 17 czerwca 1823 r. i orzecznictwa. Zarys problematyki". In *Stanowienie prawa w przeszłości. Zbiór studiów*, edited by Piotr Górecki and Dariusz Makiłła, 243–266. Warszawa: Wydawnictwo Akademii Ekonomiczno-Humanistycznej w Warszawie.

Mataniak, Mateusz. 2022b. "Visual aspects of the coexistence of courts and the Faculty of Law at the Jagiellonian University in the Free City od Krakow (1815–1846)" In *The Visualisation of Law in Academic Traditions and the Teaching of Law*, edited by Andrzej Gulczyński, 289–330. Poznań: Wydawnictwo Poznańskiego Towarzystwa Przyjaciół Nauk/Wydawnictwo Miejskie Posnania.

Meus, Konrad. 2016. "Wolne Miasto Kraków – przykład monokultury gospodarczej". In *Rzeczpospolita Krakowska 1815–1846. Materiały z sesji naukowej, 23 maja 2015 roku*, edited by Jerzy Wyrozumski, Kraków w Dziejach Narodu 35: 29–54. Kraków: Towarzystwo Miłośników Historii i Zabytków Krakowa.

Michalik, Piotr. 2020. „Consent to a Jewish Marriage in Legislation of the Free City of Cracow (1815–1846)". *Journal of European History of Law* 11, no 1: 102–109.

Michalik, Piotr. 2021. „Stosowanie przepisów prawa spadkowego Code civil przez sądy Wolnego Miasta Krakowa – sprawa Sawiczewskich". *Krakowskie Studia z Historii Państwa i Prawa* 14, no 3: 307–330.

Michalik, Piotr. 2022. „«Wstrząsające wspomnienie uzurpacji Bonapartego?» – uchwalenie zasad prawa spadkowego do kodeksu cywilnego Wolnego Miasta Krakowa". *Studia z Dziejów Państwa i Prawa Polskiego* 25: 13–36.

Michalik, Piotr. 2023. „The beginnings of the secularisation of marriage in Poland: the introduction of civil marriages and divorces in Cracow (1810–1818)". *Díké. A Márkus Dezső Összehasonlító Jogtörténeti Kutatócsoport Folyóirata* 7, no 2: 87–98.

Mohnhaupt, Heinz. 2006. "Die Gerichtspraxis zum Code civil im Königreich Westphalen zwischen Transplantation und Restauration (1807–1813)". In *Richterliche Anwendung der Code civil in seinen europäischen Geltungsbereichen außerhalb Frankreichs*, edited by Barbara Dölemeyer, Heinz Mohnhaupt and Alessandro Somma, 37–60. Frankfurt am Main: Klostermann.

Mostowik, Piotr. 2023. "Refleksje o współczesnym międzynarodowym prawie prywatnym i postępowaniu cywilnym na tle ujęcia „jurisdykcyi krajowej zewnętrznej" F. Słotwińskiego". In *Prawne zagadnienia międzynarodowego obrotu cywilnego i handlowego*, edited by Edyta Figura-Góralczyk, Radosław Flejszar, Bogusława Gnela and Piotr Mostowik, 25–48. Warszawa: C.H. Beck.

Müller, Eduard. 2004. "Le Code civil en Allemagne. Son influence générale sur le droit du pays, son adaptation dans les Pays Rhénans". In *Le Code civil 1804–2004. Livre du Bicentenaire: 2004*, 627–638. Paris: Dalloz/Litec LexisNexis.

Olszewski, Henryk, ed. 2005. *Czasopismo Prawno-Historyczne*, 57, no. 2. Poznań: Wydawnictwo Poznańskie.

Ourliac, Paul, and Jehan de Malafosse. 1971. *Historie du droit privé. Les Biens*. Paris: PUE (Presses Universitaires de France).

Osuchowski, Wacław. 1988. *Rzymskie prawo prywatne. Zarys wykładu*, Warszawa: Państwowe Wydawnictwo Naukowe.

Pańków, Stanisława. 1954. "Archiwum Wolnego Miasta Krakowa". *Archeion* 22: 103–128.

Patkaniowski, Michał. 1964. *Dzieje Wydziału Prawa Uniwersytetu Jagiellońskiego od reformy kołłątajowskiej do końca XIX stulecia. Zeszyty Naukowe Uniwersytetu Jagiellońskiego* LXXIX. *Prace Prawnicze* 13. Kraków: Wydawnictwo Uniwersytetu Jagiellońskiego.

Pauli, Lesław. 1968. *Austriacki kodeks karny z 1803 r. w Wolnym Mieście Krakowie (1815–1833). Część I. Zeszyty Naukowe Uniwersytetu Jagiellońskiego* CXCVIII. *Prace Prawnicze* 40: 5–112. Kraków: Wydawnictwo Uniwersytetu Jagiellońskiego.

Pauli, Lesław. 1970. *Austriacki kodeks karny z 1803 r. w Wolnym Mieście Krakowie (1815–1833). Część II. Zeszyty Naukowe Uniwersytetu Jagiellońskiego* CCXXXIV. *Prace Prawnicze* 46: 7–160. Kraków: Wydawnictwo Uniwersytetu Jagiellońskiego.

Pauli, Lesław. 1982. "Prawa obce w Rzeczypospolitej Krakowskiej". *Zeszyty Naukowe Uniwersytetu Jagiellońskiego* DCXXV. *Prace Prawnicze* 97: 145–158. Kraków: Wydawnictwo Uniwersytetu Jagiellońskiego.

Peguera Poch, Marta. 2009. *Aux origines de la réserve héréditaire du Code civil: la légitime en pays de coutumes (XVIe–XVIIIe siècles)*. Aix-en-Provence: Presses Universitaires d'Aix-Marseille.

Peters, Verena. 2018. *Der „germanische" Code Civil. Zur Wahrnehmung des Code Civil in den Diskussionen der deutschen Öffentlichkeit.* Tübingen: Mohr Siebeck.

Pęksa, Władysław. 1999. "Sąd Sejmowy w Rzeczypospolitej Krakowskiej". In *Dzieje wymiaru sprawiedliwości*, edited by Tadeusz Maciejewski, 253–261. Koszalin: Miscellanea. Wydawnictwo Uczelniane Bałtyckiej Wyższej Szkoły Humanistycznej.

Picard, Maurice. 1952. "Les biens". In *Traité pratique de droit civil français*, edited by Maurice Planiol and Georges Ripert, "Libraire générale de droit et de jurisprudence", vol. III. Paris: R. Pichon & R. Durand-Auzias.

Płaza, Stanisław. 1993. *Historia Prawa w Polsce. Zarys wykładu. Część II. Polska pod zaborami.* Kraków: Księgarnia Akademicka.

Płaza, Stanisław. 2002. *Historia prawa w Polsce na tle porównawczym. Część II: Polska pod zaborami*, Kraków: Księgarnia Akademicka.

Pomianowski, Piotr Z. 2015. „Funkcjonowanie francuskiego modelu rejestracji stanu cywilnego w Polsce". *Czasopismo Prawno-Historyczne* 67, no 1: 95–106.

Pomianowski, Piotr Z. 2018. *Rozwód w XIX wieku na centralnych ziemiach polskich. Praktyka stosowania Kodeksu Napoleona w latach 1808–1852.* Warszawa: Wydawnictwo Campidoglio.

Pomianowski, Piotr Z. 2022a. "Geneza i recepcja instytucji sędziego pokoju. Wybrane zagadnienia". In *Prawo i kultura: księga dedykowana Profesorowi Markowi Wąsowiczowi*, edited by Jarosław Kuisz and Anna Rosner, 317–325. Warszawa: Wydawnictwo Naukowe Scholar.

Pomianowski, Piotr Z. 2022b. *Napoleonic Divorce Law in Poland (1808–1852)*. Leiden/Boston: Brill/Nijhoff.

Probert, Rebecca. 2021. *Tying the Knot: The Formation of marriage, 1836–2020*. Cambridge/New York: Cambridge University Press.

Purchla, Jacek. 1981. "Krakowskie mosty wiślane i ich znaczenie dla rozwoju przestrzennego miasta w XIX i XX wieku". *Teka Komisji Urbanistyki i Architektury* 15: 27–40.

Ranieri, Filippo. 2005. "200 Jahre Code civil. Die Rolle des französischen Rechts in der Geschichte des europäischen Zivilrechts oder zum Aufstieg und Niedergangeines europäischen Kodifikationsmodells". In *200 Jahre Code Civil. Die napoleonische Kodifikation in Deutschland und Europa*, edited by Werner Schubert and Matthias Schmoeckel, 85–125. Köln: Böhlau Köln.

Rederowa, Danuta. 1957. "Powstanie Krakowa nowożytnego". In *Kraków. Studia nad rozwojem miasta*, edited by Jan Dąbrowski, 243–285: Kraków: Wydawnictwo Literackie.

Rémy, Philippe. 1985. "Le rôle de l'exégèse dans l'enseignement du droit au XIXe siècle". *Annales d'historie des Facultés des Droits et de la science juridique* 2: 91–105.

Rémy, Philippe. 2003/2004. "La part faite au juge", *Pouvoirs* 107: 22–36.

Robinson, Olivia F., T. David Fergus and William M. Gordon. 2000. *European legal history. Sources and institutions*, 3 ed., London: Oxford University Press.

Rosner, Anna. 1988. "Sędziowie i urzędnicy sądów pokoju w Księstwie Warszawskim". *Przegląd Historyczny* 79, no 4: 659–683.

Rosner, Anna. 1994. "Stare i nowe w organizacji i działalności sądów pokoju w Księstwie Warszawskim". *Czasopismo Prawno-Historyczne* 46, no 1–2: 69–76.

Rotwand, Bolesław. 1918. "Przysięga jako dowód w procesie cywilnym". *Kwartalnik Prawa Cywilnego i Karnego* 1, no 1–4: 446–463.

Rutkowski, Jan. 1922. *Sprawa włościańska w Polsce XVIII i XIX wieku*. Warszawa: Polska Składnica Pomocy Szkolnych.

Schubert, Werner. 1977 ed. *Französisches Recht in Deutschland zu Beginn des 19. Jahrhunderts. Zivilrecht, Gerichtsverfassungsrecht und Zivilprozessrecht*. Köln: Böhlau Köln.

Schubert, Werner. 1977. "Das französische Recht in Deutschland zu Beginn der Restaurationszeit (1814–1820)". *Zeitschrift der Savigny-Stiftung für Rechtsgeschichte – Germanistische Abteilung* 94: 129–184.

Schubert, Werner and Matthias Schmoeckel. 2005 eds. *200 Jahre Code Civil. Die napoleonische Kodifikation in Deutschland und Europa*. Köln: Böhlau Köln.

Schubert, Werner. 2011. "Die Rezeption des Code Napoléon in Deutschland und im übrigen Europa während der Napoleonischen Zeit". In *200 Jahre Badisches von 1809/1810*, edited by Christian Hattenhauer and Klaus-Peter Schroeder, 87–114. Heidelberg: Peter Lang.

Schulze, Reiner. 1994. "Französisches Recht und Europäische Rechtsgeschichte im 19. Jahrhundert". In *Französisches Zivilrecht in Europa während des 19. Jahrhunderts*, edited by Reiner Schulze, 9–36. Berlin: Dunker&Humboldt.

Sobociński, Władysław. 1964. *Historia ustroju i prawa Księstwa Warszawskiego*, "Roczniki Towarzystwa Naukowego w Toruniu" 70 (1). Toruń: Państwowe Wydawnictwo Naukowe.

Sobociński, Władysław. 1982. "Sądownictwo Księstwa Warszawskiego a problem kasacji: pierwsze pomysły i zaczątki organizacji kasacyjnej". *Czasopismo Prawno-Historyczne* 34, no 2: 141–182.

Sobociński, Władysław. 1984. "Rada Stanu Księstwa Warszawskiego jako Sąd Kasacyjny (zarys ustrojowy)". *Archeion* 77: 5–43.

Sobociński, Władysław. 1988. "Kasacja a restytucja w systemie sądowoodwoławczym Księstwa Warszawskiego". *Annales Universitatis Mariae Curie-Skłodowska*. Sectio G (35): 97–133.

Sobociński, Władysław. 1993. *Prokuratura sądu kasacyjnego w Księstwie Warszawskim*. "Studia Iuridica" 20 (1). Toruń: Towarzystwo Naukowe w Toruniu.

Sokołowski, Krzysztof P. 2016. "Nabycie nieruchomości przez Skarb Państwa na podstawie art. 713 Kodeksu Napoleona". *Rejent* 26, no 4 (300): 62–104.

Sourioux, Jean-Louis. 1989. "La doctrine française et le droit naturel dans la première moitié du XXe siècle". *Revue d'historie des Facultés des Droits et de la science juridique* 8: 155–163.

Sójka-Zielińska, Katarzyna. 1993. "Le droit privé français dans la Duché de Varsovie: transposition des principes révolutionnaires ou consolidation de l'ancien ordre?" In *Code Napoléon et son héritage. Colloque international, Łódź, 12–14 septembre 1989*, edited by Biruta Lewaszkiewicz-Petrykowska, 119–133. Łódź: Wydawnictwo Uniwersytetu Łódzkiego.

Sójka-Zielińska, Katarzyna. 1998. "Wywłaszczenie nieruchomości na cele publiczne w ustawodawstwie Królestwa Polskiego I poł. XIX w". In *Z historii państwa, prawa, miast i Polonii: prace ofiarowane Profesorowi Władysławowi Ćwikowi w czterdziestolecie Jego pracy twórczej*, edited by Józef Ciągwa and Tomasz Opas, 207–218. Rzeszów: Uniwersytet Marii Curie-Skłodowskiej. Filia.

Sójka-Zielińska, Katarzyna. 1999. "Rekurs ustawodawczy w myśli państwowej epoki Oświecenia". In *Parlamentaryzm i prawodawstwo przez wieki: prace dedykowane prof. Stanisławowi Płazie w siedemdziesiątą rocznicę urodzin*, edited by Jerzy Malec and Wacław Uruszczak, 211–220. Kraków: Wydawnictwo Uniwersytetu Jagiellońskiego.

Sójka-Zielińska, Katarzyna. 2000. "Wizerunek sędziego w kulturze prawnej epoki oświecenia". In *Prawo i ład społeczny: księga jubileuszowa dedykowana profesor Annie Turskiej*, edited by Grażyna Polkowska, 304–313. Warszawa: Wydział Prawa i Administracji Uniwersytetu Warszawskiego.

Sójka-Zielińska, Katarzyna. 2005. "Idee kodyfikacji napoleońskich. Od utopii do realizmu". *Czasopismo Prawno-Historyczne* 57, no 2: 27–42.

Sójka-Zielińska, Katarzyna. 2008. *Kodeks Napoleona. Tradycja i współczesność*. Warszawa: Wydawnictwo Prawnicze Lexis-Nexis.

Sójka-Zielińska, Katarzyna. 2009. *Wielkie kodyfikacje cywilne. Historia i współczesność.* Warszawa: Liber.

Stolleis, Michael. 2008. "The profile of the judge in the european tradition". *Trames* 12, no 2 (62–57): 204–214.

Stus, Marek. 2005. "Ewolucja zasad dziedziczenia ustawowego w prawie polskim (1918–1964). Część II". *Rejent* 15, no 11 (175): 62–80.

Szlachta, Bogdan. 2000. "Feliks Leliwa Słotwiński (1788–1863)". In *Uniwersytet Jagielloński. Złota księga Wydziału Prawa i Administracji*, edited by Jerzy Stelmach and Wacław Uruszczak, 129–134. Kraków: Wydawnictwo Uniwersytetu Jagiellońskiego.

Szpak, Jan. 1973. "Inwentaryzacja metryk parafialnych Krakowa z XVI–XIX w. oraz ksiąg stanu cywilnego z pierwszej połowy XIX w.". *Studia Historyczne* 16, no 1: 49–64.

Szymborski, Wiktor. 2014. *Collegium Broscianum.* Kraków: Księgarnia Akademicka.

Tkaczuk, Marek. 2012. "Rada familijna jako instytucja systemu opieki w Polsce w XIX i XX wieku". In *Rodzina w naukach prawnych: zbiór studiów*, edited by Marek Tkaczuk and Rita Jaworska-Stankiewicz, 179–185. Szczecin: Wydział Prawa i Administracji. Uniwersytet Szczeciński.

Travaux. 1954. = Travaux de la semaine internationale de droit, Paris 1950: l'influence du Code civil dans le monde. Association Henri Capitant pour la culture juridique française; Société de législation comparée. Paris: Éditions A. Pedone.

Urban, Jacek. 2016. "Życie religijne w Wolnym Mieście Krakowie z okręgiem" In *Rzeczpospolita Krakowska 1815–1846. Materiały z sesji naukowej, 23 maja 2015 roku*, edited by Jerzy Wyrozumski, Kraków w Dziejach Narodu 35: 123–151. Kraków: Towarzystwo Miłośników Historii i Zabytków Krakowa.

Uruszczak, Wacław. 1974. "Violentia expulsio. Z badań nad procesem posesoryjnym w prawie polskim I poł. XVI wieku". *Zeszyty Naukowe Uniwersytetu Jagiellońskiego* CCCLIX. *Prace Prawnicze* 63: 225–246.

Uruszczak, Wacław. 1990. *Korektura praw z 1532 roku. Studium historyczno-prawne.* Vol. I. *Zeszyty Naukowe Uniwersytetu Jagiellońskiego* CMLXVI. *Prace Prawnicze* 135: Warszawa-Kraków.

Uruszczak, Wacław. 1997. „Prawo francuskie w Rzeczypospolitej Krakowskiej (1815–1846)". In *Szkice z dziejów ustroju i prawa. Poświęcone pamięci Ireny Malinowskiej-Kwiatkowskiej*, edited by Marcin Kwiecień and Marian Małecki, 91–99. Kraków: Wydawnictwo Uniwersytetu Jagiellońskiego.

Uruszczak, Wacław. 2013. *Historia państwa i prawa polskiego. T. 1: (966–1795)*, 2nd ed. Warszawa: Wolters Kluwer Polska.

Uruszczak, Wacław. 2017. *Spoliatus ante omnia restituendus. Znaczenie prawa kanonicznego w rozwoju ochrony posiadania.* In Wacław Uruszczak, *Opera historico-iuridica selecta: prawo kanoniczne, nauka prawa, prawo wyznaniowe*, 461–470. Kraków: Wydawnictwo Uniwersytetu Jagiellońskiego.

Wachholz, Szczęsny. 1957. *Rzeczpospolita Krakowska. Okres od 1815 do 1830 r.* Warszawa: Wydawnictwo Prawnicze.

Wadle, Elmar. 2002. *Französisches Recht in Deutschland. Acht Beiträge zur Geschichte des 19. Jahrhunderts*. Köln: Heymanns.

Wąsowicz, Marek. 1977. "Początki Prokuratorii Generalnej Królestwa Polskiego". *Czasopismo Prawno-Historyczne* 29, no 2: 143–164.

Wąsowicz, Marek. 1979. "Prokuratoria Generalna Królestwa Polskiego w latach 1816–1866/67". *Czasopismo Prawno-Historyczne* 32, no 2: 109–147.

Wąsowicz, Marek. 2017. "Z dziejów polskich instytucji obrony interesów Skarbu Państwa. Prokuratoria Generalna Królestwa Polskiego w latach 1816–1915". In *Państwo i prawo: księga jubileuszowa 200-lecia Prokuratorii Generalnej Rzeczypospolitej Polskiej*, edited by Leszek Bosek, 41–54. Warszawa: Wydawnictwo Sejmowe.

Weill, Alex, François Terré, and Philippe Simler. 1985. *Droit civil. Les biens*. 3rd ed. Paris: Dalloz.

Witkowski, Wojciech 1984. *Sądownictwo administracyjne w Księstwie Warszawskim i Królestwie Polskim 1807–1867*. Warszawa-Łódź: Państwowe Wydawnictwo Naukowe.

Wołodkiewicz, Witold 1993. "Droit naturel et droit romain dans les travaux préparatoires du Code civil". In *Code Napoléon et son héritage. Colloque international, Łódź, 12–14 septembre 1989*, edited by Biruta Lewaszkiewicz-Petrykowska, 45–55. Łódź: Wydawnictwo Uniwersytetu Łódzkiego.

Wójcikiewicz, Włodzimierz. 1967. *Prawo hipoteczne Królestwa Polskiego*, Wrocław-Warszawa-Kraków: Zakład Narodowy im. Ossolińskich. Wydawnictwo Polskiej Akademii Nauk.

Woś, Tadeusz. 2011. *Wywłaszczanie nieruchomości i ich zwrot*. Warszawa: Lexis Nexis Polska.

Varga, Csaba 2011. *Codification as a socio-historical phenomenon*. Budapest: Szent István Társulat az Apostoli Szentszék Könyvkiadója.

Voutyras-Pierre, Anne-Marie. 1992, "Les Facultés de droit dans les départements étrangers de la France napoléonienne". *Revue d'historie des Facultés des Droits et de la science juridique* 13: 127–157.

Zimmermann, Marian. 1933. *Wywłaszczenie. Studium z dziedziny prawa publicznego*, „Archiwum Towarzystwa Naukowego we Lwowie". Lwów: Towarzystwo Naukowe we Lwowie.

Zwanzger, Michael. 2018. "Der einfluss des Code Civil auf den Privatrechtentwicklung in Deutschland". In *Europa nach Napoléon*, edited by Christoph Enders, Michael Kahlo and Andreas Mosbacher, 161–189. Paderborn: Mentis Verlag.

Żukowski, Przemysław M. 2014. *Profesorowie Wydziału Prawa Uniwersytetu Jagiellońskiego. T. 2: 1780–2012*. edited by Dorota Malec. Kraków: Wydawnictwo Uniwersytetu Jagiellońskiego.

Index of Names

Prepared by Mateusz Mataniak

Index of Places

Prepared by Mateusz Mataniak

Index of Subjects

Prepared by Mateusz Mataniak

Printed in the United States
by Baker & Taylor Publisher Services